Prentice Hall LITERATURE

All-in-One
Workbook

Grade Seven

PEARSON

Upper Saddle River, New Jersey
Boston, Massachusetts
Chandler, Arizona
Glenview, Illinois

BQ Tunes Credits
Keith London, Defined Mind, Inc., Executive Producer
Mike Pandolfo, Wonderful, Producer
All songs mixed and mastered by Mike Pandolfo, Wonderful
Vlad Gutkovich, Wonderful, Assistant Engineer
Recorded November 2007 – February 2008 in SoHo, New York City, at Wonderful, 594 Broadway

ISBN-13: 978-0-13-366812-4
ISBN-10: 0-13-366812-6

9 10 V039 13 12

CONTENTS

UNIT 5 Drama

from **Dragonwings** by Laurence Yep

A Christmas Carol: Scrooge and Marley, *Act I*, by Israel Horovitz

A Christmas Carol: Scrooge and Marley, *Act II*, by Israel Horovitz

from A Christmas Carol: Scrooge and Marley, *Act I, Scenes 2 & 5*, by Israel Horovitz

"The Monsters Are Due on Maple Street" by Rod Serling

"The People Could Fly" by Virginia Hamilton

"All Stories Are Anansi's" by Harold Courlander

"The People Could Fly" and "All Stories Are Anansi's"

"The Fox Outwits the Crow" by William Cleary
"The Fox and the Crow" by Aesop

Reading Fluency Practice and Assessment

Standardized Test Practice

Answer Sheets

Truth, performed by Becca Schack

Awareness is what we need
to know what's going on
Don't leave me in the dark
all common sense gone
What we **perceive**
is not always real
What we understand
not always the deal

Come on and shed some light
Deliver more **insight**
Come on and shed some light
so we can do what's right

Can we find the **truth**
When the answers are hidden
How do we see through
Behind the eyes of deception
Reach deep inside
and you will find
what you're looking for
what you're looking for

We can spend all night
in a heated **debate**
If we don't share our ideas

how can we collaborate
Explain all the reasons why
you do the things you do
So we can **evaluate** the situation
You see it's all about communication

Continued

Factual or **fiction**
Truth or contradiction
Real or fabrication
Aware of your own creation

Can we find the **truth**
When the answers are hidden
How do we see through
Behind the eyes of deception
Reach deep inside
and you will find
what you're looking for
what you're looking for

Child, please don't be confused
Just take my hand and let me show you
It can be simple or it can be hard
The answer often lies within you

Reveal yourself
Come show me who you are
Convince me to believe
No need to go too far
In the end I will **conclude**
a resolution
I'll have made up my mind
and know just what to do
The **evidence** will show
Help us really know
What's **believable** or crazy
Is it a dream or reality

Continued

2

Can we find the **truth**

When the answers are hidden

How do we see through

Behind the eyes of deception

Reach deep inside

and you will find

what you're looking for

what you're looking for

_____

Song Title: **Truth**

Artist / Performed by Becca Schack

Lyrics by Becca Schack

Music composed by Mike Pandolfo

Produced by Mike Pandolfo, Wonderful

Executive Producer: Keith London, Defined Mind

Unit 1: Fiction and Nonfiction
Big Question Vocabulary—1

The Big Question: Is there ever truth in fiction?

conclude: *v.* bring something to an end; other form: *conclusion*

convince: *v.* persuade someone to agree; sway someone's thinking; other form: *convincing*

evaluate: *v.* judge how good or successful something is; other forms: *evaluation, evaluating*

perceive: *v.* see or recognize something; discover; identify; other forms: *perception, perceptive*

reveal: *v.* uncover a secret; make something known; other forms: *revealing, revealed*

DIRECTIONS: *Review the vocabulary words and their definitions shown above. Then answer each question.*

1. Mr. Sanchez is a judge for the school talent show. As he watches each act in the show, which of these verbs **best** describes what he must do? Explain your answer. _____

_____

2. Ms. Chang is directing the weekly meeting of the Teachers' Association. The meeting is almost over. Which verb **best** describes what she should do? Explain your answer. _____

_____

3. The detective learned the secret identity of the Midnight Thief. He wanted to tell the newspapers the news. Which verb **best** describes what he will do? Explain your answer.

_____

4. Joanne wants her classmates to be as concerned as she is about global warming. Which verb **best** describes what she should do? Explain your answer. _____

_____

5. The fog made it difficult for us to see the mountain. Which verb **best** describes what we were trying to do? Explain your answer. _____

_____

Unit 1: Fiction and Nonfiction
Big Question Vocabulary—2

The Big Question: Is there ever truth in fiction?

awareness: *n.* a person's knowledge or understanding of a situation; other forms: *aware, unaware*

debate: *n.* a discussion between people with opposite views

      v. discuss different views on a subject; other form: *debatable*

evidence: *n.* facts, objects, or signs that prove that something is true; other form: *evident*

fiction: *n.* stories about imaginary people and events; other forms: *fictitious, fictional*

reality: *n.* what actually happens or is true; real life; other forms: *real, realism*

A. DIRECTIONS: *Review the vocabulary words listed above. On the line that precedes each question, write* **Yes** *or* **No** *to answer it. Then explain your response on the line that follows it.*

_____1. Would a book of *fiction* be the best source for facts about George Washington?

    _____

_____2. Would photographs and eyewitness reports serve as reliable *evidence* regarding what happened at a sporting event?

    _____

_____3. At a *debate*, are all participants expected to share the same opinion?

    _____

B. DIRECTIONS: *Follow each of the directions.*

1. Explain the difference between **fiction** and **reality**. Give an example of each.

    _____

    _____

    _____

2. Give three pieces of **evidence** that would raise someone's **awareness** of a fire. _____

    _____

    _____

    _____

Unit 1: Fiction and Nonfiction
Big Question Vocabulary—3

The Big Question: Is there ever truth in fiction?

believable: *adj.* able to be believed; other forms: *belief, believe, believer, believably, disbelief*

explain: *v.* describe or demonstrate something in a way that makes it clear and understandable; other form: *explanation*

factual: *adj.* based on facts; truthful; other form: *fact*

insight: *n.* personal understanding or wisdom on a subject; other form: *insightful*

truth: *n.* what can be proved, based on facts; other forms: *true, truly*

A. DIRECTIONS: *For each vocabulary word, list three things or reasons as instructed. Then, use the vocabulary word in a sentence about one of the things or reasons.*

Example: List three things that are examples of **fiction.**

a story about elves   a story about talking horses   a story about flying cats

Sentence: *In the story, the cats built an airplane and flew to a planet ruled by mice.*

---

1. List three things about cats that are *believable.*

_____ _____ _____

   Sentence: _____

2. List three things about your school that are *factual.*

_____ _____ _____

   Sentence: _____

3. Give three reasons for *explaining* safety rules to young children.

_____ _____ _____

   Sentence: _____

4. List three *insights* you have about the importance of friendship.

_____ _____ _____

   Sentence: _____

5. List three *truths* about trees.

_____ _____ _____

   Sentence: _____

Name _____ Date _____

Unit 1: Fiction and Nonfiction
Applying the Big Question

 Is there ever truth in fiction?

DIRECTIONS: *Complete the chart below to apply what you have learned about finding truth in fiction. One row has been completed for you.*

Example	Facts	Where facts are found	How the facts are revealed	How facts connect to fiction	What I learned
From Literature	Jewish families were killed and all Jews had to wear stars.	These facts were in the story "Suzy and Leah".	Suzy read Leah's journal, and Suzy's mother explained the treatment of the Jews.	The characters Suzy and Leah are fictional characters.	Some fictional stories include historical facts that can be proven.
From Literature					
From Science					
From Social Studies					
From Real Life					

Richard Peck
Listening and Viewing

Segment 1: Meet Richard Peck
- From where does Richard Peck draw his inspiration to write stories about young people?
- If you were writing a story, where might you get ideas for writing?

_____

_____

_____

_____

Segment 2: Fiction and Nonfiction
- Do you agree with Richard Peck that fiction can be "truer than fact"?
- How might a work of fiction be more convincing than a work of nonfiction, such as a newspaper article?

_____

_____

_____

_____

Segment 3: The Writing Process
- Why does Richard Peck throw out the first chapter of a book once he has written the ending?
- Which one of Richard Peck's writing methods would you use? Why?

_____

_____

_____

_____

Segment 4: The Rewards of Writing
- Why does Richard Peck believe readers "have an advantage" over people who do not read?
- How has reading helped you better understand another person, a situation, or yourself? Explain.

_____

_____

_____

_____

Name _____   Date _____

Learning About Fiction and Nonfiction

This chart compares and contrasts **fiction** and **nonfiction**:

Fiction	Nonfiction
tells about *made-up* people or animals, called **characters**: The characters experience a series of made-up events, called the **plot**; the plot takes place at a certain real or imagined time in a certain real or imagined location, which is the **setting**; the plot also contains a problem, or **conflict**, that characters must solve	tells about *real* people, animals, places, things, events, and ideas; presents facts and discusses ideas; may reflect the **historical context** of its time by making references to current events, society, and culture
may be told from the perspective of a character in the story (**first-person point of view**) or a narrator outside the story (**third-person point of view**)	is told from the **perspective** of the author
takes the form of short stories, novellas, novels	takes the form of biographies, autobiographies, memoirs, letters, journals, diaries, essays, articles, textbooks, and documents, such as application forms and instructions
to explain, inform, persuade, or entertain	to explain, inform, persuade, or entertain

A. DIRECTIONS: *Using clues in each title, write* fiction *or* nonfiction *on the line.*

_____ 1. "My Family Came From Mars"

_____ 2. "Historic Landings on the Moon"

_____ 3. *The Life of Thomas Jefferson*

_____ 4. *Jackie Rabbit, King of the Meadow*

_____ 5. "How to Make Oatmeal Bread"

B. DIRECTIONS: *Read this paragraph carefully, and decide whether it is fiction or nonfiction. Indicate your choice. Then, explain what hints led you to make your choice.*

The Ramirez family set off on their summer vacation yesterday. Luis was excited. It was the first trip that his family had taken since coming to the United States last year. Luis had brought along two books to read during the trip. He'd have plenty of time to read. After all, flying to a distant galaxy would take at least a week.

Fiction / Nonfiction: _____

Explanation: _____

Name _____ Date _____

"The Three-Century Woman" by Richard Peck
Model Selection: Fiction

Every work of **fiction** includes made-up people or animals, called **characters,** and a made-up series of events, called the **plot.** The plot may seem realistic. For example, it may be a story about students like you. On the other hand, the plot may be a fantasy. It might, for example, feature talking cats.

The plot takes place at a certain time and in a certain location, called the **setting.** The setting may or may not be real. Every plot contains a problem, or **conflict,** that one or more characters must solve.

A speaker, called the **narrator,** tells the story from a certain perspective, or **point of view.** If the narrator is a character in the story, he or she tells it from the **first-person point of view.** If the narrator is outside the story, he or she tells it from the **third-person point of view.**

Examples of fiction include novels, novellas, and short stories.

A. DIRECTIONS: *"The Three-Century Woman" is a work of fiction. Complete the following items to provide details about its characters, narrator, setting, and plot.*

1. The **characters:** _____

   _____

2. Is the **narrator** inside or outside the story? _____

3. Is the story told from the **first-person** or **third-person** point of view? _____

   _____

4. Clues that indicate the point of view: _____

   _____

5. When does the story take place? _____

   _____

6. Where does the story take place? _____

   _____

7. Is the **setting** realistic or imaginary? Explain. _____

   _____

8. Is the **plot** realistic or fantastic? _____

9. Examples of real or fantastic **plot** elements: _____

   _____

10. What **conflict,** or problem, do the characters face?

    _____

    _____

"The Fall of the *Hindenburg*" by Michael Morrison
Model Selection: Nonfiction

Nonfiction deals with *real* people, animals, places, things, events, and ideas. It may present facts or discuss ideas.

A work of nonfiction is narrated from the **point of view,** or perspective, of the author. Often nonfiction reflects the **historical context** of its time by including references to current events, society, or culture. For example, an article about the American Revolution would contain social and cultural information about the East Coast of North America in the mid-1700s.

Works of nonfiction include biographies, autobiographies, memoirs, letters, journals, diaries, essays, articles, textbooks, and various documents, such as application forms and instructions.

A. DIRECTIONS: *Answer these questions about "The Fall of the* Hindenburg.*"*

1. What real event does the article discuss?

   _____

2. On what date, and in what location, did the event take place?

   _____

3. List three facts that the author presents.

   _____

   _____

   _____

4. What conclusions can you draw about the topic, based on your reading of the article?

   _____

   _____

5. Give an example of a detail that sets a historical context for the article.

   _____

B. DIRECTIONS: *Authors have one or more purposes for writing a piece of nonfiction. For example, an author might write to explain how to do something, to tell the story of a person's life, to inform readers about a topic, to persuade readers to share an opinion, or to share a personal experience. In your opinion, what was Michael Morrison's purpose for writing "The Fall of the Hindenburg"? Support your answer by citing facts, reasons, and examples from the article.*

_____

_____

_____

Name _____ Date _____

Writing About the Big Question
What is the best way to find the truth?

Big Question Vocabulary

awareness	believable	conclude	convince	debate
evaluate	evidence	explain	factual	fiction
insight	perceive	reality	reveal	truth

A. *Use one or more words from the list above to complete each sentence.*

1. When a person has _____, he or she may know things that were not told to him or her.

2. It is sometimes difficult for someone to _____ strong feelings.

3. When someone acts indifferent toward me, I _____ that he or she does not like me.

4. When someone is very friendly and warm toward me, I _____ that he or she likes me.

B. *Answer the questions. Use at least one of the vocabulary words in each answer:*

1. Have you ever been unsure about how someone feels about you? Explain.

_____

_____

_____

2. Was the truth about the person's feelings ever revealed? If so, how? If not, what can you do to gain insight into how the person feels about you?

_____

_____

_____

C. *Complete the first sentence below. Then, answer the question to write a short paragraph connecting the sentence to the Big Question.*

One time I learned the truth about _____ when

_____

How could you use that truth in a fictional story?

_____

_____

_____

_____

Name _____ Date _____

"Papa's Parrot" by Cynthia Rylant

Reading: Use Context Clues to Unlock the Meaning

Context, the words and phrases surrounding a word, can help you understand a word you do not know. When you come across an unfamiliar word, **use context clues to unlock the meaning.** Look for a word or words that might mean the same thing or have the opposite meaning of the unfamiliar word. In addition, you may find definitions, examples, or descriptions of the unfamiliar word. For example, in this passage from "Papa's Parrot," the italicized words are clues to the meaning of *unpack*:

> *New shipments of candy and nuts* would be arriving. . . .

> ...Harry told his father that he would go to the store every day after school and <u>unpack</u> boxes. He would *sort out all the candy and nuts*.

As you read, use context clues to find possible meanings for unfamiliar words. Check the words in a dictionary after you read.

DIRECTIONS: *Read each of the following sentences or short passages from "Papa's Parrot." Look at the underlined word. Then, find other words in the passage that can be used as context clues to help you figure out the meaning of the underlined word. Write the context clue or clues on the first line. Write the meaning of the underlined word on the second line. Then, check your answer by looking up the underlined word in a dictionary.*

Hint: Sometimes the context clues appear a distance away from the unfamiliar word. For item 3, below, the context clue appears in the first paragraph of the story.

1. Harry stopped liking candy and nuts when he was around seven, but, in spite of this, he and Mr. Tillian had <u>remained</u> friends and were still friends the year Harry turned twelve.

    Context clues: _____

    Meaning of word: _____

2. At home things were different. Harry and his father joked with each other at the dinner table as they always had—Mr. Tillian <u>teasing</u> Harry about his smelly socks; Harry teasing Mr. Tillian about his blubbery stomach.

    Context clues: _____

    Meaning of word: _____

3. Though his father was fat and merely owned a candy and nut shop, Harry Tillian liked his papa. . . . Harry and his father joked with each other at the dinner table as they always had—Mr. Tillian teasing Harry about his smelly socks; Harry teasing Mr. Tillian about his <u>blubbery</u> stomach.

    Context clues: _____

    Meaning of word: _____

"**Papa's Parrot**" by Cynthia Rylant
Literary Analysis: Narrative Writing

Narrative writing is any type of writing that tells a story. The act or process of telling a story is also called **narration.**

- A narrative is usually told in chronological order—the order in which events occur in time.
- A narrative may be fiction, nonfiction, or poetry.

When you look at events in chronological order, you see that events that occur later in a narrative often depend on events that occurred earlier. For example, in "Papa's Parrot," the part of the story in which Harry walks by his father's store and hears him talking to Rocky must follow the part in which Mr. Tillian buys Rocky in the first place.

DIRECTIONS: *Below is a list of events from "Papa's Parrot." Put the events in chronological order by writing a number from 1 to 10 on the line before the event. Remember that each event has to make sense in terms of what has already occurred in the story.*

____ **A.** Harry stops going to the candy and nut shop when he sees his father talking to Rocky.

____ **B.** Harry goes to the candy and nut shop to unpack boxes and feed Rocky.

____ **C.** Harry yells at Rocky and throws peppermints at him.

____ **D.** Mr. Tillian buys a parrot, spending more money than he can afford.

____ **E.** Harry understands what Rocky means and goes to visit his father in the hospital.

____ **F.** Mr. Tillian falls ill and is taken to the hospital.

____ **G.** When they were young, Harry and his friends stopped by his father's candy and nut shop after school to buy penny candy or roasted peanuts.

____ **H.** Mr. Tillian talks to Rocky, and the two watch television together.

____ **I.** After Harry enters junior high school, he and his friends stop going to the candy and nut shop and spend more time playing video games and shopping for records.

____ **J.** The parrot says, "Hello, Rocky!" and "Where's Harry?" over and over.

Name _____ Date _____

"Papa's Parrot" by Cynthia Rylant
Vocabulary Builder

Word List

clusters   ignored   merely   perch   resumed   shipments

A. DIRECTIONS: *Think about the meaning of the italicized Word List word in each item below. Then, answer the question, and explain your answer.*

1. After his hospital stay, Mr. Tillian *resumed* his place in the candy and nut shop. Were his customers pleased?

    _____

2. While Mr. Tillian was in the hospital, Harry *ignored* his friends. Were his friends pleased?

    _____

3. When Harry threw a cluster of peppermints at the cage, Rocky clung to his *perch*. Was Rocky scared?

    _____

4. Mr. Tillian worried about the new *shipments* of candy and nuts arriving at his shop. Who would handle them?

    _____

5. In Harry's eyes, Mr. Tillian *merely* owned a candy and nut shop. Was Harry ashamed of his father's occupation?

    _____

6. Rocky's cage was next to the sign for the maple *clusters*. What other similar items does Mr. Tillian have in his store?

    _____

B. WORD STUDY The prefix *re-* means "back" or "again." Use the context of the sentences and the meaning of the prefix to explain your answer to each question.

1. If you program a song for constant *replay*, does that mean that you like it or dislike it?

    _____

2. When a football coach *repositions* the players on the field, what is he doing?

    _____

3. If you *rethink* a decision, are you happy with the choice you made?

    _____

"MK" by Jean Fritz

Writing About the Big Question

What is the best way to find the truth?

Big Question Vocabulary

awareness	believable	conclude	convince	debate
evaluate	evidence	explain	factual	fiction
insight	perceive	reality	reveal	truth

A. *Use one or more words from the list above to complete each sentence*

1. In _____, an author may mix in some truth.

2. A reader can often determine which parts of a fictional story have elements of
_____.

3. A _____ fictional story is not always true.

B. *Answer the questions.*

1. Name a fictional book, movie, or television show that was so believable, you were
convinced that at least part of it was based on truth.

_____

_____

2. Explain what elements of the fictional work were realistic.

_____

_____

_____

_____

C. *Complete the sentence below. Then, answer the question by writing a short paragraph
connecting the sentence to the Big Question.*

A story from my childhood that I would like to tell is _____

_____

If you made the story into a work of fiction, what would you change, and what
would stay the same?

_____

_____

_____

_____

_____

"**MK**" by Jean Fritz

Reading: Use Context Clues to Unlock the Meaning

Context, the words and phrases surrounding a word, can help you understand a word you do not know. When you come across an unfamiliar word, **use context clues to unlock the meaning.** Look for a word or words that might mean the same thing or have the opposite meaning of the unfamiliar word. In addition, you may find definitions, examples, or descriptions of the unfamiliar word. For example, in this passage from "MK," the italicized words are clues to the meaning of *protected:*

> The women and children going to Shanghai would be <u>protected</u> *from bullets by steel barriers erected around the deck.*

As you read, use context clues to find possible meanings for unfamiliar words. Check the words in a dictionary after you read.

DIRECTIONS: *Read each of the following sentences or short passages from "MK." Look at the underlined word. Then, find other words in the passage that can be used as context clues to help you figure out the meaning of the underlined word. Write the context clue or clues on the first line. Write the meaning of the underlined word on the second line. Then, check your answer by looking up the underlined word in a dictionary.*

1. I couldn't let on how I really felt. . . . "I'll be okay," I said, sniffing back fake tears. Sometimes it's necessary to <u>deceive</u> your parents if you love them, and I did love mine.

   Context clues: _____

   Meaning of word: _____

2. The girls were given what looked like dance cards and the boys were supposed to sign up for the talk sessions they wanted. Of course a girl could feel like a <u>wallflower</u> if her card wasn't filled up, but mine usually was.

   Context clues: _____

   Meaning of word: _____

3. It was a three-day trip across most of the <u>continent</u>, but it didn't seem long. Every minute America was under us and rushing past our windows—the Rocky Mountains, the Mississippi River, flat ranch land, small towns, forests, boys dragging school bags over dusty roads.

   Context clues: _____

   Meaning of word: _____

4. I decided that American children were <u>ignorant</u>. Didn't their teachers teach them anything?

   Context clues: _____

   Meaning of word: _____

"**MK**" by Jean Fritz
Literary Analysis: Narrative

Narrative writing is any type of writing that tells a story. The act or process of telling a story is also called **narration**.

- A narrative is usually told in chronological order—the order in which events occur in time.
- A narrative may be fiction, nonfiction, or poetry.

When you look at events in chronological order, you see that events that occur later in a narrative often depend on events that occurred earlier. In "MK," for example, the part of the story in which Jean takes her first steps on American soil must follow the part in which Jean and her family cross the Pacific Ocean to reach America.

DIRECTIONS: *Below is a list of ten events from "MK." Put the events in chronological order by writing a number from 1 to 10 on the line before the event. Remember that each event has to make sense in terms of what has already occurred in the story.*

_____ **A.** Paula, Jean's roommate at the Shanghai American School, cuts Jean's hair in a bob, the latest American style.

_____ **B.** Jean and most of the other passengers are seasick as they cross the Pacific Ocean on a steamer.

_____ **C.** Fletcher Barrett tells Jean that he is in love with her.

_____ **D.** In America, Jean wonders why her classmates are ignorant.

_____ **E.** Jean's mother enrolls Jean in the Shanghai American School.

_____ **F.** When Jean is almost ready to fall in love, her parents appear and tell her that the family is leaving China for America.

_____ **G.** When Jean meets her aunts and uncles and grandmother, she is thrilled to be part of a real family.

_____ **H.** Jean's mother learns that all of the American women and children in Wuhan must leave for Shanghai.

_____ **I.** In college, Jean reads about "real" Americans and makes a decision to write about them someday.

_____ **J.** When Jean first enters the Shanghai American School, she wonders why people make a fuss about football.

"**MK**" by Jean Fritz
Vocabulary Builder

Word List

adequate   deceive   ignorant   quest   relation   transformation

A. DIRECTIONS: *Read the incomplete paragraph below. On each line, write one of the words from the Word List. Think about the meaning of each word in the context of the paragraph.*

I was watching a quiz show one night. I tried to answer a series of questions about China. I realized I didn't know as much as I thought I did. In fact, I was (1) _____ about the country and its people. I decided to begin a search for information. My (2) _____ began at the library, where I found many books on China. Some of them were (3) _____, but others did not provide enough information to suit my purposes. Next, I checked out the Internet. There I learned about the country's topography and its rivers. A month later, I had read ten books, consulted a dozen Web sites, and watched three documentaries. I had undergone a (4) _____. I had changed from someone who knew little about China to someone who knew a great deal. I had truly learned who I was in (5) _____ to the Chinese people. I would not try to (6) _____ myself again by thinking that I was educated when I was, in fact, uneducated.

B. DIRECTIONS: *On each line, write the letter of the word whose meaning is the same as that of the Word List word.*

___ 1. quest
    A. trial   B. story   C. search   D. query

___ 2. adequate
    A. absent   B. enough   C. insufficient   D. compassionate

___ 3. deceive
    A. promise   B. yell   C. educate   D. mislead

C. WORD STUDY The prefix *in-* means "not." Use the context of the sentences and the meaning of the prefix to answer each question.

1. Why might an *indecisive* person take a long time in the candy aisle of a store?

_____

2. Why would it be a good idea to have safety education for *inexperienced* drivers?

_____

"Papa's Parrot" by Cynthia Rylant
"MK" by Jean Fritz

Integrated Language Skills: Grammar

Common and Proper Nouns

All nouns can be classified as either **common nouns** or **proper nouns.** A **common noun** names a person, place, or thing—such as a feeling or an idea. Common nouns are not capitalized unless they begin a sentence or are an important word in a title. In the following sentence, the common nouns are underlined.

> Harry had always stopped in to see his <u>father</u> at <u>work</u>.

In that sentence, the words *father* and *work* are general names for a person and a place.

A **proper noun** names a specific person, place, or thing. Proper nouns are always capitalized. In the following sentence, the proper noun is underlined.

> <u>Harry Tillian</u> liked his papa.

Harry Tillian is a proper noun because it names a specific person.

A. PRACTICE: *The following sentences are from or based on "Papa's Parrot" or "MK." Circle each proper noun, and underline each common noun.*

1. "Rocky was good company for Mr. Tillian."
2. "New shipments of candy and nuts would be arriving. Rocky would be hungry."
3. "Harry told his father that he would go to the store every day after school and unpack boxes."
4. Jean had just finished sixth grade at the British School in Wuhan.
5. "All American women and children had to catch the . . . boat to Shanghai."
6. "Mr. Barrett met us in Shanghai and drove us to their home, where his wife was on the front porch."

B. Writing Application: *Rewrite each of the following sentences. Replace as many of the common nouns as you can with a proper noun to make the information more specific.*

1. The author lived in another country when she was young.

_____

2. The boy was disappointed when his father bought a parrot.

_____

3. The author moved to another country.

_____

4. The parrot showed by his speech that the father missed his son.

_____

"Papa's Parrot" by Cynthia Rylant
"MK" by Jean Fritz

Integrated Language Skills: Support for Writing a Brief Essay

"Papa's Parrot": Use the graphic organizer below to record details that show what Harry was like before he entered junior high school and after he entered junior high school.

Before Entering Junior High	After Entering Junior High

"MK": Use this graphic organizer to record details that show Jean's feelings about America before and after she arrives in the United States.

Before Arriving in the U.S.	After Arriving in the U.S.

Now, use your notes to draft a brief compare-and-contrast essay.

from **An American Childhood** by Annie Dillard
Writing About the Big Question

What is the best way to find the truth?

Big Question Vocabulary

awareness	believable	conclude	convince	debate
evaluate	evidence	explain	factual	fiction
insight	perceive	reality	reveal	truth

A. *Use one or more words from the list above to complete each sentence.*

1. The details in a story can make a story _____.

2. Even when writing a work of fiction, it helps if there is _____ in the details.

3. Authors must have a(n) _____ of details in order to make people believe the story they are telling.

B. *Answer the questions.*

1. Add details to this sentence to make it more believable: *As I walked home, I was cold.*

   _____

   _____

   _____

2. Now, add details to the same sentence to reveal that you are writing a sentence that is fantastic and not realistic.

   _____

   _____

   _____

C. *Complete the sentence below. Then, write a short paragraph connecting the sentence to the Big Question.*

The details in a story help _____

Write a short fictional paragraph with realistic details.

_____

_____

_____

_____

_____

from **An American Childhood** by Annie Dillard

Reading: Reread and Read Ahead to Confirm Meaning

Context clues are the examples, descriptions, and other details in the text around an unfamiliar or unusual word or expression. Sometimes these clues can help you figure out what the word or expression means. When you come across an unfamiliar word, use the context clues to figure out what the word probably means. **Reread and read ahead to confirm the meaning.**

Read this example from *An American Childhood:*

But if you flung yourself <u>wholeheartedly</u> at the back of his knees—if you gathered and joined body and soul and pointed them diving fearlessly . . .

Which context clues tell you what *wholeheartedly* means? If you look for clues before and after the word, you find the phrases "flung yourself," "joined body and soul," and "pointed them diving fearlessly." These suggest that *wholeheartedly* probably means something like "completely" or "fully"—which it does.

DIRECTIONS: *Read each quotation from* An American Childhood. *Figure out the meaning of the underlined word by looking for context clues. Write the context clue or clues on the first line. Write the meaning of the word on the second line. Then, check your definitions in a dictionary.*

1. I started making an iceball—a perfect iceball, from perfectly white snow, perfectly spherical, . . . I had just <u>embarked</u> on the iceball project when we heard tire chains come clanking from afar.

   Context clues: _____

   Meaning of word: _____

2. Wordless, we split up. We were on our turf; we could lose ourselves in the neighborhood backyards, everyone for himself. I paused and considered. Everyone had <u>vanished</u> except Mikey Fahey, who was just rounding the corner of a yellow brick house.

   Context clues: _____

   _____

   Meaning of word: _____

3. You have to <u>fling</u> yourself at what you're doing, you have to point yourself, forget yourself, aim, dive.

   Context clues: _____

   Meaning of word: _____

4. Mikey and I unzipped our jackets. I pulled off my <u>sopping</u> mittens. . . . The man's lower pants legs were wet, his cuffs were full of snow.

   Context clues: _____

   Meaning of word: _____

from **An American Childhood** by Annie Dillard
Literary Analysis: Point of View

Point of view is the perspective from which a narrative is told. Point of view affects the kinds of details that are revealed to the reader.

- **First-person point of view:** The narrator is a character who participates in the action of the story and tells the story using the words *I* and *me*. The narrator can reveal only his or her own observations, thoughts, and feelings.
- **Third-person point of view:** The narrator is not a character in the story and uses third-person pronouns such as *he, she,* and *they* to refer to the characters. The narrator may know and reveal the observations, thoughts, and feelings of more than one person or character in the narrative.

Read this example from *An American Childhood:*

It was a long time before he could speak. <u>I</u> had some difficulty at first recalling why <u>we</u> were there. <u>My</u> lips felt swollen; <u>I</u> couldn't see out of the sides of <u>my</u> eyes; <u>I</u> kept coughing.

You can see from the pronouns *I, we,* and *my* that the event is being told from the first-person point of view. The speaker is there—her lips are swollen; her eyes are clouded; she is coughing.

DIRECTIONS: *Read each quotation from* An American Childhood. *Underline each pronoun that shows that the event is told from the first-person point of view. Then, on the lines that follow, briefly describe what you learned from or about the speaker.*

1. Boys welcomed me at baseball, too, for I had, through enthusiastic practice, what was weirdly known as a boy's arm.

   What I learned: _____

   _____

2. He ran after us, and we ran away from him, up the snowy Reynolds sidewalk. At the corner, I looked back; incredibly, he was still after us. . . . All of a sudden, we were running for our lives.

   What I learned: _____

   _____

3. He chased us silently over picket fences, through thorny hedges, between houses, around garbage cans, and across streets. Every time I glanced back, choking for breath, I expected he would have quit. He must have been as breathless as we were.

   What I learned: _____

   _____

Name _____ Date _____

from **An American Childhood** by Annie Dillard
Vocabulary Builder

Word List

| compelled | improvising | perfunctorily | righteous | strategy | translucent |

A. DIRECTIONS: *Think about the meaning of the underlined Word List word in each sentence. Then, answer the question.*

1. The children came up with a <u>strategy</u> for throwing snowballs at passing vehicles. Did the children have a plan? How do you know?

   _____

2. The man <u>compelled</u> Dillard to run through the neighborhood. Did she have a choice? How do you know?

   _____

3. Dillard and Mikey were <u>improvising</u> their escape route as they went along. Had they planned an escape route? How do you know?

   _____

4. When the man finally caught the kids, he said his words <u>perfunctorily</u>. Did his words hold unique meaning? How do you know?

   _____

5. Dillard describes the man's anger as <u>righteous</u>. Did he believe he was correct to be angry? How do you know?

   _____

6. Dillard's iceball was completely <u>translucent</u>. Could you see light through it? How do you know?

   _____

B. WORD STUDY: The Latin prefix *trans-* means "over," "across," or "through." Words containing the prefix *trans-* include *transfer* ("to move from one place to another") and *translator* ("someone who converts one language to another"). Consider these meanings as you answer each question.

1. Why might you need to *transfer* your records if you change schools?

   _____

2. Why might you need a *translator* in a foreign country?

   _____

"The Luckiest Time of All" by Lucille Clifton
Writing About the Big Question

What is the best way to find the truth?

Big Question Vocabulary

awareness	believable	conclude	convince	debate
evaluate	evidence	explain	factual	fiction
insight	perceive	reality	reveal	truth

A. *Use one or more words from the list above to complete each sentence.*

1. When somebody shares his or her beliefs, we must _____ whether those beliefs are consistent with our own beliefs.

2. If we _____ that our own beliefs are different, it is okay to disagree.

3. Beliefs may not be based in _____ .

B. *Answer the questions. Use at least one of the vocabulary words in each answer.*

1. Name two objects that people believe bring them good or bad luck.

   _____   _____

2. Do you believe that an object can bring you luck? Explain.

   _____

   _____

   _____

C. *Complete the sentence below. Then, answer the question to write a short paragraph connecting the sentence to the Big Question:*

In order to be believable, character's behavior' must be _____ .

In a work of fiction, what makes a character's behaviors believable? What is the advantage of having believable characters in a story?

_____

_____

_____

_____

"The Luckiest Time of All" by Lucille Clifton
Reading: Reread and Read Ahead to Confirm Meaning

Context clues are the examples, descriptions, and other details in the text around an unfamiliar or unusual word or expression. Sometimes these clues can help you figure out what the word or expression means. When you come across an unfamiliar word or expression, use the context clues to figure out what the word probably means. **Reread and read ahead to confirm the meaning.**

In "The Luckiest Time of All," the writer sometimes uses words and phrases that may mean something different from the meanings of the individual words. Look at this example:

"Somethin like the circus. Me and Ovella wanted to join that thing and see the world. Nothin wrong at home or nothin, we just wanted to travel and see new things and have <u>high</u> times."

In another context, you would probably decide that *high* means "tall" or "rising above." In this context, notice the words and phrases around the word *high:* "somethin like the circus," "see the world," and "wanted to travel and see new things." These context clues tell you that in this selection, *high* means "exciting."

DIRECTIONS: *Read each quotation from "The Luckiest Time of All." Figure out the meaning of the underlined word or expression by looking for context clues. Write the context clue or clues on the first two lines. Write the meaning of the word or expression on the next line.*

1. We got there after a good little walk and it was the <u>world</u>, Baby, such music and wonders as we never had seen! They had everything there, or seemed like it.

   Context clues: _____

   _____

   Meaning of word: _____

2. But the stone was gone from my hand and Lord, it hit that dancin dog right on his nose! Well, he <u>lit out</u> after me, poor thing. He <u>lit out</u> after me and I flew! Round and round the Silas Greene we run.

   Context clues: _____

   _____

   Meaning of word: _____

3. I stopped then and walked slow and shy to where he had picked up that poor dog to see if he was hurt, <u>cradlin</u> him and talkin to him soft and sweet.

   Context clues: _____

   Meaning of word: _____

4. He . . . helped me find my stone. . . . We search and searched and at last he <u>spied</u> it!

   Context clues: _____

   _____

   Meaning of word: _____

"The Luckiest Time of All" by Lucille Clifton
Literary Analysis: Point of View

Point of view is the perspective from which a narrative is told. Point of view affects the kinds of details that are revealed to the reader.

- **First-person point of view:** The narrator is a character who participates in the action of the story and tells the story using the words *I* and *me*. The narrator can reveal only his or her own observations, thoughts, and feelings.
- **Third-person point of view:** The narrator is not a character in the story and uses third-person pronouns such as *he, she,* and *they* to refer to the characters. The narrator may know and reveal the observations, thoughts, and feelings of more than one person or character in the narrative.

Read this example from the beginning of "The Luckiest Time of All":

Mrs. Elzie F. Pickens was rocking slowly on the porch one afternoon when her Great-granddaughter, Tee, brought her a big bunch of dogwood blooms, and that was the beginning of a story.

"Ahh, now that dogwood reminds me of the day I met your Great-granddaddy, Mr. Pickens, Sweet Tee."

The story begins by introducing two characters, Mrs. Elzie F. Pickens and her great-granddaughter, Tee. The pronoun *her* tells you that the narrative is told from the third-person point of view. In the first paragraph of dialogue, Elzie is telling her story using the pronoun *I*, but that does not mean the story is a first-person account. It is not a first-person account because Elzie is not the narrator. The narrator is quoting Elzie as she tells her story to Tee.

DIRECTIONS: *Read each numbered passage. (Two passages are from "The Luckiest Time of All," and one is about Lucille Clifton.) Underline each pronoun that tells that the passage is told from the third-person point of view. Then, on the lines that follow, briefly describe what you learned from the passage.*

1. Tee's Great-grandmother shook her head and laughed out loud.

   What I learned: _____

2. And they rocked a little longer and smiled together.

   What I learned: _____

3. Lucille Sayles Clifton was born into a large, working-class family in New York State. Although her parents were not formally educated, she learned from their example to appreciate books and poetry.

   What I learned: _____

   _____

Name _____   Date _____

"The Luckiest Time of All" by Lucille Clifton
Vocabulary Builder

Word List

    acquainted   hind   plaited   spied   twine   wonders

A. DIRECTIONS: *Think about the meaning of the underlined Word List word in each sentence. Then, answer the question.*

1. Are mountain climbers likely to use <u>twine</u> to attach themselves to each other while crossing a dangerous crevice? Why or why not?

   _____

2. If you are <u>acquainted</u> with someone, are you likely to know where he or she lives? Why or why not?

   _____

3. Are women more likely than men to have <u>plaited</u> hair? Why or why not?

   _____

4. If you catch an animal by its <u>hind</u> legs, is it likely that you approached it from the front? Why or why not?

   _____

5. Is it likely that it would be boring to see one of the Seven <u>Wonders</u> of the World? Why or why not?

   _____

6. If you <u>spied</u> an old friend, would you likely be seeing him or her in person? Why or why not?

   _____

B. WORD STUDY: The Latin prefixes *ac-/ad-* mean "motion toward," "addition to," or "nearness to." How do the meanings of the prefixes relate to the italicized words in the following sentences?

1. The key allowed me full *access* to the mansion.

   _____

2. The toddler had to *adhere* to strict rules after he ran into the street.

   _____

from **An American Childhood** by Annie Dillard
"The Luckiest Time of All" by Lucille Clifton
Integrated Language Skills: Grammar

Possessive Nouns

A **possessive noun** is a noun that shows ownership. Ownership is indicated by the use of the apostrophe.

- To form the possessive to a singular noun, add an apostrophe and *-s:*
  The black <u>car's</u> tires left tracks.

- To form the possessive of a plural noun that ends in *-s*, add only an apostrophe:
  All of the <u>cars'</u> tires left tracks.

- To form the possessive of a plural noun that does not end in *-s*, add an apostrophe and *-s:*
  The <u>children's</u> game had unexpected consequences.

A. Practice: *Each of the following sentences is based an* An American Childhood *or* "The Luckiest Time of All." *On the line, rewrite each underlined noun as a possessive. Be sure to place the apostrophe correctly to indicate that the possessive is singular or plural.*

1. The <u>boys</u> games were more exciting to Dillard than the <u>girls</u> activities.

   _____   _____

2. The <u>snowball</u> *splat* led the <u>car</u> driver to jump out and chase the children.

   _____   _____

3. The <u>boy</u> path took him through the <u>neighbors</u> front yard.

   _____   _____

4. Many years later the young <u>women</u> adventure would be the subject of the <u>girl</u> curiosity.

   _____   _____

B. Writing Application: *On the line after each description in brackets, write a possessive noun that matches the description. Make sure the possessives you choose make sense in the sentence.*

1. The [*belonging to the singular female adult*] _____ stone hit the [*belonging to the singular animal*] _____ nose.

2. The [*belonging to the plural male children*] _____ games included throwing snowballs at the [*belonging to the plural vehicle*] _____ windows.

3. The [*belonging to the singular adult male*] _____ breath came in gasps and his [*belonging to the legs of his clothing*] _____ cuffs were full of snow.

from **An American Childhood** by Annie Dillard
"The Luckiest Time of All" by Lucille Clifton
Integrated Language Skills:
Support for Writing a Description That Includes Hyperbole

To prepare to write **descriptions** that include **hyperbole,** complete the following chart, making notes about three qualities or skills a person might have.

Questions About the Quality or Skill	First Quality or Skill	Second Quality or Skill	Third Quality or Skill
What is the quality or skill?			
Who or what might have this quality or skill?			
What is exceptional about this quality or skill?			
How can I exaggerate this quality or skill?			

Now, choose one quality or skill, and use your notes to write a description of it that includes hyperbole.

Name _____ Date _____

from **Barrio Boy** by Ernesto Galarza
"**A Day's Wait**" by Ernest Hemingway

Writing About the Big Question
What is the best way to find the truth?

Big Question Vocabulary

awareness	believable	conclude	convince	debate
evaluate	evidence	explain	factual	fiction
insight	perceive	reality	reveal	truth

A. *Use one or more words from the list above to complete each sentence.*

1. The scariest stories of all deal with situations that could happen in _____.

2. To _____ how scary a story is, I listen to how hard my heart is pounding.

3. After my little brother watched the horror movie, I had to _____ to him that the "blood" was really red paint.

4. In a good detective story, the _____ is there all along.

B. *Answer the questions.*

1. Describe a situation that you faced that scared you at first.

   _____

   _____

   _____

2. How did you get over your fear? Use two vocabulary words in your answer.

   _____

   _____

   _____

C. *Complete the sentence below. Then, answer the question to write a short paragraph connecting the sentence to the Big Question.*

The most frightening situations are those in which _____

Describe a scary fictional story that you read or a scary movie that you saw. What about it was realistic? What was unrealistic?

_____

_____

_____

from **Barrio Boy** by Ernesto Galarza
"A Day's Wait" by Ernest Hemingway
Literary Analysis: Comparing Fiction and Nonfiction

Fiction is prose writing that tells about imaginary characters and events. Novels, novellas, and short stories are types of fiction. **Nonfiction** is prose writing that presents and explains ideas or tells about real people, places, objects, or events. News articles, essays, and historical accounts are types of nonfiction.

In the excerpt from *Barrio Boy,* the writer tells about an actual event in his life. In contrast, the writer of "A Day's Wait" created a narrator who tells about an imagined event in the lives of an imagined father and son.

DIRECTIONS: *Complete the following chart by answering the questions about the excerpt from* Barrio Boy *and* "A Day's Wait."

Question	*from* **Barrio Boy**	**"A Day's Wait"**
1. Who tells the story?		
2. Who are the main characters?		
3. Is there important dialogue? If so, summarize it.		
4. What important events make up the action of the story?		
5. What feelings does the main character have as events unfold?		
6. How is the main character's problem resolved?		

from **Barrio Boy** by Ernesto Galarza
"A Day's Wait" by Ernest Hemingway
Vocabulary Builder

Word List

contraption   epidemic   evidently   flushed   formidable   reassuring

A. DIRECTIONS: *Think about the meaning of the italicized word in each question. Then, answer the question.*

1. When there is an *epidemic*, why are infected people kept away from healthy people?

   _____

2. What is an example of a *formidable* school project?

   _____

3. Why might someone call a typewriter a *contraption*?

   _____

4. If Elizabeth is *evidently* healthy, how do you know that she is healthy?

   _____

5. What is a *reassuring* gesture?

   _____

6. When a hunting dog has *flushed* quail from the bushes, what has the dog done?

   _____

B. DIRECTIONS: *For each pair of related words in capital letters, write the letter of the pair of words that best expresses a* similar *relationship.*

____ 1. EPIDEMIC : DOCTORS ::
    A. hospital : nurses
    B. war : soldier
    C. sick : well
    D. medicine : science

____ 2. FORMIDABLE : UNIMPORTANT ::
    A. dangerous : great
    B. square : rectangular
    C. difficult : simple
    D. large : huge

____ 3. EVIDENTLY : SEEMINGLY ::
    A. evidence : trial
    B. slowly : quickly
    C. suddenly : sudden
    D. certainly : surely

Name _____ Date _____

from **Barrio Boy** by Ernesto Galarza
"A Day's Wait" by Ernest Hemingway
Integrated Language Skills:
Support for Writing to Compare Literary Works

To prepare to write an essay that compares and contrasts the narrators of *Barrio Boy* and "A Day's Wait," use this graphic organizer. Respond to each question by jotting down ideas about how the narrators present their stories.

Question	from *Barrio Boy*	"A Day's Wait"
Who is the narrator? What is the point of view?		
What details about the narrator are revealed?		
How is dialogue used in each work?		
How are the narrator's feelings involved in the work?		
What theme do the narrator's thoughts and actions suggest?		
How do other characters affect the narrator?		
How does the narrator bring the story to a close?		

Now, use your notes to write an essay comparing and contrasting the narrators of *Barrio Boy* and "A Day's Wait."

"All Summer in a Day" by Ray Bradbury
Writing About the Big Question

What is the best way to find the truth?

Big Question Vocabulary

awareness	believable	conclude	convince	debate
evaluate	evidence	explain	factual	fiction
insight	perceive	reality	reveal	truth

A. *Use one or more words from the list above to complete each sentence.*

1. A story about someone living on the moon cannot be _____.

2. Scientists who disagree may _____ about the possibility of life on the moon.

3. When something is _____, it is not an opinion.

B. *Answer the questions.*

1. What are the two things you would miss the most if you were away from home for a long period of time?

   _____   _____

2. What do the two things you picked reveal about you as a person? Use at least two vocabulary words in your answer.

   _____

   _____

   _____

C. *Complete the sentence below. Then, write a short paragraph connecting the sentence to the Big Question.*

If I went to live in space, I would want these things from Earth to be present:

_____.

What was true about the fictional story "All Summer in a Day"? What was unrealistic?

_____

_____

_____

_____

"All Summer in a Day" by Ray Bradbury

Reading: Recognize Details That Indicate the Author's Purpose

Fiction writers write for a variety of **purposes.** They may wish to entertain, to teach, to call to action, or to reflect on experiences. They may also wish to inform, to persuade, or to create a mood. **Recognizing details that indicate the author's purpose** can give you a richer understanding of a selection. For example, in this passage from "All Summer in a Day," Bradbury creates a mood:

> Margot stood alone. She was a very frail girl who looked as if she had been lost in the rain for years and the rain had washed out the blue from her eyes and the red from her mouth and the yellow from her hair. She was an old photograph dusted from an album.

DIRECTIONS: *Read these passages from "All Summer in a Day." Then, write the purpose or purposes you think the author had for writing that passage. Choose from these purposes: to entertain, to inform, to create a mood. A passage may have more than one purpose.*

1. It had been raining for seven years; thousands upon thousands of days compounded and filled from one end to the other with rain, with the drum and gush of water, with the sweet crystal fall of showers and the concussion of storms so heavy they were tidal waves come over the islands.

   Author's purpose: _____

2. There was talk that her father and mother were taking her back to Earth next year; it seemed vital to her that they do so, though it would mean the loss of thousands of dollars to her family.

   Author's purpose: _____

3. But they were running and turning their faces up to the sky and feeling the sun on their cheeks like a warm iron; they were taking off their jackets and letting the sun burn their arms.

   Author's purpose: _____

4. They walked slowly down the hall in the sound of cold rain. They turned through the doorway to the room in the sound of the storm and thunder, lightning on their faces, blue and terrible. They walked over to the closet door slowly and stood by it.

   Behind the closet door was only silence.

   They unlocked the door, even more slowly, and let Margot out.

   Author's purpose: _____

"All Summer in a Day" by Ray Bradbury
Literary Analysis: Setting

The **setting** of a story is the time and place of the action. In this example from "All Summer in a Day," the underlined details help establish the story's setting.

The sun came out.

It was <u>the color of flaming bronze</u> and it was <u>very large</u>. And the sky around it was <u>a blazing blue tile color</u>. And <u>the jungle burned with sunlight</u> as the children, released from their spell, rushed out, yelling, into the springtime.

- In some stories, setting is just a backdrop. The same story events might take place in a completely different setting.
- In other stories, setting is very important. It develops a specific atmosphere or mood in the story, as in the example above. There, the children joyfully rush outside to feel the sun in the springtime after seven years of constant rain. The setting may even relate directly to the story's central conflict or problem.

DIRECTIONS: *Read the name of the character or characters from "All Summer in a Day" and the passage that follows. Then, on the lines, identify the setting described in the passage and the way the character or characters feel about it. Write your response in a short sentence or two.*

1. Margot: "And once, a month ago, she had refused to shower in the school shower rooms, had clutched her hands to her ears and over her head, screaming the water mustn't touch her head."

   Setting and character's feeling about it: _____

   _____

2. Margot: "They surged about her, caught her up and bore her, protesting, and then pleading, and then crying, back into a tunnel, a room, a closet, where they slammed and locked the door. They stood looking at the door and saw it tremble from her beating and throwing herself against it."

   Setting and character's feeling about it: _____

   _____

3. The children: "The children lay out, laughing, on the jungle mattress, and heard it sigh and squeak under them, resilient and alive. They ran among the trees, they slipped and fell, they pushed each other, . . . but most of all they squinted at the sun until tears ran down their faces, they put their hands up to that yellowness and that amazing blueness and they breathed of the fresh, fresh air."

   Setting and character's feeling about it: _____

   _____

Name _____ Date _____

"**All Summer in a Day**" by Ray Bradbury
Vocabulary Builder

Word List

intermixed   resilient   savored   slackening   tumultuously   vital

A. DIRECTIONS: *Read each sentence. If the italicized word is used correctly, write* Correct *on the line. If it is not used correctly, rewrite the sentence to correct it.*

1. The speed of the rocket was *slackening* as it prepared to land on Earth.

   _____

   _____

2. It is said that water is *vital* to life; you can live without it.

   _____

   _____

3. During the calm before the storm, the wind blew *tumultuously.*

   _____

   _____

4. Because Margot was *resilient,* she could not get used to the conditions on Venus.

   _____

   _____

5. During the parade, people were *intermixed* along the packed streets.

   _____

   _____

6. During the holiday season, we never *savored* the sweet smell of pumpkin pie as it came out of the oven.

   _____

   _____

B. WORD STUDY: The Latin roots *-vit-* or *-viv-* mean "life." Words containing *-vit-* or *-viv-* include *vitality* ("liveliness"), *survive* ("to live through something"), and *revive* ("to bring back to life"). Write two sentences in which you use all three of these words.

1. _____

   _____

2. _____

   _____

3. _____

   _____

Name _____ Date _____

"Suzy and Leah" by Jane Yolen
Writing About the Big Question
What is the best way to find the truth?

Big Question Vocabulary

awareness	believable	conclude	convince	debate
evaluate	evidence	explain	factual	fiction
insight	perceive	reality	reveal	truth

A. *Use one or more words from the list above to complete each sentence.*

1. When writing historical _____, a novelist must research in order to tell the _____ about historical events.

2. The historical facts in the story may _____ readers that the story is believable.

3. Readers must have a(n) _____ of history to know that the book is based on historical events.

4. To _____ whether historical facts are true, the reader can do research.

B. *Answer the questions.*

1. Name three things that you would need to research if you were writing a story that took place one hundred years ago and you wanted to convince your readers that the setting was real.

   _____   _____   _____

2. How is the challenge to write a believable novel that takes place in the future different from the challenge of writing a believable novel that takes place in the past? Explain using at least two vocabulary words.

   _____

   _____

   _____

   _____

C. *Complete the sentence below. Then, write a short paragraph connecting the sentence to the Big Question.*

   If I were going to write a story based on a historical event, I would write about

   _____

   What kinds of facts in your story would be true? What would be fictional?

   _____

   _____

"All Summer in a Day" by Ray Bradbury **"Suzy and Leah"** by Jane Yolen

Reading: Recognize Details That Indicate the Author's Purpose

Fiction writers may write for a variety of **purposes.** They may wish to entertain, to teach, to call to action, or to reflect on experiences. They may also wish to inform, to persuade, or to create a mood. **Recognizing details that indicate the author's purpose** can give you a richer understanding of a selection. For example, the following passage from "Suzy and Leah" is written to teach readers about the background of some Eastern European Jews:

> I have a little English. But Ruth and Zipporah and the others, though they speak Yiddish and Russian and German, they have no English at all.

DIRECTIONS: *Read these passages from "Suzy and Leah." On the line that follows each passage, write the purpose or purposes you think the author had for writing that passage. Choose from these purposes:* to entertain, to inform, to create a mood. *A passage may have more than one purpose.*

1. Leah: "Today we got cereal in a box. At first I did not know what it was. Before the war we ate such lovely porridge with milk straight from our cows. And eggs fresh from the hen's nest."

   Author's purpose: _____

2. Leah: "But they made us wear tags with our names printed on them. That made me afraid. What next? Yellow stars? I tore mine off and threw it behind a bush before we went in [to the school]."

   Author's purpose: _____

3. Suzy: "Mr. Forest . . . gave me the girl with the dark braids. . . . Gee, she's as prickly as a porcupine. I asked if I could have a different kid. . . . He wants her to learn as fast as possible so she can help the others. As if she would, Miss Porcupine."

   Author's purpose: _____

4. Leah: "One day this Suzy and her people will stop being nice to us. They will remember we are not just refugees but Jews, and they will turn on us. Just as the Germans did. Of this I am sure."

   Author's purpose: _____

5. Suzy: "[Leah's] English has gotten so good. Except for some words, like victory, which she pronounces 'wick-toe-ree.' I try not to laugh. . . . She can't dance at all. She doesn't know the words to any of the top songs."

   Author's purpose: _____

Name _____ Date _____

"Suzy and Leah" by Jane Yolen
Literary Analysis: Setting

The **setting** of a story is the time and place of the action. In this example from "Suzy and Leah," the underlined details help establish the story's setting:

August 5, 1944

Dear Diary,

Today I walked past *that* place. . . . Gosh, is it <u>ugly</u>! A line of <u>rickety wooden buildings</u> just like in the army. And <u>a fence lots higher than my head</u>. <u>With barbed wire</u> on top.

- In some stories, setting is just a backdrop. The same story events might take place in a completely different setting.
- In other stories, setting is very important. It develops a specific atmosphere or mood in the story, as in the example above. There, the reader is introduced to the refugee camp through the eyes of Suzy, who has lived a privileged life. The setting may even relate directly to the story's central conflict or problem.

DIRECTIONS: *Read the name of the character from "Suzy and Leah" and the passage that follows. Then, on the lines, identify the setting described in the passage and the way the character feels about it. Write your response in a short sentence.*

1. Suzy: "With barbed wire on top. How can anyone—even a refugee—live there?"

   Setting and character's feeling about it: _____

   _____

2. Leah: "But I say no place is safe for us. Did not the Germans say that we were safe in their camps?"

   Setting and character's feeling about it: _____

   _____

3. Leah: "Zipporah braided my hair, but I had no mirror until we got to the school and they showed us the toilets. They call it a bathroom, but there is no bath in it at all, which is strange."

   Setting and character's feeling about it: _____

   _____

4. Suzy: "[Mom] said the Nazis killed people, mothers and children as well as men. In places called concentration camps. . . . It was so awful I could hardly believe it, but Mom said it was true."

   Setting and character's feeling about it: _____

   _____

"**Suzy and Leah**" by Jane Yolen
Vocabulary Builder

Word List

cupboard   falsely   penned   permanent   porridge   refugee

A. DIRECTIONS: *Read each sentence. If the italicized word is used correctly, write* Correct *on the line. If it is not used correctly, rewrite the sentence to correct it.*

1. The *refugee* fled across the border.

   _____

2. The *porridge* made a wonderful dessert.

   _____

3. The *permanent* frown on Leah's face disappeared when Suzy offered candy.

   _____

4. The teacher was correct when she *falsely* accused Sam of cheating.

   _____

5. It is common to keep items like ice cream in the kitchen *cupboard*.

   _____

6. It is easy to feel *penned* in when there are a lot of people in a small space.

   _____

B. DIRECTIONS: *Read each sentence. If the italicized word is used correctly, write* Correct *on the line. If it is not used correctly, rewrite the sentence to correct it.*

1. The *refugee* fled across the border.

   _____

2. The *porridge* made a wonderful dessert.

   _____

3. The *permanent* frown on Leah's face disappeared when Suzy offered candy.

   _____

   _____

C. WORD STUDY: The Latin root -*man*- means "hand." Explain how the meaning of the root -*man*- relates to the following uses of the word *manual.*

1. The men performed ten long hours of <u>manual</u> labor.

   _____

2. My new camera allows for both automatic and <u>manual</u> control.

   _____

3. The artist showed extraordinary <u>manual</u> dexterity in her work.

   _____

"Suzy and Leah" by Jane Yolen
Integrated Language Skills: Grammar

A **pronoun** is a word that takes the place of a noun or a group of words acting as a noun. A **nominative pronoun** is a pronoun used as a subject. An **objective pronoun** is a pronoun used as an object.

Suzy met Leah at the camp.	**She** met Leah at the camp.	Nominative pronoun
Suzy met **Leah** at the camp.	Suzy met **her** at the camp.	Objective pronoun

Some important nominative and objective pronouns:

Nominative	**Objective**
I	me
he	him
she	her
we	us
they	them

A. PRACTICE: *Read each sentence based on sentences in "All Summer in a Day" or "Suzy and Leah." Underline each nominative pronoun. Circle each objective pronoun.*

1. They hated her because she had seen the sun.
2. He gave her a shove, but she did not move away from him.
3. The thunder and rain chased them back inside, where they let her out of the closet.
4. When I looked back, she was gone, and I didn't see her again until the next day.
5. They didn't know how to peel oranges, so I taught them.
6. She loves Avi and tries to protect him.

B. Writing Application: *Rewrite each sentence by replacing each underlined noun with a pronoun. Be sure to see the difference between a nominative pronoun and an objective pronoun.*

1. The students wanted to see the sun, so the teacher let the students go outside.

   _____

2. Margot hoped to see the sun, but the students locked Margot in the closet.

   _____

3. William said Margot was a liar, but Margot stuck to Margot's story.

   _____

4. Leah refuses Suzy's candy because Leah doesn't want to look like an animal.

   _____

"All Summer in a Day" by Ray Bradbury
"Suzy and Leah" by Jane Yolen

Integrated Language Skills: Support for Writing a News Report

"All Summer in a Day": To prepare for your **news report** that tells about the day the sun appeared on Venus, complete this chart.

Question	Information in "All Summer in a Day"
Who sees the sun, and who does not see it?	
What happens when the sun is shining?	
When does the sun shine, and for how long?	
Where do the events take place?	
Why do the characters in the story respond to the sun the way they do?	

"Suzy and Leah": To prepare for your **news report** that tells about the refugee camp where Leah is living, complete this chart.

Question	Information in "Suzy and Leah"
Who is living in the camp that Suzy visits?	
What has brought Suzy to the camp?	
When are the events taking place?	
Where (in what country) is the camp?	
Why has the camp been set up?	

Now, use your notes to write a news report.

"My First Free Summer" by Julia Alvarez
Writing About the Big Question

What is the best way to find the truth?

Big Question Vocabulary

awareness	believable	conclude	convince	debate
evaluate	evidence	explain	factual	fiction
insight	perceive	reality	reveal	truth

A. *Use one or more words from the list above to complete each sentence.*

1. When an author uses autobiographical information in her writing, she _____s a personal truth.

2. When reading autobiographical fiction, the reader gains _____ into the author's real life.

3. Some works of fiction can lead to a _____ about philosophical questions.

B. *Answer the questions.*

1. Describe an event in your life that you perceived differently from someone else.

   _____

   _____

2. If you were to debate the event with the other person, would you be able to convince him or her that your version of the truth is correct? Why or why not? Use two vocabulary words in your answer.

   _____

   _____

   _____

C. *Complete the sentence below. Then, write a short paragraph connecting the sentence to the Big Question.*

Reflecting on past events _____

How might you incorporate an event from your life into a fictional story? Describe the event and a story you might create.

_____

_____

_____

_____

"My First Free Summer" by Julia Alvarez

Reading: Use Background Information to Determine the Author's Purpose

One way to determine the **author's purpose,** or reason, for writing a nonfiction work is to **use background information** that you already know about the author and topic. For example, knowing that an author grew up outside the United States might help you determine that she wrote an essay to inform readers about the country where she spent her childhood.

Although she was born in the United States, Julia Alvarez spent much of her childhood in the Dominican Republic. Near the beginning of her essay, she writes,

> That was the problem. English. My mother had decided to send her children to the American school so we could learn the language of the nation that would soon be liberating us.

The author's purpose for providing this background information is to inform readers of her reasons for studying English and attending an American school. Authors provide background information for other purposes as well—for example, to entertain or to create a mood.

DIRECTIONS: *Read each of these passages from "My First Free Summer." Decide whether the author's purpose is* to inform, to create a mood, *or* to entertain. *Write the purpose on the line following the passage. A passage may have more than one purpose.*

1. For thirty years, the Dominican Republic had endured a bloody and repressive dictatorship. From my father, who was involved in an underground plot, my mother knew that *los américanos* had promised to help bring democracy to the island.

   Author's purpose(s): _____

2. Meanwhile, I had to learn about the pilgrims with their funny witch hats, about the 50 states and where they were on the map, about Dick and Jane and their tame little pets, Puff and Spot, about freedom and liberty and justice for all—while being imprisoned in a hot classroom with a picture of a man wearing a silly wig hanging above the blackboard.

   Author's purpose(s): _____

3. The grounds on which the American school stood had been donated by my grandfather. . . . The bulk of the student body was made up of the sons and daughters of American diplomats and business people, but a few Dominicans—most of them friends or members of my family—were allowed to attend.

   Author's purpose(s): _____

Name _____   Date _____

"My First Free Summer" by Julia Alvarez
Literary Analysis: Historical Context

When a literary work is based on real events, the historical context can help you understand the action. **Historical context**—the actual political and social events and trends of the time—can explain why characters act and think the way they do. Read the following passage from "My First Free Summer." Think about what it tells you about the historical context of the selection.

> For thirty years, the Dominican Republic had endured a bloody and repressive dictatorship. From my father, who was involved in an underground plot, my mother knew that *los américanos* had promised to help bring democracy to the island.

DIRECTIONS: *Read each of these passages from "My First Free Summer." On the lines that follow, write a sentence telling how the historical context affects the action.*

1. I didn't know about my father's activities. I didn't know the dictator was bad. All I knew was that my friends who were attending Dominican schools were often on holiday to honor the dictator's birthday, the dictator's saint day, the day the dictator became the dictator, the day the dictator's oldest son was born, and so on.

    How context affects action: _____

    _____

2. But the yard replete with cousins and friends that I had dreamed about all year was deserted. Family members were leaving for the United States, using whatever connections they could drum up. The plot had unraveled. Every day there were massive arrests. The United States had closed its embassy and was advising Americans to return home.

    How context affects action: _____

    _____

3. I was about to tell her that I didn't want to go to the United States, where . . . everyone spoke English. But my mother lifted a hand for silence. "We're leaving in a few hours. I want you all to go get ready! I'll be in to pack soon." The desperate look in her eyes did not allow for contradiction. We raced off, wondering how to fit the contents of our Dominican lives into four small suitcases.

    How context affects action: _____

    _____

4. Next morning, we are standing inside a large, echoing hall as a stern American official reviews our documents. What if he doesn't let us in? What if we have to go back? I am holding my breath. My parents' terror has become mine.

    How context affects action: _____

    _____

Name _____ Date _____

"My First Free Summer" by Julia Alvarez
Vocabulary Builder

Word List

contradiction   diplomats   extenuating   repressive   summoned   vowed

A. DIRECTIONS: *Something is wrong with the following sentences. Revise each one, using the Word List word in a way that makes the sentence logical.*

1. After her first free summer, Julia *vowed* to pass all her subjects.

   Revision: _____

2. The mission of the *diplomats* was to negotiate the terms of the new car's warranty.

   Revision: _____

3. When Julia's mother *summoned* her daughters, Julia and her sister left for the beach.

   Revision: _____

4. The *repressive* government allowed complete freedom of speech and religion for all of its citizens.

   Revision: _____

5. The judge argued for a harsh sentence because of all the *extenuating* circumstances of the crime.

   Revision: _____

6. When all the witnesses offered a *contradiction* to the defendant's testimony, it was obvious that the defendant was telling the truth.

   Revision: _____

B. WORD STUDY: The Latin root *-dict-* means "to speak, assert." In the following sentences, think about the meaning of *-dict-* in each italicized word. On the line before each sentence, write *T* if the statement is true or *F* if the statement is false. Then, explain your answer.

1. _____ A *prediction* tells what happened in the past. _____

   _____

2. _____ A *dictionary* contains the roots and definitions of words. _____

   _____

3. _____ A *dictator* is the democratically elected head of a country. _____

   _____

Name _____ Date _____

from **Angela's Ashes** by Frank McCourt
Writing About the Big Question
What is the best way to find the truth?

Big Question Vocabulary

awareness	believable	conclude	convince	debate
evaluate	evidence	explain	factual	fiction
insight	perceive	reality	reveal	truth

A. *Use one or more words from the list above to complete each sentence.*

1. After some time has passed, it is easier to _____ important life events.

2. Though sometimes an event seems unimportant while it is happening, we may later gain _____ about its importance.

3. Often, in a memoir, the author will _____ the significance of events in his or her past.

B. *Answer the questions. Use one vocabulary word in each answer.*

1. What event in your life so far would you focus on in a short memoir?

   _____

   _____

   _____

2. If you could ask anyone to write a memoir, who would you ask, and why? What would you want them to tell about?

   _____

   _____

   _____

C. *Complete the sentence below. Then, answer the question with a short paragraph connecting the sentence to the Big Question.*

Things that don't seem important while they are happening _____

Give an example of a lesson that an author might learn from personal experience and how he or she may later use this experience in a work of fiction.

_____

_____

_____

_____

Name _____ Date _____

from **Angela's Ashes** by Frank McCourt
Reading: Use Background Information to Determine the Author's Purpose

One way to determine the **author's purpose,** or reason, for writing a nonfiction work is to use **background information** that you already know about the author and topic. For example, knowing that an author grew up outside the United States might help you determine that he wrote a story to inform readers about the country where he spent his youth.

Although he was born in the United States, Frank McCourt spent his childhood and teen years in Ireland. The reader learns some of this information in the excerpt from *Angela's Ashes*, which is set in the Irish hospital where the ten-year-old McCourt recovered from typhoid fever. For example, McCourt writes the following about one of the nurses in the hospital:

She's a very stern nurse from the County Kerry and she frightens me.

The author's purpose for writing this sentence is twofold: (a) to inform the reader that the story takes place in Ireland (County Kerry is a southwestern county of Ireland) and (b) to help establish a mood by portraying the harsh and frightening personality of the nurse. In addition to informing or creating a mood, an author might write a passage in order to entertain the reader.

DIRECTIONS: *Read each of these passages from the excerpt from* Angela's Ashes. *Decide whether the author's purpose is to inform, to create a mood, or to entertain. Write the purpose on the line following the passage. A passage may have more than one purpose.*

1. I have diphtheria and something else.

   What's something else?

   They don't know. They think I have a disease from foreign parts because my father used to be in Africa. I nearly died. . . .

   Author's purpose(s): _____

2. There are twenty beds in the ward, all white, all empty. The nurse tells Seamus to put me at the far end of the ward against the wall to make sure I don't talk to anyone who might be passing the door, which is very unlikely since there isn't another soul on this whole floor.

   Author's purpose(s): _____

3. [The nurse] leaves and there's silence for a while. Then Patricia whispers, Give thanks, Francis, give thanks, and say your rosary, Francis, and I laugh so hard a nurse runs in to see if I'm all right. . . .

   Author's purpose(s): _____

Name _____ Date _____

from **Angela's Ashes** by Frank McCourt
Literary Analysis: Historical Context

When a literary work is based on real events, the historical context can help you understand the action. Historical context—the actual political and social events and trends of the time—can explain why characters act and think the way they do. Read the following passage from the excerpt from *Angela's Ashes*. Think about what it tells you about the historical context of the selection.

> She tells Seamus this was the fever ward during the Great Famine long ago and only God knows how many died here brought in too late for anything but a wash before they were buried and there are stories of cries and moans in the far reaches of the night. She says 'twould break your heart to think of what the English did to us, that if they didn't put the blight on the potato they didn't do much to take it off.

DIRECTIONS: *Read each of these passages from* Angela's Ashes. *On the lines that follow, write a sentence telling how the historical context affects the action.*

1. Mam visits me on Thursdays. I'd like to see my father, too, but I'm out of danger, crisis time is over, and I'm allowed only one visitor. Besides, she says, he's back at work at Rank's Flour Mills and please God this job will last a while with the war on and the English desperate for flour. She brings me a chocolate bar and that proves Dad is working. She could never afford one on the dole.

   Historical context and effect on story: _____

   _____

2. [Seamus] says I'm not supposed to be bringing anything from a dipteria room to a typhoid room with all the germs flying around and hiding between the pages and if you ever catch dipteria on top of the typhoid they'll know and I'll lose my good job and be out on the street singing patriotic songs with a tin cup in my hand, which I could easily do because there isn't a song ever written about Ireland's sufferings I don't know. . . .

   Historical context and effect on story: _____

   _____

3. No pity. No feeling at all for the people that died in this very ward, children suffering and dying here while the English feasted on roast beef and guzzled the best of wine in their big houses, little children with their mouths all green from trying to eat the grass in the fields beyond, God bless us and save us and guard us from future famines.

   Historical context and effect on story: _____

   _____

Name _____ Date _____

from **Angela's Ashes** by Frank McCourt
Vocabulary Builder

Word List

ban   desperate   guzzle   miracle   patriotic   saluting

A. DIRECTIONS: *Write a sentence that describes each situation and shows the meaning of each vocabulary word.*

1. Why government wants to *ban* a harmful product or chemical:

_____

_____

2. Why someone might feel *desperate*:

_____

_____

3. Why one might *guzzle* a drink:

_____

_____

4. A situation that seems like—or calls for—a *miracle*:

_____

_____

5. A *patriotic* ceremony:

_____

_____

6. A situation that would call for *saluting*:

_____

_____

B. WORD STUDY: The Latin root -*sper*- means "hope." Think about the meaning of -*sper*- in each italicized word. On the line before each sentence, write *T* if the statement is true or *F* if the statement is false. Then, explain your answer.

1. _____ Someone who feels *desperate* on first seeing an exam expects to do well.

_____

2. _____ A person who is in *despair* has a negative outlook on life.

_____

3. _____ In a time of *prosperity*, most people are living in poverty.

_____

"My First Free Summer" by Julia Alvarez
from **Angela's Ashes** by Frank McCourt
Integrated Language Skills: Grammar

A **possessive pronoun** is a pronoun that shows ownership.

The football that belongs to **me**	**my** football
The video that belongs to **you**	**your** video
The idea that belongs to **her**	**her** idea
The answer that belongs to **him**	**his** answer
The house that belongs to **them**	**their** house
The decision that belongs to **us**	**our** decision

A. PRACTICE: *Underline each possessive pronoun in the sentences below.*

1. Alvarez vowed she would learn her English.
2. My mother decided to send her children to the American school.
3. I had to learn about the pilgrims with their funny witch hats.
4. The soldiers go seat by seat, looking at our faces.
5. While in the hospital, Frank wants his father to visit him.
6. When a nurse is unkind to the children, Seamus takes their side against her.

B. Writing Application: *For each sentence below, change the underlined pronoun into a possessive pronoun.*

1. Alvarez learned <u>she</u> subjects, so she could play with <u>she</u> family that summer.

    _____

2. But, she says, "<u>I</u> family were packing <u>they</u> clothing to move to America."

    _____

3. Frank McCourt liked Patricia Madigan and appreciated <u>she</u> sense of humor.

    _____

4. Mam hopes that Frank's father can keep <u>he</u> job.

    _____

5. The nurses are cruel to Frank and Patricia and take away <u>they</u> fun.

    _____

"My First Free Summer" by Julia Alvarez
from **Angela's Ashes** by Frank McCourt

Integrated Language Skills: Support for Writing a Letter

For your letter to Julia Alvarez describing what it is like to go to school in the United States or your letter to Frank McCourt describing a favorite story or poem, gather your ideas in one of the charts below.

Letter to Julia Alvarez:

Topics for Letter	My Ideas About These Topics
School hours and holidays and the school year	
Subjects and homework	
After-school activities	
Best and worst things about school	

Letter to Frank McCourt:

Topics for Letter	My Ideas About These Topics
Title of favorite story or poem	
Details about events or characters in the story, or about descriptions or sounds in the poem	
Things you liked best about the story or poem	
A reason you might recommend the story or poem to Frank McCourt	

All-in-One Workbook

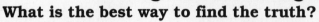

"**Stolen Day**" by Sherwood Anderson
"**The Night the Bed Fell**" by James Thurber

Writing About the Big Question

What is the best way to find the truth?

Big Question Vocabulary

awareness	believable	conclude	convince	debate
evaluate	evidence	explain	factual	fiction
insight	perceive	reality	reveal	truth

A. *Use one or more words from the list above to complete each sentence.*

1. When there are several different versions of _____, it does not mean that someone is not telling the _____.

2. People describe events differently when they _____ them differently.

3. Four different stories of the same event by four different witnesses can all be _____.

B. *Answer the questions.*

1. What are two things that you and a family member may disagree on?

   _____   _____

2. In a debate about what really happened to start an argument between you and your sibling, how do you convince your family members that your version of the truth is the correct version? Use two vocabulary words in your answer.

   _____

   _____

   _____

C. *Complete the sentence below. Then, use the writing prompt to write a short paragraph connecting the sentence to the Big Question.*

Family members may experience the same event differently because _____

_____

Write two versions of the same event. One will be your perception of the truth. The other will be a different perspective—a fictional account that someone else might think was the truth.

_____

_____

_____

Name _____ Date _____

"Stolen Day" by Sherwood Anderson
"The Night the Bed Fell" by James Thurber
Literary Analysis: Comparing Characters

A **character** is a person or an animal that takes part in the action of a literary work. In literature, you will find characters with a range of personalities and attitudes. For example, a character might be dependable and intelligent but also stubborn. One character might hold traditional values, while another might rebel against them. The individual qualities that make each character unique are called **character traits.**

Writers use the process of **characterization** to create and develop characters. There are two types of characterization:

- **Direct characterization:** The writer directly states or describes the character's traits.
- **Indirect characterization:** The writer reveals a character's personality through his or her words and actions, and through the thoughts, words, and actions of other characters.

DIRECTIONS: *To analyze the use of characterization in "Stolen Day" and "The Night the Bed Fell," complete the following chart. Answer each question with a brief example from the story. Write* not applicable *if you cannot answer a question about one of the characters.*

Character	Words that describe the character directly	What the character says and does	How other characters talk about or act toward the character
The narrator of "Stolen Day"			
The mother in "Stolen Day"			
Briggs Beall in "The Night the Bed Fell"			
The mother in "The Night the Bed Fell"			

"Stolen Day" by Sherwood Anderson
"The Night the Bed Fell" by James Thurber
Vocabulary Builder

Word List

affects   culprit   deluge   ominous   perilous   pungent   solemn

A. DIRECTIONS: *Read each sentence, paying attention to the italicized word from the Word List. If the word is used correctly, write* Correct *on the line. If it is not used correctly, write a new sentence using the word.*

1. The girl's smile was *ominous* as she happily and gently hugged her new puppy.

   _____

2. The *deluge* of rain caused the river to overflow.

   _____

3. The boy was *solemn* after he heard the good news.

   _____

4. A week of rainy weather often *affects* a person's mood negatively.

   _____

5. The mountain climbers had the most *perilous* stretch at the tip of the peak.

   _____

6. The sweet taste of peppermint ice cream was *pungent*.

   _____

7. The old lady was considered the most likely *culprit* when her purse was stolen.

   _____

B. DIRECTIONS: *Write the letter of the word that is most similar in meaning to the word from the Word List.*

____ 1. solemn
  A. joyful   B. silent   C. serious   D. cheerful

____ 2. perilous
  A. happy   B. tired   C. safe   D. dangerous

____ 3. pungent
  A. sharp   B. silly   C. serious   D. light

____ 4. culprit
  A. judge   B. criminal   C. jury   D. lawyer

____ 5. ominous
  A. easy   B. huge   C. threatening   D. pleasant

____ 6. deluge
  A. flood   B. water   C. storm   D. lightening

____ 7. affects
  A. enjoys   B. praises   C. allows   D. changes

Name _____ Date _____

"**Stolen Day**" by Sherwood Anderson
"**The Night the Bed Fell**" by James Thurber

Support for Writing to Compare Literary Works

Before you **write an essay comparing and contrasting** the narrators in "Stolen Day" and "The Night the Bed Fell," jot down your ideas in this graphic organizer. In the overlapping section of each set of boxes, write details that are true of both characters. In the sections on the left, write details that describe the narrator of "Stolen Day," and in the sections on the right, write details that describe the narrator of "The Night the Bed Fell,"

What are some of each character's traits?

Narrator of "Stolen Day":	Both:	Narrator of "The Night the Bed Fell":

What problems does each character face? How much responsibility does each character have in creating his problem?

Narrator of "Stolen Day":	Both:	Narrator of "The Night the Bed Fell":

What does the character learn from his situation? Which character learns more?

Narrator of "Stolen Day":	Both:	Narrator of "The Night the Bed Fell":

Now, use your notes to write an essay that compares and contrasts the two characters.

Conflict Resolution, performed by Tavi Fields

Yo'

It starts with a thought made from experience and what we are taught.

Then comes a different idea that doesn't mix in—

one against the other, now we have **competition.**

And where it goes depends on the ones involved,

the situation can remain or get solved.

It's your choice how you think about it, how you react to it—

that's your **attitude**, now don't you act foolish!

Keep your cool homie, and try to be patient.

Get your skills up, mainly your **communication.**

That's you expressing yourself and giving information.

How it's received depends on interpretation.

So choose your moves carefully and dare to be your best.

The more control you have on your end, the less stress (yeah, uh-huh)...

Sometimes we must lose in order to win in the end.

You gotta dust shoes off and get into the wind,

And let it take you farther than you can begin,

To imagine it happens again and again.

Sometimes we must lose in order to win in the end.

You gotta dust shoes off and get into the wind,

And let it take you farther than you can begin,

To imagine it happens again and again.

So we have two sides to the vision,

and when they're not similar we have **opposition.**

Then if we make it a contest that's a **challenge.**

Be careful how you handle it, it's best to find balance.

And if not, that's a **conflict**—pieces to the puzzle

are missin'. The mission to find them is the **struggle.**

The frustration naturally causes anger,

but when safety is threatened , that's **danger.**

Continued

Easy, self-control is a must.

If you wanna win in the end you gotta have trust

in a settlement, that's the resolution,

in other words an answer to the problem—a solution.

But you have to want it 'cause want equals desire.

It's the fire in your wishes, changing browsers into buyers.

Yo,

Sometimes we must lose in order to win in the end.

You gotta dust shoes off and get into the wind

And let it take you farther than you can begin

To imagine it happens again and again.

Sometimes we must lose in order to win in the end.

You gotta dust shoes off and get into the wind

And let it take you farther than you can begin

To imagine it happens again and again.

A lot of problems begin with **misunderstanding**—

when the point gets lost and there is confusion.

And when you make it to the end, just don't be surprised

if you have to sacrifice something 'cause that's **compromise.**

It's the solution to many **conflicts** or **disagreements**.

It's when you find middle ground, an' ease the moment.

Don't focus on the **obstacles,** the things in your way.

They'll take different forms and shapes on different days.

It's about how you get past them, that's where the lesson is.

The results, the **outcome,** that's where progression is.

And **understanding** is key to the process.

That's when you get it and eliminate the nonsense.

Word

Uh-huh, wha, yo'

Sometimes we must lose in order to win in the end.

You gotta dust shoes off and get into the wind

And let it take you farther than you can begin

To imagine it happens again and again.

Continued

Sometimes we must lose in order to win in the end.

You gotta dust shoes off and get into the wind

And let it take you farther than you can begin

To imagine it happens again and again.

Song Title: **Conflict Resolution**

Artist / Performed by Tavi Fields

Lyrics by Tavi Fields

Music composed by Mike Pandolfo, Wonderful

Produced by Mike Pandolfo, Wonderful

Executive Producer: Keith London, Defined Mind

Unit 2: Short Stories
Big Question Vocabulary—1

The Big Question: Does every conflict have a winner?

attitude: *n.* the opinion or feeling a person has about something

challenge: *n.* something that tests a person's strength, skill, or ability

     v. question or confront; other forms: *challenging, challenged*

communication: *n.* the act of speaking or writing to share ideas; other form: *communicate*

compromise: *v.* agree to accept less than originally wanted; negotiate

     n. an agreement in which people settle for less than they first wanted; other forms: *compromising, compromised*

outcome: *n.* final result of something; conclusion

A. DIRECTIONS: *Write the vocabulary word that best completes each group.*

1. settlement, negotiation, agreement, _____

2. test, trial, competition, _____

3. ending, resolution, answer, _____

4. conversation, correspondence, explanation, _____

5. thoughts, feelings, behavior, _____

B. DIRECTIONS: *Write a dialogue between two friends who are involved in a conflict. Through their discussion, they come to an agreement. Use all five vocabulary words.*

_____

_____

_____

_____

_____

_____

_____

_____

_____

_____

_____

_____

Unit 2: Short Stories
Big Question Vocabulary—2

The Big Question: Does every conflict have a winner?

competition: *n.* a contest between people or teams; other forms: *compete, competing, competed*

danger: *n.* a force or situation that may cause injury; hazard; other form: *dangerous*

desire: *n.* a strong hope or wish for something

       v. to want or hope for something; other forms: *desirable, desired*

resolution: *n.* the final solution to a problem or difficulty; other forms: *resolve*

understanding: *n.* knowledge about something, based on learning or experience

       adj. kind or forgiving; generous; other forms: *understand, understood*

Beth said this to Susan, Becky, and Danielle: "I can't believe that Sharon has decided to enter the race on Saturday. Everyone knows that that's *MY* race, and I'm determined to win it. I thought she was my friend, but I guess I was wrong. I hope someone trips her!"

Each of Beth's friends had a different reaction to what she said.

DIRECTIONS: *Use the word(s) given in parentheses to write what each friend said to Beth.*

Susan

> **(desire, competition)**

Becky

> **(understanding, danger)**

Danielle

> **(resolution)**

Unit 2: Short Stories
Big Question Vocabulary—3

The Big Question: Does every conflict have a winner?

disagreement: *n.* a situation involving a lack of agreement, which may or may not lead to an argument; other forms: *disagree, disagreeing*

misunderstanding: *n.* a mistake caused by not understanding a situation clearly

        v. not understanding something correctly; other form: *misunderstand*

obstacle: *n.* something that makes it difficult for a person to succeed; barrier

opposition: *n.* a strong disagreement regarding an issue; other forms: *oppose, opposed*

struggle: *n.* a long, hard fight against something

        v. to fight hard to succeed in a difficult task; other forms: *struggling, struggled*

A. DIRECTIONS: *Read each passage and follow the directions after it. In your answer, use the vocabulary words in parentheses, or one of their "other forms," shown above.*

1. Ramon tells Jenna to meet him "near the supermarket." Jenna waits for him next to *Brown's Market*, but Ramon doesn't show up. He is waiting near *RightPrice Groceries.*

   Describe this situation. **(misunderstanding, obstacle)** _____

   _____

2. After a long and difficult search, Jenna finally finds Ramon, but she is angry. They argue.

   Describe what takes place. **(struggle, disagreement)** _____

   _____

3. Jenna says that Ramon should have been clearer in his directions regarding where to meet. Ramon doesn't agree.

   Describe what takes place. **(misunderstanding, opposition)** _____

   _____

4. They finally come to an agreement and settle their dispute.

   Use at least two of these vocabulary words to describe the end of the story: **(resolution, understanding, compromise, communication)** _____

   _____

Name _____ Date _____

Unit 2: Short Stories
Applying the Big Question

 Does every conflict have a winner?

DIRECTIONS: *Complete the chart below to apply what you have learned about winners and losers in conflict. One row has been completed for you.*

Example	Type of Conflict	Cause	Effect	Who won or lost	What I learned
From Literature	The competition in "Amigo Brothers".	Two friends both want to win the Golden Gloves championship tournament.	They feel funny around each other at first.	Both boys won because each tried to do his best	Some conflicts do not have a loser.
From Literature					
From Science					
From Social Studies					
From Real Life					

Walter Dean Myers
Listening and Viewing

Segment 1: Meet Walter Dean Myers
- Why was it important for Walter Dean Myers to write about his community?
- What would you write about your community?

_____

_____

_____

_____

Segment 2: The Short Story
- Why would a scrapbook be a good basis for a short story?
- In what ways might Myers's short stories serve as his own scrapbook?

_____

_____

_____

_____

Segment 3: The Writing Process
- What does Myers use for inspiration for his characters?
- Would that method help you develop characters? Why or why not?

_____

_____

_____

_____

Segment 4: The Rewards of Writing
- What does Walter Dean Myers mean when he says, "Reading can make you more"?
- How has reading made you "more"?

_____

_____

_____

_____

Unit 2
Learning About Short Stories

The **short story** is a form of fiction. Certain elements are common to short stories. For example, all short stories contain **characters,** the people or animals in the story. The reasons that explain why characters act as they do are called their **motivation.** The way in which a writer reveals a character's personality and qualities is called **characterization.** There are two kinds of characterization:

- Through **direct characterization,** the writer *tells* what the character is like.
- Through **indirect characterization,** the writer *shows* what the character is like. That is, the reader must draw conclusions about the character's personality and qualities based on the character's appearance, words, and actions and what other characters say about him or her.

The **plot** is the series of events in a short story. A plot usually has five parts:

1. The **exposition** introduces the **setting** (the time and place of the story), the characters, and the basic situation.
2. The **rising action** introduces, develops, and deepens the **conflict,** or problem.
3. The **climax** is the point of highest tension, the turning point. During the climax, the characters confront the conflict.
4. During the **falling action,** the characters solve the problem, and the tension eases.
5. The **resolution** is the conclusion, when the conflict is settled and the outcome of the story is revealed.

The **theme** is a central message about life. A **universal theme** is one that is expressed in many cultures and time periods. It reflects basic human values. An example is "Crime does not pay."

A. DIRECTIONS: *On the line, write the letter of the short story element that each sentence illustrates.*

_____ 1. "Experience is a great teacher."
    A. conflict   B. theme

_____ 2. "He was a clever man."
    A. direct characterization   B. indirect characterization

_____ 3. "It was a cold winter's night."
    A. setting   B. plot

_____ 4. "Jake couldn't hold on to the rocky ledge any longer. He started to fall."
    A. resolution   B. climax

_____ 5. "Once the fire was out, we found a safe place to lie down and rest."
    A. rising action   B. falling action

B. DIRECTIONS: *On a separate sheet of paper, write the exposition of a short story. In your exposition, introduce the setting, a main character, and a basic situation. Use indirect characterization to show what your main character is like.*

"The Treasure of Lemon Brown" by Walter Dean Myers
Model Selection: Short Story

The characters in short stories are driven by **motivations**—reasons, needs, and feelings that cause them to act the way they do.

Characterization is the way in which a writer reveals a character's traits, or personal qualities. Through **direct characterization,** the writer *tells* what the character is like. Through **indirect characterization,** the writer *shows* what the character is like. With indirect characterization, the reader must draw conclusions about the character based on the character's appearance, words, and actions, as well as what other characters say about him or her.

A. DIRECTIONS: *Answer these questions about the plot, characters, characterization, and setting of "The Treasure of Lemon Brown."*

1. In the exposition, Greg is angry. What basic situation has caused his anger?

_____

2. Describe the traits, or personal qualities, of Lemon Brown.

_____

_____

3. Lemon Brown says, "Hard times caught up with me." What does he mean? Is this an example of direct or indirect characterization? Explain your answer.

_____

_____

_____

4. What conflict do Greg and Lemon Brown face?

_____

_____

5. How do Greg and Lemon Brown behave at the climax of the story?

_____

B. DIRECTIONS: *The **theme** of a story is its message about life. A **universal theme** reflects basic human values in many cultures. An example is "Hard work pays off." Answer these questions about the theme of "The Treasure of Lemon Brown."*

1. What might be the theme of "The Treasure of Lemon Brown"? Support your answer by citing details from the story.

_____

_____

2. Is the theme you stated universal? Explain why or why not.

_____

_____

Name _____ Date _____

Writing About the Big Question

Does every conflict have a winner?

Big Question Vocabulary

attitude	challenge	communication	competition
compromise	conflict	danger	desire
disagreement	misunderstanding	obstacle	opposition
outcome	resolution	struggle	understanding

A. *Use one or more words from the list above to complete each sentence.*

1. Caring for others involves _____ about their needs.

2. Lack of _____ can lead to neglect, which can create resentment.

3. When conflicts occur, both parties must be willing to _____.

4. They must approach their differences with a supportive _____.

B. *Follow the directions in responding to each of the items below.*

1. Describe a time when a person or an animal you know, or a character from a book or TV show, experienced neglect.

   _____

   _____

2. Write two sentences explaining how the preceding experience affected those involved. Use at least two of the Big Question vocabulary words.

   _____

   _____

C. *Complete the sentence below. Then, write a short paragraph in which you connect this situation to the Big Question.*

When a parent takes no interest in a child, _____

_____

_____

_____

_____

_____

_____

"**The Bear Boy**" by Joseph Bruchac

Reading: Use Prior Knowledge to Make Predictions

Predicting means making an intelligent guess about what will happen next in a story based on details in the text. You can also **use prior knowledge to make predictions.** For example, if a character in a story notices animal tracks in the snow, you can predict that the animal will play a part in the story because you know from prior knowledge that animal tracks mean that the animal is nearby.

DIRECTIONS: *Fill in the following chart with predictions as you read "The Bear Boy." Use clues from the story and your prior knowledge to make predictions. Then, compare your predictions with what actually happens. An example is shown.*

Story Details and Prior Knowledge	What I Predict Will Happen	What Actually Happens
People said that someone who followed a bear's tracks might never come back, but Kuo-Haya had never been told that. I know that if people are not warned of a danger, they may do something dangerous.	Kuo-Haya will see and follow a bear's tracks.	Kuo-Haya sees and follows a bear's tracks and finds some bear cubs.

"The Bear Boy" by Joseph Bruchac
Literary Analysis: Plot

Plot is the related sequence of events in a short story and other works of fiction. A plot has the following elements:

- **Exposition:** introduction of the setting (the time and place), the characters, and the basic situation
- **Rising Action:** events that introduce a **conflict,** or struggle, and increase the tension
- **Climax:** the story's high point, at which the eventual outcome becomes clear
- **Falling Action:** events that follow the climax
- **Resolution:** the final outcome and tying up of loose ends, when the reader learns how the conflict is resolved

In a story about a race, for example, the exposition would probably introduce the runners. The rising action might include a description of a conflict between two of the runners and some information about the start of the race. The climax might be the winning of the race by one of the runners. The falling action might include a meeting between the two runners, and the resolution might describe the end of their conflict.

DIRECTIONS: *Answer the following questions about the plot elements of "The Bear Boy."*

1. The exposition of "The Bear Boy" introduces characters and describes a setting. Who are the characters, and what is the setting?

   _____

   _____

2. How do you know that the father's neglect of Kuo-Haya is part of the rising action?

   _____

   _____

3. What happens in the climax of "The Bear Boy"?

   _____

   _____

4. Describe one event in the falling action of the story.

   _____

   _____

5. What happens in the resolution of "The Bear Boy"?

   _____

   _____

"The Bear Boy" by Joseph Bruchac
Vocabulary Builder

Word List

approvingly   canyon   guidance   initiation   neglected   timid

A. DIRECTIONS : *Use each vocabulary word by following the instructions below. Use the words in the same way they are used in "The Bear Boy," and write sentences that show you understand the meaning of the word.*

1. Use the word *timid* in a sentence about a rabbit.

   _____

2. Use the word *initiation* in a sentence about a ceremony.

   _____

3. Use the word *neglected* in a sentence about a garden.

   _____

4. Use the word *canyon* in a sentence about a vacation.

   _____

5. Use the word *approvingly* in a sentence about a grandmother.

   _____

6. Use the word *guidance* in a sentence about a coach.

   _____

B. WORD STUDY *The Latin suffix* -ance *means "the act of." Answer each of the following questions using one of these words containing* -ance: *compliance, dissonance, vigilance.*

1. Does *dissonance* describe a pleasing sound?

   _____

2. If I am in *compliance* with the rules, am I breaking them?

   _____

3. If people applaud my *vigilance,* do they consider me watchful?

   _____

Name _____ Date _____

Writing About the Big Question

Does every conflict have a winner?

Big Question Vocabulary

attitude	challenge	communication	competition
compromise	conflict	danger	desire
disagreement	misunderstanding	obstacle	opposition
outcome	resolution	struggle	understanding

A. *Use one or more words from the list above to complete each sentence.*

1. People can lose perspective during an intense _____.

2. Their only thought is to eliminate the _____ before them.

3. As a result, they may unintentionally place others in _____.

4. This can make _____ of the battle more complex.

B. *Follow the directions in responding to each of the items below.*

1. List two people whom you know or learned about in school or on the news who were affected by a battle that did not directly involve them.

   _____   _____.

2. Write two sentences describing the battle that affected one of these people, and explain how he or she was affected. Use at least two of the Big Question vocabulary words.

   _____

   _____

C. *Complete the sentence below. Then, write a short paragraph in which you connect this situation to the Big Question.*

Sometimes in a battle, innocent victims _____

_____

_____

_____

_____

_____

_____

Name _____ Date _____

"Rikki-tikki-tavi" by Rudyard Kipling
Reading: Use Prior Knowledge to Make Predictions

Predicting means making an intelligent guess about what will happen next in a story based on details in the text. You can also **use prior knowledge to make predictions.** For example, if a story introduces a mongoose and a snake and you know that mongooses and snakes are natural enemies, you can predict that the story will involve a conflict between the two animals.

DIRECTIONS: *Fill in the following chart with predictions as you read "Rikki-tikki-tavi." Use clues from the story and your prior knowledge to make predictions. Then, compare your predictions with what actually happens. An example is shown.*

Story Details and Prior Knowledge	What I Predict Will Happen	What Actually Happens
Teddy's mother says, "Perhaps he isn't really dead." I know that Rikki-tikki is the hero of the story, and heroes rarely die during a story.	The mongoose will live.	The mongoose lives.

"Rikki-tikki-tavi" by Rudyard Kipling
Literary Analysis: Plot

Plot is the related sequence of events in a short story and other works of fiction. A plot has the following elements:

- **Exposition:** introduction of the setting (the time and place), the characters, and the basic situation
- **Rising Action:** events that introduce a **conflict,** or struggle, and increase the tension
- **Climax:** the story's high point, at which the eventual outcome becomes clear
- **Falling Action:** events that follow the climax
- **Resolution:** the final outcome and tying up of loose ends, when the reader learns how the conflict is resolved

For example, in a story about a battle, the exposition would introduce the contestants. The rising action might explain the conflict between the contestants and describe events leading up to the battle. The climax might be the winning of the battle by one of the contestants. The falling action could include a celebration of the victory, and the resolution might tell about events that took place in the years following the battle.

DIRECTIONS: *Answer the following questions about the plot elements of "Rikki-tikki-tavi."*

1. Who are the characters, and what is the setting described in the exposition?

   _____

   _____

2. How do you know that the appearance of Nag is part of the rising action?

   _____

   _____

3. What happens in the climax of "Rikki-tikki-tavi"?

   _____

   _____

4. Describe one event in the falling action of the story.

   _____

   _____

5. What happens in the resolution of "Rikki-tikki-tavi"?

   _____

   _____

Name _____ Date _____

"**Rikki-tikki-tavi**" by Rudyard Kipling
Vocabulary Builder

Word List

consolation   cunningly   immensely   mourning   revived   veranda

A. DIRECTIONS: *Use each vocabulary word by following the instructions below. Use the words in the same way they are used in "Rikki-tikki-tavi," and write sentences that show you understand the meaning of the word.*

1. Use the word *revived* in a sentence about a bird.

   _____

2. Use the word *consolation* in a sentence about a race.

   _____

3. Use the word *immensely* in a sentence about an activity.

   _____

4. Use the word *veranda* in a sentence about summer.

   _____

5. Use the word *mourning* in a sentence about a dog.

   _____

6. Use the word *cunningly* in a sentence about a board game.

   _____

B. Word Study *The Latin suffix* -tion *means "the thing that is." Answer each of the following questions using one of these words containing* -tion: *humiliation, intimidation, justification.*

1. Why would a broken leg be *justification* for sitting out a soccer game?

   _____

2. Why would most people prefer that others not witness their *humiliation*?

   _____

3. If you use *intimidation* to get classmates to vote for you, how are you behaving?

   _____

"The Bear Boy" by Joseph Bruchac
"Rikki-tikki-tavi" by Rudyard Kipling
Integrated Language Skills: Grammar

Action Verbs and Linking Verbs

Verbs are words that express an action (for example, *swim* and *throw*) or a state of being (for example, *am, is, was,* and *seemed*). The verbs that express an action are called *action verbs.*

> Jessica *climbed* a mountain.

The verbs that express a state of being are called *linking verbs.* Linking verbs join the subject of a sentence with a word or expression that describes or renames the subject.

> Jessica *seems* strong.

> Jessica *is* a mountain climber.

Besides forms of *be* and *seem,* other verbs that can describe or rename a subject are *appear, look,* and *sound.*

A. Practice: *Underline the verbs in each sentence. On the line, identify each verb as an* action verb *or a* linking verb.

1. Rikki-tikki-tavi is a brave little mongoose. _____

2. Mongooses seem harmless, but they fight bravely. _____, _____

3. Rikki-tikki lives with a human family, and they love him. _____, _____

4. A snake threatens the family, and Rikki-tikki is furious. _____, _____

5. Rikki-tikki defeats the snake, and the family is very happy. _____, _____

B. Writing Application: *Write a paragraph about a time when you or someone you know was in danger. Use at least three action verbs and three linking verbs. Underline each action verb once and each linking verb twice.*

_____

_____

_____

_____

_____

_____

_____

_____

"Bear Boy" by Joseph Bruchac
"Rikki-tikki-tavi" by Rudyard Kipling

Integrated Language Skills: Support for Writing an Informative Article

Use the graphic organizer below to record details from each section of "Bear Boy" or "Rikki-tikki-tavi." Your details should tell *when, how much, how often,* or *to what extent.*

Introduction

Details:

Body

Details:

Conclusion

Details:

Now, use your notes to write a short informative article about mother bears or mongooses. Write for an audience of third-graders.

Name _____ Date _____

"**Letters from Rifka**" by Karen Hesse

Writing About the Big Question

Does every conflict have a winner?

Big Question Vocabulary

attitude	challenge	communication	competition
compromise	conflict	danger	desire
disagreement	misunderstanding	obstacle	opposition
outcome	resolution	struggle	understanding

A. *Use your own words or phrases to complete the paragraph below.*

Sometimes, if a **conflict** comes too close, families _____ to leave their

_____. If their lives continue to be in **danger**, they may even emigrate to

another _____. It can be a **challenge** to maintain a positive **attitude**

when leaving everything _____.

B. *Follow the directions in responding to each of the items below.*

1. List two groups of people you learned about in school that were forced to flee their homes as a result of war.

   _____   _____.

2. Choose one of the groups listed above, and briefly explain the **conflict** that forced its members to flee. Then, explain the **struggles** they faced in their new home.

   _____

   _____

   _____

   _____

C. *Complete the sentence below. Then, write a short paragraph in which you connect this experience to the Big Question.*

The true losers in a war are _____

_____

_____

_____

_____

_____

Name _____ Date _____

from **Letters from Rifka** by Karen Hesse
Reading: Read Ahead to Verify Predictions and Reread to Look for Details

A **prediction** is an informed guess about what will happen. Use details in the text and your own knowledge and experience to make predictions as you read. Then, **read ahead to verify predictions,** to check whether your predictions are correct.

- As you read, ask yourself whether new details support your predictions. If they do not, revise your predictions based on the new information.
- If the predictions you make turn out to be wrong, **reread to look for details** you might have missed that would have helped you make a more accurate prediction.

If it had not been for your father, though, I think my family would all be dead now: Mama, Papa, Nathan, Saul, and me.

Details in this passage can help you predict that the narrator will reveal that Rifka has escaped a dangerous situation. You can read further in the excerpt from *Letters from Rifka* to check this prediction.

DIRECTIONS: *Complete the following chart. If a prediction in the second column is correct, write* Correct *in the third column. If a prediction is wrong, write* Incorrect *in the third column. Then, in the fourth column, describe what does happen, and include a detail that would have allowed an accurate prediction. The first item has been completed as an example.*

Detail in *Letters from Rifka*	Prediction	Verification of Prediction	Event in Selection and Additional Detail
1. Tovah's father helps Rifka's family.	Tovah's father is in danger.	Incorrect	Tovah's father makes it home safely: "I am sure you and Cousin Hannah were glad to see Uncle Avrum come home today."
2. Rifka is not sure she will be able to distract the guards.	Rifka will not succeed.		
3. Nathan deserts the army.	Soldiers will look for Nathan.		
4. Rifka says, "Don't we need papers?"	Papa will find the papers.		

from **Letters from Rifka** by Karen Hesse
Literary Analysis: Characters

A **character** is a person or an animal that takes part in the action of a literary work.

- A **character's motives** are the emotions or goals that drive him or her to act one way or another. Some powerful motives are love, anger, and hope.
- **Character traits** are the individual qualities that make each character unique. These may be things such as stubbornness, sense of humor, or intelligence.

Characters' motives and qualities are important because they influence what characters do and how they interact with other characters. As you read, think about what the characters are like and why they do what they do. For example, consider this passage:

> I am sure you and Cousin Hannah were glad to see Uncle Avrum come home today. How worried his daughters must have been after the locked doors and whisperings of last night.

This passage illustrates Rifka's character traits: her caring nature and concern for others. It also suggests a motive for her actions: She wants her family to be safe.

A. DIRECTIONS: *After each character's name, write as many adjectives as you can think of that describe that character's traits.*

1. **Rifka:** _____

   _____

   _____

2. **Papa:** _____

   _____

   _____

B. DIRECTIONS: *Each quotation on the right states or hints at a motive for one of the actions on the left. On the line before each action, write the letter of the quotation that provides the motive.*

___ 1. Rifka writes to Tovah.

___ 2. Nathan deserts the army.

___ 3. Rifka distracts guards.

___ 4. Mama insists on taking candlesticks.

___ 5. Avrum helps the family escape.

A. "I've come," he said, "to warn Saul."

B. "Soon enough they will sweep down like vultures to pick our house bare."

C. "We made it!"

D. "If it had not been for your father, . . . my family would all be dead now."

E. "I knew, no matter how frightened I was, I must not let them find Nathan."

Name _____ Date _____

from **Letters from Rifka** by Karen Hesse
Vocabulary Builder

Word List

distract   emerged   huddled   peasants   precaution   regiment

A. DIRECTIONS: *Think about the meaning of the underlined word in each of these sentences. Then, answer the question.*

1. What might Rifka have done to <u>distract</u> the guards?

   _____

2. If Nathan had <u>emerged</u> from under the burlap bags, what might have happened?

   _____

3. Why had the family <u>huddled</u> in Tovah's cellar through the night?

   _____

4. Aside from a desire to join his family, why might Nathan have deserted his <u>regiment</u>?

   _____

5. Why might the <u>peasants</u> ransack homes that have been deserted?

   _____

6. Why did Rifka consider shutting Tovah out of the cellar a reasonable <u>precaution</u>?

   _____

B. WORD STUDY *The Latin root* -tract- *means "pull" or "drag." Answer each of the following questions using one of these words containing* -tract-: *attractive, protracted, retract.*

1. What are you doing when you *retract* a statement that you made?

   _____

2. What might cause a criminal trial to become *protracted*?

   _____

3. What are some things people might do to look *attractive*?

   _____

"Two Kinds" by Amy Tan

Writing About the Big Question

Does every conflict have a winner?

Big Question Vocabulary

attitude	challenge	communication	competition
compromise	conflict	danger	desire
disagreement	misunderstanding	obstacle	opposition
outcome	resolution	struggle	understanding

A. *Use one or more words from the list above to complete each sentence.*

1. It can be a _____ to try to live up to someone else's expectations.

2. People should be free to pursue the goals they truly _____.

3. Through _____, they can reach a(n) _____.

4. That way, their efforts can better achieve a positive _____.

B. *Follow the directions in responding to each of the items below.*

1. Describe a time when you did not live up to someone else's expectations or they did
   not live up to yours. _____
   _____

2. Write two or three sentences explaining how the preceding experience affected you
   and the other person involved. Use at least two of the Big Question vocabulary
   words.
   _____
   _____
   _____

C. *Complete the sentence below. Then, write a short paragraph in which you connect this
experience to the Big Question.*

When a person does not live up to someone else's expectations, the loser is _____

_____
_____
_____
_____
_____
_____

"Two Kinds" by Amy Tan

Reading: Read Ahead to Verify Predictions and Reread to Look for Details

A **prediction** is an informed guess about what will happen. Use details in the text and your own knowledge and experience to make predictions as you read. Then, **read ahead to verify predictions,** to check whether your predictions are correct.

- As you read, ask yourself whether new details support your predictions. If they do not, revise your predictions based on the new information.
- If the predictions you make turn out to be wrong, **reread to look for details** you might have missed that would have helped you make a more accurate prediction.

"Of course you can be prodigy, too," my mother told me when I was nine. "You can be best anything."

Details in this passage can help you predict that the narrator's mother will encourage her to become a prodigy. You can read further in "Two Kinds" to check this prediction.

DIRECTIONS: *Complete the following chart. If a prediction in the second column is correct, write* Correct *in the third column. If a prediction is wrong, write* Incorrect *in the third column. Then, in the fourth column, describe what does happen, and include a detail that would have allowed an accurate prediction. The first item has been completed as an example.*

Details in "Two Kinds"	Prediction	Verification of Prediction	Event in Selection and Additional Detail
1. The mother wants her daughter to be "a Chinese Shirley Temple."	The daughter will become the Chinese Shirley Temple.	Incorrect	The narrator fails at being Shirley Temple. "We didn't immediately pick the right kind of prodigy."
2. The daughter begins to think thoughts with "won'ts."	The daughter will rebel against her mother.		
3. The narrator must perform a simple piece "that sounded more difficult than it was."	She will perform well.		
4. The daughter sees her mother's offers of the piano "as a sign of forgiveness."	The daughter will take the piano.		

"Two Kinds" by Amy Tan
Literary Analysis: Characters

A **character** is a person or an animal that takes part in the action of a literary work.

- A **character's motives** are the emotions or goals that drive him or her to act one way or another. Some powerful motives are love, anger, and hope.
- **Character traits** are the individual qualities that make each character unique. These may be things such as stubbornness, sense of humor, or intelligence.

Characters' motives and qualities are important because they influence what characters do and how they interact with other characters. As you read, think about what the characters are like and why they do what they do. For example, consider this passage:

> She had come here in 1949 after losing everything in China: her mother and father, her family home, her first husband, and two daughters, twin baby girls. But she never looked back with regret. There were so many ways for things to get better.

This passage illustrates the mother's character traits: her strength and courage. It also suggests a motive for her actions: She wants things to get better.

A. DIRECTIONS: *After each character's name, write as many adjectives as you can think of that describe that character's traits.*

1. **The daughter:** _____

   _____

   _____

2. **The mother:** _____

   _____

   _____

B. DIRECTIONS: *Each quotation on the right states or hints at a motive for one of the actions on the left. On the line before each action, write the letter of the quotation that provides the motive.*

___ 1. Daughter wants to become a prodigy.

___ 2. Mother pushes her daughter to be a prodigy.

___ 3. Daughter refuses to play the piano.

___ 4. Mother offers her daughter the piano.

___ 5. Daughter begins to resist her mother's efforts to make her a prodigy.

A. I could sense her anger rising to its breaking point. I wanted to see it spill over.

B. I was filled with a sense that I would soon become *perfect*. My mother and father would adore me.

C. I saw the offer as a sign of forgiveness, a tremendous burden removed.

D. I won't let her change me, I promised myself. I won't be what I'm not.

E. "Only ask you be your best. For your sake."

Name _____   Date _____

"Two Kinds" by Amy Tan

Vocabulary Builder

Word List

conspired   debut   devastated   obedient   prodigy   reproach

A. DIRECTIONS: *Think about the meaning of the underlined word in each of these sentences. Then, answer the question.*

1. Would the daughter have been beyond <u>reproach</u> if she had become a prodigy? Why or why not?

   _____

2. How would the daughter have felt when her mother's expression <u>devastated</u> her?

   _____

3. If the mother and Old Chong <u>conspired</u> to hold a talent show, whose idea was it? How do you know?

   _____

4. What traits identify someone as a <u>prodigy</u>?

   _____

5. Where did the narrator make her musical <u>debut</u>?

   _____

6. How does an <u>obedient</u> child respond when asked to do something?

   _____

B. WORD STUDY: *The Latin root -spir- means "breath." Answer each of the following questions, using one of these words containing -spir-: respiration, inspirational, perspire.*

1. If someone's *respiration* is rapid, how is he or she breathing?

   _____

2. What makes a library an *inspirational* place?

   _____

3. When a person is in a gym, what might he or she do in order to *perspire*?

   _____

from **Letters from Rifka** by Karen Hesse
"Two Kinds" by Amy Tan
Integrated Language Skills: Grammar

Regular and Irregular Verbs

A **verb** expresses an action or a state of being. Every complete sentence needs to include at least one verb. Verbs have different forms, or tenses, that tell you when the action described took place. The four main tenses are *present, present participle, past,* and *past participle.*

Most verbs are *regular;* that is, their tenses are formed in a predictable way.

I *climb* that mountain every day.

Last month Michael *climbed* that mountain.

Jessica *has* often *climbed* that mountain.

Verbs that are *irregular* do not follow a predictable pattern.

I *am* a mountain climber.

Michael *was* a mountain climber before he broke his leg.

Jessica *has been* a mountain climber since she learned to walk.

A. PRACTICE: *Underline the verbs in each sentence. On the line, identify each verb as* regular *or* irregular. *Then, identify the tense of each verb. The tense will be* present, present participle, past, *or* past participle.

1. Her brother ran away from the army.

   Regular/Irregular: _____; **Principal part:** _____

2. The whole family fled from their home and is starting a new life.

   Regular/Irregular: _____; **Principal part:** _____

   Regular/Irregular: _____; **Principal part:** _____

3. Rifka was courageous, and she saved her family.

   Regular/Irregular: _____; **Principal part:** _____

   Regular/Irregular: _____; **Principal part:** _____

B. Writing Application: *Write a paragraph about a time when you or someone you know faced a frightening situation. Use at least three regular verbs and three irregular verbs. Underline each regular verb once and each irregular verb twice.*

_____

_____

_____

Name _____   Date _____

Integrated Language Skills: Support for Writing a Journal Entry

For your **journal entry**, put yourself in the place of the character you have chosen. Write that character's name on the line. Jot down specific events in the story. Then, imagine what you see and what you feel, and record those ideas on this chart.

My character:

_____

Event	Details from My Point of View	My Feelings About the Event

Now, use your notes to write a journal entry about the situation.

Name _____ Date _____

"**Seventh Grade**" by Gary Soto
"**Melting Pot**" by Anna Quindlen

Writing About the Big Question

Does every conflict have a winner?

Big Question Vocabulary

attitude	challenge	communication	competition
compromise	conflict	danger	desire
disagreement	misunderstanding	obstacle	opposition
outcome	resolution	struggle	understanding

A. *Use one or more words from the list above to complete each sentence.*

1. People often _____ to get along when they lack _____
   of one another's cultures.

2. This can be a(n) _____ to developing positive relationships.

3. Making an attempt at _____ can help everyone get along.

B. *Follow the directions in responding to each of the items below.*

1. List two different times when you experienced a conflict with another person.

   _____

   _____

2. Write two sentences explaining one of the preceding experiences, and describe how
   the conflict was resolved. Use at least two of the Big Question vocabulary words.

   _____

   _____

C. *Complete the sentence below. Then, write a short paragraph in which you connect this
experience to the Big Question.*

When you feel a conflict with another person, it is best to _____

_____

_____

_____

_____

_____

_____

_____

"Seventh Grade" by Gary Soto
"Melting Pot" by Anna Quindlen
Literary Analysis: Comparing Idioms

An **idiom** is an expression that cannot be understood by simply putting together the literal word-for-word meaning. Its meaning lies in a common use of the expression, which is often unique to a region or language.

For example, the sentence "This long line is for the birds!" contains an idiom. The phrase "for the birds" doesn't mean that the line is actually meant to be for birds. Some people use this expression to mean "not desirable" or "not good."

DIRECTIONS: *To analyze the use of idioms in "Seventh Grade" and "Melting Pot," complete the following chart. Jot down two or three idioms for each story. Then, answer the questions about each idiom.*

Story	Idioms	What is the literal, word-for-word meaning?	What is the intended common-use meaning?
"Seventh Grade"			
"Melting Pot"			

"Seventh Grade" by Gary Soto
"Melting Pot" by Anna Quindlen
Vocabulary Builder

Word List

bigots   elective   fluent   scowl

A. DIRECTIONS: *Think about the meaning of the italicized word in each sentence. Then, answer the question.*

1. Victor might have hoped that math would be an *elective* for seventh graders. Why? Explain your answer.

   _____

2. Many of the narrator's neighbors are *fluent* in Spanish. How do they speak the language?

   _____

3. New residents sometimes think the older residents are *bigots*. What does this mean?

   _____

4. Mr. Bueller is likely to *scowl* the next time a student speaks nonsense instead of French. How will Mr. Bueller look?

   _____

B. DIRECTIONS: *Write the letter of the word or phrase that is most similar in meaning to each Word Bank word.*

____ 1. fluent
   A. soft   C. flowing
   B. quiet   D. halting

____ 2. scowl
   A. frown   C. shovel
   B. smile   D. boat

____ 3. bigots
   A. fanatics   C. rebels
   B. racists   D. activists

____ 4. elective
   A. optional course   C. dismissal
   B. political process   D. requirement

"**Seventh Grade**" by Gary Soto
"**Melting Pot**" by Anna Quindlen

Integrated Language Skills: Support for Writing to Compare and Contrast Literary Works

Before you **write an essay comparing and contrasting** how idioms added to your interest in the stories "Seventh Grade" and "Melting Pot," jot down your ideas in this graphic organizer. For each story, choose one idiom. In the corresponding columns, write each idiom's literal and intended meanings. Then, describe how each idiom adds to our knowledge of the character or situation being described. Finally, rate the overall effectiveness of the idiom, and explain why it did or did not add interest to the story.

Story	"Seventh Grade"	"Melting Pot"
Idiom		
Literal Meaning		
Intended Meaning		
How the idiom contributes to my knowledge of the character or situation		
The overall effectiveness of the idiom in adding interest to the story		

Now, use your notes to write an essay that compares and contrasts how the idioms added to your interest in the two stories.

Name _____ Date _____

Writing About the Big Question

Does every conflict have a winner?

Big Question Vocabulary

attitude	challenge	communication	competition
compromise	conflict	danger	desire
disagreement	misunderstanding	obstacle	opposition
outcome	resolution	struggle	understanding

A. *Use one or more words from the list above to complete each sentence.*

1. We all would like to have those things that we _____ most.

2. However, a wish come true sometimes creates more _____ than joys.

3. It may even bring you into _____ with others or with your principles.

4. Your _____ toward what you want may change once you have it.

B. *Follow the directions in responding to each of the items below.*

1. List two examples of wishes that could have negative consequences if they came true.

   _____   _____

2. Write two to three sentences explaining how having one of the preceding wishes come true could turn out badly. Use at least two of the Big Question vocabulary words.

   _____

   _____

   _____

C. *Complete the sentence below. Then, write a short paragraph in which you connect this idea to the Big Question.*

Having wishes come true can sometimes _____

_____

_____

_____

_____

_____

"**The Third Wish**" by Joan Aiken

Reading: Make Inferences by Recognizing Details

Short story writers do not directly tell you everything there is to know about the characters, setting, and events. Instead, they leave it to you to **make inferences,** or logical guesses, about unstated information.

To form inferences, you must **recognize details** in the story and consider their importance. For example, in "The Third Wish," Mr. Peters finds a swan tangled up in thorns. When he moves closer and tries to free the swan, the swan hisses at him, pecks at him, and flaps its wings in a threatening way. You can use those clues to infer that the swan does not like or trust Mr. Peters.

DIRECTIONS: *The sentences in the left-hand column of this chart offer details about characters in "The Third Wish." (Some of the items are quotations from the story; some are based on the story.) In the right-hand column, describe what the details tell you about the character.*

Detail About a Character	Inference About the Character
1. Presently, the swan, when it was satisfied with its appearance, floated in to the bank once more, and in a moment, instead of the great white bird, there was a little man all in green.	
2. Mr. Peters wishes for a wife "as beautiful as the forest." A woman appears who is "the most beautiful creature he had ever seen, with eyes as blue-green as the canal, hair as dusky as the bushes, and skin as white as the feathers of swans."	
3. But as time went by Mr. Peters began to feel that [Leita] was not happy. She seemed restless, wandered much in the garden, and sometimes when he came back from the fields he would find the house empty. She would return after half an hour with no explanation of where she had been.	
4. After Leita was returned to the form of a swan, she "rested her head lightly against [Mr. Peters's] hand. . . . Next day he saw two swans swimming at the bottom of the garden, and one of them wore the gold chain he had given Leita after their marriage; she came up and rubbed her head against his hand."	

"The Third Wish" by Joan Aiken
Literary Analysis: Conflict

Most fictional stories center on a **conflict**—a struggle between opposing forces. There are two kinds of conflict:

- When there is an **external conflict,** a character struggles with an outside force, such as another character or nature.
- When there is an **internal conflict,** a character struggles with himself or herself to overcome opposing feelings, beliefs, needs, or desires. An internal conflict takes place in a character's mind.

The **resolution,** or outcome of the conflict, often comes toward the end of the story, when the problem is settled in some way.

A story can have additional, smaller conflicts that develop the main conflict. For example, in "The Third Wish," a small external conflict occurs between Mr. Peters and the swan that is tangled up in the thorns. As Mr. Peters tries to free the bird, the swan looks at him "with hate in its yellow eyes" and struggles with him. In addition, a minor internal conflict that helps develop the main conflict is Mr. Peters's difficulty in deciding what to do with his three wishes.

DIRECTIONS: *Based on details in each of the following passages from "The Third Wish," identify the conflict as* External *or* Internal. *Then, explain your answer.*

1. [Leita] was weeping, and as he came nearer he saw that tears were rolling, too, from the swan's eyes.

   "Leita, what is it?" he asked, very troubled.

   "This is my sister," she answered. "I can't bear being separated from her."

   Type of conflict: _____

   Explanation: _____

2. "Don't you love me at all, Leita?"

   "Yes, I do, I do love you," she said, and there were tears in her eyes again. "But I miss the old life in the forest."

   Type of conflict: _____

   Explanation: _____

3. She shook her head. "No, I could not be as unkind to you as that. I am partly a swan, but I am also partly a human being now."

   Type of conflict: _____

   Explanation: _____

"The Third Wish" by Joan Aiken
Vocabulary Builder

Word List

dabbling   malicious   presumptuous   rash   remote   verge

A. DIRECTIONS: *On the line, write the letter of the word whose meaning is* opposite *that of the Word List word.*

___ 1. malicious
   A. wicked   B. tangled   C. sour   D. kind

___ 2. presumptuous
   A. curious   B. modest   C. missing   D. hungry

___ 3. rash
   A. cautious   B. itchy   C. impure   D. hasty

___ 4. remote
   A. casual   B. close   C. faraway   D. controlled

___ 5. dabbling
   A. drooling   B. dipping   C. immersing   D. scratching

___ 6. verge
   A. edge   B. center   C. frame   D. bank

B. DIRECTIONS: *Think about the meaning of the italicized word in each sentence. Then, in your own words, answer the question that follows, and briefly explain your answer.*

1. The old King is *presumptuous* in believing that Mr. Peters will make three foolish wishes. Is the old King overconfident? How do you know?

   _____

2. The old King is a *malicious* character. How does he act toward Mr. Peters?

   _____

3. Mr. Peters lives in a *remote* valley. Is it close to town? How do you know?

   _____

Name _____ Date _____

"Amigo Brothers" by Piri Thomas
Writing About the Big Question

Does every conflict have a winner?

Big Question Vocabulary

attitude	challenge	communication	competition
compromise	conflict	danger	desire
disagreement	misunderstanding	obstacle	opposition
outcome	resolution	struggle	understanding

A. *Use one or more words from the list above to complete the paragraph.*

Competition between people can be healthy, but it can also lead to
_____. If you one day find yourself in _____ with a
friend, be sure to keep the lines of _____ open. If you talk things
through, you can better avoid _____ and can reach a satisfying
_____.

B. *Follow the directions in responding to each of the items below.*

1. List two different times when you experienced a conflict with a friend.

   _____

   _____

2. Write two sentences describing one of the preceding conflicts, and explain what
   helped you resolve it. Use at least two of the Big Question vocabulary words.

   _____

   _____

   _____

   _____

C. *Complete the sentence below. Then, write a short paragraph in which you connect this
situation to the Big Question.*

When a friendship is strong enough, conflicts that arise often _____

_____

_____

_____

_____

_____

Name _____ Date _____

"**Amigo Brothers**" by Piri Thomas
Reading: Make Inferences by Recognizing Details

Short story writers do not directly tell you everything there is to know about the characters, setting, and events. Instead, they leave it to you to **make inferences,** or logical guesses, about unstated information.

To form inferences, you must **recognize details** in the story and consider their importance. For example, in "Amigo Brothers," the narrator says, "While some youngsters were into street negatives, Antonio and Felix slept, ate, rapped, and dreamt positive." You can use that clue to infer that Felix and Antonio stayed out of trouble.

DIRECTIONS: *The sentences in the left-hand column of this chart offer details about the amigo brothers. In the right-hand column, describe what the details tell you about one or both of these characters.*

Detail About a Character	Inference About the Character
1. "If it's fair, *hermano,* I'm for it." Antonio admired the courage of a tugboat pulling a barge five times its welterweight size.	
2. Tony jogged away. Felix watched his friend disappear from view, throwing rights and lefts. Both fighters had a lot of psyching up to do before the big fight.	
3. Felix did a fast shuffle, bobbing and weaving, while letting loose a torrent of blows that would demolish whatever got in its way. It seemed to impress the brothers, who went about their own business.	
4. [Felix] fought off a series of rights and lefts and came back with a strong right that taught Antonio respect.	
5. The announcer turned to point to the winner and found himself alone. Arm in arm the champions had already left the ring.	

"Amigo Brothers" by Piri Thomas
Literary Analysis: Conflict

Most fictional stories center on a **conflict**—a struggle between opposing forces. There are two kinds of conflict:

- When there is an **external conflict,** a character struggles with an outside force such as another character or nature.
- When there is an **internal conflict,** a character struggles with himself or herself to overcome opposing feelings, beliefs, needs, or desires. An internal conflict takes place in a character's mind.

The **resolution,** or outcome of the conflict, often comes toward the end of the story, when the problem is settled in some way.

A story can have additional, smaller conflicts that develop the main conflict. In "Amigo Brothers," for example, a small external conflict occurs one morning as Felix and Antonio work out. There is tension between them, and Felix says, "Let's stop a while, bro. I think we both got something to say to each other." A minor internal conflict occurs when Felix mentions that he has stayed awake at night, "pulling punches" on Antonio. Felix struggles with the conflict between his wish not to harm his friend and his desire to win the fight.

DIRECTIONS: *Based on details in each of the following passages from "Amigo Brothers," identify the conflict as* External *or* Internal. *Then, explain your answer.*

1. He tried not to think of Felix, feeling he had succeeded in psyching his mind. But only in the ring would he really know.

    Type of conflict: _____

    Explanation: _____

2. He walked up some dark streets, deserted except for small pockets of wary-looking kids wearing gang colors. Despite the fact that he was Puerto Rican like them, they eyed him as a stranger to their turf.

    Type of conflict: _____

    Explanation: _____

3. Antonio was passing some heavy time on his rooftop. How would the fight tomorrow affect his relationship with Felix? After all, fighting was like any other profession. Friendship had nothing to do with it. A gnawing doubt crept in.

    Type of conflict: _____

    Explanation: _____

4. Felix and Antonio turned and faced each other squarely in a fighting pose. Felix wasted no time. He came fast, head low, half hunched toward his right shoulder, and lashed out with a straight left.

    Type of conflict: _____

    Explanation: _____

Name _____ Date _____

"Amigo Brothers" by Piri Thomas
Vocabulary Builder

Word List

devastating   dignitaries   dispelled   evading   improvised   perpetual

A. DIRECTIONS: *On the line, write the letter of the word whose meaning is* opposite *that of the Word List word.*

___ 1. perpetual
    A. permanent   B. temporary   C. strong   D. wide

___ 2. devastating
    A. confusing   B. appearing   C. harmful   D. helpful

___ 3. dispelled
    A. dispersed   B. crumbled   C. gathered   D. hypnotized

___ 4. evading
    A. confronting   B. watching   C. escaping   D. explaining

___ 5. dignitaries
    A. politicians   B. criminals   C. attorneys   D. peasants

___ 6. improvised
    A. impressive   B. rehearsed   C. through   D. unplanned

B. WORD STUDY: *The prefix* per- *means "through" or "completely." Answer each of the following questions using one of these words containing* per-: *perceive, percolate, perforate.*

1. How does a *percolator* produce coffee?

    _____

2. If I *perforate* the top of a can of engine oil, what do I do to it?

    _____

3. How can you *perceive* the difference between the colors red and blue?

    _____

"The Third Wish" by Joan Aiken
"Amigo Brothers" by Piri Thomas

Integrated Language Skills: Grammar

Adjectives

An **adjective** modifies or describes a noun or pronoun. An adjective may answer the questions *what kind? how many? which one?* or *whose?*

In this sentence, *beautiful* modifies *woman*. It tells what kind of woman appeared.

A *beautiful* <u>woman</u> suddenly appeared.

In this sentence, *two* modifies *boys*. It tells how many boys continued to run together.

Two <u>boys</u> continued to run together.

A. DIRECTIONS: *Underline the adjective or adjectives in each sentence. Then, circle the word the adjective modifies and which question it answers.*

1. Mr. Peters drove along a straight, empty stretch of road.

2. He heard strange cries coming from a distant bush.

3. A great white swan suddenly changed into a little man.

4. The grateful stranger granted Mr. Peters several wishes.

5. Mr. Peters soon had a gorgeous wife with pretty blue-green eyes.

6. Antonio was fair, lean, and lanky, while Felix was dark, short, and husky.

7. Antonio's lean form and long reach made him the better boxer.

8. Felix's short and muscular frame made him the better slugger.

9. Large posters were plastered on the walls of local shops.

10. The fighters changed from their street clothes into fighting gear.

B. Writing Application: *Write a sentence in response to each set of instructions.*

1. Write a sentence about Leita, using the adjective *attractive.*

   _____

2. Write a sentence about the forest, using the adjectives *dark* and *remote.*

   _____

3. Write a sentence about Antonio Cruz, using the adjectives *lean* and *talented.*

   _____

4. Write a sentence about Felix Vargas, using the adjectives *short* and *powerful.*

   _____

"The Third Wish" by Joan Aiken
"Amigo Brothers" by Piri Thomas

Integrated Language Skills: Support for Writing an Anecdote

Use this graphic organizer to help you prepare an anecdote that tells what might have happened if either (a) Mr. Peters had not turned Leita back into a swan or (b) Antonio or Felix had been knocked out during the fight. In the first rectangle, list details about the new ending that you imagine. In the ovals below it, describe two problems, or conflicts, that might arise as a result of the new ending. Then, in the bottom rectangle, describe one way in which the main character might act to resolve the conflict.

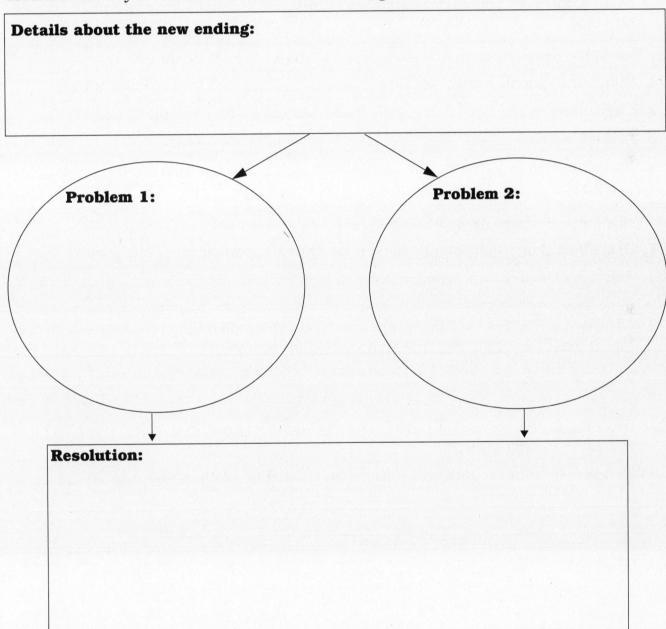

Details about the new ending:

Problem 1:

Problem 2:

Resolution:

Now, use your notes to write an anecdote telling what might have happened as a result of the new ending.

Name _____ Date _____

Writing About the Big Question

Does every conflict have a winner?

Big Question Vocabulary

attitude	challenge	communication	competition
compromise	conflict	danger	desire
disagreement	misunderstanding	obstacle	opposition
outcome	resolution	struggle	understanding

A. *Use one or more words from the list above to complete each sentence.*

1. Sometimes people have a negative _____ toward new things.

2. They may see _____ when in reality they are perfectly safe.

3. In such a case, _____ is especially important.

4. By being open to learning, you can avoid _____ and
   _____ .

B. *Follow the directions in responding to each of the items below.*

1. Describe a time when you or someone you know experienced a culture clash.

   _____

   _____

2. Write two sentences explaining how you (or they) handled the preceding experience.
   Use at least two of the Big Question vocabulary words.

   _____

   _____

C. *Complete the sentence below. Then, write a short paragraph in which you connect this situation to the Big Question.*

When people from two different worlds come together, conflict arises when _____

_____

_____

_____

_____

_____

_____

_____

Name _____ Date _____

"**Zoo**" by Edward D. Hoch

Reading: Make Inferences by Reading Between the Lines and Asking Questions

An **inference** is an intelligent guess, based on what the text tells you, about things *not* stated directly in the text. Suppose a story opens with crowds forming to wait for the arrival of an interplanetary zoo. You can infer from those details that the zoo will soon arrive.

One way to make inferences is to **read between the lines by asking questions,** such as, "Why does the writer include these details?" and "Why does the writer leave out certain information?" In the opening sentence of "Zoo," for example, we learn that "the children were always good during the month of August." The next thing we learn is that the Interplanetary Zoo comes to Chicago every year around August 23. Why does the writer open his story with these details? What conclusion can be drawn about why the children are always good in August? From these details you can infer that the children are good in August because they want their parents to take them to the interplanetary zoo.

DIRECTIONS: *Read the following passages from "Zoo," and answer the questions that follow.*

1. In the following passage, what inference can you draw from the detail that the people are clutching dollars?

   Before daybreak the crowds would form, long lines of children and adults both, each one clutching his or her dollar and waiting with wonderment to see what race of strange creatures the Professor had brought this year.

   _____

   _____

2. In the following passage, what inference can you draw about the Professor from the description of his clothing?

   Soon the good Professor himself made an appearance, wearing his many-colored rainbow cape and top hat.

   _____

3. In the following passage, what inference can you draw about the horse spiders from the way they file out of their cages, listen to Hugo's parting words, and then scurry away?

   The odd horse-spider creatures filed quickly out of their cages. Professor Hugo was there to say a few parting words, and then they scurried away in a hundred different directions, seeking their homes among the rocks.

   _____

4. In the following passage, what inference can you draw from the she-creature's reaction to her mate and offspring's arrival?

   In one house, the she-creature was happy to see the return of her mate and offspring. She babbled a greeting in the strange tongue and hurried to embrace them.

   _____

Name _____   Date _____

"Zoo" by Edward D. Hoch
Literary Analysis: Theme

A story's **theme** is its central idea, message, or insight into life. Occasionally, the author states the theme directly. More often, however, the theme is implied.

A theme is *not* the same as the subject of a work. For example, if the subject, or topic, of a story is similarities and differences, the theme will be a message about that subject, such as "differences between groups of people can keep people from seeing the ways in which they are similar."

As you read, look at what characters say and do, where the story takes place, and objects that seem important in order to determine the theme—what the author wants to teach you about life.

DIRECTIONS: *Answer the following questions about "Zoo."*

1. What is the setting? If there is more than one setting, name and briefly describe each one.

   _____

   _____

2. What do the main characters say? Summarize the words spoken by Hugo, one of the people from Earth, the female horse spider, the male horse spider, and the little one.

   Hugo: _____

   Person from Earth: _____

   She-creature: _____

   He-creature: _____

   Little creature: _____

3. How do the characters act? Describe the actions of the people in Chicago and the actions of the horse-spider creatures.

   People in Chicago: _____

   _____

   Horse spiders: _____

   _____

4. What object or objects seem important?

   _____

5. What is the subject, or topic, of "Zoo"?

   _____

6. Based on these details, what would you say is the theme of "Zoo"?

   _____

Name _____   Date _____

"Zoo" by Edward D. Hoch
Vocabulary Builder

Word List

awe   babbled   expense   garments   interplanetary   wonderment

A. DIRECTIONS: *Complete each sentence with a word from the Word List.*

1. The _____ of interplanetary travel was high, but Professor Hugo earned the money back by charging admission to his zoo.

2. The crowd gazed in _____ at the terrifying yet unusual creatures.

3. Professor Hugo's _____ zoo visited Earth, Mars, Kaan, and many other planets.

4. The creature's wife _____ happily as she greeted her husband and asked him about his trip.

5. The creatures did not wear clothes, so the _____ the humans wore seemed unnatural.

6. The children's _____ only increased as the strange array of creatures paraded before them.

B. WORD STUDY *The suffix* -ment *means "the state of." Answer each of the following questions using one of these words containing* -ment: *amusements, contentment, entertainment.*

1. What type of television show would you watch for *entertainment*?

   _____

2. Would you expect a child to complain about her *contentment*?

   _____

3. What *amusements* might a toddler enjoy?

   _____

"Ribbons" by Laurence Yep

Writing About the Big Question

Does every conflict have a winner?

Big Question Vocabulary

attitude	challenge	communication	competition
compromise	conflict	danger	desire
disagreement	misunderstanding	obstacle	opposition
outcome	resolution	struggle	understanding

A. *Use one or more words from the list above to complete each sentence.*

1. Different generations can _____ to understand one another.

2. The values of one generation can be in _____ with those of another.

3. It can be a _____ to understand one another's behaviors and beliefs.

4. Even _____ can be difficult because each may view things differently.

B. *Follow the directions in responding to each of the items below.*

1. Describe a time when you or someone you know **struggled** to **communicate** effectively with a member of another generation.

   _____

   _____

2. Explain whether both parties were able to reach an **understanding** and, if so, how. Use at least two of the Big Question vocabulary words.

   _____

   _____

C. *Complete the sentence below. Then, write a short paragraph in which you connect this situation to the Big Question.*

Family members from different generations often do not understand _____

_____

_____

_____

_____

"**Ribbons**" by Laurence Yep

Reading: Make Inferences by Reading Between the Lines and Asking Questions

An **inference** is an intelligent guess, based on what the text tells you, about things *not* stated directly in the text. One way to make inferences is to **read between the lines by asking questions,** such as, "Why does the writer include these details?" and "Why does the writer leave out certain information?" For example, "Ribbons" opens as Stacy and Ian's grandmother arrives from Hong Kong. The narrator, Stacy, says,

> Because Grandmother's . . . expenses had been so high, there wasn't room in the family budget for Madame Oblomov's ballet school. I'd had to stop my daily lessons.

Why does the writer begin with those details? What conclusion can be drawn? From these details you can infer that Stacy feels some resentment because she has had to give up her ballet lessons so that her grandmother can come from Hong Kong.

DIRECTIONS: *Read the following passages from "Ribbons," and answer the questions.*

1. What inference can you draw from Grandmother's reaction to Stacy's hug?
   When I tried to put my arms around her and kiss her, she stiffened in surprise. "Nice children don't drool on people," she snapped at me.

   _____

2. What can you infer about Grandmother's feelings about her daughter's home?
   Grandmother was sitting in the big recliner in the living room. She stared uneasily out the window as if she were gazing not upon the broad, green lawn of the square but upon a Martian desert.

   _____

3. In the following passage, what inference can you draw from these words, spoken by Stacy's mother, about Grandmother?
   [The girls' feet] were usually bound up in silk ribbons. . . . Because they were a symbol of the old days, Paw-paw undid the ribbons as soon as we were free in Hong Kong—even though they kept back the pain.

   _____

4. In the following passage, what inference about Grandmother can you draw from this attempt to show her affection for Stacy?
   She took my hand and patted it clumsily. I think it was the first time she had showed me any sign of affection.

   _____

5. What inference can you draw from Stacy's description of the invisible ribbon?
   Suddenly I felt as if there were an invisible ribbon binding us tougher than silk and satin, stronger than steel; and it joined her to Mom and Mom to me.

   _____

Name _____ Date _____

Literary Analysis: Theme

A story's **theme** is its central idea, message, or insight into life. Occasionally, the author states the theme directly. More often, however, the theme is implied.

A theme is *not* the same as the subject of a work. For example, if the subject or topic of a story is cultural differences, the theme will be a message about that, such as "cultural differences can be overcome by communication."

As you read, look at what characters say and do, where the story takes place, and which objects seem important in order to determine the theme—what the author wants to teach you about life.

DIRECTIONS: *Answer the following questions about "Ribbons."*

1. What is the setting? Briefly describe it.

   _____

2. What do the main characters say? Summarize the important statements made by Grandmother, Mom, and Stacy.

   Grandmother: _____

   _____

   Mom: _____

   _____

   Stacy: _____

   _____

3. How do the characters act? Describe the important actions of Grandmother and Stacy.

   Grandmother: _____

   _____

   _____

   Stacy: _____

   _____

   _____

4. What objects seem important?

   _____

5. What is the subject, or topic, of "Ribbons"?

   _____

6. Based on your answers above, what would you say is the theme of "Ribbons"?

   _____

"Ribbons" by Laurence Yep
Vocabulary Builder

Word List

coax   exertion   furrowed   laborious   meek   sensitive

A. DIRECTIONS: *Complete each sentence with a word from the Word List.*

1. Because Grandmother's feet had been bound when she was young, she found walking and climbing stairs _____ activities.

2. Stacy loved ballet so much that she hardly realized that it was _____ until she collapsed from exhaustion after each lesson.

3. Because the binding of her feet was painful physically and emotionally, Grandmother was _____ about her feet.

4. Stacy hoped that she could _____ Grandmother into paying attention to her by explaining her love of ballet.

5. In many cultures it is expected that a daughter will be _____ and never challenge her parents' requests.

6. Unsure of what to say to her daughter, Stacy's mother _____ her brow in concentration.

B. WORD STUDY: *The suffix -ious means "full of." Answer each of the following questions using one of these words containing -ious: delicious, harmonious, industrious.*

1. How does an *industrious* worker perform her job?

   _____

2. Why would most people prefer a *harmonious* tune over a *dissonant* one?

   _____

3. How would a hungry child respond to a *delicious* meal?

   _____

"Zoo" by Edward D. Hoch
"Ribbons" by Laurence Yep
Integrated Language Skills: Grammar

Adverbs

An **adverb** is a word that modifies or describes a verb, an adjective, or another adverb. Adverbs provide information by answering the questions *how? when? where? how often?* or *to what extent?* Many adverbs end in the suffix *-ly.*

In the first sentence, the adverb, *always,* tells how often the children are good. In the second sentence, the adverb, *outside,* tells where the car stops:

The children were *always* <u>good</u> during the month of August.

A car <u>stopped</u> *outside.*

A. DIRECTIONS: *Underline the adverb in each sentence once, and circle the word it modifies. Then, write the question that the adverb answers.*

1. The sides slowly slid up to reveal the familiar barred cages. _____

_____

2. The citizens of Earth clustered around as Professor Hugo's crew quickly collected the waiting dollars._____

_____

3. The odd horse-spider creatures filed quickly out of their cages._____

_____

4. The little one enjoyed it especially. _____

_____

5. Mom bowed formally as Grandmother reached the porch. _____

_____

B. Writing Application: *Write a sentence in response to each set of instructions. Underline the word or phrase that the adverb you use modifies.*

1. Use *quickly* in a sentence about catching a school bus.

_____

2. Use *never* in a sentence about a food you dislike.

_____

3. Use *gently* in a sentence about something you do.

_____

4. Use *always* in a sentence about something else you do.

_____

5. Use *finally* in a sentence about a process that involves several steps.

_____

Name _____ Date _____

"Zoo" by Edward D. Hoch
"Ribbons" by Laurence Yep

Integrated Language Skills: Support for Writing a Letter to the Editor

Use this graphic organizer to organize your thoughts before writing your letter to the editor as a response to either "Zoo" or "Ribbons." In the top center box, write your topic (Zoo Animals or Extra Schooling). At the top of each column, list a position on the topic. Then, write down advantages and disadvantages of each position.

Topic:

Position:

Advantages: _____

_____

_____

_____

_____

_____

_____

_____

Disadvantages: _____

_____

_____

_____

_____

_____

_____

_____

Position:

Advantages: _____

_____

_____

_____

_____

_____

_____

_____

Disadvantages: _____

_____

_____

_____

_____

_____

_____

_____

Decide which position you want to take, and draft a letter to the editor of a local newspaper in support of your position. Use your notes to back up your opinion with reasons and details that will persuade readers to take your side.

Name _____ Date _____

"After Twenty Years" by O. Henry
"He—y, Come On O—ut!" by Shinichi Hoshi

Writing About the Big Question

Does every conflict have a winner?

Big Question Vocabulary

attitude	challenge	communication	competition
compromise	conflict	danger	desire
disagreement	misunderstanding	obstacle	opposition
outcome	resolution	struggle	understanding

A. *Use one or more words from the list above to complete each sentence.*

1. Our expectations are based on our _____ of how the world works.

2. When things take an unexpected turn, the _____ may be unwelcome.

3. It can be a _____ to accept this new turn of events.

4. On the other hand, the _____ may be a pleasant surprise.

B. *Follow the directions in responding to each of the items below.*

1. List two different times when things turned out differently from what you expected.

   _____

   _____

2. Write two sentences explaining one of the preceding experiences, and describe how you reacted at the time. Use at least two of the Big Question vocabulary words.

   _____

   _____

   _____

C. *Complete the sentence below. Then, write a short paragraph in which you connect this situation to the Big Question.*

When things turn out differently from what you expected, it can be _____

_____

_____

_____

_____

_____

"After Twenty Years" by O. Henry
"He—y, Come On O—ut!" by Shinichi Hoshi

Literary Analysis: Irony

Irony involves a contradiction or contrast of some kind. In **situational irony** (or **irony of situation**), something takes place that a character or reader does not expect to happen. For example, a student voted Most Likely to Succeed ends up going to prison.

In **verbal irony,** a writer, speaker, or character says something that deliberately contradicts or blurs what he or she actually means. Think of a man who has been dreading a reunion with his best friend from twenty years before. When they meet, he says, "I've been *so* looking forward to seeing you." That is verbal irony.

In **dramatic irony,** the reader or audience knows or understands something that a character or speaker does not. For example, readers know that the apple Snow White is about to bite into is poisoned, but Snow White does not know it. That is dramatic irony.

As you read "After Twenty Years" and "He—y, Come On O—ut!" look for situational irony in particular.

DIRECTIONS: *Answer the following questions.*

1. What is the general situation, or the plot? Describe it briefly.

   "After Twenty Years": _____

   _____

   "He—y, Come On O—ut!": _____

   _____

2. What outcome do you expect?

   "After Twenty Years": _____

   "He—y, Come On O—ut!": _____

3. What happens? How does the story end?

   "After Twenty Years": _____

   "He—y, Come On O—ut!": _____

4. What details in the story lead you to expect a certain outcome? Describe one or two details, and state what they lead you to expect.

   "After Twenty Years": _____

   _____

   "He—y, Come On O—ut!": _____

   _____

5. What is ironic about the ending of the story?

   "After Twenty Years": _____

   "He—y, Come On O—ut!": _____

"After Twenty Years" by O. Henry
"He—y, Come On O—ut!" by Shinichi Hoshi
Vocabulary Builder

Word List

apparent   destiny   intricate   plausible   proposal   simultaneously   spectators

A. DIRECTIONS: *Revise each sentence so that the italicized vocabulary word is used logically. Be sure to use the vocabulary word in your new sentence.*

1. The plot of the short story was so *intricate* that we followed it easily.

   _____

2. The *destiny* of a criminal is likely to include time spent as a police officer.

   _____

3. The two men arrived *simultaneously,* one reaching the doorway an hour after the other.

   _____

4. Because there were many *spectators* when the crime was committed, no eyewitnesses could testify at the trial.

   _____

5. The *apparent* smile on the face of the scientist was not visible to anyone.

   _____

6. The *plausible* explanation made sense to no one.

   _____

7. Because he offered no solution, everyone accepted the concessionaire's *proposal.*

   _____

B. DIRECTIONS: *Write the letter of the word whose meaning is most similar to that of the Word Bank word.*

____ 1. intricate
      A. complicated   B. tiny   C. simple   D. intelligent
____ 2. simultaneously
      A. genuinely   B. apart   C. together   D. separately
____ 3. apparent
      A. obvious   B. hidden   C. deceptive   D. similar

"After Twenty Years" by O. Henry
"He—y, Come On O—ut!" by Shinichi Hoshi

Integrated Language Skills: Support for Writing to Compare Literary Works

Before you write an essay that compares your reaction to "After Twenty Years" with your reaction to "He—y, Come On O—ut!" use this graphic organizer to consider how irony is used in the two stories.

What details make the story believable or realistic?

"After Twenty Years":

"Hey—y, Come On O—ut!":

How does the believability or the realism of the story affect your response? Do you prefer a believable story to a fantasy one? Why or why not?

"After Twenty Years":

"Hey—y, Come On O—ut!":

What is the story's message? Is the message easy to understand? Why or why not?

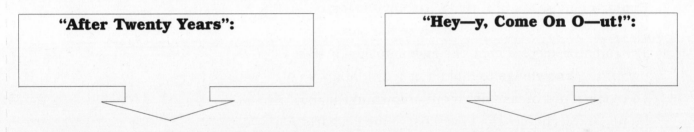

"After Twenty Years":

"Hey—y, Come On O—ut!":

When you respond to a story, are you influenced by the difficulty of understanding its message? Why or why not?

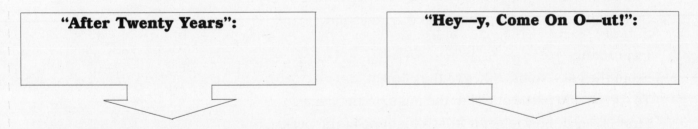

"After Twenty Years":

"Hey—y, Come On O—ut!":

Now, use your notes to write an essay in which you compare your reactions to the use of irony in "After Twenty Years" and "He—y, Come On O—ut!"

 **BQ Tunes**

The Expert, performed by Hydra

Yeah... Unh... yea... Hydra... yea... Blitzkrieg... yea....

I want it all
From the cars, to the bikes to the planes,
To the books, to the stars, to the mike, to the games,
First I'll learn how to get it, that's just one of the perks.
Cus' I also want to learn how they work.
Call me the expert.

Nah, you can't give me a car and just hand me the keys /
I need to learn how to drive it not to crash into trees /
And aside from my safety, there's something else that's got me /
Exploring more about it that's just my **curiosity** /
So I pop open the hood and **analyze** the parts /
The radiator keeps it cool, the engine makes it start /
I want the **knowledge** to build it or tear it apart /
To repair it if it breaks down out of town in the dark /
So no Mr. Mechanic, can't overcharge me for parts /
Or sell me things I don't need please I've studied the art /
I **understand** the diagrams and the tune up charts /
So change your tune up man, I'm way too smart! Yup!

I want it all
From the cars, to the bikes to the planes,
To the books, to the stars, to the mike, to the games,
First I'll learn how to get it, that's just one of the perks.
Cus' I also want to learn how they work.
Call me the expert.

I'll learn it all
But **evaluate** things that you learn / some things are more important than others
of more concern /
I'll learn it all

Continued

Investigate to reach your objective / find out all the details like a good detective /

I'll learn it all

Inquire with those well informed on the topic / if they don't know what they're saying information is toxic

I'll learn it all

Y'all know what I mean, don't let somebody tell you what's true, find out for yourself... Feel me?

See ever since I was a freshman (yes then)

If there was something I wanted to know I'd go and ask a **question** /

Jus' because I got an answer doesn't mean I would accept them /

To be sure it was right, the truth and nothing less than /

I might set up an **experiment**, prep them and test them /

Research gave me **information** in a note book I kept them /

Examine findings carefully like a doctors dissection /

Once I knew I had the right answer I could get some rest then /

Everybody was impressed an' yeah I liked how it felt /

But the real reason I did it to get the facts for myself /

That's what's gonna help me keep putting platinum plaques on my shelf /

Discover everything I can that'll keep me on top /

If you don't seek out the knowledge you'll eventually flop /

It's better not to be so foolish / Nah, it's not the way /

Who wants to **interview** somebody with nothing to say? Huh, huh?

I want it all

From the cars to the bikes to the planes,

To the books to the stars to the mike to the games,

First I'll learn how to get it, that's just one of the perks.

Cus' I also want to learn how they work.

Call me the expert.

Continued

I want it all

From the cars to the bikes to the planes,

To the books to the stars to the mike to the games,

First I'll learn how to get it, that's just one of the perks.

Cus' I also want to learn how they work.

Call me the expert.

Song Title: **The Expert**
Artist / Performed by Hydra
Vocals: Rodney "Blitz" Willie
Lyrics by Rodney "Blitz" Willie
Music composed by Keith "Wild Child" Middleton
Produced by Keith "Wild Child" Middleton
Technical Production: Mike Pandolfo, Wonderful
Executive Producer: Keith London, Defined Mind

Name _____ Date _____

Unit 3: Types of Nonfiction
Big Question Vocabulary—1

The Big Question: What should we learn?

analyze: *v.* to study something's pieces and parts in order to understand it better; other forms: *analyzing, analyzed, analysis*

curiosity: *n.* a desire to learn about or know something; other form: *curious*

facts: *n.* pieces of information that are known to be true; other forms: *fact, factual*

interview: *n.* a meeting in which a person is asked questions
    v. to ask a person questions for a specific purpose; other form: *interviewed*

knowledge: *n.* information and understanding that someone gains through learning or experience; other form: *know*

DIRECTIONS: *List three items as instructed. Then answer each question.*

1. List three questions that arouse your *curiosity.*

   _____   _____   _____

   What might you do to satisfy your curiosity about one of these things? _____

   _____

2. List three famous people whom you would like to *interview.*

   _____   _____   _____

   What would be your first question to one of these people? _____

   _____

3. What *facts* would you use to help a child gain *knowledge* about your state?

   _____   _____   _____

   Which fact would be most interesting to the child? Explain. _____

   _____

4. What three steps might help a student to *analyze* a poem?

   _____   _____   _____

   Why is it important to work carefully when you *analyze* something? _____

   _____

Unit 3: Types of Nonfiction
Big Question Vocabulary—2

The Big Question: What should we learn?

discover: *v.* to uncover information that you did not know before; other forms: *discovery, discovered, discovering*

evaluate: *v.* to decide how good, useful, or successful something is; other forms: *evaluation, evaluating, evaluated*

experiment: *n.* a test that shows why things happen or why something is true

               v. to perform a test to gather new information; other form: *experimenting*

explore: *v.* to discuss or think about something thoroughly; other form: *exploration*

inquire: *v.* to ask someone for information about a topic; other forms: *inquired, inquiring*

A. DIRECTIONS: *Underline the* **synonym** *(the word or phrase closest in meaning) to each vocabulary word.*

1. **discover**   a. test   b. try to see   c. find out
2. **evaluate**   a. judge   b. criticize   c. uncover
3. **experiment**   a. find   b. visualize   c. test
4. **explore**   a. overlook   b. analyze   c. decide
5. **inquire**   a. question   b. consider   c. respond

B. DIRECTIONS: *Complete each sentence by writing the correct vocabulary word in the blank space. Three possible choices are shown in parentheses.*

1. To begin his research on the rings of Saturn, Ramon went to the school librarian to _____ about the facts. *(experiment, inquire, evaluate)*

2. Cheryl performed two tests to _____ the purity of the water. *(experiment, inquire, evaluate)*

3. You can _____ many facts about animals by studying how they interact. *(experiment, discover, explore)*

4. To _____ for clues about its meaning, Jeb and I examined the strange painting carefully. *(explore, evaluate, inquire)*

5. To make his salad more delicious, the chef decided to _____ with different seasonings. *(discover, explore, experiment)*

Unit 3: Types of Nonfiction
Big Question Vocabulary—3

The Big Question: What should we learn?

examine: *v.* to look at something carefully in order to learn more about it; other forms: *examined, examining, examination, exam*

information: *n.* facts and details about a topic; other forms: *informative, inform*

investigate: *v.* to try to find out the truth about something, such as the details of a crime; other forms: *investigation, investigating, investigated*

question: *n.* a sentence or phrase used to ask for information

v. to have doubts about something; other forms: *questioning, questioned*

understand: *v.* to know how or why something happens or what it is like; other forms: *understood, understanding*

A. DIRECTIONS: *Review the vocabulary words and their definitions. Then write the one that belongs in each group of related words.*

1. knowledge, wisdom, truths, _____

2. check, explore, inquire, _____

3. inspect, study, watch, _____

4. know, learn, grasp, _____

5. challenge, debate, ask, _____

B. DIRECTIONS: *On the line before each sentence, write True if the statement is true, or False if it is false. If the statement is false, rewrite the sentence so that it is true.*

_____1. Most *information* is based on opinions that cannot be proved true.

_____

_____2. If you *examine* the stars through a telescope, you will see them clearly.

_____

_____3. If you don't *understand* the question, you'll probably get the right answer.

_____

_____4. A person who *investigates* a crime is often guilty.

_____

_____5. It is rude and unnecessary to *question* the claims in an advertisement.

_____

All-in-One Workbook
123

Name _____ Date _____

Unit 3: Types of Nonfiction
Applying the Big Question

What should we learn?

DIRECTIONS: *Complete the chart below to apply what you have learned about what we should learn. One row has been completed for you.*

Example	Type of knowledge	Why it is important	Effect it will have	What I learned
From Literature	Understanding different cultures, as in "Conversational Ballgames."	To be able to better relate to people who are different from us.	More tolerance and better relationships.	When with people from another culture, don't assume that your own customs are the norm.
From Literature				
From Science				
From Social Studies				
From Real Life				

Richard Mühlberger
Listening and Viewing

Segment 1: Meet Richard Mühlberger
- Why do you think Richard Mühlberger chose to write art history books?
- Do you agree with the writing advice given to Mühlberger by a fellow writer "to stick to the masters"?

_____

_____

_____

Segment 2: The Essay
- According to Richard Mühlberger, what are some characteristics of essays?
- When would you write an essay, and why?

_____

_____

_____

Segment 3: The Writing Process
- Why is it very important to Richard Mühlberger to write in precise, detailed language when writing about a painting?
- Why do you think Richard Mühlberger chooses to write his books in a "conversational tone"?

_____

_____

_____

Segment 4: The Rewards of Writing
- What does Richard Mühlberger hope that his readers will gain by reading books about art?
- Why do you think books about art are important?

_____

_____

_____

All-in-One Workbook
125

Learning About Nonfiction

An author has a specific **purpose for writing** an essay or article. Often, that purpose is to explain, to entertain, to inform, or to persuade. An essay or an article uses one or more of these **formats:**

- Expository writing: presents facts, discusses ideas, or explains a process
- Persuasive writing: attempts to persuade the reader to adopt a particular point of view or take a particular course of action
- Reflective writing: addresses an event or experience and gives the writer's insights about its importance
- Humorous writing: entertains the audience by evoking laughter
- Narrative writing: tells about real-life experiences
- Descriptive writing: appeals to the reader's senses of sight, hearing, taste, smell, and touch
- Analytical writing: breaks a large idea into parts to help the reader see how they work together as a whole

A. DIRECTIONS: *The following are titles of nonfiction essays or articles. Circle the letter of the answer choice that shows the best format for each title. Then, circle the letter of the answer choice that shows the purpose that the author probably had for writing the article.*

1. "How to Build a Doghouse"
   Format: A. persuasive   **B.** expository   **C.** narrative   **D.** reflective
   Purpose: A. to explain   **B.** to entertain

2. "Don't Throw That Cardboard and Paper in the Trash!"
   Format: A. persuasive   **B.** analytical   **C.** narrative   **D.** humorous
   Purpose: A. to entertain   **B.** to persuade

3. "Moving to Tucson Changed My Life"
   Format: A. persuasive   **B.** expository   **C.** analytical   **D.** reflective
   Purpose: A. to persuade   **B.** to share insights

B. DIRECTIONS: *Below are essay topics and their purpose. Write the format that you would use to write each essay. Explain your choice. Refer to the bulleted list above as needed for help.*

Topic: how to draw a face   Purpose: to explain
Format choice/reason: <u>expository; it explains a process</u>.

1. Topic: a strange animal   Purpose: to entertain
   Format choice/reason: _____

2. Topic: vote for a certain candidate   Purpose: to persuade
   Format choice/reason: _____

3. Topic: The Civil War   Purpose: to present ideas
   Format choice/reason: _____

"What Makes a Rembrandt a Rembrandt?" by Richard Mühlberger
Model Selection: Nonfiction

Nonfiction writing is about real people, places, objects, ideas, and experiences. Here are some common types:

Type of Nonfiction	Description
Biography	the life story of a real person, written by another person
Autobiography	the author's account of his or her own life
Media Accounts	true stories written for newspapers, magazines, television, or radio
Essays and Articles	short nonfiction works about a particular subject

Nonfiction writing must be organized to present information logically and clearly. Writers use **chronological organization** (they present details in time order); **comparison-and-contrast organization** (they show similarities and differences); **cause-and-effect organization** (they show relationships among events); and **problem-and-solution organization** (they identify a problem and present a solution).

DIRECTIONS: *On the lines below, answer these questions about "What Makes a Rembrandt a Rembrandt?"*

1. What type of nonfiction writing is "What Makes a Rembrandt a Rembrandt?" Explain.

   _____

2. How is the first paragraph in "Two Handsome Soldiers" organized? Explain.

   _____

   _____

3. What two real people are the most important in this article?

   _____

4. Why does Richard Mühlberger use an expository format for sections of "What Makes a Rembrandt a Rembrandt?"

   _____

5. Often, nonfiction writers have more than one purpose for writing an article or essay. Which *two* purposes did Richard Mühlberger have for writing this article? Check your choices.

   _____ A. to persuade his city to form a militia company as a social club
   _____ B. to entertain readers with a humorous event
   _____ C. to explain Rembrandt's painting techniques
   _____ D. to explain why Banning Cocq was a great Dutch soldier
   _____ E. to inform readers with facts about the painting *Night Watch*

"**Life Without Gravity**" by Robert Zimmerman
Writing About the Big Question

What should we learn?

Big Question Vocabulary

analyze	curiosity	discover	evaluate	examine
experiment	explore	facts	information	inquire
interview	investigate	knowledge	question	understand

A. *Choose one word from the list above to complete each sentence. There may be more than one right answer.*

1. Anna's _____ about other people helped her learn about different cultures.

2. It can be fun to _____ new neighborhoods in your hometown.

3. Try to ask each new acquaintance at least one _____ about her life.

B. *Follow the directions in responding to each of the items below.*

1. List two different times that you learned something outside of school. Write your response in complete sentences.

   _____

   _____

2. Choose one of the experiences you listed in number 1. Write two sentences describing that experience. Use at least two of the Big Question vocabulary words. You may use the words in different forms (for example you can change *analyze* to *analyzing*).

   _____

   _____

C. *Complete the sentence below. Then, write a short paragraph in which you connect this sentence to the big question.*

Our assumptions about unfamiliar experiences are _____

   _____

   _____

"**Life Without Gravity**" by Robert Zimmerman

Reading: Adjust Your Reading Rate to Recognize Main Ideas and Key Points

The **main idea** is the central point of a passage or text. Most articles and essays have a main idea. Each paragraph or passage in the work also has a main idea, or **key point.** The main idea of a paragraph is usually stated in a **topic sentence.** The paragraph then supplies **supporting details** that give examples, explanations, or reasons.

When reading nonfiction, **adjust your reading rate to recognize main ideas and key points.**

- **Skim** the article to get a sense of the main idea before you begin reading. Look over the text quickly, looking for text organization, topic sentences, and repeated words.
- **Scan** the text when you need to find answers to questions or to clarify or find supporting details. Run your eyes over the text, looking for a particular word or idea.
- **Read closely** to learn what the main ideas are and to identify the key points and supporting details.

A. DIRECTIONS: *Scan each paragraph below to find answers to the questions that follow.*

Our bodies are adapted to Earth's gravity. Our muscles are strong in order to overcome gravity as we walk and run. Our inner ears use gravity to keep us upright. And because gravity wants to pull all our blood down into our legs, our hearts are designed to pump hard to get blood up to our brains.

1. What parts of the body are discussed in this paragraph?

_____

In microgravity, you have to learn new ways to eat. Don't pour a bowl of cornflakes. Not only will the flakes float all over the place, the milk won't pour. Instead, big balls of milk will form. You can drink these by taking big bites out of them, but you'd better finish them before they slam into a wall, splattering apart and covering everything with little tiny milk globules.

2. What foods are mentioned in this paragraph?

_____

B. DIRECTIONS: *Now, read the paragraphs closely. Answer these questions.*

1. What is the main idea of the first paragraph?

_____

2. What are two details that support that main idea?

_____

3. What is the main idea of the second paragraph?

_____

4. What are two details that support that main idea?

_____

Name _____ Date _____

"**Life Without Gravity**" by Robert Zimmerman
Literary Analysis: Expository Essay

An **expository essay** is a short piece of nonfiction that explains, defines, or interprets ideas, events, or processes. The way in which the information is organized and presented depends on the specific topic of the essay. Writers organize the main points of their essays logically, to aid readers' comprehension. They may organize information in one of these ways or in a combination of ways:

- Comparison and contrast
- Cause and effect
- Chronological order
- Problem and solution

"Life Without Gravity" is an expository essay that explains an idea. It uses cause and effect to make the explanation clear. In the paragraph below, the details help readers understand some of the effects of weightlessness.

> Worse, weightlessness can sometimes be downright unpleasant. Your body gets upset and confused. Your face puffs up, your nose gets stuffy, your back hurts, your stomach gets upset, and you throw up.

DIRECTIONS: *The left-hand column of the following chart names parts of the human body that are affected by weightlessness. In the right-hand column, write the effect—in your own words—as it is described in "Life Without Gravity." If one effect causes yet another effect, describe the second effect as well.*

Body Part	Effects of Weightlessness
The blood	Weightlessness causes _____ _____
The spine	Weightlessness causes _____ _____
The bones	Weightlessness causes _____ _____
The muscles	Weightlessness causes _____ _____
The stomach	Weightlessness causes _____ _____

Name _____ Date _____

"Life Without Gravity" by Robert Zimmerman
Vocabulary Builder

Word List

 blander   feeble   globules   manned   readapted   spines

A. DIRECTIONS: *On the short line, write* T *if the following statement is true and* F *if it is false. Then, explain your answer in a complete sentence.*

____ 1. Animals' *spines* are very strong.

_____

____ 2. A *feeble* voice is one that can be heard across a room.

_____

____ 3. Foods made without pepper are *blander* than the same foods prepared with pepper.

_____

____ 4. All astronauts have successfully *readapted* to life on Earth.

_____

____ 5. *Manned* space flight is considered too dangerous at this time.

_____

____ 6. Floating *globules* help astronauts exercise their muscles in space.

_____

B. WORD STUDY: *The suffix -ness from Old English means "the condition or quality of being." Read the following sentences. Use your knowledge of the suffix -ness to write a full sentence to answer each question. Include the italicized word in your answer.*

1. What are some of the ways that *weightlessness* is enjoyable?

_____

2. How can living in space cause *feebleness*?

_____

3. Why is it important for astronauts to have a *willingness* to try new things?

_____

"Conversational Ballgames" by Nancy Masterson Sakamoto
Writing About the Big Question

What should we learn?

Big Question Vocabulary

analyze	curiosity	discover	evaluate	examine
experiment	explore	facts	information	inquire
interview	investigate	knowledge	question	understand

A. *Choose one word from the list above to complete each sentence. There may be more than one right answer.*

1. _____ an older person in your family to learn about history.

2. _____ is often gained after a lifetime of experience.

3. It can take time to learn to _____ someone from another culture.

B. *Follow the directions in responding to each of the items below.*

1. List two different times that you learned something about a person from another culture. Write your response in complete sentences.

_____

_____

2. Choose one of the experiences you listed in number 1. Write two or more sentences describing that experience. Use at least two of the Big Question vocabulary words in your answer. You may use the words in different forms (for example, you can change *analyze* to *analyzing*).

_____

_____

C. *Complete the sentence below. Then, write a short paragraph in which you connect this sentence to the big question.*

Cultural knowledge can _____

_____

_____

Name _____ Date _____

"Conversational Ballgames" by Nancy Masterson Sakamoto
Reading: Adjust Your Reading Rate to Recognize Main Ideas and Key Points

The **main idea** is the central point of a passage or text. Most articles and essays have a main idea. Each paragraph or passage in the work also has a main idea, or **key point.**

The main idea of a paragraph is usually stated in a **topic sentence**—a sentence that identifies the key point. The paragraph then supplies **supporting details** that give examples, explanations, or reasons.

When reading nonfiction, **adjust your reading rate to recognize main ideas and key points.**

- **Skim** the article to get a sense of the main idea before you begin reading. Look over the text quickly, looking for text organization, topic sentences, and repeated words.
- **Scan** the text when you need to find answers to questions or to clarify or find supporting details. Run your eyes over the text, looking for a particular word or idea.
- **Read closely** to learn what the main ideas are and to identify the key points and supporting details.

A. DIRECTIONS: *Scan each paragraph below to find answers to the questions that follow.*

A western-style conversation between two people is like a game of tennis. If I introduce a topic, a conversational ball, I expect you to hit it back. If you agree with me, I don't expect you simply to agree and do nothing more. I expect you to add something—a reason for agreeing, another example, or an elaboration to carry the idea further. But I don't expect you always to agree. I am just as happy if you question me, or challenge me, or completely disagree with me. Whether you agree or disagree, your response will return the ball to me.

1. What game does the author discuss in this paragraph? _____

A Japanese-style conversation, however, is not at all like tennis or volleyball. It's like bowling. You wait for your turn. And you always know your place in line. It depends on such things as whether you are older or younger, a close friend or a relative stranger to the previous speaker, in a senior or junior position, and so on.

2. What game does the author discuss in this paragraph? _____

B. DIRECTIONS: *Now, read the paragraphs closely for main ideas and supporting details.*

1. What is the main idea of the first paragraph?

_____

2. What are two details that support that main idea?

_____

3. What is the main idea of the second paragraph?

_____

4. What are two details that support that main idea?

_____

Name _____ Date _____

"Conversational Ballgames" by Nancy Masterson Sakamoto
Literary Analysis: Expository Essay

An **expository essay** is a short piece of nonfiction that explains, defines, or interprets ideas, events, or processes. The way in which the information is organized and presented depends on the specific topic of the essay. Writers organize the main points of their essays logically, to aid readers' comprehension. They may organize information in one of these ways or in a combination of ways:

- Comparison and contrast
- Cause and effect
- Chronological order
- Problem and solution

"Conversational Ballgames" is an expository essay that explains two processes. It uses comparison and contrast to make the explanation clear. In the paragraph below, the details set up the differences between Japanese and western styles of conversation.

Japanese-style conversations develop quite differently from western-style conversations. And the difference isn't only in the languages. I realized that just as I kept trying to hold western-style conversations even when I was speaking Japanese, so my English students kept trying to hold Japanese-style conversations even when they were speaking English.

DIRECTIONS: *Use this chart to compare and contrast Japanese-style conversation and western-style conversation. In the left-hand column, write five characteristics of western-style conversations as those conversations are described in "Conversational Ballgames." In the right-hand column, describe how the Japanese style differs from, or is similar to, each characteristic described on the left.*

Western-Style Conversation	Japanese-Style Conversation
1.	
2.	
3.	
4.	
5.	

"Conversational Ballgames" by Nancy Masterson Sakamoto
Vocabulary Builder

Word List

elaboration   indispensable   murmuring   parallel   suitable   unconsciously

A. DIRECTIONS: *Think about the meaning of the italicized word in each sentence. Then, answer the question.*

1. If two lines run *parallel* to each other, what do you know about them?

   _____

2. If a speaker is *murmuring*, what might he or she be asked to do?

   _____

3. Why might someone who is learning Japanese say that a dictionary is *indispensable*?

   _____

4. If you were engaged in a conversation about cultural differences, and someone asked you for *elaboration*, what would you do?

   _____

5. If two cultures had different ideas about *suitable* times for serious conversation, would holding a meeting be simple or difficult?

   _____

6. Why is it hard to stop doing something if you do it *unconsciously*?

   _____

B. WORD STUDY: *The suffix -able means "capable or worthy of being." Read the following sentences. Use your knowledge of the suffix -able to write a full sentence to answer each question.*

1. Does a *capable* person need help?

   _____

2. If an experience is *enjoyable*, are you eager to have it end?

   _____

3. Is a *breakable* plate a good choice for a picnic?

   _____

Name _____ Date _____

Integrated Language Skills: Grammar

Conjunctions

Conjunctions connect words or groups of words. **Coordinating conjunctions,** such as *but, and, nor, for, so, yet,* and *or,* connect words or groups of words that have a similar function in a sentence. They might connect two or more nouns, adjectives, adverbs, groups of words, or sentences. In the following examples, the coordinating conjunctions are in bold type. The words they connect are underlined.

Connecting nouns:	<u>Bones</u> **and** <u>muscles</u> become weak in outer space.
Connecting verbs:	How can people <u>talk</u> **and** <u>eat</u> at the same time?
Connecting adjectives:	A conversation can be <u>interesting</u>, <u>exciting</u>, **or** <u>boring</u>.
Connecting sentences:	<u>Becoming an astronaut is difficult</u>, **but** <u>it is also rewarding</u>.

A. PRACTICE: *Circle the coordinating conjunction in each sentence. Then, underline the words, groups of words, or sentences that the conjunction connects.*

1. Some astronauts adjust well to living without gravity, but others have problems.
2. Zero gravity is hard on the bones and the muscles.
3. Astronauts are not surprised by zero gravity, for they are trained to expect it.
4. Sakamoto had mastered Japanese, yet she was having trouble communicating.
5. In western conversations, someone may agree, question, or challenge.
6. Sakamoto learned the art of Japanese conversation, so she was able to participate fully.

B. Writing Application: *Complete the following instructions by writing sentences about "Life Without Gravity" or "Conversational Ballgames." In each sentence that you write, use the coordinating conjunction in the way described.*

1. Join two nouns with the conjunction *and.* _____

_____

2. Join two verbs with the conjunction *or.* _____

_____

3. Join two sentences with the conjunction *but.* _____

_____

4. Join two groups of words with the conjunction *or.* _____

_____

5. Join two adjectives with the conjunction *yet.* _____

_____

"Life Without Gravity" by Robert Zimmerman
"Conversational Ballgames" by Nancy Masterson Sakamoto

Integrated Language Skills:
Support for Writing an Analogy

An **analogy** makes a comparison between two or more things that are similar in some ways, but otherwise unalike. A good analogy can spice up your writing, make the reader smile, or explain a difficult concept.

Analogies often take the form of a compound sentence with two parts joined by the phrase "is like." For example, A is like B. The two halves of the sentence usually have a parallel structure. For example,

A NOUN without a NOUN is like A NOUN without a NOUN.

___{first half}_____connector _____{second half___.

Before you write an analogy of your own, practice by completing this chart.

A	connector	B
Life without gravity	is like	French fries without ketchup.
Life without gravity	is like	spaghetti without _____.
Life without gravity	is like	(noun) _____ without _____.
	is like	
Communicating with someone from another culture	is like	hiking blindfolded.
Communicating with someone from another culture	is like	singing _____.
Communicating with someone from another culture	is like	_____.

Now, use a separate piece of paper to write three complete analogies. Use the beginning phrases provided in the chart or come up with your own.

"I Am a Native of North America" by Chief Dan George
Writing About the Big Question

What should we learn?

Big Question Vocabulary

analyze	curiosity	discover	evaluate	examine
experiment	explore	facts	information	inquire
interview	investigate	knowledge	question	understand

A. *Choose one word from the list above to fill the blanks in the sentences below. There may be more than one right answer.*

1. Many Americans wish to _____ Native American culture.

2. Like many Americans, Chief George has _____ of two cultures.

3. If you could _____ Chief George, what _____ would you ask him?

B. *Follow the directions in responding to each of the items below.*

1. List two different times that you learned something new about your own country. Write your response in complete sentences.

   _____

   _____

2. Choose one of the experiences you listed in number 1. Write two sentences describing that experience. Use at least two of the Big Question vocabulary words. You may use the words in different forms (for example you can change *analyze* to *analyzing*).

   _____

   _____

C. *Complete the sentence below. Use the completed sentence as the beginning of a short paragraph in which you discuss the big question.*

In order for people to live together in a society, they must _____

   _____

   _____

"I Am a Native of North America" by Chief Dan George
Reading: Make Connections Between Key Points and Supporting Details to Understand the Main Idea

The **main idea** is the most important thought or concept in a work or a passage of text. Sometimes the author directly states the main idea of a work and then provides key points that support it. These key points are supported in turn by details such as examples and descriptions. Other times the main idea is unstated. The author gives you *only* the key points or supporting details that add up to a main idea. To understand the main idea, **make connections between key points and supporting details.** Notice how the writer groups details. Look for sentences that pull details together.

In this passage from "I Am a Native of North America," Chief George states key points and provides details that support the main idea of the essay:

> I am afraid my culture has little to offer yours. But my culture did prize friendship and companionship. It did not look on privacy as a thing to be clung to, for privacy builds up walls and walls promote distrust. My culture lived in big family communities, and from infancy people learned to live with others.

DIRECTIONS: *Write the main idea of Chief George's essay on the line below. Then, read each passage, and write its key point and the details that support it.*

Main idea: _____

And beyond this acceptance of one another there was a deep respect for everything in nature that surrounded them. My father loved the earth and all its creatures. The earth was his second mother. The earth and everything it contained was a gift from See-see-am . . . and the way to thank this great spirit was to use his gifts with respect.

1. **Key point:** _____

2. **Details:** _____

_____

Love is something you and I must have. We must have it because our spirit feeds upon it. We must have it because without it we become weak and faint. Without love our self-esteem weakens. Without it our courage fails. Without love we can no longer look out confidently at the world. Instead we turn inwardly and begin to feed upon our own personalities and little by little we destroy ourselves.

3. **Key point:** _____

4. **Details:** _____

_____

"I Am a Native of North America" by Chief Dan George
Literary Analysis: Reflective Essay

A **reflective essay** is a brief prose work that presents a writer's feelings and thoughts, or reflections, about an experience or idea. The purpose is to communicate these thoughts and feelings so that readers will respond with thoughts and feelings of their own. As you read a reflective essay, think about the ideas the writer is sharing. Think about whether your responses to the experience or idea are similar to or different from the writer's.

In this passage from "I Am a Native of North America," Chief George reflects on life in apartment buildings:

> I see people living in smoke houses hundreds of times bigger than the one I knew. But the people in one apartment do not even know the people in the next and care less about them.

Chief George thinks about how neighbors do not know one another and concludes that they do not care about one another.

A. DIRECTIONS: *In the second column of the chart, summarize Chief George's thoughts about each experience described in the first column. Then, in the third column, write your response. That is, describe your own thoughts on the subject.*

Experience	Author's Thoughts	My Thoughts
1. Chief George describes his grandfather's smoke house.		
2. Chief George's father finds him killing fish "for the fun of it."		
3. Chief George sees his culture disappearing.		

B. DIRECTIONS: *Write the first paragraph of a reflective essay of your own. Include a description of an experience and your thoughts about it. Write on one of these topics:*

- the role of nature in your life
- the importance of tradition in your life
- the meaning of family in your life

_____

_____

_____

_____

"I Am a Native of North America" by Chief Dan George
Vocabulary Builder

Word List

communal   distinct   hoarding   integration   justifies   promote

A. DIRECTIONS: *Use the italicized word in each sentence in a sentence of your own.*

1. Chief George seeks to *promote* a greater understanding of Native American culture.

   _____

2. Chief George suggests that *communal* living teaches people to respect one another.

   _____

3. A critical situation sometimes *justifies* a drastic solution.

   _____

4. Social scientists can identify many *distinct* cultures in North America.

   _____

5. Native American culture does not prize the *hoarding* of private possessions.

   _____

6. Many peoples see *integration* into American culture as inevitable.

   _____

B. WORD STUDY: *The Latin root* -just *means "law" or "right." Read the following sentences. Use your knowledge of the Latin root* -just *to write a full sentence to answer each question.*

1. If a decision is *unjust*, is it fair?

   _____

2. If there is no *justification* for your mistake, are you free from blame?

   _____

3. Is a *justifiable* complaint one that should be taken seriously?

   _____

All-in-One Workbook
141

"**Volar: To Fly**" by Judith Ortiz Cofer
Writing About the Big Question

What should we learn?

Big Question Vocabulary

analyze	curiosity	discover	evaluate	examine
experiment	explore	facts	information	inquire
interview	investigate	knowledge	question	understand

A. *Choose one word from the list above and use it to complete each sentence. There may be more than one right answer.*

1. Imagine the places you could _____ if you knew how to fly.

2. Children often like to _____ with different personalities.

3. Judith seems to _____ her parents' feelings very well.

B. *Follow the directions in responding to each of the items below.*

1. List two different times that you learned something new about your parents. Write your response in complete sentences.

   _____

   _____

2. Choose one of the experiences you listed in number 1. Write two or more sentences describing that experience. Use at least two of the Big Question vocabulary words. You may use the words in different forms (for example you can change *analyze* to *analyzing*).

   _____

   _____

C. *Complete the sentence below. Use the completed sentence as the beginning of a short paragraph in which you discuss the big question.*

Family connections are _____

_____

_____.

"**Volar: To Fly**" by Judith Ortiz Cofer

Reading: Make Connections Between Key Points and Supporting Details to Understand the Main Idea

The **main idea** is the most important thought or concept in a work or a passage of text. Sometimes, the author directly states the main idea of a work and then provides key points that support it. These key points are supported in turn by details such as examples and descriptions. Other times, the main idea is unstated. The author gives *only* the key points or supporting details that add up to a main idea. To understand the main idea, **make connections between key points and supporting details.** Notice how the writer groups details. Look for sentences that pull details together.

In this passage from "Volar: To Fly," Judith Ortiz Cofer states a key point and provides details that support the main idea of the essay:

> At twelve I was an avid consumer of comic books—*Supergirl* being my favorite. I spent my allowance of a quarter a day on two twelve-cent comic books or a double issue for twenty-five. I had a stack of *Legion of Super Heroes* and *Supergirl* comic books in my bedroom closet that was as tall as I.

DIRECTIONS: *Write the main point of Cofer's essay "Volar: To Fly" on the line below. Then, read each passage, and write its key point and the details that support it.*

Main idea: _____

From up there, over the rooftops, I could see everything, even beyond the few blocks of our barrio; with my X-ray vision I could look inside the homes of people who interested me. Once I saw our landlord, whom I knew my parents feared, sitting in a treasure-room dressed in an ermine coat and a large gold crown. He sat on the floor counting his dollar bills. I played a trick on him. Going up to his building's chimney, I blew a little puff of my super-breath into his fireplace, scattering his stacks of money so that he had to start counting all over again.

1. **Key point:** _____

2. **Details:** _____

I could more or less program my Supergirl dreams in those days by focusing on the object of my current obsession. This way I "saw" into the private lives of my teachers, and in the last days of my childish fantasy and the beginning of adolescence, into the secret room of the boys I liked.

3. **Key point:** _____

4. **Details:** _____

"Volar: To Fly" by Judith Ortiz Cofer
Literary Analysis: Reflective Essay

A **reflective essay** is a brief prose work that presents a writer's feelings and thoughts, or reflections, about an experience or idea. The purpose is to communicate these thoughts and feelings so that readers will respond with thoughts and feelings of their own. As you read a reflective essay, think about the ideas the writer is sharing. Think about whether your responses to the experience or idea are similar to or different from the writer's.

In this passage from "Volar: To Fly," Judith Ortiz Cofer describes the view from her kitchen window:

> The view was of a dismal alley that was littered with refuse thrown from windows. The space was too narrow for anyone larger than a skinny child to enter safely, so it was never cleaned.

Judith Ortiz Cofer considers this view and dreams of flying away from the city.

A. DIRECTIONS: *In the second column of the chart, summarize Judith Ortiz Cofer's thoughts about each experience described in the first column. Then, in the third column, write your response. That is, describe your own thoughts on the subject.*

Experience	Author's Thoughts	My Thoughts
1. Reading comic books		
2. "Seeing" her neighbors and friends in dreams		
3. Overhearing her mother's desire to fly		

B. DIRECTIONS: *Write the first paragraph of a reflective essay of your own. Include a description of an experience and your thoughts about it. Write on one of these topics:*

- the role of nature in your life
- the importance of tradition in your life
- the meaning of family in your life

_____

_____

_____

_____

_____

Name _____ Date _____

Vocabulary Builder

Word List

adolescence   avid   dismal   interrupted   obsession   refuse

A. DIRECTIONS: *Use the italicized word in each sentence in a sentence of your own.*

1. Before she reached *adolescence*, Judith Ortiz Cofer dreamed of flying.

   _____

2. Judith Ortiz Cofer was an *avid* reader of comic books.

   _____

3. The view out of the kitchen window was *dismal*.

   _____

4. As a child, Judith Ortiz Cofer never *interrupted* her parents' quiet time together.

   _____

5. Sometimes an *obsession* can affect our dreams.

   _____

6. *Refuse* littered the air shaft outside of Judith Ortiz Cofer's childhood apartment.

   _____

B. WORD STUDY: *The Latin root -rupt- means "break" or "burst." Read the following sentences. Use your knowledge of the Latin root -rupt- to write a full sentence to answer each question.*

1. Would a quiet conversation *disrupt* science class?

   _____

2. If a water main *ruptured*, would traffic be heavy?

   _____

3. Could a baby sleep through a *disruption*?

   _____

"I Am a Native of North America" by Chief Dan George
"Volar: To Fly" by Judith Ortiz Cofer
Integrated Language Skills: Grammar

Prepositions and Prepositional Phrases

A **preposition** relates a noun or pronoun that follows the preposition to another word in the sentence. In *The key is in the lock,* the preposition *in* relates *lock* to *key.* These are some common prepositions:

above	beyond	in	of	over	under
behind	for	inside	on	through	up
below	from	into	outside	to	with

A **prepositional phrase** begins with a preposition and ends with the noun or pronoun that follows it. In *The key is in the lock,* the prepositional phrase is *in the lock.*

A. DIRECTIONS: *The following sentences are from "I Am a Native of North America" and "Volar: To Fly." In each sentence, underline each preposition and circle the prepositional phrases.*

1. I blew a little puff of my super-breath into his fireplace.
2. I can still see him as the sun rose above the mountaintop in the early morning.
3. There was a deep respect for everything in nature.
4. In my dream I climbed the stairs to the top of our apartment building.
5. I could look inside the homes of people who interested me.
6. In the course of my lifetime I have lived in two distinct cultures.
7. I remember, as a little boy, fishing with him up Indian River.
8. I could see everything, even beyond the few blocks of our barrio.

B. Writing Application: *Write a paragraph about an artistic talent that you or someone you know possesses. Use at least three prepositional phrases. Underline each preposition, and circle the prepositional phrases.*

_____

_____

_____

_____

_____

_____

Name _____ Date _____

Integrated Language Skills: Support for Writing an Outline

To prepare to write an **outline** of "I Am a Native of North America" or "Volar: To Fly," create a word web. Write the main idea in the center circle. In each of the circles around it, write a key point. In the circles around each key point, write details that support the key point.

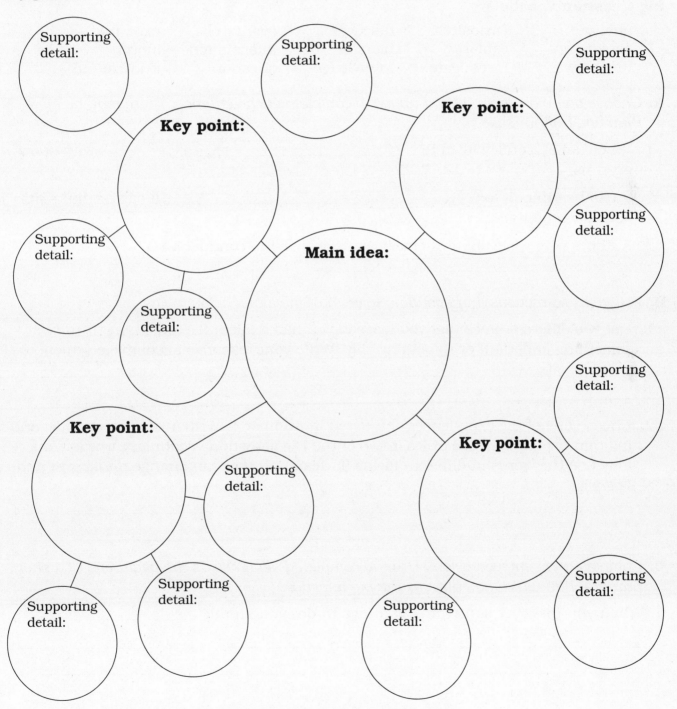

Now, use your word web to make an outline of the essay.

Name _____ Date _____

"A Special Gift: The Legacy of Snowflake Bentley" by Barbara Eaglesham
"No Gumption" by Russell Baker

Writing About the Big Question

What should we learn?

Big Question Vocabulary

analyze	curiosity	discover	evaluate	examine
experiment	explore	facts	information	inquire
interview	investigate	knowledge	question	understand

A. *Choose one word from the list above to complete each sentence. There may be more than one right answer.*

1. "Snowflake" Bentley liked to _____ with snow crystals.

2. It can be difficult to _____ a career that suits your personality.

3. Authors who write about themselves never need to conduct an

   _____ .

B. *Follow the directions in responding to each of the items below.*

1. List two different times that you learned you had a talent for something. It can be something important or something silly. Write your response in complete sentences.

   _____

   _____

2. Choose one of the experiences you listed in number 1. Write two sentences describing that experience. Use at least two of the Big Question vocabulary words. You may use the words in different forms (for example you can change *analyze* to *analyzing*).

   _____

   _____

C. *Complete the sentence below. Use the completed sentence as the beginning of a short paragraph in which you discuss the big question.*

When you discover something you love to do, you should _____

   _____

   _____ .

"A Special Gift: The Legacy of 'Snowflake' Bentley" by Barbara Eaglesham
"No Gumption" by Russell Baker

Literary Analysis: Comparing Biography and Autobiography

In an **autobiography**, a person tells his or her own life story. Writers may write about their own experiences to explain their actions, to provide insight into their choices, or to show the personal side of an event.

In contrast, in a **biography**, a writer tells the life story of another person. Writers of biographies often write to analyze a person's experiences and actions. Biographies often present their subject as an example from which readers can learn a lesson.

Some biographies and autobiographies are short essays that focus on a particular episode in the subject's life.

Both biography and autobiography focus on actual events and offer insight to explain a person's actions or ideas. However, the forms have these important differences:

Biography	**Autobiography**
• More objective	• More personal
• Based on research	• Based on memory and emotion

A. Read the following sentences. Determine whether they belong to an autobiography or a biography. Use the line provided to explain your answer.

1. I was born in Detroit during the Depression.

_____ **autobiography/biography Explanation:** _____

_____

2. As children, my brother and I often whispered secrets late into the night.

_____ **autobiography/biography Explanation:** _____

_____

3. Historians agree that Jimmy Carter has been very productive since he left the presidency.

_____ **autobiography/biography Explanation:** _____

_____

B. Complete the following sentences:

1. Autobiographies are _____, _____, _____.
   One thing I like about autobiographies is _____.

2. Biographies are _____, _____, _____. I would like to read a biography of the following people: _____.

"A Special Gift: The Legacy of 'Snowflake' Bentley" by Barbara Eaglesham
"No Gumption" by Russell Baker
Vocabulary Builder

Word List

aptitude	crucial	evaporated	gumption
hexagons	microscope	negatives	paupers

A. DIRECTIONS: *Use the italicized word in each sentence in a sentence of your own.*

1. Russell Baker had an *aptitude* for writing.

   _____

2. Baker's mother thinks gumption is *crucial* to success in life.

   _____

3. The snow crystals *evaporated* quickly.

   _____

4. *Gumption* may be something you are born with.

   _____

5. Honeycombs are a grid of *hexagons*.

   _____

6. Ordinary objects look different under the *microscope*.

   _____

7. *Negatives* must not get wet.

   _____

8. He achieved great success, even though his father and grandfather were *paupers*.

   _____

B. DIRECTIONS: *Write the letter of the word that is most similar in meaning to the word from the Word List.*

____ 1. aptitude
   A. talent   B. desire   C. joy   D. luck

____ 2. crucial
   A. dull   B. ugly   C. minor   D. important

____ 3. evaporated
   A. vanished   B. melted   C. dried up   D. disappeared

____ 4. gumption
   A. talent   B. drive   C. personality D. good looks

____ 5. hexagons
   A. six-sided figures B. shapes   C. curses   D. seven-sided figures

____ 6. paupers
   A. poor people   B. dancers   C. thieves   D. leaders

Name _____ Date _____

"A Special Gift: The Legacy of 'Snowflake' Bentley" by Barbara Eaglesham
"No Gumption" by Russell Baker

Writing Support for Comparing Literary Works

	(Biography) "Snowflake" Bentley	**(Autobiography) Russell Baker**
How was each character influenced by his parents?		
What is your overall impression of the person?		
What kind of information helped you form your opinion?		
Which person do you feel you understand better?		

Now, use your notes to write an essay in which you compare and contrast what you learned about "Snowflake" Bentley with what you learned about Russell Baker.

Name _____ Date _____

"The Eternal Frontier" by Louis L'Amour
Writing About the Big Question

What should we learn?

Big Question Vocabulary

analyze	curiosity	discover	evaluate	examine
experiment	explore	facts	information	inquire
interview	investigate	knowledge	question	understand

A. *Choose one word from the list above to complete each sentence. There may be more than one right answer.*

1. Do you believe the desire to _____ is part of human nature?

2. Astronauts need the traits of bravery and _____.

3. I read an interesting _____ with a space shuttle astronaut.

B. *Follow the directions in responding to each of the items below.*

1. What do you think can be learned from space travel? Write at least two complete sentences, using one or more of the Big Question vocabulary words. You may use the words in different forms (for example you can change *analyze* to *analyzing*).

   _____

   _____

2. What do you think can be learned from traveling to another city, state or country? Write at least two complete sentences, using one or more of the Big Question vocabulary words. You may use the words in different forms (for example you can change *experiment* to *experiments*).

   _____

   _____

C. *Complete the sentence below. Use the completed sentence as the beginning of a short paragraph in which you discuss the big question.*

When we stop asking questions about the unknown _____

_____

_____

Name _____ Date _____

"The Eternal Frontier" by Louis L'Amour
Reading: Fact and Opinion

When you read nonfiction, it is important to be able to distinguish between fact and opinion. A **fact** is something that can be proved true. An **opinion** is a person's judgment or belief. It may be supported by factual evidence, but it cannot be proven.

As you read, **recognize clue words that indicate an opinion,** as in the phrases "I believe" and "in my opinion." Also look for words such as *always, never, must, cannot, best, worst,* and *all,* which may indicate a broad statement that reveals a personal judgment. Emotional statements are also often clues to opinion.

You can tell that the statement below from "The Eternal Frontier" is an opinion because it cannot be proven. Another hint is that it contains the word *must.*

What is needed now is leaders with perspective; we need leadership on a thousand fronts, but they must be men and women who can take the long view and help to shape the outlines of our future.

DIRECTIONS: *Identify each of the following quotations from "The Eternal Frontier" as a fact or an opinion. Then, briefly explain your answer. For quotations identified as opinions, point out any words or phrases that indicate it is an opinion.*

1. "All that has gone before is preliminary."

    Fact / Opinion: _____ **Explanation:** _____

    _____

2. "In 1900 there were 144 miles of surfaced road in the United States. Now there are over 3,000,000."

    Fact / Opinion: _____ **Explanation:** _____

    _____

3. "There will always be the nay-sayers, those who cling to our lovely green planet as a baby clings to its mother."

    Fact / Opinion: _____ **Explanation:** _____

    _____

4. "We have a driving need to see what lies beyond [the frontier] . . ."

    Fact / Opinion: _____ **Explanation:** _____

    _____

5. "We landed men on the moon; we sent a vehicle beyond the limits of the solar system, a vehicle still moving farther and farther into that limitless distance."

    Fact / Opinion: _____ **Explanation:** _____

    _____

6. "Nor is the mind of man bound by any limits at all."

    Fact / Opinion: _____ **Explanation:** _____

    _____

"The Eternal Frontier" by Louis L'Amour
Literary Analysis: Persuasive Essay

A **persuasive essay** is a piece of nonfiction that presents a series of arguments to convince readers that they should believe or act in a certain way. Below are some techniques that are often used in persuasive essays. When you read a persuasive essay, be aware of these techniques; you will need to decide whether they are powerful enough to persuade you to accept the author's ideas.

- **Appeals to authority:** using the opinions of experts and well-known people
- **Appeals to emotion:** using words that convey strong feeling
- **Appeals to reason:** using logical arguments backed by statistics and facts

DIRECTIONS: *In the left-hand column of the following chart, copy down statements from "The Eternal Frontier" that include appeals to emotion. In the right-hand column, copy down statements that include appeals to reason. Find at least two examples of each kind of appeal. (The essay does not make any appeals to authority.)*

Appeals to Emotion	Appeals to Reason

"The Eternal Frontier" by Louis L'Amour
Vocabulary Builder

Word List

antidote	atmospheric	destiny	frontier	impetus	preliminary

A. DIRECTIONS: *Answer each question in a complete sentence. In your answer, use one of the Word List words in place of the italicized word or phrase.*

1. What *unexplored region* might you want to learn more about?

_____

2. Can you recommend a *cure* for an hour spent working in the hot sun?

_____

3. What is the *driving force* behind studying for a test?

_____

4. What kind of examination might be given *before* a major examination?

_____

5. What is one important use of the gases *surrounding Earth*?

_____

6. Do you believe humankind will find its *future* in space?

_____

B. WORD STUDY: *The Latin root -peti- means "to ask for," "to request," or "to strive after." Read the following sentences. Use your knowledge of the Latin root -peti- to write a full sentence to answer each question. Include the italicized word in your answer.*

1. When you *petition* your principal, are you hoping for a response?

_____

2. Can *competition* motivate a person to improve her skills?

_____

3. Does *repetition* help you learn new words?

_____

Name _____ Date _____

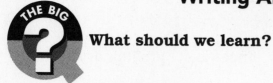

"All Together Now" by Barbara Jordan
Writing About the Big Question
What should we learn?

Big Question Vocabulary

analyze	curiosity	discover	evaluate	examine
experiment	explore	facts	information	inquire
interview	investigate	knowledge	question	understand

A. *Replace the italicized word in the sentence below with one of the vocabulary words above. The meaning of the sentence should stay the same. There may be more than one right answer.*

1. The *details* Barbara Jordan shared in her essay changed the way I saw race relations _____.

2. Barbara Jordan wants us to *study* our own circle of friends _____.

3. It is interesting to *think about* what makes people prejudiced _____.

B. *Follow the directions in responding to each of the items below.*

1. Describe one person you have met who was very different from you. Write your response in complete sentences. Use at least one of the Big Question vocabulary words. You may use the words in different forms (for example you can change *explore* to *exploration*).

    _____

    _____

2. Write two sentences describing what you learned from the person described in question 1. Use at least one of the Big Question vocabulary words. You may use the words in different forms (for example, you can change *analyze* to *analyzing*).

    _____

    _____

C. *Complete the sentence below. Use the completed sentence as the beginning of a short paragraph in which you discuss the Big Question.*

Asking questions can help _____

_____

_____

"All Together Now" by Barbara Jordan
Reading: Fact and Opinion

When you read nonfiction, it is important to be able to distinguish between fact and opinion. A **fact** is something that can be proven true. An **opinion** is a person's judgment or belief. It may be supported by factual evidence, but it cannot be proven.

As you read, **recognize clue words that indicate an opinion,** as in the phrases "I believe" and "In my opinion." Also look for words such as *always, never, must, cannot, best, worst,* and *all,* which may indicate a broad statement that reveals a personal judgment. Emotional statements are also often clues to opinion.

You can tell that this statement from "All Together Now" is an opinion because it cannot be proven. Another hint is that it contains the phrase "I don't believe":

> Frankly, I don't believe that the task of bringing us all together can be accomplished by government.

DIRECTIONS: *Identify each of the following quotations from "All Together Now" as a* fact *or an* opinion. *Then, briefly explain your answer. For quotations identified as opinions, point out any words or phrases that indicate it is an opinion.*

1. President Lyndon B. Johnson pushed through the Civil Rights Act of 1964, which remains the fundamental piece of civil rights legislation in this century.

   Fact / Opinion: _____   **Explanation:** _____

   _____

2. One thing is clear to me: We, as human beings, must be willing to accept people who are different from ourselves.

   Fact / Opinion: _____   **Explanation:** _____

   _____

3. Children learn ideas and attitudes from the adults who nurture them.

   Fact / Opinion: _____   **Explanation:** _____

   _____

4. I absolutely believe that children do not adopt prejudices unless they absorb them from their parents or teachers.

   Fact / Opinion: _____   **Explanation:** _____

   _____

5. It is possible for all of us to work on this at home, in our schools, at our jobs.

   Fact / Opinion: _____   **Explanation:** _____

   _____

"All Together Now" by Barbara Jordan
Literary Analysis: Persuasive Essay

A **persuasive essay** is a piece of nonfiction that presents a series of arguments to convince readers that they should believe or act in a certain way. Below are some techniques that are often used in persuasive essays. When you read a persuasive essay, be aware of these techniques; you will need to decide whether they are powerful enough to persuade you to accept the author's ideas.

- **Appeals to authority:** using the opinions of experts and well-known people
- **Appeals to emotion:** using words that convey strong feeling
- **Appeals to reason:** using logical arguments backed by statistics and facts

DIRECTIONS: *In the first column of the following chart, copy statements from "All Together Now" that include appeals to authority. In the second column, copy statements that include appeals to emotion. In the third column, copy statements that include appeals to reason. Find at least one example of each kind of appeal.*

Appeals to Authority	Appeals to Emotion	Appeals to Reason

Name _____ Date _____

"**All Together Now**" by Barbara Jordan
Vocabulary Builder

Word List

culminated   equality   fundamental   legislation   optimist   tolerant

A. DIRECTIONS: *Answer each question in a complete sentence. In your answer, use one of the Word List words in place of the italicized word or phrase.*

1. In what way have civil rights *laws* changed this country?

   _____

2. What is the *basic* rule for getting along with others?

   _____

3. What happens when people are not *accepting* of others' differences?

   _____

4. Are you *someone who takes the most hopeful view of matters*?

   _____

5. Barbara Jordan's career *reached its highest point* when she was elected to the United States House of Representatives.

   _____

6. This country was founded on the idea that everyone should enjoy *the same rights*.

   _____

B. WORD STUDY: *The Latin root -leg- means "law." Use your knowledge of the Latin root -leg- to write a full sentence to answer each question. Include the italicized word in your answer.*

1. Is a thief likely to give a *legitimate* account of his actions?

   _____

2. Would you expect an honest person to do something *illegal*?

   _____

3. Is it *legal* to cross the street when the sign reads DON'T WALK?

   _____

"The Eternal Frontier" by Louis L'Amour
"All Together Now" by Barbara Jordan
Integrated Language Skills: Grammar

Subjects and Predicates

Every sentence has two parts: the **subject** and the **predicate.** The **subject** describes whom or what the sentence is about. The **simple subject** is the noun or pronoun that states exactly whom or what the sentence is about. The **complete subject** includes the simple subject and all of its modifiers.

The **predicate** is a verb that tells what the subject does, what is done to the subject, or what the condition of the subject is. The **simple predicate** is the verb or verb phrase that tells what the subject of the sentence does or is. It includes the simple predicate and any modifiers or complements.

In the following example, the simple subject and the simple predicate are in bold type. The complete subject is underlined once, and the complete predicate is underlined twice.

Louis L'Amour, a writer of novels about the American West, **has written** a persuasive essay about the importance of space exploration.

A. PRACTICE: *In each sentence, underline the simple subject once and the simple predicate twice.*

1. Louis L'Amour writes about the importance of space travel.

2. In L'Amour's view, outer space is the next frontier.

3. All of humankind longs for exploration and discovery.

4. According to Barbara Jordan, we can win the fight against prejudice.

5. Little children do not hate other people.

6. People learn to hate from parents and teachers.

B. WRITING APPLICATION: *In a paragraph of at least four sentences, describe a place you would like to explore. Underline each simple subject once and each simple predicate twice.*

_____

_____

_____

_____

_____

_____

_____

"The Eternal Frontier" by Louis L'Amour
"All Together Now" by Barbara Jordan

Integrated Language Skills:
Support for Writing a Persuasive Essay

Prepare to write a brief **persuasive essay** on one of the following topics:

- A letter to community leaders telling them how people in the community can promote tolerance
- A letter to government leaders advising them about space travel.

Organize your thoughts by completing the chart below. In the left-hand column, write down the goals you would like to see achieved by government or your community. In this column, explain any challenges elected officials or community members might face in trying to achieve the goal.

In the right-hand column, describe the persuasive technique you will use to make each point. Your choices are to:

- **Appeal to authority** by using opinions of experts and well-known people

- **Appeal to reason** by using logical arguments backed by facts.

- **Appeal to emotion** by using words that convey strong feelings

Points	Persuasive Techniques

Now, use the ideas you have gathered to write your persuasive letter.

"The Real Story of a Cowboy's Life" by Geoffrey C. Ward
Writing About the Big Question

What should we learn?

Big Question Vocabulary

analyze	curiosity	discover	evaluate	examine
experiment	explore	facts	information	inquire
interview	investigate	knowledge	question	understand

A. *Replace the italicized word in the sentence below with one of the vocabulary words above. The meaning of the sentence should stay the same. There may be more than one right answer.*

1. It was a good idea to *ask* cowboys about what their lives were really like

    _____.

2. It is difficult to *estimate* how many cattle were on the range at once

    _____.

3. This essay helped me *find out about* another way of life

    _____.

B. *Follow the directions in responding to each of the items below.*

1. Write about a job that you'd like to know more about and explain why. Write your response in complete sentences. Use at least one of the Big Question vocabulary words. You may change the form of the word (for example, you can change *information* to *inform.*)

    _____

    _____

2. Write about a job that you'd never want to do and explain why. Write your response in complete sentences. Use at least one of the Big Question vocabulary words. You may change the form of the word (for example, you can change *discover* to *discovery.*)

    _____

    _____

C. *Complete the sentence below. Use the completed sentence as the beginning of a short paragraph in which you discuss the big question.*

Talking to people who participated in an event can _____

    _____

    _____

"The Real Story of a Cowboy's Life" by Geoffrey C. Ward
Reading: Use Resources to Check Facts

A **fact** is information you can prove. An **opinion** is a judgment.

Fact: The big herds . . . carried with them a disease . . . that devastated domestic livestock.

Opinion: The settlers' hostility was entirely understandable.

Be aware that some writers present opinions or beliefs as facts. To get to the truth, **use resources to check facts.**

Resource	Characteristics
almanac	a collection of facts and statistics on the climate, planets, stars, people, places, events, and so on, updated yearly
atlas	a collection of maps
biographical dictionary	an alphabetical listing of famous or historically significant persons with identifying information and dates of birth and death
dictionary	an alphabetical listing of words with their pronunciation and definition
encyclopedia	an alphabetically organized collection of articles on a broad range of subjects
reliable Web sites	Internet pages and articles on an extremely wide variety of topics, sponsored by individuals, companies, governments, and organizations

DIRECTIONS: *Read these passages from "The Real Story of a Cowboy's Life." Then, identify each one as a fact or an opinion. If the statement is a fact, indicate the best resource for checking it.*

1. Most Texas herds numbered about 2,000 head with a trail boss and about a dozen men in charge though herds as large as 15,000 were also driven north with far larger escorts.

   Fact/opinion: _____ **Resource:** _____

2. Regardless of its ultimate destination, every herd had to ford a series of rivers—the Nueces, the Guadalupe, the Brazos, the Wichita, the Red.

   Fact/opinion: _____ **Resource:** _____

3. After you crossed the Red River and got out on the open plains . . . it was sure a pretty sight to see them strung out for almost a mile, the sun shining on their horns.

   Fact/opinion: _____ **Resource:** _____

4. Initially, the land immediately north of the Red River was Indian territory, and some tribes charged tolls for herds crossing their land payable in money or beef.

   Fact/opinion: _____ **Resource:** _____

"The Real Story of a Cowboy's Life" by Geoffrey C. Ward
Literary Analysis: Word Choice and Diction

A writer's **word choice** and **diction** are important elements of his or her writing. The specific words a writer uses can make writing difficult or easy to read, formal or informal. Diction includes not only the vocabulary the writer uses but also the way in which the sentences are put together. Here are some questions writers consider when deciding which words to use:

- What does the audience already know about the topic? If an audience is unfamiliar with a topic, the writer will have to define technical vocabulary or use simpler language.
- What feeling will this work convey? Word choice can make a work serious or funny, academic or personal. The length and style of the sentences can make a work simple or complex.

In this passage from "The Real Story of a Cowboy's Life," notice that the author uses both technical vocabulary (*point, swing, drag*) and informal language ("eating dust"):

The most experienced men rode "point" and "swing," at the head and sides of the long herd; the least experienced brought up the rear, riding "drag" and eating dust.

DIRECTIONS: *Read each passage. Then, on the lines that follow, write down examples of technical vocabulary, formal language, and informal language. If there are no examples of a particular kind of language, write* none.

1. If . . . the cattle started running you'd hear that low rumbling noise along the ground and the men on herd wouldn't need to come in and tell you, you'd know—then you'd jump for your horse and get out there in the lead, trying to head them and get them into a mill before they scattered. It was riding at a dead run in the dark, with cut banks and prairie dog holes all around you, not knowing if the next jump would land you in a shallow grave.

   Technical vocabulary: _____

   Informal language: _____

   Formal language: _____

2. The big herds ruined their crops, and they carried with them a disease, spread by ticks and called "Texas fever," that devastated domestic livestock. Kansas and other territories along the route soon established quarantine lines, called "deadlines," at the western fringe of settlement, and insisted that trail drives not cross them.

   Technical vocabulary: _____

   Informal language: _____

   Formal language: _____

Name _____ Date _____

"The Real Story of a Cowboy's Life" by Geoffrey C. Ward
Vocabulary Builder

Word List

discipline   diversions   emphatic   gauge   longhorns   ultimate

A. DIRECTIONS: *Write the correct word from the Word List on each line.*

1. The teammates want to win the next match, but their _____ goal is to win the championship.

2. The fair offered games, rides, and a few other _____.

3. The cowboys tried to _____ the mood of the cattle by the way the animals moved and the cries they uttered.

4. Bosses like Charles Goodnight needed to impose _____ along the trail.

5. Settlers had an _____ message for cowboys: STAY OUT!

6. _____ are a type of cattle popular in Texas.

B. WORD STUDY: *The Latin root -vers- means "to turn." Use your knowledge of the Latin root -vers- to write a full sentence to answer each question. Include the italicized word in your answer.*

1. If you *reverse* direction do you go the opposite way?

_____

2. If you behave in a *subversive* manner are you being supportive?

_____

3. Can a *versatile* employee handle many different responsibilities?

_____

"**Rattlesnake Hunt**" by Marjorie Kinnan Rawlings
Writing About the Big Question

What should we learn?

Big Question Vocabulary

analyze	curiosity	discover	evaluate	examine
experiment	explore	facts	information	inquire
interview	investigate	knowledge	question	understand

A. *Choose one word from the list above to complete each sentence. There may be more than one right answer.*

1. Journalists often _____ dozens of experts before writing an article.

2. Sometimes it's impossible to _____ why something frightens us.

3. The scientist did an _____ to learn how many rattlesnakes he could catch.

B. *Follow the directions in responding to each of the items below.*

1. Write about a time when you learned about something that frightens you. Write your response in complete sentences. Use at least one of the Big Question vocabulary words. You may use the words in different forms (for example you can change *analyze* to *analyzing*).

   _____

   _____

2. Write about a common fear you find difficult to understand. Write your response in complete sentences. Use at least one of the Big Question vocabulary words. You may use the words in different forms (for example you can change *analyze* to *analyzing*).

   _____

   _____

C. *Complete the sentence below. Use the completed sentence as the beginning of a short paragraph in which you discuss the big question.*

The more we understand something, _____

_____

_____

"**Rattlesnake Hunt**" by Marjorie Kinnan Rawlings
Reading: Use Resources to Check Facts

A **fact** is information you can prove. An **opinion** is a judgment.

Fact: Ross Allen is a young herpetologist from Florida.

Opinion: "The scientific and dispassionate detachment of the material and the man made a desirable approach to rattlesnake territory."

Be aware that some writers present opinions or beliefs as facts. To get to the truth, **use resources to check facts.** You can confirm whether a statement is accurate by using one of these resources:

Resource	Characteristics
almanac	a collection of facts and statistics on the climate, planets, stars, people, places, events and so on, updated yearly
atlas	a collection of maps
geographical dictionary	an alphabetical listing of places with statistical and factual information about them and perhaps some maps
dictionary	an alphabetical listing of words with their pronunciations and definitions
encyclopedia	an alphabetically organized collection of articles on a broad range of subjects
reliable Web sites	Internet pages and articles on an extremely wide variety of topics, sponsored by individuals, companies, governments, and organizations

DIRECTIONS: *Read these passages from and about "Rattlesnake Hunt." Then, identify each one as a* fact *or an* opinion. *If the statement is a fact, indicate the best resource for checking it.*

1. Big Prairie, Florida, is south of Arcadia and west of the northern tip of Lake Okeechobee.

   Fact/opinion: _____   **Resource:** _____

2. Snakes take on the temperature of their surroundings. They can't stand too much heat for that reason, and when the weather is cool, as now, they're sluggish.

   Fact/opinion: _____   **Resource:** _____

3. Snakes are not cold and clammy.

   Fact/opinion: _____   **Resource:** _____

4. The next day was magnificent. The air was crystal, the sky was aquamarine.

   Fact/opinion: _____   **Resource:** _____

5. A rattler will lie quietly without revealing itself if a man passes by and it thinks it is not seen.

   Fact/opinion: _____   **Resource:** _____

"**Rattlesnake Hunt**" by Marjorie Kinnan Rawlings
Literary Analysis: Word Choice and Diction

A writer's **word choice** and **diction** are important elements of his or her writing. The specific words a writer uses can make writing difficult or easy to read, formal or informal. Diction includes not only the vocabulary the writer uses but also the way in which the sentences are put together. Here are some questions writers consider when deciding which kinds of words to use:

- What does the audience already know about the topic? If an audience is unfamiliar with a topic, the writer will have to define technical vocabulary or use simpler language.
- What feeling will this work convey? Word choice can make a work serious or funny, academic or personal. The length or style of the sentences can make a work simple or complex.

In this passage from "Rattlesnake Hunt," note that the author uses formal language and difficult vocabulary, but she also uses the informal word *varmints:*

> The scientific and dispassionate detachment of the material and the man made a desirable approach to rattlesnake territory. As I had discovered with the insects and varmints, it is difficult to be afraid of anything about which enough is known.

DIRECTIONS: *Read each passage. Then, on the lines that follow, write down examples of technical vocabulary, formal language, and informal language. If there are no examples of a particular kind of language, write* none.

1. They lived in winter, he said, in gopher holes, coming out in the midday warmth to forage, and would move ahead of the flames and be easily taken.

   Technical vocabulary: _____

   Informal language: _____

   Formal language: _____

2. After the rattlers, water snakes seemed innocuous enough. We worked along the edge of the stream and here Ross did not use his L-shaped steel.

   Technical vocabulary: _____

   Informal language: _____

   Formal language: _____

3. Yet having learned that it was we who were the aggressors; that immobility meant complete safety; that the snakes, for all their lightning flash in striking, were inaccurate in their aim, . . . suddenly I understood that I was drinking in freely the magnificent sweep of the horizon, with no fear of what might be at the moment under my feet.

   Technical vocabulary: _____

   Informal language: _____

   Formal language: _____

"Rattlesnake Hunt" by Marjorie Kinnan Rawlings
Vocabulary Builder

Word List

adequate   arid   desolate   forage   mortality   translucent

A. DIRECTIONS: *Write* true *if a statement is true and* false *if it is false. Then, explain your answer.*

1. If a region is *arid*, crops will grow there easily.

   True/false: _____ **Explanation:** _____

   _____

2. If a character in a book faces his *mortality,* he believes he will live forever.

   True/false: _____ **Explanation:** _____

   _____

3. If a scene in a movie is set in a *desolate* location, the mood will likely be lonely.

   True/false: _____ **Explanation:** _____

   _____

4. If you will be around dangerous animals, it is important to take *adequate* precautions.

   True/false: _____ **Explanation:** _____

   _____

5. *Forage* can be an important part of cattle's diet.

   True/false: _____ **Explanation:** _____

   _____

6. Windows are never *translucent.*

   True/false: _____ **Explanation:** _____

   _____

B. WORD STUDY: *The Latin root* -sol- *means "alone." Use your knowledge of the Latin root* -sol- *to write a full sentence to answer each question. Include the italicized word in your answer.*

1. How many people can play a game of *solitaire?*

   _____

2. If you seek *solitude,* do you want others around?

   _____

3. Would many people play a *solo* at one time?

   _____

Name _____ Date _____

Compound Subjects and Predicates

A **compound subject** contains two or more subjects that share the same verb. A **compound predicate** contains two or more verbs that share the same subject. Both compound subjects and compound predicates are joined by conjunctions such as *and, or, but,* and *nor.*

Compound subject:	<u>Discipline</u> *and* <u>planning</u> were essential to the success of a cattle drive.
Compound predicate:	"The snake <u>did</u> not <u>coil</u>, *but* <u>lifted</u> its head *and* <u>whirred</u> its rattles lightly."

A. PRACTICE: *In these sentences, underline the compound subjects once and the compound predicates twice.*

1. On trail rides, cowboys keep the herd together and guide them along the trail.
2. Trail bosses and cowboys work together to keep the cattle safe.
3. Sometimes bosses pay homesteaders or face their anger.
4. Most trail bosses forbid gambling and punish cowboys for drinking.
5. Rattlesnakes warn intruders but strike quickly.
6. Snakes and other reptiles are cold-blooded.
7. Sun and warm temperatures bring snakes out of hiding.
8. Snake catchers must move carefully or suffer the consequences.

B. Writing Application: *Imagine that you are describing an attempt at catching a rattlesnake. Follow these instructions.*

1. Write a sentence with a compound predicate; use *walked* and *searched.*

   _____

   _____

2. Write a sentence with a compound subject; use *insects* and *snakes.*

   _____

   _____

3. Write a sentence with a compound predicate; use *hissed* and *rattled.*

   _____

   _____

4. Write a sentence with a compound predicate; use *found* and *caught.*

   _____

   _____

"The Real Story of a Cowboy's Life" by Geoffrey C. Ward
"Rattlesnake Hunt" by Marjorie Kinnan Rawlings

Integrated Language Skills: Support for Writing an Adaptation

Prepare to write an **adaptation** of one of the incidents described in "Rattlesnake Hunt" or "The Real Story of a Cowboy's Life," by completing the following graphic organizer. First note the incident you plan to adapt and the audience you plan to present your adaptation to. For examples, tell the incident to a group of kindergartners or a class of students learning English. Then, in the first column of the chart, copy down the incident. In the second column, write your adaptation, keeping your audience in mind. Finally, look carefully at your adaptation. See if you can simplify it even further. In the last column, note your revisions.

Incident: _____

Audience: _____

Passage	Adaptation	Revision of Adaptation

Now, use your notes to write a final draft of your adaptation.

Name _____ Date _____

"**Alligator**" by Bailey White
"**The Cremation of Sam McGee**" by Robert Service
Writing About the Big Question

What should we learn?

Big Question Vocabulary

analyze	curiosity	discover	evaluate	examine
experiment	explore	facts	information	inquire
interview	investigate	knowledge	question	understand

A. *Choose one word from the list above to complete each sentence. There may be more than one right answer.*

1. I think _____ made the alligator visit shore.

2. The characters in "The Cremation of Sam McGee" hoped to _____ gold.

3. I would like to _____ the Yukon.

B. *Follow the directions in responding to each of the items below.*

1. Write about what makes you laugh. Write your response in complete sentences. Use at least one of the Big Question vocabulary words. You may use the words in different forms (for example you can change *analyze* to *analyzing*).

   _____

   _____

2. Explain one way you think laughter is important. Write your response in complete sentences. Use at least one of the Big Question vocabulary words. You may use the words in different forms.

   _____

   _____

C. *Complete the sentence below. Use the completed sentence as the beginning of a short paragraph in which you discuss the big question.*

The funniest things happen when _____

   _____

   _____.

Name _____ Date _____

Literary Analysis: Comparing Humorous Essays

Humorous essays are works of nonfiction meant to amuse readers. To entertain, authors may use one or more of these comic techniques:

- presenting an illogical, inappropriate, improper, or unusual situation
- contrasting reality with characters' mistaken views
- exaggerating the truth or exaggerating the feelings, ideas, and actions of characters

While most humorists want to entertain the reader, many also want to convey a serious message.

Writers of humorous essays often develop the humor through the characters they present. For example, humorous characters are central to "Alligator" and "The Cremation of Sam McGee."

DIRECTIONS: *Explain your answers to the following questions, using examples from the selections.*

Question	"Alligator"	"The Cremation of Sam McGee"
1. Does the essay describe illogical, inappropriate, improper, or unusual situations?		
2. Does the writer contrast reality with characters' mistaken views?		
3. Does the writer exaggerate the truth or the feelings, ideas, and actions of characters?		
4. Which character did you find the most humorous? How is that character's appearance described? How are his or her actions described? What does the character say, or what do other characters say about him or her, to add to the humor?		

"Alligator" by Bailey White
"The Cremation of Sam McGee" by Robert Service
Vocabulary Builder

Word List

bellow   cattails   exultant   loathed   whimper

A. DIRECTIONS: *Read each sentence, paying attention to the italicized word from the Word List. Then, explain whether the sentence makes sense. If it does not make sense, rewrite the sentence using the Word List word correctly, or write a new sentence using the word.*

1. On our trip to the desert, we found *cattails* growing everywhere.

   Explanation: _____

   New sentence: _____

2. The crowds in the arena *bellow* when the referee makes an unfair call.

   Explanation: _____

   New sentence: _____

3. When she discovered she had come in last place, the student was *exultant*.

   Explanation: _____

   New sentence: _____

4. We hated to hear our dog *whimper* when we left him home alone.

   Explanation: _____

   New sentence: _____

5. Maria *loathed* eating things she found delicious.

   Explanation: _____

   New sentence: _____

B. DIRECTIONS: *Write the letter of the word that is most similar in meaning to the word from the Word List.*

____ 1. exultant
   A. depressed   B. overjoyed   C. safe   D. dangerous

____ 2. cattails
   A. plants   B. clothes   C. cat   D. pattern

____ 3. bellow
   A. write   B. shout   C. whisper   D. read

____ 4. whimper
   A. sing   B. shout   C. whine   D. drive

____ 5. loathed
   A. hated   B. loved   C. cherished   D. ignored

Name _____ Date _____

"**Alligator**" by Bailey White
"**The Cremation of Sam McGee**" by Robert Service
Integrated Language Skills:
Support for Writing to Compare Literary Works

To prepare to write an essay **comparing humorous essays,** complete this graphic organizer.

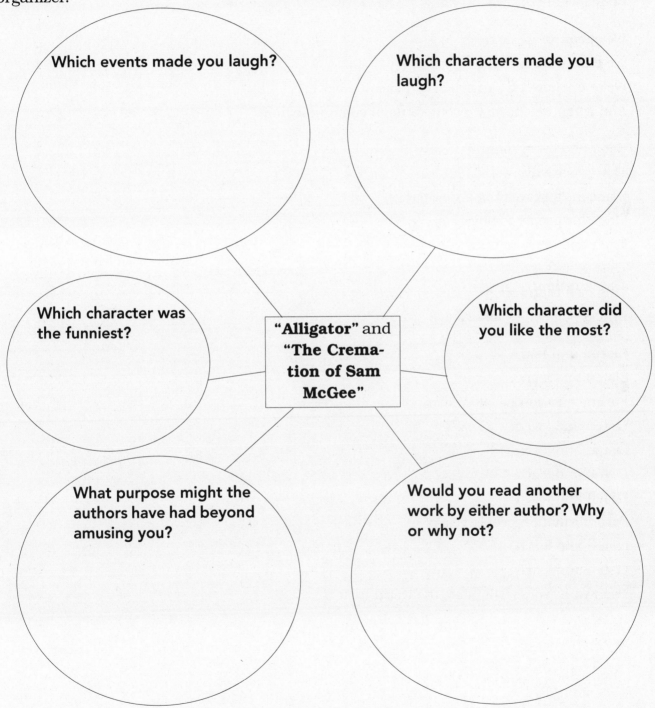

Which events made you laugh?

Which characters made you laugh?

Which character was the funniest?

"**Alligator**" and "**The Crema-tion of Sam McGee**"

Which character did you like the most?

What purpose might the authors have had beyond amusing you?

Would you read another work by either author? Why or why not?

Now, use your notes to write an essay explaining why you found "Alligator" funnier than "The Cremation of Sam McGee" or why you found "The Cremation of Sam McGee" funnier than "Alligator."

 **BQ Tunes**

Listen & Learn, performed by Nina Zeitlin

Listen, can you hear me?
Learn what you need to know

We **speak** to the listener
We **communicate** the information
We're **enriched** by knowledge (makes us better)
And when we share, we contribute to communication

Each and every minute
That passes by
Someone's **producing** a new gadget
Made for people to buy
Each and every minute
That passes by
This new **technology**
Enters someone's mind's eye

Listen and **learn**
Listen and learn
For information people yearn
Listen and learn
Listen and learn
Listen and learn
Listen and learn
For information people yearn
Listen and learn
Listen and learn
Then your words will make the world turn

Continued

To play our favorite music

To **transmit** the words we say

Show an **entertaining** movie, or my favorite TV show

On whatever media we chose today (we chose today)

Teach ourselves how to use it

To learn and to be **informed**

To speak and to **express** ourselves

Choosing one from the other, we might be torn but

Listen and **learn**

Listen and learn

For information people yearn

Listen and learn

Listen and learn

Listen and learn

Listen and learn

For information people yearn

Listen and learn

Listen and learn

Then your words will make the world turn

There will always be something new

People **react,** they respond to the next big thing

Who's **producing** the greatest **media** toy? (**media** toy)

No matter what form of communication this year brings, ya gotta...

Listen and **learn**

Listen and learn

For information people yearn

Listen and learn

Listen and learn

Listen and learn

Listen and learn

Continued

For information people yearn

Listen and learn

Listen and learn

Then your words will make the world turn

———————————————————

Song Title: **Listen & Learn**

Artist / Performed by Nina Zeitlin

Guitar: Josh Green

Drums/Bass: Mike Pandolfo

Keys: Mike Pandolfo & Nina Zeitlin

Conga: Vlad Gutkovich

Lyrics by Nina Zeitlin

Music composed by Mike Pandolfo & Nina Zeitlin

Produced by Mike Pandolfo, Wonderful

Executive Producer: Keith London, Defined Mind

Name _____ Date _____

Unit 4: Poetry
Big Question Vocabulary—1

The Big Question: What is the best way to communicate?

communicate: *v.* to exchange information with others; other forms: *communication, communicating, communicated*

elaborate: *v.* to give more details or information about a topic

　　　　adj. having a lot of small parts or details put together in a complicated way; other forms: elaborated, elaborating, elaboration

entertain: *v.* to amuse or interest others in a way that makes them happy; other forms: *entertainment, entertaining, entertained*

generate: *v.* to create or develop new ideas on a topic; other forms: *generated, generator*

listen: *v.* to pay attention to what someone is saying; other forms: *listening, listened, listener*

A. DIRECTIONS: *Read each sentence carefully. Each one describes an action that is the* **opposite** *of the action that a vocabulary word describes. Identify each vocabulary word. Write it on the line following the word* **Opposite***.*

> **Example:** He wanted to *open* the door.　Opposite:_____shut_____

1. I decided to *ignore* what he said.　　　　　**Opposite:** _____

2. Let's *simplify* this complicated issue.　　　**Opposite:** _____

3. He will bore the audience with that performance.　**Opposite:** _____

4. She wanted to *conceal* her ideas.　　　　　**Opposite:** _____

5. He wanted us to *use his old plans and ideas.*　**Opposite:** _____

B. DIRECTIONS: *Complete each sentence by adding the correct vocabulary word.*

1. The school principal asked the students to _____ new ideas about improving school safety.

2. If you don't _____ carefully, you won't hear the beautiful, soft call of the Baltimore oriole.

3. I didn't understand the math problem, so I asked the teacher to _____ on the directions.

4. To _____ with each other effectively, you must speak clearly and listen carefully.

5. Using rich, vivid words and humorous situations will help you to _____ your readers.

Unit 4: Poetry
Big Question Vocabulary—2

The Big Question: What is the best way to communicate?

contribute: *v.* to share or give something of value to others; other form: *contribution*

express: *v.* to use words or actions to show thoughts and feelings; other forms: *expression, expressing, expressed*

learn: *v.* to gain knowledge and understanding of information; other forms: *learning, learned*

produce: *v.* to create something; other forms: *production, producing, produced, producer*

teach: *v.* to help someone learn by giving them information; other forms: *teacher, taught*

DIRECTIONS: *List three things as instructed. Then, use the vocabulary word in a sentences about one of the things. You may use one of its other forms, as shown above.*

1. List three ways that a person might use to *express* happiness.

   _____   _____   _____

   Sentence: _____

2. List three things that grandparents and other older people can *teach* young people.

   _____   _____   _____

   Sentence: _____

3. List three things that a person might *produce* with a pencil and paper.

   _____   _____   _____

   Sentence: _____

4. List three ways that a person might *contribute* to his or her neighborhood or community.

   _____   _____   _____

   Sentence: _____

5. List three things that you consider to be the most important things for a young child to *learn*.

   _____   _____   _____

   Sentence: _____

Unit 4: Poetry
Big Question Vocabulary—3

The Big Question: What is the best way to communicate?

enrich: *v.* to improve the quality of something; other forms: *enrichment, enriching, enriched*

inform: *v.* to share facts or information with someone; other forms: *information, informed*

media: *n.* institutions or items that present news and other information, including newspapers, magazines, television programs, and Internet sources; other form: *medium*

technology: *n.* machines and equipment that are based on modern knowledge about science; other forms: *technological, technologies*

transmit: *v.* to send a message or signal, through such sources as radios, televisions, or the Internet; other forms: *transmission, transmitting, transmitted*

A. DIRECTIONS: *Give an example of each of the following.*

1. a *technology* that you use at school: _____

2. something that you *transmitted* to someone electronically: _____

3. a way to *enrich* a friendship: _____

4. a fact that you'd like to *inform* people about: _____

5. a specific form of the *media* that you respect as a news source: _____

B. DIRECTIONS: *Imagine that you are a scientist who just discovered life on another planet. On the lines below, write a summary of your findings, telling how you made your discovery, what messages the people sent to you and how they sent them, and why you feel your discovery might improve life on Earth. Use each of the vocabulary words.*

_____

_____

_____

_____

_____

_____

_____

_____

_____

Name _____ Date _____

Unit 4: Poetry
Applying the Big Question

What is the best way to communicate?

DIRECTIONS: *Complete the chart below to apply what you have learned about communication. One row has been completed for you.*

Example	Type of communication	Purpose	Pros	Cons	What I learned
From Literature	Writing about meaningful family lessons.	To share an important life lesson.	Conveys a personal story to a broader audience.	The audience for poetry is smaller than media, such as TV.	A metaphor's lesson can apply many people.
From Literature					
From Science					
From Social Studies					
From Real Life					

Pat Mora
Listening and Viewing

Segment 1: Meet Pat Mora
- Why does Pat Mora use both English and Spanish when she writes?
- What are some reasons that it is important to read literature by or about people of many different cultures?

_____

_____

_____

_____

Segment 2: Poetry
- Why does Pat Mora write the last line of "The Desert Is My Mother" in Spanish?
- What effect do the Spanish lines in this poem have on you as a reader?

_____

_____

_____

_____

Segment 3: The Writing Process
- How does Pat Mora prepare to begin writing?
- Which one of her writing strategies would you use, and why?

_____

_____

_____

_____

Segment 4: The Rewards of Writing
- How are poetry readings particularly rewarding to Pat Mora?
- Has a certain piece of literature had a strong impact on you as a reader? Explain.

_____

_____

_____

_____

Name _____ Date _____

Learning About Poetry

Poetry is the most musical, and often the most imaginative, of all literary forms. A common characteristic of poetry is **figurative language,** which is writing or speech that is not meant to be taken literally, or as though it is realistic.

FIGURATIVE LANGUAGE	• **metaphor:** describes one thing as if it were something else *(You are the sunshine of my life.)*
	• **simile:** uses *like* or *as* to compare two unlike things *(Your smile is as bright as the sun.)*
	• **personification:** gives human qualities to a nonhuman thing *(The sun smiled on our picnic.)*
	• **symbol:** something that represents something else *(The flag is a symbol of our country; a dove is a symbol of peace.)*

A. DIRECTIONS: *On the lines, write the letter of the type of figurative language used in each line of poetry.*

___ 1. bubbly and bright like a mountain stream

A. simile

___ 2. a bright lantern that welcomed me home

B. metaphor

___ 3. your eyes are moonlight to my earth

C. symbol

___ 4. the apple pie that means "home"

D. personification

B. DIRECTIONS: *Follow each direction by writing an original phrase or sentence.*

1. Use a metaphor to write about the moon.

_____

2. Use a simile to write about a dog.

_____

3. Use personification to write about a clock.

_____

4. Write a sentence containing a symbol.

_____

The Poetry of Pat Mora
Model Selection: Poetry

In addition to figurative language, Pat Mora's three poems contain examples of **sound devices,** or writing or speech that adds a musical quality.

SOUND DEVICES	• **alliteration:** repetition of consonant sounds at the beginning of words (*a busy bee*)
	• **repetition:** use of a sound, word, or group of words more than once (*the beat of the drum and the beat of my heart*)
	• **onomatopoeia:** use of words that imitate sounds (*quack, bang*)
	• **rhyme:** repetition of sounds at the ends of words (*sit, lit, hit*)
	• **meter:** arrangement of stressed and unstressed syllables (*The day began at eight o'clock.*)

A. DIRECTIONS: *Answer these questions about the characteristics in Pat Mora's poems.*

1. In the first stanza of "Maestro," what verb is an example of onomatopoeia?

   _____

2. What example of repetition appears in the first five lines of "Bailando"?

   _____

3. What type of sound device is represented by the word *whispers*?

   _____

4. What type of sound device is represented by the phrase *the snow's silence*?

   _____

B. DIRECTIONS: *In these poems, Pat Mora speaks of family members. On the lines below, write your own short poem about a family member or friend. Include at least two examples of figurative language and sound devices.*

   _____

   _____

   _____

   _____

   _____

   _____

"The Rider" by Naomi Shihab Nye, **"Seal"** by William Jay Smith, **Haiku** by Buson

Writing About the Big Question

What is the best way to communicate?

Big Question Vocabulary

communicate	contribute	enrich	entertain	express
inform	learn	listen	media	produce
react	speak	teach	technology	transmit

A. *Use one or more words from the list above to complete each sentence.*

1. Helping others to _____ new skills is a good way to communicate.

2. One way to communicate what you know is to _____ a skill to someone else.

3. When you _____ your knowledge to others, they find out about you as well as your subject.

4. You can use _____ such as computers to communicate your knowledge.

B. *Answer each question with a complete sentence.*

1. Write down two things you have taught another person. Use at least two of the Big Question vocabulary words.

   _____

   _____

2. Write two sentences explaining how you communicated the knowledge you taught.

   _____

   _____

C. *In "Poetry Collection 1," three poets use different forms to share their thoughts or observations. Complete these sentences:*

Through poetry, writers **communicate** _____.

I most enjoy reading poems that **express** _____.

Poetry Collection: Naomi Shihab Nye, William Jay Smith, Buson
Reading: Ask Questions to Draw a Conclusion

Drawing conclusions means arriving at an overall judgment or idea by pulling together several details. By drawing conclusions, you recognize meanings that are not directly stated. **Asking questions** can help you identify details and make connections that lead to a conclusion. You might ask yourself questions such as these:

- What details does the writer include and emphasize?
- How are the details related?
- What do the details mean all together?

Consider, for example, this haiku by Buson:

After the moon sets,

slow through the forest, shadows

drift and disappear

What do the details suggest? The moon has set, so it must be morning. Why, though, do "shadows / drift and disappear"? Is it because it has grown darker or because it has grown lighter, because the sun is rising? The reader might conclude that Buson's haiku vividly evokes the darkness that precedes dawn.

DIRECTIONS: *Complete the following chart. First, ask a question about the poem. Then, record the details that prompted the question. Finally, write a conclusion that you can draw based on the question and the related details.*

Poem	Question	Details Relating to Question	Conclusion
"The Rider"			
"Seal"			
"O foolish ducklings"			
"Deep in a windless wood"			

Poetry Collection: Naomi Shihab Nye, William Jay Smith, Buson
Literary Analysis: Forms of Poetry

There are many different **forms of poetry.** A poet will follow different rules depending on the structure of a poem. These are the three forms represented by the poems in this collection:

- A **lyric poem** expresses the poet's thoughts and feelings about a single image or idea in vivid, musical language.
- In a **concrete poem,** the poet arranges the letters and lines to create a visual image that suggests the poem's subject.
- **Haiku** is a traditional form of Japanese poetry that is often about nature. In a traditional haiku, the first line always has five syllables, the second line always has seven syllables, and the third line always has five syllables.

DIRECTIONS: *Write your responses to the following questions.*

1. If you were to rewrite "The Rider" as a concrete poem, what shape would you use to express the main idea of the poem? Why?

   _____

   _____

2. If you were to rewrite "Seal" as a haiku, what seven-syllable line might you write that contained the phrase "Quicksilver-quick"?

   _____

3. If you were to rewrite one of Buson's haiku as a lyric poem, on what single image would you focus? Why?

   _____

   _____

4. If you were to rewrite "The Rider" as a haiku, what would one of your lines be?

   _____

5. If you were to rewrite "Seal" as a lyric poem, how would you change it? Why?

   _____

   _____

Name _____ Date _____

Word List

luminous   minnow   swerve   translates   utter   weasel

A. DIRECTIONS: *Provide an explanation for your answer to each question.*

1. Would you be able to see *luminous* stars in a clear night sky?

   _____

   _____

2. If someone did not *utter* a word, would she be likely to win a debate?

   _____

   _____

3. Would you be likely to see a *weasel* in the Large Mammals section of a zoo?

   _____

   _____

4. Would a driver likely go into a *swerve* to avoid hitting something in the road?

   _____

   _____

5. Would you find a *minnow* in a forest?

   _____

   _____

6. If someone *translates* a poem into English, could you read it?

   _____

   _____

B. WORD STUDY: *The Latin root* -lum- *means "light." Write a sentence that answers each question, using the italicized word.*

1. If a soccer field is *illuminated*, what time of day is the game probably being played?

   _____

2. What part of the ocean is a *bioluminescent* fish likely to live in?

   _____

3. If someone is a *luminary* in the field of medicine, what do people probably think of the person?

   _____

"**Winter**" by Nikki Giovanni, "**Forsythia**" by Mary Ellen Solt, **Haiku** by Matsuo Bashō

Writing About the Big Question

What is the best way to communicate?

Big Question Vocabulary

communicate	contribute	enrich	entertain	express
inform	learn	listen	media	produce
react	speak	teach	technology	transmit

A. *Use one or more words from the list above to complete each sentence.*

1. One of the most direct ways to get to know someone is to _____ to the person in a conversation.

2. When you have a conversation, is it important to _____ to what the other person says.

3. The way you _____ to someone's statements may show in your face or body.

4. You can use facial expressions and body language to _____ your feelings.

B. *Answer each question with a complete sentence.*

1. Describe a facial expression and what it can communicate to another person. Use a Big Question vocabulary word in your description.

   _____

   _____

2. Describe an example of body language and what it can communicate to another person. Use a Big Question vocabulary word in your description.

   _____

   _____

C. *In "Poetry Collection 2," each poem describes an aspect of nature. Complete this sentence:*

Descriptive language can **contribute** to _____

_____

_____.

Poetry Collection: Nikki Giovanni, Mary Ellen Solt, Bashō
Reading: Ask Questions to Draw a Conclusion

Drawing conclusions means arriving at an overall judgment or idea by pulling together several details. By drawing conclusions, you recognize meanings that are not directly stated. **Asking questions** can help you identify details and make connections that lead to a conclusion. You might ask yourself questions such as these:

- What details does the writer include and emphasize?
- How are the details related?
- Taken together, what do all the details mean?

Consider, for example, this haiku by Bashō:

On sweet plum blossoms

The sun rises suddenly.

Look, a mountain path!

What do those details mean? As the sun rises, it shines on a blossoming plum tree. You can conclude that it is a spring morning.

DIRECTIONS: *Complete the following chart. First, ask a question about the poem. Then, record the details that prompted the question. Finally, write a conclusion that you can draw based on the question and the related details.*

Poem	Question	Details Relating to Question	Conclusion
"Winter"			
"Forsythia"			
"Has spring come indeed?"			
"Temple bells die out"			

Name _____   Date _____

There are many different **forms of poetry.** A poet will follow different rules, depending on the structure of a poem. These are the three forms represented by poems in this collection:

- A **lyric poem** expresses the poet's thoughts and feelings about a single image or idea in vivid, musical language.
- In a **concrete poem,** the poet arranges the letters and lines to create a visual image that suggests the poem's subject.
- **Haiku** is a traditional form of Japanese poetry that is often about nature. In a traditional haiku, the first line always has five syllables, the second line always has seven syllables, and the third line always has five syllables.

DIRECTIONS: *Write your answers to the following questions.*

1. If you were to rewrite one of Bashō's haiku as a concrete poem, what shape would you use to express the main idea? Why?

   _____

   _____

   _____

2. If you were to rewrite "Winter" as a haiku, what seven-syllable line might you write that contained the phrase "Bears store fat"?

   _____

3. If you were to rewrite "Forsythia" as a lyric poem, on what single idea would you focus? Why?

   _____

   _____

   _____

4. If you were to rewrite "Forsythia" as a haiku, what would one of your lines be?

   _____

5. If you were to rewrite one of Bashō's haiku as a lyric poem, how would you change it? Why?

   _____

   _____

   _____

Poetry Collection: Nikki Giovanni, Mary Ellen Solt, Bashō
Vocabulary Builder

Word List

burrow   forsythia   fragrant   telegram

A. DIRECTIONS: *Provide an explanation for your answer to each question.*

1. Would you see a *forsythia* flowering in the fall?

_____

2. Would a *telegram* be likely to include a long description?

_____

3. Would an animal *burrow* in the sand to escape an enemy?

_____

4. Would a bouquet of roses smell *fragrant*?

_____

B. WORD STUDY: *The Greek root -gram- means "write, draw, or record." Write a sentence that answers each question, using the italicized word.*

1. What could an *electrocardiogram* show about your heart?

_____

2. What does a *grammarian* study?

_____

3. What might be an *anagram* of the word "bat"?

_____

Poetry Collections: Naomi Shihab Nye, William Jay Smith, Buson;
Nikki Giovanni, Mary Ellen Solt, Bashō

Integrated Language Skills: Grammar

Infinitives and Infinitive Phrases

An **infinitive** is a verb that acts as a noun, an adjective, or an adverb. An infinitive usually begins with the word *to*.

Some dogs like *to swim*. (infinitive as a noun serving as the object of the verb *like*)

To travel is my objective. (infinitive as a noun serving as the subject of the sentence)

Paris is the city *to visit*. (infinitive as an adjective modifying the noun *city*)

Everyone waited *to hear*. (infinitive as an adverb modifying the verb *waited*)

An **infinitive phrase** is an infinitive plus its own modifiers or complements.

Some dogs like *to swim all year round*. (phrase serving as object of the verb *like*)

To travel in Europe is my objective. (phrase serving as subject of the sentence)

Paris is the city *to visit in the spring*. (phrase modifying the noun *city*)

Everyone waited *to hear the news*. (phrase modifying the verb *waited*)

A. PRACTICE: *Underline the infinitive in each sentence, and circle any infinitive phrases.*

1. In "Winter," the speaker goes outside to air her quilts.
2. To create a poem that looks like a forsythia bush was the aim of Mary Ellen Solt.
3. In "The Rider," the roller skater wants to escape his loneliness.
4. In one of Buson's haiku, "not one leaf dares to move."
5. In "Seal," the seal loves to swim fast.

B. Writing Application: *Review the poems in these collections. Then, write a sentence that captures your reaction to each poem and includes an infinitive or an infinitive phrase.*

1. **"The Rider":** _____

   _____

2. **"Seal":** _____

   _____

3. **One of Buson's haiku:** _____

   _____

4. **"Winter":** _____

   _____

5. **"Forsythia":** _____

   _____

6. **One of Bashō's Haiku:** _____

   _____

Name _____ Date _____

Integrated Language Skills: Support for Writing a Lyric Poem, Concrete Poem, or Haiku

In the chart below, write details that you might use in your poem.

Subject: _____

Vivid Descriptions	Action Words	Thoughts	Feelings

Now, use the details you have collected to draft a **lyric poem, concrete poem,** or **haiku.**

Name _____ Date _____

"Life" by Naomi Long Madgett, **"The Courage that My Mother Had"** by Edna St. Vincent Millay, **"Loo-Wit"** by Wendy Rose

Writing About the Big Question

What is the best way to communicate?

Big Question Vocabulary

communicate	contribute	enrich	entertain	express
inform	learn	listen	media	produce
react	speak	teach	technology	transmit

A. *Use one or more words from the list above to complete each sentence.*

1. The _____, such as newspapers and television, is a useful way to communicate.

2. News articles can _____ you about important events and issues.

3. Stories about other cultures can _____ your understanding about how others live.

4. Reading and listening to the news can _____ a greater understanding of the world.

B. *Answer each question with a complete sentence.*

1. Write two things you have learned about other cultures from newspapers or television. Use two Big Question vocabulary words in your response.

   _____

   _____

2. Explain how your knowledge of other cultures has helped you understand the world more fully. Use two Big Question vocabulary words in your response.

   _____

   _____

C. *In Poetry Collection 3, each poem includes one or more comparisons between objects or ideas. Complete this sentence:*

When you make connections between unrelated things, you **enrich**

_____ and **learn** _____.

All-in-One Workbook
196

Poetry Collection: Naomi Long Madgett, Wendy Rose, Edna St. Vincent Millay
Reading: Connect the Details to Draw a Conclusion

A **conclusion** is a decision or an opinion that you reach after considering the details in a literary work. **Connecting the details** can help you draw conclusions as you read. For example, if the speaker in a poem uses the words *spits, growls, snarls, trembling, shudder, unravel,* and *dislodge,* you might conclude that he or she is expressing dissatisfaction, anger, or some aspect of violence. As you read, identify important details. Then, look at the details together and draw a conclusion about the poem or the speaker.

DIRECTIONS: *In the first column of the chart below are details from the poems in this collection. Consider each set of details, and use them to draw a conclusion about the poem. Write your conclusion in the second column.*

Details	Conclusion
"Life": • The speaker says that life is a toy. • The toy ticks for a while, amusing an infant. • The toy, a watch, stops running.	
"Loo-Wit": • The old woman is "bound" by cedar. • Huckleberry "ropes" lie around her neck. • Machinery operates on her skin.	
"The Courage That My Mother Had": • The speaker's mother had courage. • The speaker has a brooch her mother wore. • The speaker wants her mother's courage.	

Name _____ Date _____

Poetry Collection: Naomi Long Madgett, Wendy Rose, Edna St. Vincent Millay
Literary Analysis: Figurative Language

Figurative language is language that is not meant to be taken literally. Writers use figures of speech to express ideas in vivid and imaginative ways. Common figures of speech include the following:

- A **simile** compares two unlike things using a word such as *like* or *as*.
- A **metaphor** compares two unlike things by stating that one thing is another thing. In an **extended metaphor,** several related comparisons extend over a number of lines.
- **Personification** gives human characteristics to a nonhuman subject.
- A **symbol** is an object, a person, an animal, a place, or an image that represents something else.

Look at this line from "Life." What figure of speech does the speaker use?

Life is but a toy that swings on a bright gold chain.

The speaker uses a metaphor to compare life to a toy, one "that swings on a bright gold chain."

DIRECTIONS: *As you read the poems in this collection, record the similes, metaphors, extended metaphors, personification, and symbols.*

Poem	Passage	Figurative Language
"Life"		
"Loo-Wit"		
"The Courage That My Mother Had"		

Poetry Collection: Naomi Long Madgett, Wendy Rose, Edna St. Vincent Millay
Vocabulary Builder

Word List

crouches   dislodge   fascinated   granite   prickly   unravel

A. DIRECTIONS: *Read each sentence, paying attention to the italicized word. Then, explain whether the sentence makes sense. If it does not make sense, rewrite the sentence or write a new sentence, using the italicized word correctly.*

1. The angry woman *crouches* as she stretches herself on her bumpy bed.

   Explanation: _____

   New sentence: _____

2. If you *dislodge* the stones, they may start an avalanche.

   Explanation: _____

   New sentence: _____

3. Anita was so *fascinated* by the movie that she fell asleep.

   Explanation: _____

   New Sentence: _____

4. The sweater was so well made that it began to *unravel*.

   Explanation: _____

   New sentence: _____

5. The rough wool sweater felt *prickly* and uncomfortable.

   Explanation: _____

   New Sentence: _____

6. The piece of *granite* dissolved in the hard rain.

   Explanation: _____

   New Sentence: _____

B. WORD STUDY: *The Latin suffix -ly means "like; in the manner of." Answer each question, using the italicized word with the suffix added.*

1. How can you tell if someone is *brave*?

   _____

2. What might a person who is *ambitious* do at work?

   _____

3. Why is it important to be *careful* when you are hiking?

   _____

Name _____ Date _____

"Mother to Son" by Langston Hughes, "The Village Blacksmith" by Henry Wadsworth Longfellow, "Fog" by Carl Sandburg

Writing About the Big Question

What is the best way to communicate?

Big Question Vocabulary

communicate	contribute	enrich	entertain	express
inform	learn	listen	media	produce
react	speak	teach	technology	transmit

A. *Use one or more words from the list above to complete each sentence.*

1. Some people like to _____ others through music, dance, or acting.

2. The arts are a good way to _____ your thoughts and feelings.

3. When you _____ to a musician or actor, you can hear the feelings of both the performer and the composer or playwright.

4. A performer can _____ thoughts and feelings in the audience, too.

B. *Answer each question with a complete sentence.*

1. Describe two times when you have listened to a musical or dramatic piece that moved you.

   _____

   _____

2. Explain how you reacted to one of the preceding experiences. Tell what feelings or thoughts it produced in you.

   _____

   _____

C. *In Poetry Collection 4, the poets use evocative language to make their poems memorable. Complete this sentence:*

Words that **express** strong emotions _____.

_____

_____

_____

_____

Name _____ Date _____

Poetry Collection: Langston Hughes, Henry Wadsworth Longfellow, Carl Sandburg

Reading: Connect the Details to Draw a Conclusion

A **conclusion** is a decision or an opinion that you reach after considering the details in a literary work. **Connecting the details** can help you draw conclusions as you read. For example, if the speaker in a poem uses the words *tacks*, *splinters*, *boards*, *bare*, and *dark*, you might conclude that he or she wishes to create an image of hardship. As you read, identify important details. Then, look at the details together and draw a conclusion about the poem or the speaker.

DIRECTIONS: *In the first column of the chart below are details from the poems in this collection. Consider each set of details, and use them to draw a conclusion about the poem. Write your conclusion in the second column.*

Details	Conclusion
"Mother to Son": • The speaker describes the staircase she has climbed: it had tacks, splinters, bare boards, and places with no light. • The speaker is still climbing.	
"The Village Blacksmith": • On the blacksmith's brow is "honest sweat." • The blacksmith "owes not any man." • The blacksmith works long and hard.	
"Fog": • The fog arrives "on little cat feet." • The fog sits "on silent haunches." • The fog looks "over harbor and city / . . . and then moves on."	

Name _____ Date _____

Poetry Collection: Langston Hughes, Henry Wadsworth Longfellow, Carl Sandburg
Literary Analysis: Figurative Language

Figurative language is language that is not meant to be taken literally. Writers use figures of speech to express ideas in vivid and imaginative ways. Common figures of speech include the following:

- A **simile** compares two unlike things using a word such as *like* or *as.*
- A **metaphor** compares two unlike things by stating that one thing is another thing. In an **extended metaphor,** several related comparisons extend over a number of lines.
- **Personification** gives human characteristics to a nonhuman subject.
- A **symbol** is an object, a person, an animal, a place, or an image that represents something else.

Look at this line from "The Village Blacksmith." What figure of speech does the speaker use?

And the muscles of his brawny arms

Are strong as iron bands.

The speaker uses a simile to compare the blacksmith's muscles to iron bands.

DIRECTIONS: *As you read the poems in this collection, record the similes, metaphors, extended metaphors, personification, and symbols you find in the poems.*

Poem	Passage	Figurative Language
"Mother to Son"		
"The Village Blacksmith"		
"Fog"		

Name _____ Date _____

Poetry Collection: Langston Hughes, Henry Wadsworth Longfellow, Carl Sandburg
Vocabulary Builder

Word List

brawny   crystal   haunches   parson   sinewy   wrought

A. DIRECTIONS: *Read each sentence, paying attention to the italicized word. Then, explain whether the sentence makes sense. If it does not make sense, rewrite the sentence or write a new sentence, using the italicized word correctly.*

1. The cheetah sprang from its *haunches* to bring down the fleeing antelope.

   Explanation: _____

   New sentence: _____

2. Because the blacksmith was *brawny,* he easily lifted the heavy sledgehammer.

   Explanation: _____

   New sentence: _____

3. The *sinewy* construction worker could carry only the lightest loads.

   Explanation: _____

   New sentence: _____

4. The *crystal* vase shattered when it hit the ground.

   Explanation: _____

   New Sentence: _____

5. The *parson* had always been too shy to speak in public.

   Explanation: _____

   New Sentence: _____

6. The bracelet was *wrought* from white gold.

   Explanation: _____

   New Sentence: _____

B. WORD STUDY: *The Latin suffix -y means "marked by, having." Answer each question, using the italicized word with the suffix added.*

1. How does a person who feels *anger* behave?

   _____

2. How would someone who learns with *ease* probably do in school?

   _____

3. Why is it important not to make a *mess* on a test paper?

   _____

Poetry Collections: Naomi Long Madgett, Wendy Rose, Edna St. Vincent Millay;
Langston Hughes, Henry Wadsworth Longfellow, Carl Sandburg

Integrated Language Skills: Grammar

Appositives and Appositive Phrases

An **appositive** is a noun or pronoun that is placed after another noun or pronoun to identify, rename, or explain it. In the following sentence, the appositive is underlined:

In "Fog," the poet compares an animal, a <u>cat</u>, to fog.

An **appositive phrase** is a noun or pronoun, along with any modifiers, that is placed after another noun or pronoun to identify, rename, or explain it. In the following sentence, the appositive is underlined; the words that make up the appositive phrase are in italics:

Longfellow made the village blacksmith, *an honest and reliable <u>man</u>*, into a hero.

A. PRACTICE: *In each sentence, underline the appositive phrase. Then, circle the noun that the appositive phrase identifies or explains.*

1. Loo-Wit, a volcano, is about to erupt.
2. Death, an old man, lets the watch run down.
3. The speaker in "The Courage That My Mother Had" mentions New England, a region in the northeast.
4. The speaker in "The Courage That My Mother Had" compares her mother's courage to granite, a hard rock.
5. The village blacksmith weeps when he hears the voice of his daughter, a singer in the choir.
6. In "Mother to Son," a poem by Langston Hughes, a mother gives advice to her son.

B. Writing Application: *Use each phrase in brackets as an appositive phrase in the sentence that follows it. Set off each phrase with commas or dashes.*

1. [a beautiful golden pin] In "The Courage That My Mother Had," the speaker's mother has given the speaker a brooch.

_____

_____

2. [a blanket of white mist] In "Fog," fog covers a harbor.

_____

3. [a symbol of an easy life] The mother in "Mother to Son" speaks of the crystal stair.

_____

_____

Name _____ Date _____

Poetry Collections: Naomi Long Madgett, Wendy Rose, Edna St. Vincent Millay; Langston Hughes, Henry Wadsworth Longfellow, Carl Sandburg

Integrated Language Skills: Support for Writing an Extended Metaphor

Use the word web below to collect ideas for an **extended metaphor** about a quality or an idea, such as love, loyalty, life, or death. Decide on the quality or idea, and then decide what you will compare it to. It may be an object, an animal, or an idea. Write your ideas in the center of the web. Then, complete the web by writing down ideas that relate to your central idea. Use vivid images and descriptive language. Your extended metaphor may include similes, metaphors, personification, and symbols.

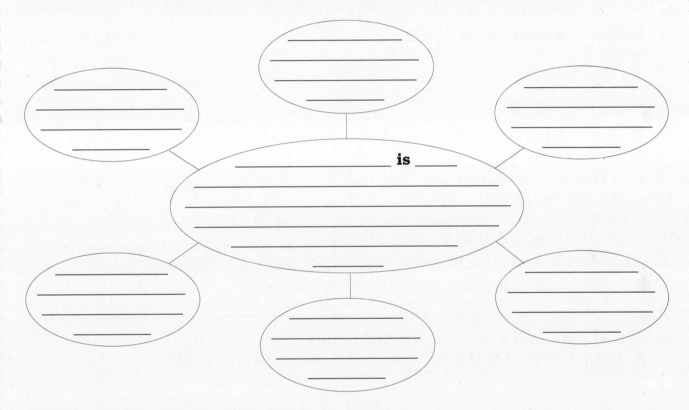

Now, use your notes to write an extended metaphor about a quality or an idea. Be sure to use vivid images and descriptive language.

"The Highwayman" by Alfred Noyes and **"How I Learned English"** by Gregory Djanikian
Writing About the Big Question

What is the best way to communicate?

Big Question Vocabulary

communicate	contribute	enrich	entertain	express
inform	learn	listen	media	produce
react	speak	teach	technology	transmit

A. *Use one or more words from the list above to complete each sentence.*

1. Words are a great way to _____ with other people.

2. You can _____ yourself to others through the words you choose.

3. When you _____, what you say tells others about yourself.

4. Your choice of words can _____ to others' understanding of you.

B. *Answer each question with a complete sentence.*

1. Write the words you might speak to introduce yourself to someone new.

   _____

   _____

2. Explain what you would like to communicate about yourself to someone you have just met. Use two Big Question vocabulary words in your response.

   _____

   _____

C. *In each of these narrative poems, people communicate in an unconventional way. Complete this sentence:*

_____ can be more expressive than words.

Name _____ Date _____

Poetry by Alfred Noyes and Gregory Djanikian
Literary Analysis: Comparing Narrative Poems

Narrative poetry combines elements of fiction and poetry to tell a story. Like short stories, narrative poetry usually includes characters, setting, plot, conflict, and point of view. Like other poems, narrative poetry uses sound devices, such as rhythm and rhyme, to bring out the musical qualities of the language. It also uses figurative language to create memorable images, or word pictures.

Narrative poetry is well suited to a wide range of stories. For example, narrative poems may tell romantic tales about knights and ladies, heroic deeds, amazing events, or larger-than-life characters. In contrast, the form may be used to relate everyday stories about ordinary people.

The poems presented in this collection blend elements of fiction and poetry in a memorable way. As you read these poems, look for ways in which each one blends the elements of narration and poetry.

DIRECTIONS: *Complete this chart about the narrative poems in this collection. In the second column, briefly describe the poem's plot and conflict. In the third column, describe the sound devices and/or figurative language in the poem.*

Poem	Plot and Conflict	Poetic Devices
"The Highwayman"		
"How I Learned English"		

Name _____ Date _____

Poetry by Alfred Noyes and Gregory Djanikian
Vocabulary Builder

Word List

bound   strive   torrent   transfixed   whimper   writhing

A. DIRECTIONS: *Pay attention to the way the italicized vocabulary word is used in each sentence. Decide whether each statement is true or false. Write T or F. Then, explain your answer.*

1. If a dog were *bound* to a tree, it would be free to roam.

   T / F: _____ **Explanation:** _____

2. Someone *writhing* in pain is lying still.

   T / F: _____ **Explanation:** _____

3. A *torrent* of rain is likely to cause a river to overflow its banks.

   T / F: _____ **Explanation:** _____

4. If children *whimper,* they are probably content.

   T / F: _____ **Explanation:** _____

5. Someone *transfixed* by fear is running to escape danger.

   T / F: _____ **Explanation:** _____

6. People who *strive* are usually very lazy.

   T / F: _____ **Explanation:** _____

B. WORD STUDY: *Change each underlined word into another form from its word family. Answer the question using the new word.*

1. What can cause a small waterfall to become a *torrent*?

   _____

2. Why are people often *transfixed* when they watch a scary movie?

   _____

3. Why should a wound be *bound*?

   _____

Poetry by Alfred Noyes and Gregory Djanikian
Integrated Language Skills: Support for Writing to Compare Literary Works

Use this chart to take notes for an essay comparing and contrasting the stories that are told in the narrative poems in this collection.

Point of Comparison	"The Highwayman"	"How I Learned English"
Who narrates the poem? Is it a character in the poem or someone outside the poem?		
Is there any suspense? If so, when does it occur, and why?		
How do the poetic elements increase my interest in or my appreciation of the story?		

Now, use your notes to write an essay comparing and contrasting the poems' stories.

Name _____ Date _____

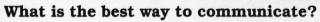

"Sarah Cynthia Sylvia Stout Would Not Take the Garbage Out" by Shell Silverstein,
"Weather" by Eve Merriam, **"One"** by James Berry

Writing About the Big Question

What is the best way to communicate?

Big Question Vocabulary

communicate	contribute	enrich	entertain	express
inform	learn	listen	media	produce
react	speak	teach	technology	transmit

A. *Use one or more words from the list above to complete each sentence.*

1. _____ has made it much faster and easier for people to communicate.

2. It is possible to _____ messages almost instantly.

3. One problem with this form of communication is that people don't see or _____ directly with each other.

4. They cannot see how others _____ to what they say.

B. *Answer each question with a complete sentence.*

1. Think of a time when you sent a message using technology, such as instant messaging or text messaging, that cause a problem. Describe how the other person reacted to the message.

   _____

   _____

2. Explain how the other person would have reacted differently if you had spoken directly with him or her.

   _____

   _____

C. *In "Poetry Collection 1," the poems have a pleasing musical quality. Complete this sentence:*

The use of musical language can **produce** _____.

Poetry Collection: Shel Silverstein, Eve Merriam, James Berry
Reading: Read Aloud According to Punctuation in Order to Paraphrase

When you **paraphrase,** you restate something in your own words. To paraphrase a poem, you must first understand it. **Reading aloud according to punctuation** can help you identify complete thoughts in a poem and therefore grasp its meaning. Because poets do not always complete a sentence at the end of a line, pausing simply because a line ends can interfere with your understanding of the meaning. Follow these rules when you read aloud:

- Keep reading when a line has no end punctuation.
- Pause at commas, dashes, and semicolons.
- Stop at end marks, such as periods, question marks, or exclamation points.

As you read poetry, allow the punctuation to help you paraphrase the poet's ideas.

DIRECTIONS: *The following items are from "Sarah Cynthia Sylvia Stout Would Not Take the Garbage Out," "Weather," or "One." Read each item aloud, following the rules above. Then, paraphrase the lines. That is, restate them in your own words.*

1. Dot a dot dot dot a dot dot
   Spotting the windowpane.

   _____

   _____

2. Nobody can get into my clothes for me
   or feel my fall for me, or do my running.
   Nobody hears my music for me, either.

   _____

   _____

3. Poor Sarah met an awful fate,
   That I cannot right now relate
   Because the hour is much too late.
   But children, remember Sarah Stout
   And always take the garbage out!

   _____

   _____

   _____

   _____

   _____

Name _____   Date _____

Literary Analysis: Sound Devices

Sound devices create musical effects that appeal to the ear. Here are some common sound devices used in poetry:

- **Onomatopoeia** is the use of words whose sounds suggest their meaning:

  The explosion made a thunderous <u>boom</u>. The snake uttered a <u>hiss</u>.

- **Alliteration** is the repetition of sounds at the beginnings of words:

  <u>She</u> <u>s</u>ells <u>s</u>ea <u>s</u>hells by the <u>s</u>ea <u>s</u>hore.

- **Repetition** is the repeated use of words, phrases, and/or rhythms:

  I said, "Come," / I said, "Sit," / My dog would have none of it.

In the last example, there is repetition of both the words (*I said*) and the rhythm. In poetry, a line may contain more than one sound device.

DIRECTIONS: *The following items are from "Sarah Cynthia Sylvia Stout Would Not Take the Garbage Out," "Weather," or "One." Read each item, and decide which sound devices the lines contain. Then, identify the sound devices in each line by writing* Onomatopoeia, Alliteration, *and/or* Repetition. *An item may contain more than one sound device.*

1. Prune pits, peach pits, orange peel

   _____

2. Crusts of black burned buttered toast

   _____

3. A spatter a scatter a wet cat a clatter
   A splatter a rumble outside.

   _____

4. And mirrors can show me multiplied
   Many times

   _____

5. Umbrella umbrella umbrella umbrella
   Bumbershoot barrel of rain.

   _____

6. Sarah Cynthia Sylvia Stout
   Would not take the garbage out!

   _____

7. Slosh a galosh slosh a galosh
   Slither and slather and glide

   _____

Poetry Collection: Shel Silverstein, Eve Merriam, James Berry
Vocabulary Builder

Word List

curdled   expectancy   rancid   slather   stutter   withered

A. DIRECTIONS: *Read each item, and think about the meaning of the italicized word from the Word List. Then, answer the question, and explain your answer.*

1. The *withered* flowers had been in the vase for a week. Were the flowers brightly colored?

   _____

2. The hungry twins found *rancid* cheese in the refrigerator. Would they have thrown it out or eaten it?

   _____

3. The suspect began to *stutter* when he was questioned. Was he nervous? How can you tell?

   _____

4. The milk has *curdled* in the bottle. Would you drink it?

   _____

5. The girl stared out the window with *expectancy*. Why was she probably looking out?

   _____

6. At the beach, Nora was careful to *slather* on sunscreen. Was this a good idea?

   _____

B. WORD STUDY: *The Latin suffix -ancy mean "the state of being." Decide whether each statement is true or false. Write T or F. Then, explain your answer.*

1. The baby was still in its *infancy*.

   T / F: _____ **Explanation:** _____

2. Someone who shows *hesitancy* is sure of himself or herself.

   T / F: _____ **Explanation:** _____

3. A diamond is likely to shine with great *brilliancy*.

   T / F: _____ **Explanation:** _____

"Full Fathom Five" by William Shakespeare, **"Onomatopoeia"** by Eve Merriam,
"Train Tune" by Louise Bogan

Writing About the Big Question

What is the best way to communicate?

Big Question Vocabulary

communicate	contribute	enrich	entertain	express
inform	learn	listen	media	produce
react	speak	teach	technology	transmit

A. *Use one or more words from the list above to complete each sentence.*

1. When you have a problem with a friend, you can _____
   your opinion by talking it over.

2. It is important to _____ to your friend's
   opinions, too.

3. Listening well and speaking honestly can _____
   a friendship.

B. *Answer each question with a complete sentence.*

1. Describe two occasions when you have expressed an opinion to a friend. Use two of
   the Big Question vocabulary words.

   _____

   _____

2. Choose one of the discussions above. Explain how the discussion helped to enrich
   your friendship.

   _____

   _____

C. *In "Poetry Collection 2," each poem uses sound to create an image or to bring about a
certain mood. Complete this sentence:*

When you really **listen**, you can _____.

Poetry Collection: William Shakespeare, Eve Merriam, Louise Bogan
Reading: Read Aloud According to Punctuation in Order to Paraphrase

When you **paraphrase,** you restate something in your own words. To paraphrase a poem, you must first understand it. **Reading aloud according to punctuation** can help you identify complete thoughts in a poem and therefore grasp its meaning. Because poets do not always complete a sentence at the end of a line, pausing simply because a line ends can interfere with your understanding of the meaning. Follow these rules when you read aloud:

- Keep reading when a line has no end punctuation.
- Pause at commas, dashes, and semicolons.
- Stop at end marks, such as periods, question marks, or exclamation points.

As you read poetry, allow the punctuation to help you paraphrase the poet's ideas.

DIRECTIONS: *The following items are from "Full Fathom Five," "Onomatopoeia," or "Train Tune." Read each item aloud, following the rules above. Then, paraphrase the lines. That is, restate them in your own words.*

1. spurts,
   finally stops sputtering
   and plash!
   gushes rushes splashes
   clear water dashes.

   _____

   _____

   _____

2. Back through lightning
   Back through cities
   Back through stars
   Back through hours

   _____

   _____

   _____

3. Sea nymphs hourly ring his knell;
   Ding-dong.
   Hark! Now I hear them ding-dong bell.

   _____

   _____

   _____

Poetry Collection: William Shakespeare, Eve Merriam, Louise Bogan
Literary Analysis: Sound Devices

Sound devices create musical effects that appeal to the ear. Here are some common sound devices used in poetry:

- **Onomatopoeia** is the use of words whose sounds suggest their meaning:
The saw cut through the tree with a <u>buzz</u>. The librarian <u>murmured</u> her answer.
- **Alliteration** is the repetition of sounds at the beginnings of words:
<u>P</u>eter <u>P</u>iper <u>p</u>icked a <u>p</u>eck of <u>p</u>ickled <u>p</u>eppers.
- **Repetition** is the repeated use of words, phrases, and/or rhythms:
<u>The leaves blew</u> up, / <u>The leaves blew</u> down, / <u>The leaves blew</u> all around the town.

In the last example, there is repetition of both the words (*The leaves blew*) and the rhythm. In poetry, a line may contain more than one sound device.

DIRECTIONS: *The following items are from "Full Fathom Five," "Onomatopoeia," or "Train Tune." Read each item, and decide which sound devices the lines contain. Then, identify the sound devices in each line by writing* Onomatopoeia, Alliteration, *and/or* Repetition. *An item may contain more than one sound device.*

1. Full fathom five thy father lies

   _____

2. The rusty spigot
   sputters,
   utters
   a splutter

   _____

3. Back through clouds
   Back through clearing
   Back through distance
   Back through silence

   _____

4. finally stops sputtering
   and plash!
   gushes rushes splashes
   clear water dashes

   _____

5. Nothing of him that doth fade
   But doth suffer a sea change
   Into something rich and strange.

   _____

All-in-One Workbook
216

Name _____ Date _____

Poetry Collection: William Shakespeare, Eve Merriam, Louise Bogan
Vocabulary Builder

Word List

fathoms   garlands   groves   smattering   spigot   sputters

A. DIRECTIONS: *Read each item, and think about the meaning of the italicized word from the Word List. Then, answer the question, and explain your answer.*

1. If a plumber says you need a new *spigot*, should you purchase a device to keep water from running down the drain?

   _____

2. If a person *sputters* as she speaks, is she likely to be calm?

   _____

3. If there are orange *groves* on your property, are there trees on your property?

   _____

4. If you are measuring the depths of a lake, would you measure in *fathoms*?

   _____

5. If you were hit by a *smattering* of raindrops, would you need to change your clothes?

   _____

6. If someone decorates her house with *garlands*, would it probably smell good?

   _____

B. WORD STUDY: *The Latin suffix -less means "without." Decide whether each statement is true or false. Write T or F. Then, explain your answer.*

1. You could trust someone who is *careless* with your most prized possession.

   T / F: _____ **Explanation:** _____

2. A movie that seems *endless* is very long or very dull.

   T / F: _____ **Explanation:** _____

3. A *joyless* person is almost always happy.

   T / F: _____ **Explanation:** _____

Poetry Collections: Shel Silverstein, Eve Merriam, James Berry; William Shakespeare, Eve Merriam, Louise Bogan

Integrated Language Skills: Grammar

Independent and Subordinate Clauses

A **clause** is a group of words with its own subject and verb. There are two types of clauses: independent clauses and subordinate clauses. An **independent clause** expresses a complete thought and can stand alone as a sentence.

A **subordinate clause** (also called a **dependent clause**) has a subject and a verb, but it does not express a complete thought. Therefore, it cannot stand alone as a sentence. The following sentence contains both an independent clause and a subordinate clause. The subject in each clause is underlined once, and the verb is underlined twice. The subordinate clause appears in italics:

> Shel Silverstein was a cartoonist and a writer, *though he also composed songs.*

A subordinate clause may appear either before or after the independent clause:

> *Though he also composed songs,* Shel Silverstein was a cartoonist and a writer.

A. DIRECTIONS: *In each sentence, underline the independent clause once and the subordinate clause twice.*

1. Eve Merriam's lifelong love was poetry even though she wrote fiction, nonfiction, and drama.
2. Because language and its sound gave Eve Merriam great joy, she tried to communicate her enjoyment by writing poetry for children.
3. Berry moved to the United States when he was seventeen.
4. If Berry had not lost his job as a telegraph operator, he might not have become a writer.
5. Because he did not play ball or dance when he was young, Shel Silverstein began to draw and write.
6. Silverstein began to draw cartoons after he served in the military.

B. Writing Application: *Rewrite each sentence by adding a subordinate clause.*

1. Sarah Stout was a stubborn young woman.

   _____

2. The rain spotted the windowpane.

   _____

3. Anyone can dance like me.

   _____

4. The drowned man's bones had turned to coral.

   _____

Name _____ Date _____

Integrated Language Skills: Support for Writing a Poem Called "Alliteration"

Use this chart as you draft a **poem** called "Alliteration."

"Alliteration": A Poem
Alliteration, defined by the textbook: "Alliteration is the repetition of sounds at the beginning of words."
Alliteration, defined in my own words: _____ _____ _____
Example of alliteration: Peter Piper picked a peck of pickled peppers.
My own example of alliteration: _____ _____ _____ _____ _____
My poem, combining my definition of alliteration with my examples of alliteration: _____ _____ _____ _____ _____ _____ _____ _____

Look over your poem to be sure your examples work. Do they contain words that begin with the same sound? Then, check your definition. Does it correctly define alliteration? Revise your poem before creating your final draft.

All-in-One Workbook

"Annabel Lee" by Edgar Allan Poe, **"Martin Luther King"** by Raymond R. Patterson,
"I'm Nobody" by Emily Dickinson

Writing About the Big Question

What is the best way to communicate?

Big Question Vocabulary

communicate	contribute	enrich	entertain	express
inform	learn	listen	media	produce
react	speak	teach	technology	transmit

A. *Use one or more words from the list above to complete each sentence.*

1. An argument with someone can _____ feelings
   of anger, or it can work out problems.

2. Arguing can actually be a good way to _____.

3. When you argue, you need to _____ yourself
   clearly.

4. Use positive words and a calm tone of voice when you _____.

B. *Answer each question with a complete sentence.*

1. Describe an argument you have had in which you were able to communicate with the
   other person. Use at least two Big Question vocabulary words.

   _____

   _____

2. Explain how you expressed yourself in the argument, describing the words you used
   and your tone of voice.

   _____

   _____

C. *In "Poetry Collection 1," the poets present people and ideas about which they feel
passionate. Complete these sentences:*

Words can be used to **produce** _____.
The way people **react** can _____.

Poetry Collection: Edgar Allan Poe, Raymond Richard Patterson, Emily Dickinson

Reading: Reread in Order to Paraphrase

To **paraphrase** means to restate or explain something in your own words. When you paraphrase lines of poetry, you make the meaning clear to yourself. If you are unsure of a poem's meaning, **reread** the parts that are difficult. Follow these steps:

- Look up unfamiliar words, and replace them with words you know.
- Restate the line or passage using your own everyday words.
- Reread the passage to make sure that your version makes sense.

Look at these lines from the poem "Martin Luther King":

He came upon an age / Beset by grief, by rage

The first line tells you that King "came upon an age." If you look up "come upon" in a dictionary, you will learn that it means "meet by chance." In this case, you might use a looser definition: "happen to live in." *Age* can refer to the number of years a person has lived or to a period in history. In this case, it refers to a period of history when African Americans did not have the same rights as white Americans.

If you looked up *beset,* you would discover that one of its meanings is "troubled." You probably know that *grief* is a synonym for *sorrow* or *sadness* and that *rage* is a synonym for *anger.* Now you have all the ingredients for a paraphrase of the line. It might look like this:

He happened to live at a time that was troubled by sorrow and anger.

DIRECTIONS: *Read these passages from "Annabel Lee," "Martin Luther King," and "I'm Nobody." Following the process described above, write a paraphrase of each passage.*

1. "A wind blew out of a cloud by night / Chilling my Annabel Lee; /
   So that her highborn kinsmen came / And bore her away from me, /
   To shut her up in a sepulcher / In this kingdom by the sea."

   _____

   _____

   _____

2. "He came upon an age / Beset by grief and rage—
   His love so deep, so wide / He could not turn aside."

   _____

   _____

   _____

3. "How dreary to be Somebody! / How public like a Frog /
   To tell your name the livelong June / To an admiring Bog!"

   _____

   _____

Name _____ Date _____

Poetry Collection: Edgar Allan Poe, Raymond Richard Patterson, Emily Dickinson
Literary Analysis: Rhythm, Meter, and Rhyme

Rhythm and rhyme make poetry musical. **Rhythm** is a poem's pattern of stressed (´) and unstressed (˘) syllables.

Meter is a poem's rhythmical pattern. It is measured in *feet,* or single units of stressed and unstressed syllables. In the examples below, stressed and unstressed syllables are marked, and the feet are separated by vertical lines (|). The first line of "Annabel Lee" contains four feet, and the second line contains three feet. The two lines of "Martin Luther King" contain three feet each.

Rhyme is the repetition of sounds at the ends of lines. The two words that rhyme in the lines from "Martin Luther King" are underlined.

It was MAN | -y and MAN | -y a YEAR | a-GO. | / In a KING | -dom BY | the SEA.

He CAME | up-ON | an AGE | be-SET | by GRIEF, | by RAGE.

A. DIRECTIONS: *Mark the stressed (´) and unstressed (˘) syllables in these lines. Then, show the meter by drawing a vertical rule after each foot.*

1. But our love it was stronger by far than the love / Of those who were older than we

2. His passion, so profound, / He would not turn around.

B. DIRECTIONS: *The words that end each line of "Annabel Lee" and "Martin Luther King" are listed in the following items. In each item, circle each word that rhymes with another word. Then, draw lines to connect all the words that rhyme with each other in that item.*

1. ago sea know Lee thought me

2. child sea love Lee Heaven me

3. ago sea night Lee came me sepulcher sea

4. Heaven me know sea chilling Lee

5. love we we above sea soul Lee

6. dreams Lee Lee side bride sea sea

7. age rage / wide aside / profound around / Earth worth / be free

Poetry Collection: Edgar Allan Poe, Raymond Richard Patterson, Emily Dickinson
Vocabulary Builder

Word List

banish   coveted   envying   kinsmen   passion   profound

A. DIRECTIONS: *Read each sentence, and think about the meaning of the italicized word from the Word List. Then, answer the question, and explain your answer.*

1. The speaker in "Annabel Lee" says that the angels *coveted* the love between him and Annabel Lee. Did the angels criticize their love?

   _____

2. The speaker in "Martin Luther King" says that King's feeling was *profound*. Did King feel very strongly?

   _____

3. The speaker in "I'm Nobody" says that "they" will *banish* her if they find out that she is a Nobody. Will "they" accept her in their social circle?

   _____

4. The speaker in "Annabel Lee" says the angels were *envying* the love he and Annabel shared. Did the angels want love for themselves?

   _____

5. Annabel Lee's *kinsmen* took her away from the speaker. Were they related to her?

   _____

6. The speaker of "Martin Luther King" says that King felt a deep *passion*. Was King's feeling one of despair?

   _____

B. WORD STUDY: *The Latin prefix* im- *means "in, into, toward." Use the meaning of the italicized word in each question to write an answer.*

1. If someone had a tooth *implanted*, what would the result be?

   _____

2. What would it look like if you *imprinted* a picture on a T-shirt?

   _____

3. If your car is *impounded*, what has happened to it?

   _____

Name _____ Date _____

"Jim" by Gwendolyn Brooks, **"Father William"** by Lewis Carroll,
"Stopping by Woods on a Snowy Evening" by Robert Frost

Writing About the Big Question

What is the best way to communicate?

Big Question Vocabulary

communicate	contribute	enrich	entertain	express
inform	learn	listen	media	produce
react	speak	teach	technology	transmit

A. *Use one or more words from the list above to complete each sentence.*

1. When you take part in a poetry slam, you can _____
   an audience with poetry.

2. You _____ yourself through your poetry to the
   audience.

3. Your audience can _____ about you as they
   _____ to your poems.

B. *Answer each question with a complete sentence.*

1. Describe a poem you have listened to or read that you found moving or entertaining.
   _____

   _____

2. Explain why the poem entertained you, and explain what you learned from it. Use at
   least two Big Question vocabulary words in your response.
   _____

   _____

C. *In "Poetry Collection 2," each poem uses rhythm and rhyme to create a musical quality.*
   Complete this sentence:

   Messages that **entertain** as well as **inform** _____.

All-in-One Workbook
224

Poetry Collection: Gwendolyn Brooks, Lewis Carroll, Robert Frost
Reading: Reread in Order to Paraphrase

To **paraphrase** means to restate or explain something in your own words. When you paraphrase lines of poetry, you make the meaning clear to yourself. If you are unsure of a poem's meaning, **reread** the parts that are difficult. Follow these steps:

- Look up unfamiliar words, and replace them with words you know.
- Restate the line or passage using your own everyday words.
- Reread the passage to make sure that your version makes sense.

Look at these lines from "Father William":

"In my youth," said his father, "I took to the law

  And argued each case with my wife;

And the muscular strength which it gave to my jaw

  Has lasted the rest of my life."

The first line tells you that Father William "took to the law." If you look up *law* in a dictionary, you will learn that one of its meanings is "the legal profession." Father William is saying that he was a lawyer. That knowledge will help you understand the second line: Father William prepared for his legal cases by arguing them with his wife. You probably know or can guess that *muscular* has to do with muscles. Now you have all the ingredients to write a paraphrase of the verse. It might look like this:

"When I was young," Father William said, "I was a lawyer

  And I talked over every case with my wife;

And as a result, I developed strong jaw muscles

  That I still have today."

DIRECTIONS: *Read these passages from "Jim," "Father William," and "Stopping by Woods on a Snowy Evening." Following the process described above, write a paraphrase of each passage.*

1. The sun should drop its greatest gold / On him.

   _____

2. "In my youth," said the sage, as he shook his gray locks, / "I kept all my limbs very supple / By the use of this ointment—one shilling the box—/ Allow me to sell you a couple?"

   _____

   _____

   _____

3. He gives his harness bells a shake / To ask if there is some mistake. / The only other sound's the sweep / Of easy wind and downy flake.

   _____

   _____

   _____

Poetry Collection: Gwendolyn Brooks, Lewis Carroll, Robert Frost
Literary Analysis: Rhythm, Meter, and Rhyme

Rhythm and rhyme make poetry musical. **Rhythm** is a poem's pattern of stressed (´) and unstressed (˘) syllables.

Meter is a poem's rhythmical pattern. It is measured in *feet,* or single units of stressed and unstressed syllables. In the examples below, stressed and unstressed syllables are marked, and the feet are separated by vertical lines (|). The first line of "Father William" contains four feet, and the second line contains three feet. The two lines of "Stopping by Woods on a Snowy Evening" contain four feet each.

"You are OLD, | Fa-ther WILL- | iam," the YOUNG | man SAID, |

And your HAIR | has be-COME | ver-y WHITE" |

Rhyme is the repetition of sounds at the ends of lines. The two words that rhyme in the lines from "Stopping by Woods on a Snowy Evening" are underlined.

My LIT- | tle HORSE | must THINK | it QUEER |

to STOP | with-OUT | a FARM- | house NEAR |

A. DIRECTIONS: *Mark the stressed (´) and unstressed (˘) syllables in these lines. Then, show the meter by drawing a vertical rule after each foot.*

1. "You are old," said the youth, "as I mentioned before. / And have grown most uncommonly fat."

2. He gives his harness bells a shake / To ask if there is some mistake. / The only other sound's the sweep / Of easy wind and downy flake.

B. DIRECTIONS: *The words that end each verse of "Jim," "Father William," and "Stopping by Woods on a Snowy Evening" are listed in the following items. In each item, circle each word that rhymes with another word. Then, draw lines to connect all the words that rhyme with each other in that item.*

1. boy Jim gold him / sick in bread medicine / room see baseball Terribly

2. said white head right / son brain none again before fat door that

3. locks supple box couple / weak suet beak do it law wife jaw life

4. suppose ever nose clever / enough airs stuff downstairs

5. know though here snow / queer near lake year

6. shake mistake sweep flake / deep keep sleep sleep

Poetry Collection: Gwendolyn Brooks, Lewis Carroll, Robert Frost
Vocabulary Builder

Word List

downy   harness   incessantly   sage   supple   uncommonly

A. DIRECTIONS: *Read each item, and think about the meaning of the italicized word from the Word List. Then, answer the question, and explain your answer.*

1. Father William stands on his head *incessantly*. Does he stand on his head for an hour at a time, taking breaks when he gets tired?

   _____

2. Father William is a *sage*. Would he be likely to do well on a quiz show?

   _____

3. Father William used an ointment to keep his joints *supple*. Was he likely to have had trouble bending down to tie his shoes?

   _____

4. The snow falls in *downy* flakes. Is the snow heavy?

   _____

5. The horse wears a *harness* with bells. Does the harness keep it warm?

   _____

6. Father William has grown *uncommonly* fat. Is it usual for someone to become so fat?

   _____

B. WORD STUDY: *The Latin prefix* un- *means "not." Answer each question by adding* un- *to each italicized word and using the new word in your response.*

1. What would happen if you were not *prepared* for a test?

   _____

2. Is a fantasy movie likely to have only *realistic* characters?

   _____

3. Is it hard to sleep in a *comfortable* bed?

   _____

Poetry Collections: Edgar Allan Poe, Raymond Richard Patterson, Emily Dickinson; Gwendolyn Brooks, Lewis Carroll, Robert Frost

Integrated Language Skills: Grammar

Sentence Structure

A **simple sentence** is an independent clause. That is, it is a group of words that has a subject and a verb and can stand by itself as a complete thought.

A **compound sentence** consists of two or more independent clauses that are joined by a conjunction such as *and, but, or,* or *for.*

> Lewis Carroll was a mathematician, <u>but</u> he also wrote stories and poetry.

A **complex sentence** contains one independent clause and one or more subordinate clauses. In this sentence, the subordinate clause is underlined:

> <u>Although he was a mathematician</u>, Lewis Carroll also wrote novels.

A. DIRECTIONS: *Identify each sentence below by writing* Simple, Compound, *or* Complex.

1. Gwendolyn Brooks lived in an area of Chicago known as Bronzeville, and one of her volumes of poetry is called *A Street in Bronzeville.*

   _____

2. Although she was primarily a poet, Brooks published a novel, *Maud Martha.*

   _____

3. Gwendolyn Brooks served as the poet laureate of Illinois.

   _____

4. Lewis Carroll's *Alice's Adventures in Wonderland* has been translated into more than thirty languages.

   _____

5. Carroll liked to write nonsense verse, and he invented nonsense characters, such as the Snark, the Jabberwock, and the twins Tweedledee and Tweedledum.

   _____

B. Writing Application: *Write a short paragraph in which you describe your reaction to one of the poems in these collections. Tell what you liked most about the poem and why it appeals to you. Use at least one simple sentence, one compound sentence, and one complex sentence. Label your sentences by writing* Simple, Compound, *or* Complex *in parentheses after each one.*

_____

_____

_____

_____

_____

Name _____ Date _____

Integrated Language Skills: Support for Writing a Paraphrase

Use these charts to draft a **paraphrase** of one of the six poems you have read. In the first chart, write down unfamiliar words from the poem, their dictionary definition, and the definition restated in your own words. In the second chart, write each line of the poem in the first column. In the second column, restate the meaning of the line in your own words. If you are paraphrasing "Father William," finish your paraphrase on a separate sheet of paper.

Title of poem: _____

Word to Look Up	Dictionary Definition	Definition in My Own Words

Poem, Line by Line	Paraphrase, Line by Line

Now, read over your paraphrase to make sure it has the same meaning as the original. Make your revisions as you prepare your final draft.

Poetry by Walt Whitman and E. E. Cummings
Writing About the Big Question

What is the best way to communicate?

Big Question Vocabulary

communicate	contribute	enrich	entertain	express
inform	learn	listen	media	produce
react	speak	teach	technology	transmit

A. *Use one or more words from the list above to complete each sentence.*

1. You can _____ with others by speaking, writing, or through the arts.

2. All communication helps you _____ about other people.

3. Communication can _____ your life and the lives of others.

B. *Respond to each item with a complete sentence.*

1. Describe your favorite way to communicate and tell when you are likely to use it. Use at least two Big Question vocabulary words.

   _____

   _____

   _____

2. Explain why you prefer to communicate in the way you have chosen. Tell how it helps you express yourself and learn about other people.

   _____

   _____

   _____

C. In the poetry of Whitman and Cummings, the writers use imagery to paint vivid pictures in the minds of readers. Think about the Big Question as you complete the sentence.

   Descriptive words can enrich a piece of writing because _____ .

   _____

   _____

   _____

Name _____   Date _____

Poetry by Walt Whitman and E. E. Cummings
Literary Analysis: Comparing Imagery

In poetry, an **image** is a word or phrase that appeals to one or more of the five senses. Writers use **imagery** to bring poetry to life with descriptions of how their subjects look, sound, feel, taste, and smell.

Both "Miracles" and "in Just—" contain images that appeal to the senses. For example, "wade with naked feet along the beach" appeals to the sense of touch, and "the little lame balloonman" appeals to sight.

DIRECTIONS: *Read each image in the first column, and mark an X in the column or columns to indicate the sense or senses that the image appeals to. The first fifteen images are from "Miracles"; the last nine are from "in Just—."*

Image	Sight	Hearing	Touch	Taste	Smell
1. "walk the streets of Manhattan"					
2. "dart my sight over the roofs"					
3. "stand under trees in the woods"					
4. "talk by day with any one I love"					
5. "sit at table at dinner with the rest"					
6. "look at strangers opposite me"					
7. "honeybees busy around the hive"					
8. "animals feeding in the fields"					
9. "birds, or . . . insects in the air"					
10. "the sundown"					
11. "stars shining so quiet and bright"					
12. "thin curve of the new moon"					
13. "fishes that swim the rocks"					
14. "the motion of the waves"					
15. "the ships with men in them"					
16. "the world is mud-luscious"					
17. "little lame balloonman whistles"					
18. "eddieandbill come running"					
19. "from marbles and piracies"					
20. "the world is puddle-wonderful"					
21. "queer old balloonman whistles"					
22. "bettyandisbel come dancing"					
23. "from hop-scotch and jump-rope"					

Name _____ Date _____

Vocabulary Builder

Word List
   distinct   exquisite

A. DIRECTIONS: *Complete these word maps by writing synonyms, antonyms, and an example sentence for each vocabulary word.*

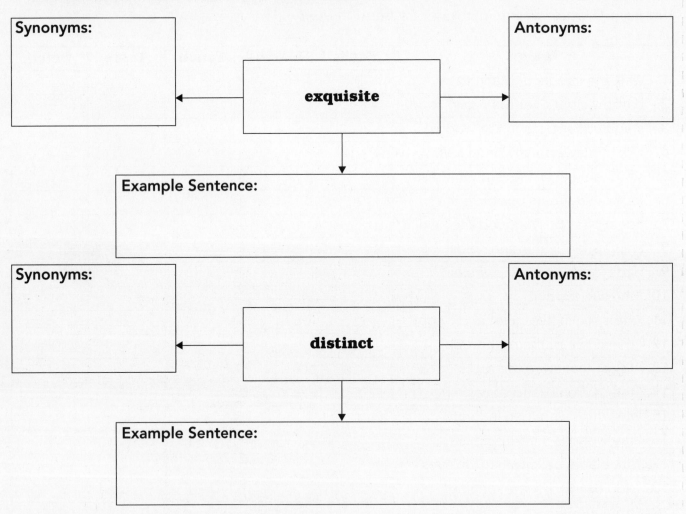

Synonyms:		Antonyms:
	exquisite	

Example Sentence:

Synonyms:		Antonyms:
	distinct	

Example Sentence:

B. DIRECTIONS: *Write the letter of the word or words whose meaning is most nearly* the same as *the word from the Word List.*

____ 1. exquisite
      A. quaint   **B.** significant   **C.** costly   **D.** beautiful

____ 2. distinct
      A. blurry   **B.** separate   **C.** similar   **D.** pure

Poetry by Walt Whitman and E. E. Cummings

Integrated Language Skills: Support for Writing to Compare Literary Works

Use the following graphic organizers as you prepare to write an essay recommending either "Miracles" or "in Just—" to someone your age.

Imagery from "Miracles" that appeals to me:

Sight	Hearing	Touch

Imagery from "in Just—" that appeals to me:

Sight	Hearing	Touch

Which poem's imagery is fascinating or strange? What about it is fascinating or strange?

_____

_____

Which poem is more musical? Why?

_____

_____

Which poem's images do I find more meaningful? Why?

_____

_____

_____

Now, use your notes to write an essay about the poem that you would recommend.

True Identity, performed by Carolyn Sills and the Boss Tweed Band

People make **assumptions**, think their opinion must be true,
that your **image**, or how you present yourself, is the actual you.
So if you think that their opinion is **biased** or personally skewed,
just be yourself so they can rightfully **define** and describe you.

You can't **ignore**, or not acknowledge, who you are.
Your looks and your **appearance** will only take you so far.
So **appreciate** and be grateful for what makes you one of a kind
and show the world, reveal to them, what's really on your mind

Your **reaction** or response to life's daily ins and outs
is all some people need to think they know what you're all about.
So if you want to **reflect** or show how you truly are inside,
make use of your features and characteristics, to imitate is simply to hide.

You can't **ignore**, or not acknowledge, who you are.
Your looks and **appearance** will only take you so far.
So **appreciate** and be grateful for what makes you one of a kind
and show the world, reveal to them, what's really on your mind

How other people see things, **perceptions**, can hold true
if you refuse to concentrate or focus on the real you.

So if you think they have the wrong **perspective** or point of view,
Just make sure that your identity, your true self, is shining through.

Continued

You can't **ignore**, or not acknowledge, who you are.

Your looks and **appearance** will only take you so far.

So **appreciate** and be grateful for what makes you one of a kind

and show the world, **reveal** to them, what's really on your mind

and show the world, **reveal** to them, what's really on your mind

and show the world, **reveal** to them, what's really on your mind

---

Song Title: **True Identity**
Artist / Performed by Carolyn Sills and the Boss Tweed Band
Vocals & Bass Guitar: Carolyn Sills
Guitar: Gerard Egan
Drums: Vlad Gutkovich
Lyrics by Carolyn Sills
Music composed by Carolyn Sills & the Boss Tweed Band

Unit 5: Drama
Big Question Vocabulary—1

 The Big Question: Do others see us more clearly than we see ourselves?

appreciate: *v.* to understand something's importance or value; other form: *appreciation*

assumption: *n.* a decision that something is true, without definite proof; other form: *assume*

bias: *n.* the act of favoring one group of people over another; other form: *biased*

define: *v.* to describe something correctly and thoroughly; other forms: *definition, defined*

reveal: *v.* to expose something that has been hidden or secret; other forms: *revealed, revealing*

A. DIRECTIONS: *In the chart, write a synonym and an antonym for each vocabulary word. Choose your answers from the words and phrases in the box. You will not use all of them.*

| theory | fairness | distort | be thankful | be happy | be ungrateful | hide |
| characterize | uncover | proof | pride | concentrate | prejudice | |

Word	Synonym	Antonym
1. appreciate		
2. assumption		
3. bias		
4. define		
5. reveal		

B. DIRECTIONS: *Write a humorous short story about a man who receives a large parrot for a pet. At first he is unhappy because he doesn't like birds. However, the parrot is so clever that the man changes his mind. Use all five vocabulary words.*

_____

_____

_____

_____

_____

_____

Unit 5: Drama
Big Question Vocabulary—2

The Big Question: Do others see us more clearly than we see ourselves?

appearance: *n.* the way a person looks to other people; other forms: *appear, appearing*

focus: *v.* to direct one's attention to one specific thing; other forms: *focusing, focused*

identify: *v.* to recognize and correctly name something; other forms: *identification, identified*

ignore: *v.* to act as if something has not been seen or heard; other forms: *ignoring, ignorant*

perspective: *n.* a special way to think about something, usually influenced by one's personality and experiences

A. DIRECTIONS: *Write the vocabulary word that best completes each group of related words.*

1. avoid, neglect, forget, _____

2. attitude, viewpoint, thoughts, _____

3. looks, image, personality, _____

4. concentrate, stare, study, _____

5. classify, define, describe, _____

B. DIRECTIONS: *On the line before each sentence, write* True *if the statement is true, or* False *if it is false. If the statement is false, rewrite the sentence so that it is true.*

_____1. A person's *appearance* is his or her innermost thoughts.

_____

_____2. If the fire alarm goes off, the best course of action is to *ignore* it.

_____

_____3. To board an airplane, you must carry a suitcase in order to *identify* yourself.

_____

_____4. Activities that require you to *focus* carefully include sleeping and daydreaming.

_____

_____5. A person's *perspective* is often based on opinions and attitudes.

_____

Name _____   Date _____

Unit 5: Drama
Big Question Vocabulary—3

The Big Question: Do others see us more clearly than we see ourselves?

characteristic: *n.* a special quality or feature that is typical of someone or something

image: *n.* the way a person appears to others; other forms: *images, imagination, imagine*

perception: *n.* the unique way you think about someone or something; other form: *perceive*

reaction: *n.* a response to someone or something in the form of thoughts, words, or actions; other forms: *react, reactionary*

reflect: *v.* to express or show through gestures or actions; other forms: *reflection, reflected*

Karen said this to Mario, Heidi, and Ramon: "I saw a really strange looking man on the subway. He gave me a spooky feeling. Maybe he was a magician. Anyway, he was carrying a huge bag. I peeked inside and almost fainted with shock. It was a painting—a painting of ME!"

Each of Karen's friends had a different reaction to what she said.

DIRECTIONS: *Use the word(s) shown to write what each friend said to Karen.*

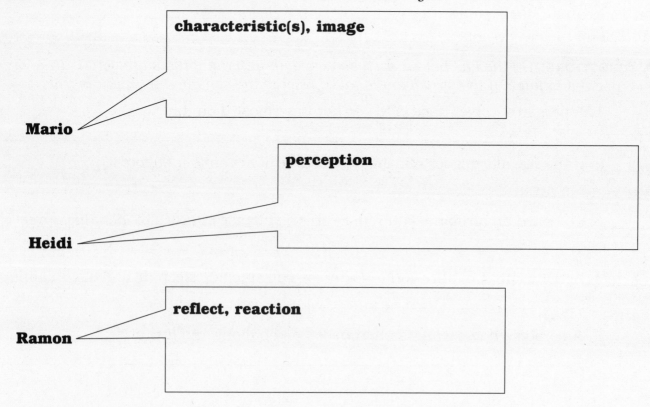

Mario

characteristic(s), image

Heidi

perception

Ramon

reflect, reaction

Name _____ Date _____

Unit 5: Drama
Applying the Big Question

Do others see us more clearly than we see ourselves?

DIRECTIONS: *Complete the chart below to apply what you have learned about how people form impressions of others. One row has been completed for you.*

Example	Who/What is Judged	Who does the Judging	Is the judgment fair	What I learned
From Literature	Goodman in "The Monsters . . .	His neighbors	No, it is based on the fact that he is an "oddball"	Fear can change the way people see others
From Literature				
From Science				
From Social Studies				
From Real Life				

Name _____ Date _____

Laurence Yep
Listening and Viewing

Segment 1: Meet Laurence Yep
- Why did Laurence Yep identify with the themes he encountered in science fiction?
- Does it surprise you that he chose to write science fiction? Why or why not?

_____

_____

_____

_____

Segment 2: Drama
- According to Yep, what are the differences between a drama and a novel?
- Which form, the drama or the novel, might be more difficult to write? Why?

_____

_____

_____

_____

Segment 3: The Writing Process
- Why does Yep adjust his drafts as he writes?
- What method of Yep's would you be most inclined to try in your own writing? Why?

_____

_____

_____

_____

Segment 4: The Rewards of Writing
- What does Yep think literature can do for young readers?

_____

_____

_____

_____

Learning About Drama

Drama is a story told in dialogue by performers in front of an audience. The **playwright** is the author of a drama, which may also be called a *play*. The play itself is written in segments, called **acts.** Acts are often divided into **scenes.**

A playwright uses **characterization** to create believable characters. To advance the action, the playwright creates **dramatic speech.** Two types of dramatic speech are **dialogue,** conversation between two or more characters, and **monologue,** a long speech by a single character. A monologue often reveals a character's thoughts and feelings.

Stage directions describe the scenery and tell how the characters move and speak. The **set** is the construction onstage that suggests the time and place of the action (the setting). **Props** are small movable items that make the set look realistic.

Two types of drama are comedy and tragedy. A **comedy** has a happy ending. It often features ordinary characters in funny situations. In a **tragedy,** the events lead to the downfall of the main character. The main character may be an ordinary person, but the traditional tragic hero is a man of great significance, such as a king.

A. DIRECTIONS: *Read the following excerpt from a drama. Then, answer the questions.*

[*The FISCHERS' kitchen, 7 A.M. MRS. FISCHER sits at kitchen table, reading a newspaper. The door opens. BECKY rushes in. She wears school clothes and carries a book bag.*]

BECKY. Mom! I overslept! I'll miss the tryouts for the play. Why didn't you wake me?

MRS. FISCHER [*getting up from the table*]. Calm down. Let me make you some breakfast.

BECKY [*almost shouting*]. Breakfast? I'm already late!

MRS. FISCHER [*patiently*]. No, dear, you're early. It's Saturday. Tryouts aren't until Monday.

1. Describe the set. _____

2. What props are used? _____

3. Quote a stage direction that tells how a character speaks.

_____

4. Quote a stage direction that tells how a character moves.

_____

5. Is the passage a dialogue or a monologue? Explain.

_____

6. Is this scene more likely from a comedy or a tragedy? Explain. _____

_____

from **Dragonwings** by Laurence Yep
Model Selection: Drama

Dragonwings is a **drama,** or *play,* a story told in dialogue and meant to be performed by actors before an audience. Laurence Yep is the **playwright,** the author of the play. A play is written in segments. You have read just one segment, a **scene.** In a full-length work, several scenes usually make up an **act,** and several acts make up the play.

To advance the action, Yep wrote **dramatic speech.** Most of the excerpt from *Dragonwings* contains **dialogue,** conversation between several characters. One section might be considered a **monologue,** a long speech by a single character. A monologue often reveals a character's thoughts and feelings.

Stage directions describe the scenery and sound effects and tell how the characters move and speak. The **set** is the construction onstage that suggests the time and place of the action (the setting). **Props** are small movable items that make the set look realistic.

In a drama, as the **main character** develops, the audience should identify with his or her emotions. The **climax** of a drama, the moment of greatest tension, concerns the main character in some way. With the climax comes some insight or revelation.

A. DIRECTIONS: *Answer these questions about Scene 9 of* Dragonwings.

1. What is the setting? _____

2. What props is Moon Shadow most likely using during his opening speech?

   _____

3. Describe one sound effect that is used. _____

4. After Windrider takes off in the airplane, Moon Shadow speaks these lines:

   I thought he'd fly forever and ever. Up, up to heaven and never come down. But then . . . Dragonwings came crashing to earth. Father had a few broken bones, but it was nothing serious. Only the aeroplane was wrecked. . . . Father didn't say much, just thought a lot I figured he was busy designing the next aeroplane. . . .

   What type of dramatic speech would you call this passage? Explain your answer.

   _____

5. Who is the main character? How can you tell?

   _____

B. DIRECTIONS: *What is the climax of events in Scene 9 of* Dragonwings? *What insight does Windrider gain in response to the climax? What insight does Moon Shadow gain?*

_____

_____

_____

All-in-One Workbook
242

Name _____ Date _____

"A Christmas Carol: Scrooge and Marley, *Act 1*" by Israel Horowitz

Writing About the Big Question

Do others see us more clearly than we see ourselves?

Big Question Vocabulary

appearance	appreciate	assumption	bias	characteristic
define	focus	identify	ignore	image
perception	perspective	reaction	reflect	reveal

A. *Choose one word from the list above to complete each sentence. There may be more than one right answer.*

1. Over time, Betsy learned to _____ her mother's fashion advice.

2. Sometimes you know what a word means, but find it hard to _____.

3. Eric's hard work in the gym helped quicken his _____ time.

B. *Follow the directions in responding to each of the items below.*

1. List two different times when you learned something new about yourself. Write your response in complete sentences.

_____

_____

2. Choose one of the experiences you listed in number 1. Write three or more sentences describing that experience. Use at least two of the Big Question vocabulary words. You may use the words in different forms (for example you can change *reflect* to *reflection*).

_____

_____

C. *Complete the sentence below. Use the completed sentence as the topic sentence in a short paragraph about the big question.*

The way we treat others reveals _____

_____

_____

A Christmas Carol: Scrooge and Marley, *Act I,* by Israel Horovitz
Reading: Preview a Text to Set a Purpose for Reading

When you **set a purpose for reading,** you decide what you want to get from a text. Setting a purpose gives you a focus as you read. These are some of the reasons you might have for reading something:

- to learn about a subject
- to be entertained
- to gain understanding
- to prepare to take action or make a decision
- to find inspiration
- to complete a task

In order to set a purpose, **preview a text** before you read it. Look at the title, the pictures, the captions, the organization, and the beginnings of passages. If you already have a purpose in mind, previewing will help you decide whether the text will fit that purpose. If you do not have a purpose in mind, previewing the text will help you determine one.

DIRECTIONS: *Read the passages from Act I of* A Christmas Carol: Scrooge and Marley *indicated below, and then complete each item.*

1. Following the list of "The People of the Play," read the information labeled "The Place of the Play." Where is the play set?

   _____

2. Read the information labeled "The Time of the Play." When does the play take place?

   _____

3. What purpose or purposes might you set based on that information?

   _____

   _____

4. The illustrations that accompany the text of Act I of the play are photographs from a production of the play. Look at those photographs now, but ignore the one of the ghostly character in chains. How are the characters dressed?

   _____

5. Based on that information, what purpose might you set for reading Act I of the play?

   _____

6. Read the opening lines of Act I, Scene 1, spoken by a character called Marley. Then, look at the photograph of the ghostly character in chains. What purpose might you set based on that information?

   _____

A Christmas Carol: Scrooge and Marley, *Act I,* by Israel Horovitz
Literary Analysis: Dialogue

Dialogue is a conversation between characters. In a play, the characters are developed almost entirely through dialogue. Dialogue also advances the action of the plot and develops the conflict.

In the script of a dramatic work, you can tell which character is speaking by the name that appears before the character's lines. In this example of dialogue, you are introduced to two of the characters in *A Christmas Carol: Scrooge and Marley:*

NEPHEW. [*Cheerfully; surprising* SCROOGE] A merry Christmas to you, Uncle! God save you!

SCROOGE. Bah! Humbug!

NEPHEW. Christmas a "humbug," Uncle? I'm sure you don't mean that.

SCROOGE. I do! Merry Christmas? What right do you have to be merry? What reason have you to be merry? You're poor enough!

In just a few words apiece, the characters establish a conflict between them. The nephew thinks Christmas is a joyful holiday, and Scrooge thinks it is nonsense. This conflict will reappear throughout the play until it is resolved. Those lines of dialogue also give you a look at the character traits of Scrooge and his nephew. Scrooge is quarrelsome and unpleasant; the nephew is upbeat and friendly.

DIRECTIONS: *Answer the following questions about this passage from* A Christmas Carol: Scrooge and Marley, *Act I, Scene 2.*

PORTLY MAN. . . . [*Pen in hand; as well as notepad*] What shall I put you down for, sir?

SCROOGE. Nothing!

PORTLY MAN. You wish to be left anonymous?

SCROOGE. I wish to be left alone! [*Pauses; turns away; turns back to them*] Since you ask me what I wish, gentlemen, that is my answer. I help to support the establishments that I have mentioned; they cost enough: and those who are badly off must go there.

THIN MAN. Many can't go there; and many would rather die.

SCROOGE. If they would rather die, they had better do it, and decrease the surplus population. . . .

1. How many characters are speaking? Who are they?

   _____

2. What is Scrooge like in this scene?

   _____

3. How is he different from the men he is talking to?

   _____

   _____

4. Based on the identification of the characters, whom would you expect to speak next?

   _____

Name _____ Date _____

A Christmas Carol: Scrooge and Marley, *Act 1*, by Israel Horovitz
Vocabulary Builder

Word List

conveyed   destitute   gratitude   implored   morose   void

A. DIRECTIONS: *Think about the meaning of the italicized word from the Word List in each sentence. Then, answer the question, and explain your answer.*

1. Marley *implored* Scrooge to pay attention to him. Did Marley ask casually?

   _____

2. Scrooge was *morose*. Did he enjoy celebrating Christmas?

   _____

3. Are the *destitute* able to save money?

   _____

4. Scrooge looked into the *void*. Did he see anything?

   _____

5. In Act I, Scene 3, of *A Christmas Carol: Scrooge and Marley*, has Scrooge *conveyed* his fear?

   _____

6. Do Fezziwig's employees feel *gratitude*?

   _____

B. WORD STUDY: *The Latin root -grat- means "thankful, pleasing." Read the following sentences. Use your knowledge of the root -grat- to write a full sentence to answer each question. Include the italicized word in your answer.*

1. If you are *grateful*, is it likely that someone has done something nice for you?

   _____

2. Is *gratitude* an unhappy emotion?

   _____

3. Would you value a *gratifying* friendship?

   _____

Name _____ Date _____

A Christmas Carol: Scrooge and Marley, *Act I,* by Israel Horovitz
Integrated Language Skills: Grammar

Interjections

An **interjection** is a part of speech that exclaims and expresses a feeling, such as pain or excitement. It may stand on its own or it may appear within a sentence, but it functions independently of the sentence—it is not related to it grammatically. If an interjection stands on its own, it is set off with a period or an exclamation point. If it appears in a sentence, it is set off with commas.

<u>Wow</u>, look at that sunset!

My pants are covered with mud. <u>Yuck</u>!

<u>Boy</u>, do my legs ache after climbing all those stairs.

Here are some common interjections:

Boy	Hmmm	Oh	Ugh	Whew	Yikes
Hey	Huh	Oops	Well	Wow	Yuck

A. DIRECTIONS: *Rewrite each item. Punctuate the sentence or pair of sentences to set off the interjections. Some sentences or pairs of sentences may be written in more than one way.*

1. Oops the cat spilled his food all over the floor

   _____

2. Ouch I dropped the hammer on my foot

   _____

3. I worked for two hours in the hot sun Whew

   _____

4. Hmmm I think this CD costs way too much

   _____

5. Hey do not go near that downed electric wire

   _____

B. WRITING APPLICATION: *Write three sentences using interjections. Be sure to punctuate the sentences correctly.*

1. _____

2. _____

3. _____

Name _____ Date _____

A Christmas Carol: Scrooge and Marley, *Act I*, by Israel Horovitz

Integrated Language Skills: Support for Writing a Letter

Use this form to prepare to **write a letter** to Scrooge.

Salutation

State your main point: Scrooge is missing out in life by being cranky and negative with the people around him.

State a specific thing that Scrooge is missing out on. Include a detail from the play or from your experience to support your point.

State another specific thing that Scrooge is missing out on. Include a detail from the play or from your experience to support your point.

Conclude with a summary or a request that Scrooge change his behavior.

Closing, Signature

Dear _____,

_____

_____

_____

_____

_____

_____

_____

_____

_____

_____

_____

_____

_____

_____

_____

_____

_____

_____

_____

_____

_____

_____

_____

_____

Now, prepare a final draft of your letter.

Name _____ Date _____

Writing About the Big Question

Do others see us more clearly than we see ourselves?

Big Question Vocabulary

appearance	appreciate	assumption	bias	characteristic
define	focus	identify	ignore	image
perception	perspective	reaction	reflect	reveal

A. *Choose one word from the list above to complete each sentence. There may be more than one right answer.*

1. Do you think someone's _____ can tell you something about their personality?

2. The players felt that the coach had a _____ against short players.

3. Luke found it difficult to _____ on his work in the noisy classroom.

B. *Follow the directions in responding to each of the items below.*

1. Make a list of four or more different ways people can communicate. For example, people can communicate by *telephone*. Write your response in a complete sentence.

   _____

   _____

2. Choose one of the means of communication you listed in question 1. Write three or more sentences describing the good and bad points of communicating that way. Use at least two of the Big Question vocabulary words. You may use the words in different forms (for example you can change *reflect* to *reflection*).

   _____

   _____

C. *Complete the sentence below. Then, write a short paragraph in which you connect this sentence to the big question.*

In order to change, we must first identify _____

_____

_____

Name _____ Date _____

A Christmas Carol: Scrooge and Marley, *Act II*, by Israel Horovitz
Reading: Adjust Your Reading Rate to Suit Your Purpose

Setting a purpose for reading is deciding before you read what you want to get out of a text. The purpose you set will affect the way you read.

Adjust your reading rate to suit your purpose. When you read a play, follow these guidelines:

- Read stage directions slowly and carefully. They describe action that may not be revealed by the dialogue.
- Read short lines of dialogue quickly in order to create the feeling of conversation.
- Read longer speeches by a single character slowly in order to reflect on the character's words and look for clues to the message.

DIRECTIONS: *Read the following passages, and answer the questions that follow each one.*

MAN # **1.** Hey, you, watch where you're going.

MAN # **2.** Watch it yourself, mate!

[PRESENT *sprinkles them directly, they change.*]

MAN # **1.** I pray go in ahead of me. It's Christmas. You be first!

MAN # **2.** No, no. I must insist that YOU be first!

1. How would you read the preceding dialogue? Why?

   _____

2. How would you read the stage directions? Why?

   _____

3. What important information do the stage directions contain? How does it affect your understanding of the lines that follow it?

   _____

   _____

   _____

PRESENT. Mark my words, Ebenezer Scrooge. I do not present the Cratchits to you because they are a handsome, or brilliant family. They are not handsome. They are not brilliant. They are not well-dressed, or tasteful to the times. Their shoes are not even waterproofed by virtue of money or cleverness spent. So when the pavement is wet, so are the insides of their shoes and the tops of their toes. They are the Cratchits, Mr. Scrooge. They are not highly special. They are happy, grateful, pleased with one another, contented with the time and how it passes. They don't sing very well, do they? But, nonetheless, they do sing . . . [*Pauses*] think of that, Scrooge. Fifteen shillings a week and they do sing . . . hear their song until its end.

4. How would you read the preceding passage? Why?

   _____

   _____

Name _____ Date _____

A Christmas Carol: Scrooge and Marley, _Act II_, by Israel Horovitz
Literary Analysis: Stage Directions

Stage directions are the words in the script of a drama that are not spoken by characters. When a play is performed, you can see the set, the characters, and the movements, and you can hear the sound effects. When you read a play, you get this information from the stage directions. Stage directions are usually printed in italic type and set off by brackets or parentheses.

DIRECTIONS: _Read the following passages, and answer the questions that follow each one._

[BOB CRATCHIT _enters, carrying_ TINY TIM _atop his shoulder. He wears a threadbare and fringe-less comforter hanging down in front of him._ TINY TIM _carries small crutches and his small legs are bound in an iron frame brace._]

1. Who appears in this scene?

   _____

2. What does the description of Bob Cratchit reveal about the Cratchit family?

   _____

3. What does the description of Tiny Tim reveal about him?

   _____

   _____

SCROOGE. Specter, something informs me that our parting moment is at hand. I know it, but I know not how I know it.

[FUTURE _points to the other side of the stage. Lights out on_ CRATCHITS. FUTURE _moves slow-ing, gliding . . ._ FUTURE _points opposite._ FUTURE _leads_ SCROOGE _to a wall and a tombstone. He points to the stone._]

Am I that man those ghoulish parasites so gloated over?

4. Who appears in this scene? How do you know?

   _____

   _____

5. What do the stage directions reveal that the dialogue does not reveal?

   _____

   _____

   _____

Name _____ Date _____

A Christmas Carol: Scrooge and Marley, *Act II,* by Israel Horovitz
Vocabulary Builder

Word List

astonish   audible   compulsion   intercedes   meager   severe

A. DIRECTIONS: *Think about the meaning of the italicized word from the Word List in each sentence. Then, answer the question, and explain your answer.*

1. Scrooge's new attitude will *astonish* his family. Will they be surprised by it?

   _____

2. Scrooge has a *compulsion* to go with each of the ghosts. Can he easily resist going?

   _____

3. Mrs. Cratchit's judgment of Scrooge is *severe.* Does she think highly of him?

   _____

4. Scrooge paid Cratchit a *meager* salary. Was the salary generous?

   _____

5. The actor's voice is *audible* when he whispers. Can the audience hear him?

   _____

6. The Ghost of Christmas Future *intercedes* on Scrooge's behalf. Does the ghost help Scrooge?

   _____

B. WORD STUDY: *The Latin prefix* inter- *means "between, among." Read the following sentences. Use your knowledge of the prefix* inter- *to write a full sentence to answer each question. Include the italicized word in your answer.*

1. Have your parents ever *interceded* on your behalf?

   _____

2. If a ball is *intercepted*, does it reach its destination?

   _____

3. Is a highway *intersection* a place where two roads meet?

   _____

A Christmas Carol: Scrooge and Marley, *Act II,* by Israel Horovitz
Integrated Language Skills: Grammar

Double Negatives

Double negatives occur when two negative words appear in a sentence, but only one is needed. Examples of negative words are *nothing, not, never,* and *no.* You can correct a double negative by revising the sentence.

Incorrect	Correct
I do <u>not</u> have <u>no</u> homework tonight.	I do <u>not</u> have <u>any</u> homework tonight.
You <u>never</u> said <u>nothing</u> about that movie.	You <u>never</u> said <u>anything</u> about that movie.

A. DIRECTIONS: *Put a checkmark (✓) next to each sentence that uses a negative word correctly. Put an ✗ next to each sentence that contains a double negative.*

____ 1. Do not ever say nothing to Mom about the surprise party.

____ 2. You never told me anything about your new coach.

____ 3. The team never had time to make a comeback.

____ 4. We do not have no reason to get up early tomorrow.

____ 5. They did not have no money for the movie.

B. Writing Application: *Rewrite each sentence to eliminate the double negative.*

1. We do not have no bread for sandwiches.

   _____

2. The spy never had no intention of giving himself up.

   _____

3. This article does not have nothing to do with our assignment.

   _____

4. They are not going to no championship game tonight.

   _____

5. Our dog will not ever eat no food she does not like.

   _____

A Christmas Carol: Scrooge and Marley, *Act II,* by Israel Horovitz
Integrated Language Skills: Support for Writing a Tribute

To prepare to write a **tribute,** or an expression of admiration, to the changed Ebenezer Scrooge, answer the following questions.

What is Scrooge like before the change?

_____

_____

What anecdotes—brief stories that make a point—illustrate Scrooge's character before the change?

_____

_____

_____

_____

_____

What causes Scrooge to change?

_____

_____

_____

What is Scrooge like after the change?

_____

_____

What anecdotes illustrate Scrooge's character after the change?

_____

_____

_____

_____

_____

Now, write a draft of your tribute to Scrooge. Be sure to explain how Scrooge has changed and why his new behavior deserves to be honored. Use this space to write your first draft.

_____

_____

_____

_____

_____

Name _____   Date _____

from **A Christmas Carol: Scrooge and Marley,** *Act I, Scenes 2 & 5* by Israel Horovitz

Writing About the Big Question

Do others see us more clearly than we see ourselves?

Big Question Vocabulary

appearance	appreciate	assumption	bias	characteristic
define	focus	identify	ignore	image
perception	perspective	reaction	reflect	reveal

A. *Choose one word from the list above to complete each sentence. There may be more than one right answer.*

1. The wrong _____ will lead to the wrong conclusion.

2. It is important to _____ on life's big events.

3. Her family members tried not to _____ the plans for the surprise party.

B. *Follow the directions in responding to each of the items below.*

1. Think of at least three adjectives or descriptive phrases that you feel describe you well. List the adjectives or phrases in a complete sentence.

   _____

   _____

2. Write at least two sentences describing an article of clothing that makes you feel special. Write your response in complete sentences. Use at least one of the Big Question vocabulary words. You may use the words in different forms (for example, you can change *reveal* to *reveals*).

   _____

   _____

C. *Complete the sentence below. Then, write a short paragraph in which you connect this sentence to the Big Question.*

   Over time, people change _____

   _____

   _____

Name _____ Date _____

from **A Christmas Carol: Scrooge and Marley,** *Act 1, Scenes 2 & 5* by Israel Horovitz
Literary Analysis: Comparing Characters

A **character** is a person who takes part in a literary work. Like main characters in stories and novels, main characters in dramas have traits that make them unique. These may include qualities such as dependability, intelligence, selfishness, and stubbornness. The characters in dramas have motives, or reasons, for behaving the way they do. For example, one character may be motivated by compassion, while another may be motivated by guilt.

When you read a drama, pay attention to what each character says and does, and note the reactions those words and actions spark in others. Notice what those words and actions reveal about the character's traits and motives.

In drama, one way to develop a character is through a **foil,** a character whose behavior and attitude contrast with those of the main character. With a foil, audiences can see good in contrast with bad or generousness in contrast with selfishness.

DIRECTIONS: *Answer the following questions to compare the older Scrooge with Fezziwig.*

Question	Scrooge	Fezziwig
1. What does the character say?		
2. What does the character do?		
3. How does the character react to Christmas?		
4. What do other characters say to or about him?		
5. What adjectives describe the character?		

from **A Christmas Carol: Scrooge and Marley,** *Act I, Scenes 2 & 5* by Israel Horovitz
Vocabulary Builder

Word List

fiddler   snuffs   suitors

A. DIRECTIONS: *Complete the word maps by writing a definition, synonyms, and an example sentence for each word from the Word List.*

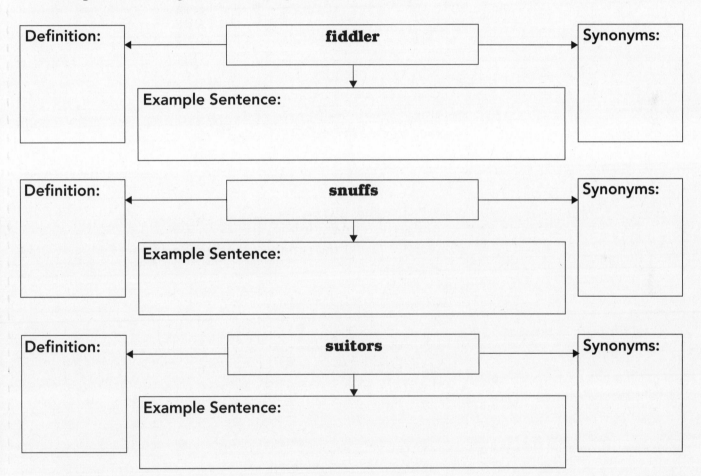

B. DIRECTIONS: *Write the letter of the word whose meaning is* most like *that of the word from the Word List.*

_____ 1. fiddler
   A. crab   B. musician   C. violinist   D. tinkerer

_____ 2. snuffs
   A. sniffs   B. erases   C. blots   D. extinguishes

_____ 3. suitors
   A. boyfriends   B. tailors   C. lawyers   D. apprentices

from A Christmas Carol: Scrooge and Marley, *Act I, Scenes 2 & 5* by Israel Horovitz
Support for Writing to Compare Literary Works

Use this graphic organizer to gather notes for an essay in which you compare and contrast Fezziwig and Scrooge.

Scrooge   **Fezziwig**

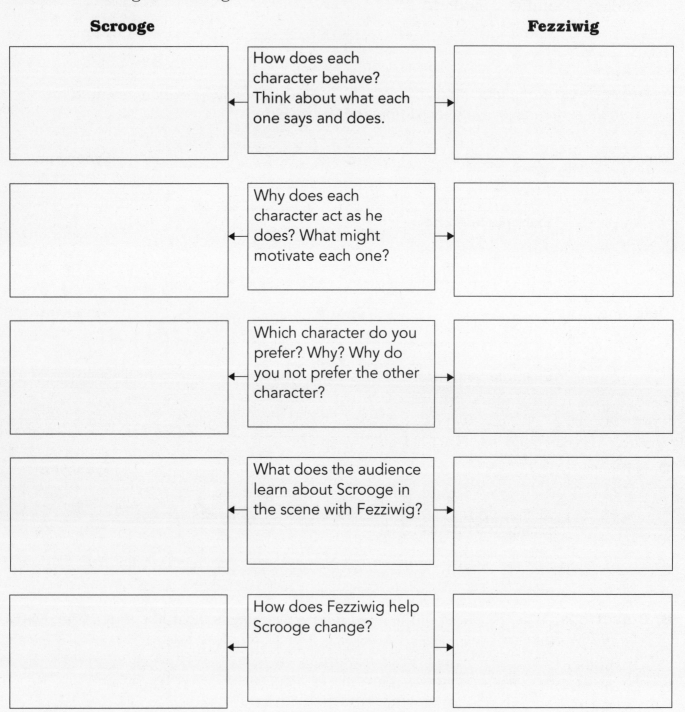

How does each character behave? Think about what each one says and does.

Why does each character act as he does? What might motivate each one?

Which character do you prefer? Why? Why do you not prefer the other character?

What does the audience learn about Scrooge in the scene with Fezziwig?

How does Fezziwig help Scrooge change?

Now, use your notes to write an essay comparing and contrasting Fezziwig and Scrooge. Be sure to discuss how each character's actions and words help the playwright make a point about Scrooge and his behavior.

Name _____ Date _____

"The Monsters Are Due on Maple Street" by Rod Serling
Writing About the Big Question

Do others see us more clearly than we see ourselves?

Big Question Vocabulary

appearance	appreciate	assumption	bias	characteristic
define	focus	identify	ignore	image
perception	perspective	reaction	reflect	reveal

A. *Choose one word from the list above to complete each sentence. There may be more than one right answer.*

1. Most people have one _____ that is more notice-able than the others.

2. Sometimes it is hard to _____ your talents.

3. It is dangerous to _____ your shortcomings.

B. *Follow the directions in responding to each of the items below.*

1. List at least four ways that kids project an image to others.

   _____

   _____

2. Do you think school uniforms are a good idea? Write three or more sentences explaining your position. Use at least two of the Big Question vocabulary words. You may use the words in different forms (for example, you can change *reflect* to *reflection*).

   _____

   _____

C. *Complete the sentence below. Then, write a short paragraph in which you connect this sentence to the Big Question.*

When we are afraid, our reactions can sometimes _____

   _____

   _____

"The Monsters Are Due on Maple Street" by Rod Serling

Reading: Distinguish Between Important and Unimportant Details to Write a Summary

A **summary** is a brief statement that presents only the main ideas and most important details. Summarizing helps you review and understand what you are reading. To summarize, you must first **distinguish between important and unimportant details.** Ask yourself questions like these:

- Is the detail necessary to an understanding of the literary work?
- Would the work hold together without the inclusion of this information?

As you read, pause periodically to recall and restate only the key events and important details.

DIRECTIONS: *Read these summaries of portions of "The Monsters Are Due on Maple Street." Then, answer the questions that follow each summary.*

It is an ordinary September evening on Maple Street when a roar is heard and a flash is seen. The power goes off, and telephones and portable radios stop working. One neighbor leaves to see what is happening on another street. Another neighbor says that he will go downtown to find out what is going on. For no explainable reason, his car will not start. He and a third neighbor decide to walk downtown. Tommy, a fourteen-year-old boy who wears eyeglasses, tells the men not to go. Tommy tells the crowd that what is happening is like every story about aliens he has read. He says that before they land, aliens send a family that looks human to live in a community and prepare for the aliens' arrival.

1. What is the main idea of the preceding summary?

   _____

2. Which detail in the preceding summary is unnecessary?

   _____

After Les Goodman's car starts on its own, the neighbors become suspicious of Goodman. A neighbor says that she has seen him standing on his porch in the middle of the night, looking at the sky. Goodman explains that he often has insomnia. He compares his neighbors to frightened rabbits. He says that they are letting a nightmare begin.

3. What is the main idea of the preceding summary?

   _____

   _____

4. Which detail in the preceding summary is unimportant? How do you know it is unimportant?

   _____

Name _____ Date _____

"The Monsters Are Due on Maple Street" by Rod Serling
Literary Analysis: A Character's Motives

A character's motives are the reasons for his or her actions. Motives are usually related to what a character wants, needs, or feels. Powerful motives include love, anger, fear, and greed. As you read, think about what motivates each character.

DIRECTIONS: *Read the following passages from "The Monsters Are Due on Maple Street." Then, answer the questions that follow, about the characters' motives.*

STEVE. It isn't just the power failure, Charlie. If it was, we'd still be able to get a broadcast on the portable.

[*There's a murmur of reaction to this.* STEVE *looks from face to face and then over to his car.*]

STEVE. I'll run downtown. We'll get this all straightened out.

1. What are Steve's motives for volunteering to go downtown?

   _____

   _____

GOODMAN. I just don't understand it. I tried to start it and it wouldn't start. You saw me. All of you saw me.

[*And now, just as suddenly as the engine started, it stops and there's a long silence that is gradually intruded upon by the frightened murmuring of the people.*]

GOODMAN. I don't understand. I swear . . . I don't understand. What's happening?

DON. Maybe you better tell us. Nothing's working on this street. Nothing. No lights, no power, no radio. . . . Nothing except one car—yours!

[*The people pick this up and now their murmuring becomes a loud chant filling the air with accusations and demands for action. Two of the men . . . head toward* GOODMAN, *who backs away, backing into his car and now at bay.*]

GOODMAN. Wait a minute now. You keep your distance—all of you. So I've got a car that starts by itself—well, that's a freak thing. I admit it. But does that make me some kind of a criminal or something? I don't know why the car works—it just does!

2. Which speaker appears to be motivated by confusion? _____

3. Which speaker appears to be motivated by suspicion? _____

4. What emotion or emotions appear to be motivating Goodman after the crowd has accused him? _____

5. Why might Goodman be feeling this emotion? _____

   _____

Name _____ Date _____

Vocabulary Builder

Word List

defiant   flustered   metamorphosis   persistently   sluggishly   transfixed

A. DIRECTIONS: *Read each sentence, and think about the meaning of the italicized word from the Word List. Then, answer the question, and explain your answer.*

1. Would you expect a *flustered* person to speak clearly?

   _____

2. If a heavy rain fills a riverbed, will the river move *sluggishly*?

   _____

3. If someone *persistently* asks a question, would you assume that she is eager to know the answer?

   _____

4. Would a *defiant* child be likely to refuse to do his chores?

   _____

5. If a rude person undergoes a *metamorphosis*, is she likely to continue to be rude?

   _____

6. If a person is *transfixed* by a performance, does he find it interesting?

   _____

B. WORD STUDY: *The Latin root -sist- means "stand." Read the following sentences. Use your knowledge of the root -sist- to write a full sentence to answer each question. Include the italicized word in your answer.*

1. Is an *assistant* someone who competes with you?

   _____

2. If you *insist* on doing something, are you expressing yourself in a firm manner?

   _____

3. Is a *persistent* person going to give up easily?

   _____

"The Monsters Are Due on Maple Street" by Rod Serling
Integrated Language Skills: Grammar

Sentence Functions and Endmarks

Sentences are classified into four categories, according to their function.

Category, Function, and Endmark	Example
A **declarative sentence** makes a statement. It ends with a period. (.)	Monsters are due on Maple Street.
An **interrogative sentence** asks a question. It ends with a question mark. (?)	What is going on?
An **imperative sentence** gives a command. It ends with a period or an exclamation point. (. or !)	Do not leave town. Watch out!
An **exclamatory sentence** calls out or exclaims. It ends with an exclamation point. (!)	Hey! How frightened we were!

Note that the subject of an imperative sentence is always the word *you*, and it is never stated: *(You) do not leave town. (You) watch out!*

Also note that in your writing, you should use exclamatory sentences as if they were a powerful spice. For the greatest effect, use them sparingly.

A. DIRECTIONS: *Add the correct endmark to each sentence. Then, identify the sentence as* declarative, interrogative, imperative, *or* exclamatory.

1. Where did you go on your field trip on Saturday _____ _____

2. We drove to a quarry and looked for fossils _____ _____

3. What cool fossils _____ _____

4. This one is a trilobite _____ _____

5. Don't drop it _____ _____

6. Next time we go, you should come with us _____ _____

7. Will you tell me when you plan to go again _____ _____

B. Writing Application: *Write a short dialogue between two characters. Use at least one of each kind of sentence. Label your sentences* dec *for declarative,* int *for interrogative,* imp *for imperative, and* exclam *for exclamatory.*

_____

_____

_____

_____

Name _____ Date _____

"The Monsters Are Due on Maple Street" by Rod Serling
Integrated Language Skills: Support for Writing a Summary

A **summary** is a brief statement that presents only the main ideas and most important details of a literary work. Summarizing helps you review and understand what you are reading.

To summarize, you must first distinguish between important and unimportant details. Ask yourself questions like the following:

- Is this detail necessary for my understanding of the literary work?

- Would the literary work hold together without this information?

Use the following chart to take notes for your summary of Act 1 or Act 2 of the screenplay. Fill in the left-hand column first. Finish this column by stating the theme, or underlying meaning, of the act. Then, go through the right-hand column, and verify that each fact you are including reflects the act's meaning.

	Supports Underlying Meaning?
Main Idea #1:	(Y/N)
Supporting Detail:	(Y/N)
Supporting Detail:	(Y/N)
Supporting Detail:	(Y/N)
Main Idea #2	(Y/N)
Supporting Detail:	(Y/N)
Supporting Detail:	(Y/N)
Supporting Detail:	(Y/N)
Underlying Meaning:	

Now, write a draft of your summary. Include only those ideas and supporting details that reflect the underlying meaning of the screenplay.

All-in-One Workbook
264

Name _____ Date _____

from **Grandpa and the Statue** by Arthur Miller
"My Head Is Full of Starshine" by Peg Kehret
Writing About the Big Question
Do others see us more clearly than we see ourselves?

Big Question Vocabulary

appearance	appreciate	assumption	bias	characteristic
define	focus	identify	ignore	image
perception	perspective	reaction	reflect	reveal

A. *Choose one word from the list above to complete each sentence. There may be more than one right answer.*

1. Some musicians work very hard to create the right _____ for their band.

2. An older person's _____ on a problem may be different from a child's.

3. What we see, smell, taste, hear and feel adds up to our _____ of the world.

B. *Follow the directions in responding to each of the items below.*

1. List at least two different ways people may get the wrong impression of another person. Write your response in complete sentences.

_____

_____

2. If you could see yourself as others do, would you want to? Write at least three sentences explaining your position. Use at least two of the Big Question vocabulary words. You may use the words in different forms (for example, you can change *reflect* to *reflection*).

_____

_____

C. *Complete the sentence below. Then, write a short paragraph in which you connect this sentence to the Big Question.*

The best way to understand a person is to _____

_____

_____

from **Grandpa and the Statue** by Arthur Miller

"My Head Is Full of Starshine" by Peg Kehret

Literary Analysis: Comparing Dramatic Speeches

Dramatic speeches are performed by actors in a drama or play. Whether spoken by a character who is onstage alone or given by a character who is part of a larger scene, these speeches move the action of the story forward and help define the conflict in a play. There are two main types of dramatic speeches:

- **Monologues** are long, uninterrupted speeches that are spoken by a single character. They reveal the private thoughts and feelings of the character.
- **Dialogues** are conversations between characters. They reveal characters' traits, develop conflict, and move the plot forward.

Grandpa and the Statue is a dialogue, and "My Head Is Full of Starshine" is a monologue. As you read these selections, consider what you learn about the characters. Also, think about how other key information is revealed.

DIRECTIONS: *Answer the following questions about the excerpts from* Grandpa and the Statue *and "My Head Is Full of Starshine."*

1. In the excerpt from *Grandpa and the Statue,* what does the audience learn about Monaghan's character?

_____

_____

2. What conflict is revealed in Monaghan and Sheean's dialogue in the excerpt from *Grandpa and the Statue*?

_____

_____

3. In the excerpt from *Grandpa and the Statue,* what does Monaghan reveal about himself in the speech about his experiences when he first came to America?

_____

_____

4. How does the reader learn about the writer's tendency to daydream in "My Head Is Full of Starshine"?

_____

_____

5. What does the writer reveal about her feelings toward having library fines in "My Head Is Full of Starshine"?

_____

_____

from **Grandpa and the Statue** by Arthur Miller
"My Head Is Full of Starshine" by Peg Kehret
Vocabulary Builder

Word List

peeved   potential   practical   rummaging

A. DIRECTIONS: *Read each sentence, paying attention to the italicized word from the Word List. Then, answer each question, and explain your answer.*

1. If you accidentally threw away a diamond ring, might you be *rummaging* through the trash?

    _____

2. Is a *practical* person one who daydreams and puts things off until the last minute?

    _____

3. Is a relaxed, easygoing person likely to be easily *peeved*?

    _____

4. Is someone with great *potential* as an athlete likely to compete in the Olympics someday?

    _____

B. DIRECTIONS: *Write the letter of the word whose meaning is* most like *that of the word from the Word List.*

____ 1. peeved
    A. outgoing   **B.** happy   **C.** realistic   **D.** annoyed

____ 2. practical
    A. happy   **B.** realistic   **C.** strong   **D.** imaginative

____ 3. rummaging
    A. reselling   **B.** organizing   **C.** searching   **D.** destroying

____ 4. potential
    A. capability   **B.** intelligence   **C.** sharpness   **D.** volume

Name _____ Date _____

from **Grandpa and the Statue** by Arthur Miller
"My Head Is Full of Starshine" by Peg Kehret

Support for Writing to Compare Dramatic Speeches

Use this graphic organizer to take notes for your essay comparing and contrasting the dramatic speech by Monaghan in the excerpt from *Grandpa and the Statue* with the one by the speaker in "My Head Is Full of Starshine."

Which ideas in the speech are familiar to you? _____
_____
_____
_____
_____
_____

With which ideas in the speech do you agree or disagree? _____
_____
_____
_____
_____
_____

Which character do you relate to more? Why?
_____
_____
_____
_____
_____
_____
_____
_____

The speaker in "My Head Is Full of Starshine"

Monaghan in *Grandpa and the Statue*

From which character do you think you learn more? Why? _____
_____
_____
_____
_____
_____
_____
_____

Which ideas in the speech are familiar to you? _____
_____
_____
_____
_____
_____

With which ideas in the speech do you agree or disagree? _____
_____
_____
_____
_____
_____

Now, use your notes to write a draft of an essay comparing and contrasting the two speeches.

BQ Tunes

Solidarity, performed by the Fake Gimms

We have a **common** goal to achieve
Yea, what we want is the same.
We share a place, our home, our **community**.
We have a stake in the game.

It's bigger than you.
It's bigger than me, too.

Just a single **individual** trying to succeed.
It's not so easy by yourself,
You've got to work as a **team**.

It's bigger than you.
It's bigger than me, too.

Part of the **culture** stems from **tradition**.
The ways that we're defined.
These are the things that bring us together,
The things that **unify**.

It's bigger than you.
It's bigger than me, too.

Our **duty** and obligation,
Stand as one, a **group** of many in solidarity.
A **family** with a **unique** plan.
More effective than a single man.
To make a change when it matters.
Now.

Now.

I am a product of my surroundings,
Of my **environment**.
I have a **custom** and it defines how I live.

It's bigger than you.

It's bigger than me, too.

Ethnicity and identity might show them where we're from,

But **diversity** and difference will serve to make us strong.

It's bigger than you.

It's bigger than me, too.

Song Title: **Solidarity**

Artist / Performed by the Fake Gimms

Vocals & Guitar: Joe Pfeiffer

Guitar: Greg Kuter

Bass Guitar: Jared Duncan

Drums: Tom Morra

Lyrics by the Fake Gimms

Produced by the Fake Gimms

Studio Production: Mike Pandolfo, Wonderful

Executive Producer: Keith London, Defined Mind

Unit 6: Themes in the Oral Tradition
Big Question Vocabulary—1

The Big Question: Community or individual: Which is more important?

common: *adj.* shared with others, such as mutual ideas or interests

community: *n.* a town or neighborhood in which a group of people live; other forms: *communal, communities*

culture: *n.* the ideas, beliefs, and customs that are shared by people in a society; other forms: *cultural, cultured*

individual: *n.* a person; other form: *individually*

unique: *adj.* single, one of a kind

A. DIRECTIONS: *Follow each direction.*

1. Explain the difference between something that is **common** and something that is **unique.** Provide an example of each. _____

   _____

2. Explain the relationship between an **individual** and his or her **community.** _____

   _____

3. Provide three examples of **culture**—ideas, beliefs, or customs shared by people living in your community or in the United States at large.

   _____

   _____

   _____

B. DIRECTIONS: *Provide an example of each of the following.*

1. a common interest shared by you and a friend: _____

   _____

2. a community in which you would like to live someday: _____

   _____

3. a foreign culture of your family, neighbors, or friends: _____

   _____

4. an individual whom you admire: _____

   _____

5. a characteristic or feature that makes you unique: _____

   _____

Unit 6: Themes in the Oral Tradition
Big Question Vocabulary—2

The Big Question: Community or individual: Which is more important?

custom: *n.* a tradition shared by people from the same culture; other form: *customary.*

diversity: *n.* a variety of different ideas, cultures, or objects; other form: *diverse*

environment: *n.* the setting in which an individual lives; other form: *environmental*

group: *n.* several people or things that are together; other forms: *grouping, grouped*

duty: *n.* conduct due to parents and superiors; tasks, conduct, service, or functions that arise from one's position; other form: *dutiful*

DIRECTIONS: *Answer each question.*

1. Many snakes and colorful birds reside in a rain forest. Which vocabulary word **best** describes where they live? Explain your answer. _____

   _____

2. Sally takes care of her sisters every day when she comes home from school. Which vocabulary word **best** describes this situation? Explain your answer. _____

   _____

3. Every May 1, my sister and I make May baskets. Then we deliver them to our neighbors. Which vocabulary word **best** describes this annual event? Explain your answer.

   _____

4. Everyone interested in running the marathon got together to share their ideas about training. Which vocabulary word **best** describes these individuals? Explain your answer.

   _____

5. The restaurant serves Italian, Spanish, English, African, and German foods. Which vocabulary word **best** describes the menu? Explain your answer. _____

   _____

Unit 6: Themes in the Oral Tradition
Big Question Vocabulary—3

The Big Question: Community or individual: Which is more important?

ethnicity: *n.* the race or national group to which an individual belongs; other form: *ethnic*

family: *n.* a group of people who are related to each other; other forms: *families, familiar*

team: *n.* a group of people who work together to achieve a common goal

tradition: *n.* a belief or custom that has existed for a long time; other form: *traditional*

unify: *v.* to combine two or more things to form a single unit; other form: *unified*

DIRECTIONS: *Answer each question.*

1. Which vocabulary word is an **antonym** for the word *separate* ? Explain their opposite meanings.

   _____

2. Chico and Manny's family came to this country from Spain. Which vocabulary word **best** describes their family's roots? Explain your answer. _____

3. The students in my class broke into small groups to create radio plays. Which vocabulary word **best** describes each group? Explain your answer. _____

   _____

4. On Valentine's Day each year, my mother and her friend Mrs. Ortiz make delicious heart-shaped cookies. Which vocabulary word **best** describes this annual event? Explain your answer. _____

   _____

5. I have four brothers and fifteen cousins. Which vocabulary word **best** describes this group? Explain your answer. _____

   _____

Name _____   Date _____

Unit 6: Themes in the Oral Tradition
Applying the Big Question

Community or individual—which is more important?

DIRECTIONS: Complete the chart below to apply what you have learned about the importance of the community and the individual. One row has been completed for you.

Example	What does the individual want?	What does the community want?	Who won or lost	What I learned
From Literature	Ixtla wants to marry Popo	Ixtla to rule the kingdom	Nobody, because Ixtla dies of a broken heart	Sometimes individuals cannot be forced to do what others wish of them
From Literature				
From Science				
From Social Studies				
From Real Life				

Jon Scieszka
Listening and Viewing

Segment 1: Meet Jon Scieszka
- How did Jon Scieszka choose his audience? Scieszka reads all different types of literature.
- How do you think this helps him come up with writing ideas?

_____

_____

_____

_____

Segment 2: Themes in the Oral Tradition
- Why is Jon Scieszka "amazed" by fairy tales, myths, and legends?
- Why do you think that the retelling of these stories over time is important?

_____

_____

_____

_____

Segment 3: The Writing Process
- Who is Lane Smith, and how is he involved in Jon Scieszka's writing process?
- Why are illustrations important in fairy tales, myths, and fables like the stories that Jon Scieszka writes?

_____

_____

_____

_____

Segment 4: The Rewards of Writing
- Why is being a writer rewarding to Jon Scieszka?
- Why do you think that reading is a valuable activity for young people in today's age of technology?

_____

_____

_____

_____

All-in-One Workbook
275

Learning About the Oral Tradition

The sharing of stories, cultures, and ideas by word of mouth is called the **oral tradition.** Here are common elements of the oral tradition.

- The **theme** is a central idea, message, or insight that a story reveals.
- A **moral** is a lesson about life that is taught by a story.
- **Heroes** and **heroines** are larger-than-life figures whose virtues and deeds are often celebrated in stories from the oral tradition.
- **Storytelling** calls on the talents and personality of the teller to bring the narrative to life. Storytelling techniques include **hyperbole,** or the use of exaggeration or overstatement, and **personification,** the giving of human characteristics to a non-human subject.

Many stories have been written down for readers. Categories of stories in the oral tradition that have been committed to paper include the following.

- **Myths** are ancient tales that describe the actions of gods, goddesses, and the heroes who interact with them.
- **Legends** are traditional stories about the past. They are based on real-life events or people, but they are more fiction than fact.
- **Folk tales** tell about ordinary people. These stories reveal the traditions and values of a culture and teach a lesson about life.
- **Tall tales** are folk tales that contain hyperbole.
- **Fables** are brief animal stories that contain personification. Fables often end with a moral or lesson.
- **Epics** are long narrative poems about a hero who engages in a dangerous journey.

A. DIRECTIONS: *The following items are elements of stories in the oral tradition. Decide which of the two terms matches the preceding description. Underline your choice.*

1. A woman spins cloth out of gold.   hyperbole   personification
2. The god Apollo drives his chariot across the sky.   myth   legend
3. Baseball great Babe Ruth hits the ball into another state.   fable   legend
4. The sun refuses to shine on an evil character's birthday.   personification   theme
5. It is best to be prepared.   moral   hero

B. DIRECTIONS: *On the lines below, write a plot summary for an original fable. Include one or more animal characters, and include an example of personification. End your fable with a moral. Use a separate sheet of paper if more space is needed.*

_____

_____

_____

"Grasshopper Logic," "The Other Frog Prince," and "duckbilled platypus vs. beefsnakstik®" by Jon Scieszka and Lane Smith
Model Selection: The Oral Tradition

Jon Scieszka entertains readers with his comical versions of traditional **fairy tales** and **fables. Fables** are brief animal stories that contain personification. Fables often end with a moral or lesson. These three short selections are humorous examples of stories in the **oral tradition**—the sharing of stories, cultures, and ideas by word of mouth. Elements of the oral tradition include the following.

- The **theme** is a central idea, message, or insight that a story reveals.
- A **moral** is a lesson about life that is taught by a story. An example of a moral is "Hard work leads to success."
- **Hyperbole** is a deliberate exaggeration or overstatement. It is often used to create humor. For example, a man might be as strong as an ox.
- **Personification** is the granting of human characteristics to a nonhuman subject. This would include a talking fox or an angry tree.

A. DIRECTIONS: *Answer the following questions.*

1. Give an example of hyperbole from "Grasshopper Logic." Tell why it is a hyperbole.

_____

_____

2. How does the ending of "The Other Frog Prince" differ from the ending of the traditional "Frog Prince" fairy tale?

_____

_____

3. What types of characters are in "duckbilled platypus vs. beefsnakstik®," and in what specific ways are they examples of personification?

_____

_____

B. DIRECTIONS: *On the lines below, describe the specific ways in which the grasshopper and his mother talk and act like humans.*

_____

_____

_____

_____

_____

_____

Name _____ Date _____

"Icarus and Deadalus" by Josephine Preston Peabody

Writing About the Big Question

Community or individual: Which is more important?

Big Question Vocabulary

common	community	culture	custom	diversity
duty	environment	ethnicity	family	group
individual	team	tradition	unify	unique

A. *Use one or more words from the list above to complete each sentence.*

1. I used a lot of paper printing drafts of a _____
   research project.

2. My teammate was concerned about the impact on the _____ .

3. We decided it was our _____ to recycle.

4. That way we could balance our _____ needs
   with those of the earth.

B. *Follow the directions in responding to each of the items below.*

1. Describe a time when you became so focused on getting what you wanted that you
   failed to consider the consequences of your actions.

   _____

   _____

2. Write two sentences explaining how the preceding experience affected those around
   you, such as friends or family. Use at least two of the Big Question vocabulary
   words.

   _____

   _____

   _____

C. *Complete the sentence below. Then, write a short paragraph in which you connect this
experience to the big question.*

When an individual becomes too focused on his or her own desires, _____

_____

_____

_____

_____

_____

Name _____ Date _____

Reading: Ask Questions to Analyze Cause-and-Effect Relationships

A **cause** is an event, an action, or a feeling that produces an **effect,** or result. In some literary works, multiple causes result in one single effect. In other works, a single cause results in multiple effects. Effects can also become causes for events that follow. The linking of causes and effects propels the action forward.

As you read, **ask questions** such as "What happened?" and "What will happen as a result of this?" **to analyze cause-and-effect relationships.**

DIRECTIONS: *Use the following graphic organizer to analyze some of the cause-and-effect relationships in "Icarus and Daedalus." The first response has been filled in as an example. Where there is no box in which to write the question you would ask yourself, ask the question mentally, and then write the effect in the next box.*

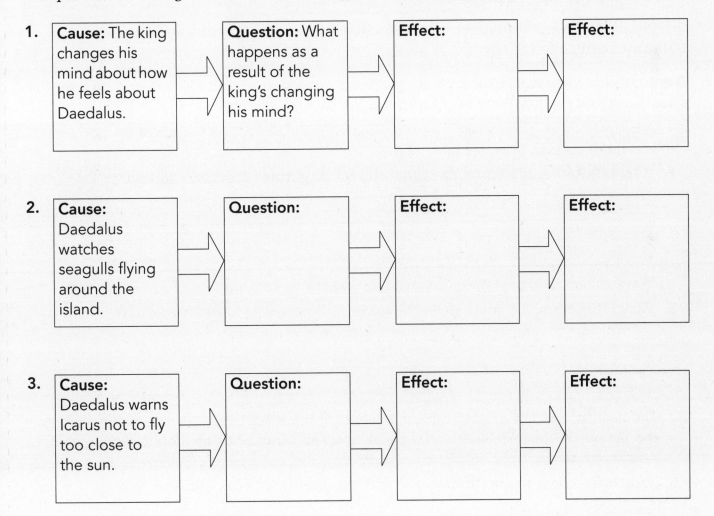

1. **Cause:** The king changes his mind about how he feels about Daedalus.

Question: What happens as a result of the king's changing his mind?

Effect:

Effect:

2. **Cause:** Daedalus watches seagulls flying around the island.

Question:

Effect:

Effect:

3. **Cause:** Daedalus warns Icarus not to fly too close to the sun.

Question:

Effect:

Effect:

"Icarus and Daedalus" by Josephine Preston Peabody
Literary Analysis: Myth

Since time began, people have tried to understand the world around them. Ancient peoples created **myths**—stories that explain natural occurrences and express beliefs about right and wrong. Every culture has its own collection of myths, or *mythology*. In many myths, gods and goddesses have human traits, and human heroes have superhuman traits. Myths explore universal themes and explain the world in human terms.

Most myths perform some of the following functions:

- explain natural occurrences
- express beliefs about right and wrong
- show gods or goddesses with human traits
- show human heroes with superhuman traits
- explore universal themes

Not all myths perform all of those functions, however. "Icarus and Daedalus" illustrates only a few of them.

DIRECTIONS: *Read each excerpt from "Icarus and Daedalus" that follows, and answer the question about the functions of a myth that the excerpt illustrates.*

Among all those mortals who grew so wise that they learned the secrets of the gods, none was more cunning than Daedalus.

1. Which function of a myth does the excerpt illustrate? How can you tell?

_____

_____

_____

"Remember," said the father, "never to fly very low or very high."

2. Which function of a myth does the excerpt illustrate? How can you tell?

_____

_____

_____

The nearest island he named Icaria, in memory of the child; but he, in heavy grief, went to the temple of Apollo in Sicily, and there hung up his wings as an offering. Never again did he attempt to fly.

3. Which function of a myth does the excerpt illustrate? How can you tell?

_____

_____

_____

Name _____ Date _____

"Icarus and Daedalus" by Josephine Preston Peabody
Vocabulary Builder

Word List

aloft   captivity   liberty   reel   sustained   vacancy

A. DIRECTIONS: *Write the letter of the word that means the same or about the same as the word from the Word List.*

____ 1. vacancy
    A. property
    B. appointment
    C. emptiness
    D. discount

____ 2. sustained
    A. supported
    B. starved
    C. deprived
    D. competed

____ 3. liberty
    A. dependence
    B. freedom
    C. history
    D. agreement

____ 4. aloft
    A. in the air
    B. still
    C. trapped
    D. on the ground

____ 5. reel
    A. punch
    B. sing
    C. unravel
    D. stagger

____ 6. captivity
    A. exterior
    B. prison
    C. resort
    D. arrangement

B. WORD STUDY: *The Latin root -vac- means "empty." Answer each of the following questions using one of these words containing -vac-: vacancy, vacuous, vacuum.*

1. Why would you look for a *vacancy* sign if you needed to rent a room?

_____

2. What has been done to a jar that is *vacuum* packed?

_____

3. Why would a *vacuous* TV show not be worth watching?

_____

"Demeter and Persephone" by Anne Terry White
Writing About the Big Question
Community or individual: Which is more important?

Big Question Vocabulary

common	community	culture	custom	diversity
duty	environment	ethnicity	family	group
individual	team	tradition	unify	unique

A. *Use one or more words from the list above to complete each sentence.*

1. Zach and his dad had a _____ of washing their cars on Sunday.

2. However, their local _____ was experiencing a water shortage.

3. They had a _____ to consider the impact of their actions on others.

4. They decided to forgo the carwash for the _____ good of the town.

B. *Follow the directions in responding to each of the items below.*

1. Describe a time when you or someone you know was faced with a decision that would affect a large number of people. _____
   _____

2. Write two sentences explaining the decision and how it affected those involved. Use at least two of the Big Question vocabulary words.
   _____
   _____

C. *Complete the sentence below. Then, write a short paragraph in which you connect this situation to the big question.*

When making a decision that will affect the greater community, it is one's duty to

_____
_____
_____
_____
_____
_____

Name _____ Date _____

Reading: Ask Questions to Analyze Cause-and-Effect Relationships

A **cause** is an event, an action, or a feeling that produces an **effect,** or result. In some literary works, multiple causes result in one single effect. In other works, a single cause results in multiple effects. Effects can also become causes for events that follow. The linking of causes and effects propels the action forward.

As you read, **ask questions** such as "What happened?" and "What will happen as a result of this?" **to analyze cause-and-effect relationships.**

DIRECTIONS: *Use the following graphic organizer to analyze some of the cause-and-effect relationships in "Demeter and Persephone." The first response has been filled in as an example. Where there is no box in which to write the question you would ask yourself, ask the question mentally, and then write the effect in the next box.*

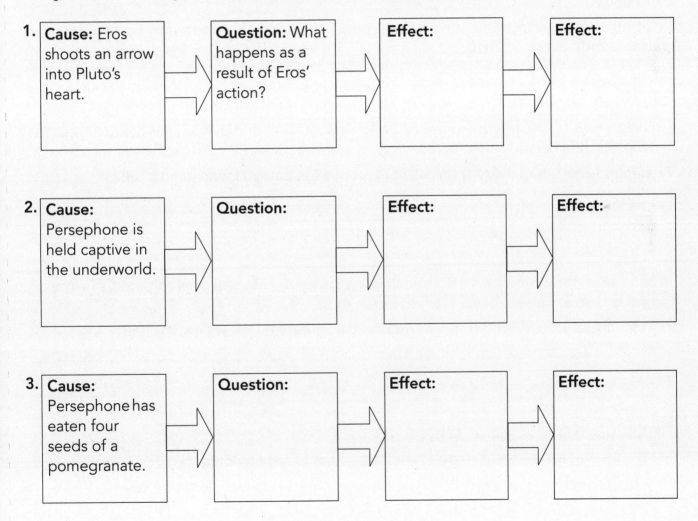

1. | **Cause:** Eros shoots an arrow into Pluto's heart. | **Question:** What happens as a result of Eros' action? | **Effect:** | **Effect:**

2. | **Cause:** Persephone is held captive in the underworld. | **Question:** | **Effect:** | **Effect:**

3. | **Cause:** Persephone has eaten four seeds of a pomegranate. | **Question:** | **Effect:** | **Effect:**

"Demeter and Persephone" by Anne Terry White
Literary Analysis: Myth

Since time began, people have tried to understand the world around them. Ancient peoples created **myths**—stories that explain natural occurrences and express beliefs about right and wrong. Every culture has its own collection of myths, or *mythology.* In many myths, gods and goddesses have human traits, and human heroes have superhuman traits. Myths explore universal themes and explain the world in human terms.

Most myths perform some of the following functions:

- explain natural occurrences
- express beliefs about right and wrong
- show gods or goddesses with human traits
- show human heroes with superhuman traits
- explore universal themes

Not all myths perform all of those functions, however. "Demeter and Persephone" illustrates only a few of them.

DIRECTIONS: *Read each excerpt from "Demeter and Persephone" that follows, and answer the question about the function of a myth that the excerpt illustrates.*

Deep under Mt. Aetna, the gods had buried alive a number of fearful, fire-breathing giants. The monsters heaved and struggled to get free. And so mightily did they shake the earth . . .

1. Which function of a myth does the excerpt illustrate? How can you tell?

_____

_____

_____

Now an unaccustomed warmth stole through his veins. His stern eyes softened. . . . The god looked at Persephone and loved her at once.

2. Which function of a myth does the excerpt illustrate? How can you tell?

_____

_____

_____

It seemed that all mankind would die of hunger.

"This cannot go on," said mighty Zeus. "I see that I must intervene."

3. Which function of a myth does the excerpt illustrate? How can you tell?

_____

_____

_____

"Demeter and Persephone" by Anne Terry White
Vocabulary Builder

Word List

abode   defies   dominions   intervene   monarch   realm

A. DIRECTIONS: *Revise each sentence so that it makes sense.*

1. Zeus is pleased when a god or goddess <u>defies</u> his orders.

   _____

2. When the world is calm and at peace, Zeus is likely to <u>intervene</u>.

   _____

3. The <u>monarch</u> bowed before his subjects.

   _____

4. Pluto rules supreme outside his <u>dominions</u>.

   _____

5. Within the <u>realm</u> of fantasy, imagination is restrained.

   _____

6. With its cheerful fire and sweet scent, the Queen's <u>abode</u> gave her a sense of danger.

   _____

B. WORD STUDY: *The Latin root -dom- means "master" or "building." Answer each of the following questions using one of these words containing -dom-: domicile, dominant, domesticate.*

1. What do people do in a *domicile*?

   _____

2. If you are a *dominant* figure in politics, what kind of position would you hold?

   _____

3. What happens when you *domesticate* an animal?

   _____

"Icarus and Daedalus" by Josephine Preston Peabody
"Demeter and Persephone" by Anne Terry White
Integrated Language Skills: Grammar

Punctuation: Colons

A **colon** looks like two periods, one above the other (:). Colons are used to introduce a list that follows an independent clause.

To make wings, Daedalus gathered the following materials: feathers, wax, and thread.

A. PRACTICE: *Each of the following sentences is missing a colon. Rewrite the sentences, and insert a colon in the correct place.*

1. All of the characters in "Demeter and Persephone" are gods or goddesses Aphrodite, Eros, Pluto, Persephone, Demeter, Zeus, and Hermes.

   _____

   _____

2. Daedalus warns Icarus not to do these things fly too low, fly too high, and fly too far from him.

   _____

   _____

B. Writing Application: *Write two sentences about Greek mythology. In each sentence, use a colon to introduce a list.*

_____

_____

_____

_____

_____

_____

_____

_____

_____

_____

_____

_____

"Icarus and Daedalus" by Josephine Preston Peabody
"Demeter and Persephone" by Anne Terry White

Integrated Language Skills: Support for Writing a Myth

Use the following graphic organizer to take notes for a **myth** you will write to explain a natural phenomenon. You do not have to respond to each prompt in the chart in the order in which it appears, but you should probably decide on the phenomenon you want to explain before you decide on anything else. You might describe the problem and the resolution next and then work on the characters. Coming up with the title may be the last thing you do.

Natural phenomenon that myth will explain:
Title of myth:
Names and traits of characters—how they look, what they do, what they say to one another:
_____
_____
_____
_____
_____
_____
_____
_____
Problem to be solved and creative way in which it will be solved:
_____
_____
_____
_____
_____
_____
_____
_____
_____

Now, write the first draft of your myth.

Name _____ Date _____

Writing About the Big Question

Community or individual: Which is more important?

Big Question Vocabulary

common	community	culture	custom	diversity
duty	environment	ethnicity	family	group
individual	team	tradition	unify	unique

A. *Use one or more words from the list above to complete each sentence.*

1. Gary's volunteer _____ was made up of twenty workers.

2. Each worker contributed something _____ to the project.

3. As they worked together, they developed a strong sense of _____.

4. The work was hard, but they stayed focused on their _____ goal.

B. *Follow the directions in responding to each of the items below.*

1. List two different times when you worked with others on a school or community project.

   _____.

   _____.

2. Write two sentences explaining how your involvement in one of the preceding projects made you feel. Use at least two of the Big Question vocabulary words.

   _____

   _____

   _____

   _____

C. *Complete the sentence below. Then, write a short paragraph in which you connect this situation to the big question.*

Protecting a community sometimes requires that individuals _____

_____

_____

_____

_____

Name _____ Date _____

"**Tenochtitlan: Inside the Aztec Capital**" by Jacqueline Dineen
Reading: Reread to Look for Connections That Indicate Cause-and-Effect Relationships

A **cause** is an event or a situation that produces an **effect,** or the result produced. In a story or an essay, each effect may eventually become a cause for the next event. This series of events results in a cause-and-effect chain, which propels the action forward.

As you read, think about the causes and effects of events. If you do not see a clear cause-and-effect relationship in a passage, **reread to look for connections** in the text. Look for words and phrases that identify cause-and-effect relationships—for example, *because, due to, for that reason, therefore,* and *as a result.*

DIRECTIONS: *Read the following sequences of events. Underline any words or phrases that help you identify a cause-and-effect relationship. Then, identify each event as a* cause, *an* effect, *or both* cause and effect.

_____ 1. The Aztecs were excellent engineers.

_____ 2. Therefore, they were able to build three causeways linking the island city to the mainland.

_____ 3. Because of their skill as engineers, they were also able to build bridges that could be removed.

_____ 4. As a result, they could prevent their enemies from reaching the city.

_____ 5. The land around Lake Texcoco was dry.

_____ 6. Because the land was dry, the Aztecs built ditches to irrigate the land.

_____ 7. As they dug, they piled up the earth from the ditches in shallow parts of the lake, thus forming swamp gardens.

_____ 8. Because they had formed swamp gardens, they had land on which to grow crops.

_____ 9. Because they had land on which to grow crops, a portion of the population was able to grow its own food.

_____ 10. Two of the lakes that fed into Lake Texcoco contained salt water.

_____ 11. For that reason, the Aztecs built an embankment to keep out the salt water.

_____ 12. The embankment also protected the city from floods.

Name _____ Date _____

Literary Analysis: Legends and Facts

A **legend** is a traditional story about the past. Legends are based on facts that have grown into fiction over generations of retelling. Legends usually include these elements: a larger-than-life hero or heroine; fantastic events; roots, or a basis, in historical facts; and actions and events that reflect the culture that created the legend.

A **fact** is something that can be proved true. We uncover facts about ancient cultures by studying a variety of sources: written material, paintings, objects, and excavated ruins. When historians are unable to prove a theory about the past, they may speculate, or make a guess, based on the available evidence.

DIRECTIONS: *Read each excerpt from "Tenochtitlan: Inside the Aztec Capital." Then, circle whether the statement describes a* fact *or a* speculation, *and explain how you know.*

1. The Aztecs . . . built three causeways over the swamp to link the city with the mainland.

   Fact / Speculation: _____

   _____

2. These bridges could be removed to leave gaps, and this prevented enemies from get-ting to the city.

   Fact / Speculation: _____

   _____

3. The Spaniards' first view of Tenochtitlan was described by one of Cortés's soldiers, Bernal Diaz.

   Fact / Speculation: _____

   _____

4. Tenochtitlan was built in a huge valley, the Valley of Mexico.

   Fact / Speculation: _____

   _____

5. Archaeologists think that when Tenochtitlan was at its greatest, about one million people lived in the Valley of Mexico.

   Fact / Speculation: _____

   _____

6. Historians are not sure how many people in Tenochtitlan were farmers, but they think it may have been between one third and one half of the population.

   Fact / Speculation: _____

   _____

"Tenochtitlan: Inside the Aztec Capital" by Jacqueline Dineen
Vocabulary Builder

Word List

causeways   goblets   irrigation   nobility   outskirts   reeds

A. DIRECTIONS: *Read each item, and think about the meaning of the underlined word from the Word List. Then, answer each question, and explain your answer.*

1. Poorer people lived on the <u>outskirts</u> of Tenochtitlan. Did they live near the Temple Mayor?

   _____

   _____

2. <u>Reeds</u> were cut down in the swamps, dried, and woven into baskets. Are reeds trees?

   _____

   _____

3. The host passed <u>goblets</u> to his guests. Was he serving food?

   _____

   _____

4. People used <u>causeways</u> to travel to the mainland. Did they travel through tunnels?

   _____

   _____

5. The Aztecs dug <u>irrigation</u> ditches around their chinampas. Did these ditches carry water?

   _____

   _____

6. The <u>nobility</u> lived in homes near the city center. Would their homes be smaller than the farmers' homes?

   _____

   _____

B. WORD STUDY: *The prefix* out- *means "outside" or "more than." Answer each of the following questions using one of these words containing* out-: *outcast, outlaw, outplays.*

1. Why would you expect an *outcast* to have few friends?

   _____

2. Why might an *outlaw* be wanted by the police?

   _____

3. What happens when an opposing team *outplays* your team?

   _____

Name _____ Date _____

Writing About the Big Question

Community or individual: Which is more important?

Big Question Vocabulary

common	community	culture	custom	diversity
duty	environment	ethnicity	family	group
individual	team	tradition	unify	unique

A. *Use one or more words from the list above to complete each sentence.*

1. Cassie's coach begins each new season with a special _____.

2. She always hosts a _____ dinner the night before the first game.

3. Cassie doesn't want to go this year, but she feels it is her _____.

4. The coach sees the dinner as a way to _____ the team.

B. *Follow the directions in responding to each of the items below.*

1. List two examples that show the value of tradition or community involvement.

   _____

   _____

2. Write two sentences describing one of the preceding examples and explain how it benefits those involved. Use at least two of the Big Question vocabulary words.

   _____

   _____

   _____

   _____

C. *Complete the sentences below. Then, write a short paragraph in which you connect this idea to the big question.*

Tradition and **duty** to one's **community** should _____

_____

_____

_____

_____

Name _____ Date _____

"Popocatepetl and Ixtlaccihuatl" by Juliet Piggott Wood

Reading: Reread to Look for Connections That Indicate Cause-and-Effect Relationships

A **cause** is an event or a situation that produces an **effect,** or the result produced. In a story or an essay, each effect may eventually become a cause for the next event. This series of events results in a cause-and-effect chain, which propels the action forward.

As you read, think about the causes and effects of events. If you do not see a clear cause-and-effect relationship in a passage, **reread to look for connections** in the text. Look for words and phrases that identify cause-and-effect relationships—for example, *because, due to, for that reason, therefore,* and *as a result.*

DIRECTIONS: *Read the following sequences of events. Underline any words or phrases that help you identify a cause-and-effect relationship. Then, identify each event as a* cause, *an* effect, *or both* cause and effect.

_____ 1. The Emperor wants Ixtla to rule the empire after he dies.

_____ 2. Therefore, Ixtla becomes more serious and more studious.

_____ 3. Ixtla also studies harder because she has fallen in love.

_____ 4. The Emperor becomes ill.

_____ 5. As a result, he rules the empire less effectively.

_____ 6. Because the empire has grown weaker, enemies are emboldened to surround it.

_____ 7. Because enemies surround the empire, the Emperor commands his warriors to defeat them.

_____ 8. Jealous warriors tell the Emperor that Popo has been killed in battle.

_____ 9. The Emperor tells Ixtla that Popo has died.

_____ 10. Because she is heartbroken and does not want to marry anyone but Popo, Ixtla grows sick and dies.

_____ 11. When Popo learns the circumstances of Ixtla's death, he kills the warriors who lied to the Emperor.

_____ 12. Popo grieves for Ixtla.

_____ 13. Therefore, Popo instructs the warriors to build two pyramids.

_____ 14. Popo stands atop the second pyramid, holding a burning torch.

_____ 15. Over time, the pyramids became mountains.

"Popocatepetl and Ixtlaccihuatl" by Juliet Piggott Wood
Literary Analysis: Legends and Facts

A **legend** is a traditional story about the past. A legend generally starts out as a story based on **fact**—something that can be proved true. Over the course of many generations, however, the story is retold and transformed into fiction. It becomes a legend.

Every culture has its own legends to immortalize real people who were famous in their time. Most legends include these elements:

- a larger-than-life hero or heroine
- fantastic events
- roots, or a basis, in historical facts
- actions and events that reflect the culture that created the legend

A powerful Aztec emperor wants to pass his kingdom on to his daughter, Ixtlaccihuatl, or Ixtla. Ixtla studies hard so that she will be worthy of this role. She loves Popocatepetl, or Popo, a brave and strong warrior in the service of the emperor. The emperor, Ixtla, and Popo are three larger-than-life characters who will form the basis of the legend.

DIRECTIONS: *Read each excerpt from "Popocatepetl and Ixtlaccihuatl." On the line, identify the element or elements of a legend that the passage reflects, and briefly explain how you recognized the element.*

1. The pass through which the Spaniards came to the ancient Tenochtitlan is still there, as are the volcanoes on each side of that pass. Their names have not been changed. The one to the north is Ixtlaccihuatl and the one on the south of the pass is Popocatepetl.

   Element of legend: _____

   Explanation: _____

2. There was once an Aztec Emperor in Tenochtitlan. He was very powerful. Some thought he was wise as well, whilst others doubted his wisdom.

   Element of legend: _____

   Explanation: _____

3. As time went on natural leaders emerged and, of these, undoubtedly Popo was the best. Finally it was he, brandishing his club and shield, who led the great charge of running warriors across the valley, with their enemies fleeing before them.

   Element of legend: _____

   Explanation: _____

4. So Popocatepetl stood there, holding the torch in memory of Ixtlaccihuatl, for the rest of his days.
   The snows came and, as the years went by, the pyramids of stone became high white-capped mountains.

   Element of legend: _____

   Explanation: _____

"**Popocatepetl and Ixtlaccihuatl**" by Juliet Piggott Wood
Vocabulary Builder

Word List

decreed   feebleness   relish   routed   shortsightedness   unanimous

A. DIRECTIONS: *Answer each question after thinking about the meaning of the underlined word from the Word List. Then, explain your answer.*

1. When the Emperor <u>decreed</u> that the triumphant warrior would marry his daughter, did he ask a question?

   _____

2. Would the story have ended happily if the warriors' support for Popo had been <u>unanimous</u>?

   _____

3. Would the Emperor have shown <u>shortsightedness</u> by considering the needs of his kingdom after his death?

   _____

4. When the warriors <u>routed</u> the enemy, did the battles continue?

   _____

5. Did the Emperor's <u>feebleness</u> inspire him to lead his warriors into battle?

   _____

6. Did Ixtla <u>relish</u> the idea of marrying Popo?

   _____

B. WORD STUDY: *The Latin prefix* uni- *means "having or consisting of only one." Answer each of the following questions using one of these words containing* uni-*: unicycle, unicorn, unite.*

1. Why would it be challenging to balance on a *unicycle*?

   _____

2. What is a *unicorn* said to have on its forehead?

   _____

3. If two separate groups *unite*, what do they form?

   _____

All-in-One Workbook
295

"Tenochtitlan: Inside the Aztec Capital" by Jacqueline Dineen
"Popocatepetl and Ixtlaccihuatl" by Juliet Piggott Wood
Integrated Language Skills: Grammar

Commas and Semicolons

A **comma** (,) is used in the following ways:

Function	Example
to separate two independent clauses that are joined by a conjunction	One mountain is called Popocatepetl, and the other one is called Ixtlaccihuatl.
to separate three or more words, phrases, or clauses in a series	There were goblets for pulque and other drinks, graters for grinding chilis, and storage pots of various designs.
after an introductory word, phrase, or clause	Unfortunately, some warriors were jealous of Popo. On an island in a swampy lake, the Aztecs built a city. As the city grew, more and more land was drained.

The **semicolon** (;) looks like a period above a comma. It has two main uses:

Function	Example
to join independent clauses that are not joined by a conjunction	One mountain is called Popocatepetl; the other one is called Ixtlaccihuatl.
to separate items in a series when one or more of the items itself contains a comma	The three main characters in the legend are the Emperor; his daughter, Ixtla; and Popo, a warrior.

A. PRACTICE: *Each sentence is missing one or more commas or semicolons. Rewrite each sentence with the correct punctuation.*

1. The family consisted of a couple their married children and their grandchildren.

   _____

2. Aztec houses were very plain everyone slept on mats of reeds.

   _____

B. WRITING APPLICATION: *Write two sentences about the Aztecs. In one, use one or more semicolons, and in the other, use one or more commas.*

_____

_____

_____

_____

All-in-One Workbook
296

Name _____ Date _____

Integrated Language Skills: Support for Writing a Description

Use this chart to take notes as you prepare to write a **description** of Tenochtitlan or Ixtla. Write down as many details as you can to describe the various aspects of the city or of Ixtla's character. Include verbs and adjectives that appeal to the five senses: sight, touch, taste, smell, and hearing.

Background information about Tenochtitlan (When was it built? Where was it located?) or about Ixtla (Who is she? What is she like? What is expected of her?):
Physical description of Tenochtitlan or Ixtla:
Activities in which Ixtla or the residents of Tenochtitlan take part:

Now, use your notes to write a draft of a description of the city of Tenochtitlan or the character of Ixtla. Be sure to use vivid verbs and adjectives that will make your description interesting to your readers. Use words that appeal to the senses of sight, touch, taste, smell, and hearing.

Name _____ Date _____

"To the Top of Everest" by Samantha Larson
"The Voyage from Tales from the Odyssey" by Mary Pope Osborne
Writing About the Big Question

Community or individual: Which is more important?

Big Question Vocabulary

common	community	culture	custom	diversity
duty	environment	ethnicity	family	group
individual	team	tradition	unify	unique

A. *Use one or more words from the list above to complete each sentence.*

1. The _____ of rock climbers prepared for their journey.

2. They had a _____ goal of reaching the summit.

3. They were awed by the _____ of flora and fauna around them.

4. They felt fortunate to be in such a beautiful _____ .

B. *Follow the directions in responding to each of the items below.*

1. List two times when you traveled to a new place. _____ .

_____

2. Write two sentences describing one of the preceding experiences, and explain how it affected your view of the world. Use at least two of the Big Question vocabulary words.

_____

_____

C. *Complete the sentence below. Then, write a short paragraph in which you connect this idea to the big question.*

Travel enriches an individual's view of the world. A community of travelers

_____

_____

_____

_____

_____

_____

_____

"To the Top of Everest" by Samantha Larson
"The Voyage from Tales from the Odyssey" by Mary Pope Osborne
Literary Analysis: Comparing Universal Themes

A universal theme is a message about life that is expressed regularly in many different cultures and time periods. Universal themes include the importance of courage, the power of love, and the danger of greed. Universal themes are often found in epics, or stories or long poems about the adventures of a larger-than-life hero. Epic tales usually focus on the hero's bravery, strength, and success in battle or adventure. In addition to telling the story of a hero, an epic is a portrait of the culture that produced it. The following **epic conventions** are traditional characteristics of this form of literature:

- An epic involves a dangerous journey, or *quest*, that the hero must take.
- Gods or powerful characters help the hero.
- The setting of an epic is broad, covering several nations or even the universe.
- The style is serious and formal.

Because epics have become an important part of the literature of different cultures, they often inspire the works of later generations. For example, it is not unusual to find an allusion, or reference, to the ancient Greek epic the *Odyssey* in a contemporary adventure story. As you read "To the Top of Everest" and "The Voyage from Tales from the Odyssey," look for the use of epic conventions in the stories.

DIRECTIONS: *Use the following chart to compare "To the Top of Everest" and "The Voyage from Tales of the Odyssey." If the information to answer a question does not appear in the selection, write* information not mentioned.

Questions	"To the Top of Everest"	"The Voyage from Tales from the Odyssey"
1. What is the setting?		
2. What dangerous journey is undertaken?		
3. Who helps along the journey?		
4. What is the character's attitude?		
5. What obstacles must be overcome?		
6. What is the outcome?		

"To the Top of Everest" by Samantha Larson
"The Voyage from Tales from the Odyssey" by Mary Pope Osborne
Vocabulary Builder

Word List

designated   impervious   inflicted   saturation

A. DIRECTIONS: *Think about the meaning of each italicized word from the Word List. Then, explain whether the sentence makes sense. If it does not make sense, write a new sentence. In the new sentence, use the italicized word correctly.*

1. Jenna *inflicted* comfort with her gentle touch.

   Explanation: _____

   New sentence: _____

2. The leaky bottle resulted in the *saturation* of Emma's cotton bib.

   Explanation: _____

   New sentence: _____

3. We *designated* our star player as our choice for team captain.

   Explanation: _____

   New sentence: _____

4. Her proud smile suggested she was *impervious* to our compliments.

   Explanation: _____

   New sentence: _____

B. DIRECTIONS: *Write the letter of the word that means the same or about the same as the word from the Word List.*

____ 1. designated
   A. designed   C. described
   B. arranged   D. marked

____ 2. impervious
   A. unaffected   C. lazy
   B. angry   D. bored

____ 3. inflicted
   A. stopped   C. caused
   B. soothed   D. increased

"To the Top of Everest" by Samantha Larson
"The Voyage from Tales from the Odyssey" by Mary Pope Osborne
Support for Writing to Compare Universal Themes

Use this graphic organizer to take notes for an **essay** in which you compare and contrast the themes of "To the Top of Everest" and "The Voyage from Tales from the Odyssey."

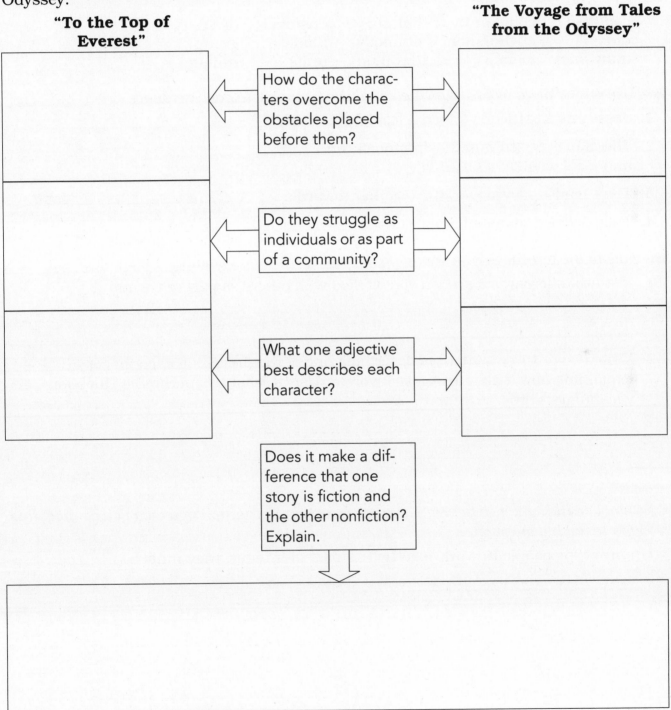

"To the Top of Everest"

"The Voyage from Tales from the Odyssey"

How do the characters overcome the obstacles placed before them?

Do they struggle as individuals or as part of a community?

What one adjective best describes each character?

Does it make a difference that one story is fiction and the other nonfiction? Explain.

Now, use your notes to write an essay comparing and contrasting the themes of "To the Top of Everest" and "The Voyage from Tales from the Odyssey."

"Sun and Moon in a Box" by Ricahrd Erdoes and Alfonso Ortiz

Writing About the Big Question

Community or individual: Which is more important?

Big Question Vocabulary

common	community	culture	custom	diversity
duty	environment	ethnicity	family	group
individual	team	tradition	unify	unique

A. *Use one or more words from the list above to complete each sentence.*

1. Jesse and his friends joined a local fundraising _____.

2. The money raised would help protect the _____
   and local wildlife.

3. The friends enjoyed working together toward a _____ goal.

4. They decided to make it an annual _____ .

B. *Follow the directions in responding to each of the items below.*

1. List two different times when you worked with others as part of a team.

   _____

   _____

2. Write two or three sentences describing one of the preceding experiences and
   explaining how it affected those involved. Use at least two of the Big Question
   vocabulary words. _____

   _____

   _____

   _____

C. *Complete the sentence below. Then, write a short paragraph in which you connect this
   idea to the big question.*

   In order for people to work together as part of a team, they must _____

   _____

   _____

   _____

   _____

   _____

   _____

   _____

Name _____   Date _____

"Sun and Moon in a Box" by Richard Erdoes and Alfonso Ortiz
Reading: Use Prior Knowledge to Compare and Contrast

A **comparison** tells how two or more things are alike. A **contrast** tells how two or more things are different. When you **compare and contrast,** you recognize similarities and differences. You can often understand an unfamiliar concept by **using your prior knowledge to compare and contrast.** For example, you may understand an ancient culture better if you look for ways in which it is similar to and different from your own culture. You also might find similarities and differences between a story told long ago and one that is popular today. To compare and contrast stories, ask questions such as "What does this event bring to mind?" or "Does this character make me think of someone I know or have read about?"

DIRECTIONS: Read each passage from "Sun and Moon in a Box." In the second column of the chart, write a question that will help you compare or contrast the passage to something else you have read or to something or someone you know or know about. In the third column, write the answer to your question. The first item has been completed as an example.

Passage from "Sun and Moon in a Box"	Question Based on My Prior Knowledge	Comparison or Contrast
1. Coyote and Eagle were hunting. Eagle caught rabbits. Coyote caught nothing but grasshoppers. Coyote said, "Friend Eagle, my chief, we make a great hunting pair."	How are these characters like Wile E. Coyote and Road Runner in the cartoons I used to watch?	Road Runner is a bird, but not an eagle, and Wile E. Coyote tries to catch him. Here, the coyote and the eagle seem to be friends.
2. Whenever [the Kachinas] wanted light they opened the lid and let the sun peek out. Then, it was day. When they wanted less light, they opened the box just a little for the moon to look out.		
3. After a while Coyote called Eagle, "My chief, let me have the box. I am ashamed to let you do all the carrying." "No," said Eagle, "You are not reliable. You might be curious and open the box."		
4. [Coyote] sat down and opened the box. In a flash, . . . icy winds made all living things shiver. Then, before Coyote could put the lid back, . . . snow fell down from heaven and covered the plains and the mountains.		

"Sun and Moon in a Box" by Richard Erdoes and Alfonso Ortiz

Literary Analysis: Cultural Context

Stories such as fables, folk tales, and myths are influenced by cultural context. **Cultural context** is the background, customs, and beliefs of the people who originally told them. Knowing the cultural context of a work will help you understand and appreciate it. You can keep track of the cultural context of a work by considering these elements: the *title* of the selection, the *time* in which it takes place, the *place* in which it takes place, the *customs* of the characters, the *beliefs* that are expressed or suggested.

Consider this passage from "Sun and Moon in a Box":

Now, at this time, the earth was still soft and new. There was as yet no sun and no moon.

The passage tells you that the folk tale is set in the distant past, before Earth looked as it does today and before there was a sun and a moon. From the cultural context, you can infer that the people who told the tale believed there was a time when Earth existed, but the sun and the moon as yet did not.

DIRECTIONS: *Read each passage from "Sun and Moon in a Box." In the second column of the chart, indicate which element of the cultural context—*time, place, customs, *or* beliefs—*the passage illustrates. Then, explain your choice. Tell why you think the example shows the element you have chosen.*

Passage from "Sun and Moon in a Box"	Element of Cultural Context and Explanation
1. [Eagle and Coyote] went toward the west. They came to a deep canyon.	
2. Whenever [the Kachinas] wanted light they opened the lid and let the sun peek out. . . . When they wanted less light, they opened the box just a little for the moon to look out.	
3. "Let us steal the box," said Coyote. "No, that would be wrong," said Eagle. "Let us just borrow it."	
4. Eagle grabbed the box and . . . Coyote ran after him on the ground. After a while Coyote called Eagle: "My chief, let me have the box. I am ashamed to let you do all the carrying."	

"Sun and Moon in a Box" by Richard Erdoes and Alfonso Ortiz
Vocabulary Builder

Word List

cunning   curiosity   pestering   regretted   relented   reliable

A. DIRECTIONS: *Circle* T *if the statement is* true *or* F *if it is* false. *Then, explain your answer.*

1. A car that starts only half the time is *reliable.*

   T / F _____

   _____

2. A teacher who refuses her students' pleas to make a test easier has *relented.*

   T / F _____

   _____

3. Someone who always gets caught cheating is *cunning.*

   T / F _____

   _____

4. A man who thoroughly disliked a movie, probably *regretted* going to see it.

   T / F _____

   _____

5. Parents would be charmed by a child who is *pestering* them.

   T / F _____

   _____

6. A gossipy neighbor's *curiosity* naturally leads him to mind his own business.

   T / F _____

   _____

B. WORD STUDY: *The Latin suffix* -ity *means "state, quality, or condition of." Answer each of the following questions using one of these words containing* -ity: *elasticity, sincerity, predictability.*

1. How might you test an object's *elasticity?*

   _____

2. What might lead you to question a person's *sincerity?*

   _____

3. Why might you appreciate a coworker's *predictability?*

   _____

"**How the Snake Got Poison**" by Zora Neale Hurston

Writing About the Big Question

Community or individual: Which is more important?

Big Question Vocabulary

common	community	culture	custom	diversity
duty	environment	ethnicity	family	group
individual	team	tradition	unify	unique

A. *Use one or more words from the list above to complete each sentence.*

1. As an _____ , Snake had the right to protect himself.

2. However, he presented a threat to members of the larger _____.

3. They lived in an _____ of fear and anxiety.

4. For the _____ good of all involved, compromise was necessary.

B. *Follow the directions in responding to each of the items below.*

1. List a time when your needs or the needs of someone you know were in conflict with the needs of family, neighbors, classmates, or any larger community.

   _____

   _____

2. Write two sentences explaining the preceding experience and describe how the situation was resolved. Use at least two of the Big Question vocabulary words.

   _____

   _____

   _____

C. *Complete the sentence below. Then, write a short paragraph in which you connect this situation to the big question.*

When the needs of the **individual** and the needs of the larger **group** are in conflict,

_____

_____

_____

_____

_____

_____

Name _____ Date _____

Reading: Use Prior Knowledge to Compare and Contrast

A **comparison** tells how two or more things are alike. A **contrast** tells how two or more things are different. When you **compare and contrast,** you recognize similarities and differences. You can often understand an unfamiliar concept by **using your prior knowledge to compare and contrast.** For example, you may understand an ancient culture better if you look for ways in which it is similar to and different from your own culture. You also might find similarities and differences between a story told long ago and one that is popular today. To compare and contrast stories, ask questions such as "What does this event bring to mind?" or "Does this character make me think of someone I know or have read about?"

DIRECTIONS: *Read each passage from "How the Snake Got Poison." In the second column of the chart, write a question that will help you compare or contrast the passage to something else you have read or to something or someone you know or know about. In the third column, write the answer to your question. The first item has been completed as an example.*

Passage from "How the Snake Got Poison"	Question Based on My Prior Knowledge	Comparison or Contrast
1. "Ah ain't so many, God, you put me down here on my belly in de dust and everything trods upon me and kills off my generations. Ah ain't got no kind of protection at all."	How does this snake compare with Nag and Nagaina in the story "Rikki-tikki-tavi"?	Like this snake, Nag and Nagaina can talk. They also have a problem protecting themselves and their unborn children.
2. "God, please do somethin' 'bout dat snake. He' layin' in de bushes there wid poison in his mouf and he's strikin' everything dat shakes de bushes. He's killin' up our generations."		
3. "Lawd, you know Ah'm down here in de dust. Ah ain't got no claws to fight wid, and Ah ain't got no feets to git me out de way. All Ah kin see is feets comin' to tromple me. Ah can't tell who my enemy is. . . ."		
4. "Well, snake, I don't want yo' generations all stomped out and I don't want you killin' everything else dat moves. Here take dis bell and tie it to yo' tail."		

"**How the Snake Got Poison**" by Zora Neale Hurston
Literary Analysis: Cultural Context

Stories such as fables, folk tales, and myths are influenced by cultural context. **Cultural context** is the background, customs, and beliefs of the people who originally told them. Knowing the cultural context of a work will help you understand and appreciate it. You can keep track of the cultural context of a work by considering these elements: the *title* of the selection, the *time* in which it takes place, the *place* in which it takes place, the *customs* of the characters, the *beliefs* that are expressed or suggested.

Consider this passage from "How the Snake Got Poison":

Well, when God made de snake he put him in de bushes to ornament de ground.

The passage tells you that the folk tale is set in the distant past. From the cultural context, you can infer that the people who told the tale held beliefs about the purpose of the snake in nature.

DIRECTIONS: *These passages from "How the Snake Got Poison" illustrate the folk tale's cultural context by suggesting beliefs held by the people who told the tale. In the second column of the chart, tell what belief the passage illustrates.*

Passage from "How the Snake Got Poison"	Suggested Belief
1. God . . . said, "Ah didn't mean for nothin' to be stompin' you snakes lak dat. You got to have some kind of a protection. Here, take dis poison and put it in yo' mouf and when they tromps on you, protect yo'self."	
2. "Snake, . . . Ah didn't mean for you to be hittin' and killin' everything dat shake de bush. I give you dat poison and tole you to protect yo'self when they tromples on you. But you killin' everything dat moves."	
3. "Here take dis bell and tie it to yo' tail. When you hear feets comin' you ring yo' bell and if it's yo' friend, he'll be keerful. If it's yo' enemy, it's you and him."	

Name _____ Date _____

"How the Snake Got Poison" by Zora Neale Hurston
Vocabulary Builder

Word List

immensity   ornament   suit   varmints

A. DIRECTIONS: *Circle* T *if the statement is* true *or* F *if it is* false. *Then, explain your answer.*

1. Colored lights and Chinese lanterns will *ornament* a backyard party.

   T / F _____

   _____

2. An *immensity* can easily be fenced in.

   T / F _____

   _____

3. A bright green dress *suits* a rosy complexion.

   T / F _____

   _____

4. Gardeners hope their gardens will attract *varmints*.

   T / F _____

   _____

B. WORD STUDY: *The Latin suffix* -ity *means "state, quality, or condition of." Answer each of the following questions using one of these words containing* -ity: *marketability, integrity, enmity.*

1. Why should a company consider the *marketability* of its products?

   _____

2. Why might a politician who lacks *integrity* lose an election?

   _____

3. How would you respond to someone who treats you with *enmity*?

   _____

Name _____   Date _____

Integrated Language Skills: Grammar

Capitalization is the use of uppercase letters (*A, B, C,* and so on). Capital letters signal the beginning of a sentence or a quotation and identify proper nouns and proper adjectives. **Proper nouns** include the names of people, geographical locations, specific events and time periods, organizations, languages, and religions. **Proper adjectives** are derived from proper nouns.

Use of Capital Letter	Example
Sentence beginning	**T**he coyote was a bad swimmer. **H**e nearly drowned.
Quotation	The snake said, "**Y**ou know I'm down here in the dust."
Proper nouns	They traveled through the **S**outhwest.
Proper adjectives	Coyote might have run as far as the **M**exican border.

A. PRACTICE: *Rewrite each sentence below. Use capitalization correctly.*

1. the character named coyote suggested that they steal the box.

   _____

2. the folk tale takes place in the american southwest, perhaps in present-day arizona or new mexico.

   _____

   _____

3. coyote said to eagle, "this is a wonderful thing."

   _____

4. "i do not trust you," eagle said many times. "you will open that box."

   _____

B. Writing Application: *Write a short episode telling what Coyote might have done after he let the sun and the moon escape from the box. Include at least one quotation, one proper noun, and one proper adjective. Use capitalization correctly.*

_____

_____

_____

_____

_____

Name _____ Date _____

"Sun and Moon in a Box" by Richard Erdoes and Alfonso Ortiz
"How the Snake Got Poison" by Zora Neale Hurston

Integrated Language Skills: Support for Writing a Plot Summary

Use this chart to take notes for a **plot summary** of "Sun and Moon in a Box" or "How the Snake Got Poison."

Plot Summary

Setting:		
Major character 1:	**Major character 2:**	
Main event from beginning of folk tale:	**Main event from middle of folk tale:**	**Main event from end of folk tale:**
Final outcome:		

Now, use your notes to write your **plot summary.** Be sure to include all the information called for on the chart.

Name _____ Date _____

Community or individual: Which is more important?

Big Question Vocabulary

common	community	culture	custom	diversity
duty	environment	ethnicity	family	group
individual	team	tradition	unify	unique

A. *Use one or more words from the list above to complete each sentence.*

1. America has not always embraced the _____ of its population.

2. Some people were discriminated against because of their _____.

3. When people came together as a _____ , they made a difference.

4. There was power in their _____ that could not be denied.

B. *Follow the directions in responding to each of the items below.*

1. List two different groups of people who struggled against oppression.

   _____   _____

2. Write two sentences describing what helped unify one of the preceding groups in their efforts. Use at least two of the Big Question vocabulary words.

   _____

   _____

   _____

C. *Complete the sentence below. Then, write a short paragraph in which you connect this situation to the big question.*

In order to unify people who share a common struggle, _____

_____

_____

_____

_____

_____

_____

_____

"The People Could Fly" by Virginia Hamilton

Reading: Use a Venn Diagram to Compare and Contrast

When you **compare and contrast,** you recognize similarities and differences. You can compare and contrast elements in a literary work by **using a Venn diagram** to examine character traits, situations, and ideas. First, reread the text to locate the details you will compare. Then, write the details on a diagram like the ones shown below. Recording these details will help you understand the similarities and differences in a literary work.

DIRECTIONS: *Fill in the Venn diagrams as directed to make comparisons about elements of "The People Could Fly."*

1. Compare Toby and Sarah. Write characteristics of Toby in the left-hand oval and characteristics of Sarah in the right-hand oval. Write characteristics that they share in the overlapping part of the two ovals.

Toby　　　　　　　　　　　**Both**　　　　　　　　　　　**Sarah**

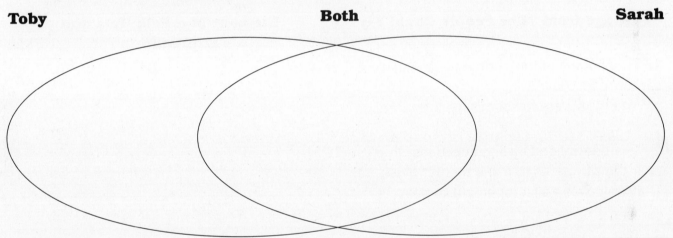

2. Compare the enslaved people with the Overseer and Driver. Write characteristics of the enslaved people in the left-hand oval and characteristics of the Overseer and Driver in the right-hand oval. Write characteristics that they share in the overlapping part of the two ovals.

Enslaved People　　　　　　　　　**Both**　　　　　　**Overseer and Driver**

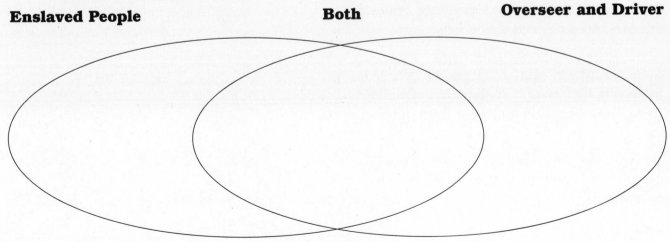

"The People Could Fly" by Virginia Hamilton
Literary Analysis: Folk Tale

A **folk tale** is a story that is composed orally and then passed from person to person by word of mouth. Although folk tales originate in this **oral tradition,** many of them are eventually collected and written down. Similar folk tales are told by different cultures throughout the world. Such folk tales have common character types, plot elements, and themes. Folk tales often teach a lesson about life and present a clear separation between good and evil. Folk tales are part of the oral tradition that also includes fairy tales, legends, myths, fables, tall tales, and ghost stories.

DIRECTIONS: *Read each passage from "The People Could Fly." In the second column of the chart, indicate whether the passage* teaches a lesson about life *or whether it* clearly presents good, clearly presents evil, *or presents a clear distinction between the two. Then, explain your choice. Tell why you think the example shows the element you have chosen.*

Passage from "The People Could Fly"	Element of a Folk Tale and Explanation
1. Then, many of the people [in Africa] were captured for Slavery. . . . The folks were full of misery, then.	
2. The one called Driver cracked his whip over the slow ones to make them move faster. That whip was a slice-open cut of pain.	
3. The . . . woman fell to the earth. The old man that was there, Toby, came and helped her to her feet.	
4. A young man slave fell from the heat. The Driver come and whipped him. Toby come over and spoke words to the fallen one.	
5. "Take us with you!" . . . Toby couldn't take them with him. Hadn't the time to teach them to fly. They must wait for a chance to run.	
6. The slaves who could not fly told about the people who could fly to their children. When they were free.	

Name _____ Date _____

"The People Could Fly" by Virginia Hamilton
Vocabulary Builder

Word List

croon   hoed   mystery   scorned   shed   shuffle

A. DIRECTIONS: *Write the letter of the word or group of words that means* the opposite of *the vocabulary word.*

___ 1. scorned
   A. commanded   B. resigned   C. appreciated   D. hired

___ 2. croon
   A. sing softly   B. speak quietly   C. speak haltingly   D. sing loudly

___ 3. shuffle
   A. jump   B. walk quickly   C. drag   D. pull into

___ 4. mystery
   A. ritual   B. secret   C. explanation   D. magic

___ 5. shed
   A. put on   B. pull down   C. take off   D. drop

___ 6. hoed
   A. dug   B. straightened   C. released   D. planted

B. WORD STUDY: *The Greek root* -myst- *means "a secret rite." Answer each of the following questions using one of these words containing* -myst-: *mystified, mystical, mystic.*

1. How would you reply if you were *mystified* by a friend's request?

_____

_____

2. When might an ancient artifact be considered a *mystical* object?

_____

_____

3. Why might someone seek guidance from a *mystic*?

_____

_____

Name _____ Date _____

Writing About the Big Question

Community or individual: Which is more important?

Big Question Vocabulary

common	community	culture	custom	diversity
duty	environment	ethnicity	family	group
individual	team	tradition	unify	unique

A. *Use one or more words from the list above to complete each sentence.*

1. The two con men targeted a _____ of small-town residents.

2. They worked as a _____ to gain the residents' trust.

3. They offered a free seminar and created a friendly _____ .

4. Once they had what they wanted, both _____ disappeared.

5. After that, the _____ was wary of strangers offering free advice.

B. *Follow the directions in responding to each of the items below.*

1. List two people you have heard or read about who exploited others for personal gain.

   _____   _____

2. Write two sentences describing one of the preceding incidents and how it affected those involved. Use at least two of the Big Question vocabulary words.

   _____

   _____

   _____

C. *Complete the sentence below. Then, write a short paragraph in which you connect this situation to the big question.*

When an individual exploits others for personal gain, _____

   _____

   _____

   _____

   _____

"All Stories Are Anansi's" by Harold Courlander

Reading: Use a Venn Diagram to Compare and Contrast

When you **compare and contrast,** you recognize similarities and differences. You can compare and contrast elements in a literary work by **using a Venn diagram** to examine character traits, situations, and ideas. First, reread the text to locate the details you will compare. Then, write the details on a diagram like the ones shown below. Recording these details will help you understand the similarities and differences in a literary work.

DIRECTIONS: *Fill in the Venn diagrams as directed to make comparisons about elements of "All Stories Are Anansi's."*

1. Compare Anansi and Onini, the great python. Write characteristics of Anansi in the left-hand oval and characteristics of Onini in the right-hand oval. Write characteristics that they share in the overlapping part of the two ovals.

Anansi   **Both**   **Onini**

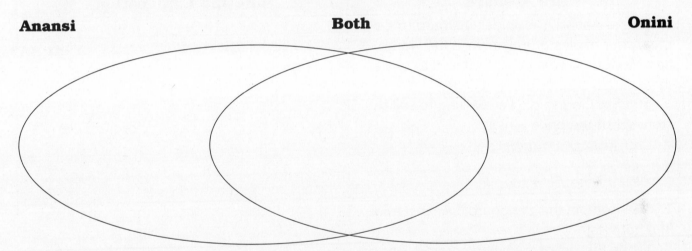

2. Compare Mmoboro, the hornets, with Osebo, the leopard. Write characteristics of the hornets in the left-hand oval and characteristics of the leopard in the right-hand oval. Write characteristics that they share in the overlapping part of the two ovals.

Hornets   **Both**   **Leopard**

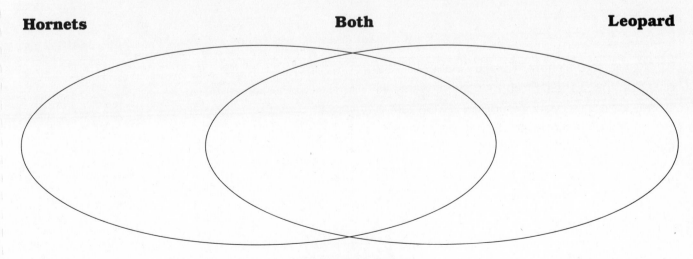

"All Stories Are Anansi's" by Harold Courlander
Literary Analysis: Folk Tale

A **folk tale** is a story that is composed orally and then passed from person to person by word of mouth. Although folk tales originate in this **oral tradition,** many of them are eventually collected and written down. Similar folk tales are told by different cultures throughout the world. Such folk tales have common character types, plot elements, and themes. Folk tales often teach a lesson about life and present a clear separation between good and evil. Folk tales are part of the oral tradition that also includes fairy tales, legends, myths, fables, tall tales, and ghost stories.

DIRECTIONS: *Read each passage from "All Stories Are Anansi's." In the second column of the chart, indicate what value or lesson about life the passage teaches. Then, explain your choice.*

Passage from "All Stories Are Anansi's"	Value or Lesson About Life and Explanation
1. Kwaku Anansi, the spider, yearned to be the owner of all stories known in the world, and he went to Nyame and offered to buy them. The Sky God said: "I am willing to sell the stories, but the price is high."	
2. "Go here, in this dry gourd," Anansi told [the hornets]. . . . When the last of them had entered, Anansi plugged the hole with a ball of grass, saying: "Oh, yes, but you are really foolish people!"	
3. Nyame said to him: "Kwaku Anansi, . . . I will give you the stories. From this day onward, all stories belong to you. Whenever a man tells a story, he must acknowledge that it is Anansi's tale."	

"All Stories Are Anansi's" by Harold Courlander
Vocabulary Builder

Word List

acknowledge   dispute   gourd   opinion   python   yearned

A. DIRECTIONS: *Write the letter of the word that means the same or about the same as the vocabulary word.*

____ 1. yearned
   A. rejected   B. questioned   C. desired   D. ignored

____ 2. gourd
   A. cup   B. fork   C. platter   D. knife

____ 3. acknowledge
   A. taunt   B. challenge   C. credit   D. dismiss

____ 4. python
   A. panther   B. snake   C. cougar   D. spider

____ 5. opinion
   A. statement   B. fact   C. statistic   D. belief

____ 6. dispute
   A. argument   B. lie   C. error   D. agreement

B. WORD STUDY: *The root -know- means "to understand." Answer each of the following questions using one of these words containing -know-: unknowingly, acknowledge, knowledgeable.*

1. How might you *unknowingly* hurt a friend's feelings?

   _____

   _____

2. How would you *acknowledge* a friend's presence?

   _____

   _____

3. Why would you ask a *knowledgeable* person a difficult question?

   _____

   _____

"The People Could Fly" by Virginia Hamilton
"All Stories Are Anansi's" by Harold Courlander

Integrated Language Skills: Grammar

Abbreviations

An **abbreviation** is a shortened form of a word or phrase. Most abbreviations end with a period, but many do not, and some may be written either with or without a period. Most dictionaries have entries for abbreviations, so look them up if you are not sure of the correct form. Note which abbreviations are written with periods, which ones are not, and which ones appear in capital letters in these lists:

Titles of persons: Mr. Ms. Mrs.

Days of the week: Sun. Mon. Tues. Wed. Thurs. Fri. Sat. Sun.

Months of the year: Jan. Feb. Mar. Apr. Aug. Sept. Oct. Nov. Dec.

Times of day: a.m. p.m.

Street designations: Ave. Blvd. Pl. St.

State postal abbreviations: AL AK AZ AR CA CO CT DE FL GA HI ID IL IN IA KS KY LA ME MD MA MI MN MS MO MT NE NV NH NJ NM NY NC ND OH OK OR PA RI SC SD TN TX UT VT VA WA WV WI WY

Organizations: NAACP UN YMCA

Units of measure: in. ft. yd. lb. qt. gal. *but* mm cm m mg g ml dl l

A. PRACTICE: *Rewrite each sentence below, and abbreviate the words in italics.*

1. James lives at 115 Elm *Street*, Pleasant Valley, *Nebraska.*

   _____

2. The gardener said that if your yard measures 50 *feet* (16.6 *yards*) by 40 *feet* (13.3 *yards*), you will need 2 *pounds* of fertilizer.

   _____

   _____

3. *Mister* Raymond works for the *United Nations*.

   _____

B. Writing Application: *Compose an e-mail message to a friend. Tell about something you have done recently. Use at least five abbreviations. If you are not sure of the correct form, look up the abbreviation in a dictionary.*

_____

_____

_____

_____

_____

Name _____ Date _____

Integrated Language Skills: Support for Writing a Review

Use this chart to take notes for a **review** of "The People Could Fly" or "All Stories Are Anansi's."

Notes for Review

Element of the Tale	My Opinion of the Element	Details From the Tale That Support My Opinion
Characters		
Description		
Dialogue		
Plot		

Now, write a draft of your review. Tell readers whether or not you think they will enjoy the folktale. Remember to support your opinions with details from the tale.

Name _____ Date _____

"The Fox Outwits the Crow" by William Cleary
Writing About the Big Question

Community or individual: Which is more important?

Big Question Vocabulary

common	community	culture	custom	diversity
duty	environment	ethnicity	family	group
individual	team	tradition	unify	unique

A. *Use one or more words from the list above to complete each sentence.*

1. People enjoyed listening to Leslie's _____ singing voice.

2. She frequently sang at _____ gatherings.

3. She felt it was her _____ to share her gift with others.

4. She did not want to use her talent for _____ gain.

B. *Follow the directions in responding to each of the items below.*

1. List two works of literature from which you have learned something significant.

   _____   _____

2. Write two sentences describing one of the works and what it taught you. Use at least two of the Big Question vocabulary words.

   _____

   _____

   _____

   _____

C. *Complete the sentence below. Then, write a short paragraph in which you connect this experience to the big question.*

   One of the purposes of literature is to teach individuals how to _____

   _____

   _____

   _____

   _____

   _____

"The Fox Outwits the Crow" by William Cleary
"The Fox and the Crow" by Aesop

Literary Analysis: Comparing Tone

The **tone** of a literary work is the writer's attitude toward his or her subject and characters. The tone can often be described by a single adjective, such as *formal, playful,* or *respectful.* To determine the tone of each selection, notice the words and phrases that the authors use to express their ideas.

The theme is a central message in a literary work. A theme can usually be expressed as a general statement about life. Although a theme may be stated directly in the text, it is more often presented indirectly. To figure out the theme of a work, look at what it reveals about people or life.

A. DIRECTIONS: *Compare the tone of the two selections by completing this chart. Choose one adjective to describe each passage. Use* serious, formal, informal, *or* playful.

"The Fox Outwits the Crow"	Adjective	"The Fox and the Crow"	Adjective
1. One day a young crow snatched a fat piece of cheese. . . .		A Fox once saw a Crow fly off with a piece of cheese in its beak. . . .	
2. A fox . . . got a whiff of the cheese, / The best of his favorite hors d'oeuvres, . . .		"That's for me, as I am a Fox," said Master Reynard, . . .	
3. Hey, you glamorous thing, / Does your voice match your beautiful curves?		"I feel sure your voice must surpass that of other birds, just as your figure does."	

B. DIRECTIONS: *Answer the following questions to determine the theme of each work.*

1. What are the characters' key traits?

   Poem: _____

   Fable: _____

2. What is the main conflict in the story?

   Poem: _____

   Fable: _____

3. What happens as a result?

   Poem: _____

   Fable: _____

4. What general statement about life does this outcome suggest?

   Poem: _____

   Fable: _____

"The Fox Outwits the Crow" by William Cleary
"The Fox and the Crow" by Aesop
Vocabulary Builder

Word List

flatterers   glossy   hors d'oeuvres   malice   surpass   whiff

A. DIRECTIONS: *Circle* T *if the statement is true or* F *if the statement is false. Then, explain your answer.*

1. A true bloodhound can follow someone's trail after getting only a *whiff* of the person's odor.

   T / F _____

2. *Flatterers* are honest and sincere.

   T / F _____

3. Something that is *glossy* has a rough finish.

   T / F _____

4. Most people would feel *malice* toward someone who has harmed them.

   T / F _____

5. *Hors d'oeuvres* are served after the main course.

   T / F _____

6. For a person to *surpass* expectations, he or she must do better than expected.

   T / F _____

B. DIRECTIONS: *For each pair of words in CAPITAL LETTERS, write the letter of the pair of words that best expresses a similar relationship.*

____ 1. OUTDO : SURPASS ::
    A. lose : win
    B. talk : remember
    C. work : play
    D. throw : toss

____ 2. WHIFF : SCENT ::
    A. sight : hearing
    B. good : bad
    C. love : adoration
    D. eyes : nose

____ 3. MALICE : GOODWILL ::
    A. stroll : walk
    B. painter : artist
    C. large : humongous
    D. blame : praise

"The Fox Outwits the Crow" by William Cleary
"The Fox and the Crow" by Aesop

Support for Writing to Compare Reactions to Tone and Theme

Use this graphic organizer to take notes for an essay that compares your reaction to the tone and theme in "The Fox Outwits the Crow" with your reaction to the tone and theme in "The Fox and the Crow."

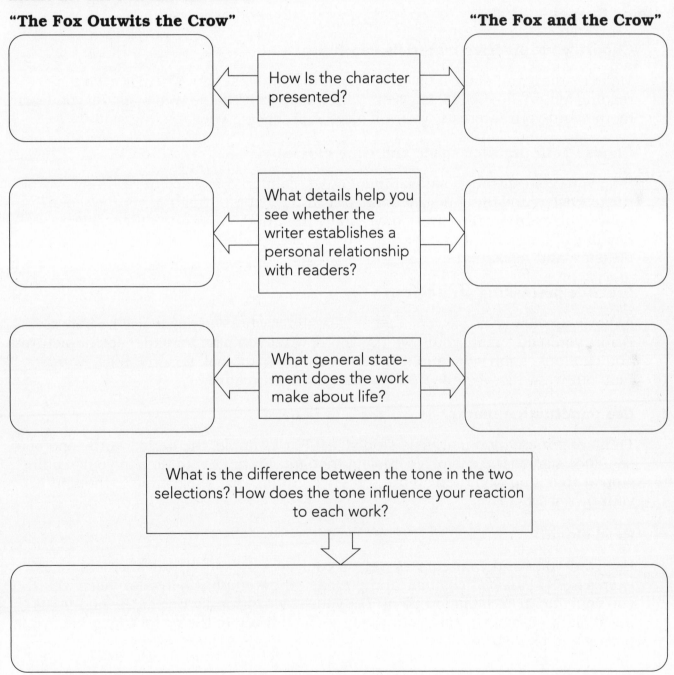

"The Fox Outwits the Crow"   **"The Fox and the Crow"**

How Is the character presented?

What details help you see whether the writer establishes a personal relationship with readers?

What general statement does the work make about life?

What is the difference between the tone in the two selections? How does the tone influence your reaction to each work?

Now, use your notes to write an essay in which you compare your reaction to the tone and theme of "The Fox Outwits the Crow" with your reaction to the tone and theme of "The Fox and the Crow."

All-in-One Workbook
325

Tips for Improving Your Reading Fluency

You've probably heard the expression "Practice makes perfect." Through your own experiences, you know that practice improves all types of skills. If you play a guitar, you know that practicing has made you a better player. The same is true for sports, for crafts, and for reading. The following tips will help you to practice skills that will lead to reading **fluency**—the ability to read easily, smoothly, and expressively.

Choose your practice materials carefully.

Make reading fun! Make a list of subjects that interest you. Then, search for reading materials—books, magazines, newspapers, reliable Web sites. As you learn more about your interests, you will also be practicing your reading skills.

Choose your practice space and time carefully.

Help your concentration skills. Find a quiet, comfortable place to read—away from the television and other distractions. Get in the habit of treating yourself to an hour of pleasure reading every day—apart from homework and other tasks. Reading about interesting topics in a quiet, comfortable place will provide both pleasure and relaxation.

Practice prereading strategies.

A movie preview gives viewers a good idea about what the movie will be about. Before you read, create your own preview of what you plan to read. Look at pictures and captions, subheads, and diagrams. As you scan, look for unfamiliar words. Find out what those words mean before you start reading.

Use punctuation marks.

Think of punctuation marks as stop signs. For example, the period at the end of a sentence signals the end of a complete thought. From time to time in your reading, stop at that stop sign. Reread the sentence. Summarize the complete thought in your own words.

Read aloud.

Use your voice and your ears as well as your eyes. Read phrases and sentences expressively. Pause at commas and periods. Show emphasis in your voice when you come to an exclamation point. Let your voice naturally rise at the end of a question. If possible, record your reading. Then listen to the recording, noting your pacing and expression.

Pause to ask questions.

Stop reading after a short amount of time (for example, five minutes) or at the end of a meaty paragraph. Look away from the text. Ask yourself questions—What are the main ideas? What message does the author want me to get? What might happen next? If the answers seem unclear, reread—either silently or aloud. Find the answers!

Use what you know.

As you read an informational article, think about what you already know about the topic. Use your knowledge and ideas as background information. Doing so will help you to understand new ideas. As you read fiction or a personal narrative, think about your own experiences. If you have been in a situation that is similar to that of a fictional character, you will be better able to understand his or her feelings, actions, and goals.

Talk about it.

Ask a friend or family member to read what you have read. Take turns reading aloud together, listening to both content and expression. Then discuss what you read. Share, compare, and contrast your ideas. Doing so will reinforce your knowledge of the content of what you read, and may provide new and interesting perspectives about the topic.

Reading Fluency Assessment Passage 1

Nonverbal communication is vital to expressing people's true thoughts and feelings. We watch how others move and stand when they speak; we hear the tone of their voice and notice their facial expressions and body language. All of this information is extremely important. Just think about it—has a person's[50] exquisite smile ever meant more to you than a hundred words that this individual might have spoken?

Signing is another critical form of communication. For those who can neither hear nor communicate verbally, signing is a powerful tool for listening and speaking. Many parents today are teaching their very young[100] children to sign so that they can communicate before they are able to talk.

Going beyond these forms of daily nonverbal communication are art forms created to speak to us without words. For example, the ancient art of drumming is considered a universal form of communication. As you listen to[150] people playing in a drum circle, you can feel their emotions. A drumbeat can sound serious or humorous, powerful or lighthearted. Drummers can tell entire stories. A drumbeat can take you to the top of a mountain or to the depths of the brilliant ocean.

Other art forms work wordlessly,[200] too: Rather than hearing a message, you see it. For example, a mime is a person who acts out complete scenes while remaining mute. Often appearing in slippered feet, mimes try to avoid creating any sounds. Even when a scene calls for jostling or other usually noisy encounters, a mime[250] succeeds in showing the action quietly. Watching a mime perform is like seeing a woodpecker at work through a soundproof window. You can hear what is happening but only in your mind. Through the silence, you can think more deeply about the action you see.[295]

950L

Check Your Understanding

1. Which of the following is not a form of nonverbal communication?

   a. signing
   b. smiling
   c. singing
   d. miming

2. Name two emotions that can be created by a drumbeat.

   _____

   _____

Reading Fluency Assessment Passage 2

Shoes protect our feet, but how they look has always seemed to matter as much as their ability to save our feet from cold, injury, and dirt. The first shoes were simply animal skins wrapped around the feet. Around the 1400s, however, shoes were becoming quite fancy.

Men who were[50] rich wore shoes with very long, pointed toes. Ribbons tied around the knees were used to hold the toes off the ground. After a day of trying to walk in such shoes, the wearers no doubt headed home quickly to their sore and aching feet!

Workers wore less complex shoes,[100] often with leather or wood bottoms strapped on to the feet with leather ties. At home, people might have worn soft fabric slippers. They would keep them on even after saying good-night and going to bed. What could feel better than toasty warm feet while you sleep?

In the 1850s,[150] an American shoemaker developed a machine that could sew the upper parts of shoes to their soles. He sold the rights of ownership to the machine to a factory owner, whereupon the first mass-produced shoes could be made. Since then, we have had shoes for every type of activity. We[200] have sports shoes, work shoes, and dress shoes. If you want, you can even find a pair of shoes to match your purse. In fact, our society might be described as shoe crazy. You can see people with one pair of shoes on their feet and another pair slung across[250] their shoulders.

Shoe fashion is big business today. Colors, styles, and materials are offered in huge variety. When you watch the brunettes and redheads on fashion show runways, be sure to look at their feet. These models will be wearing the latest shoe fashions to match their outfits.[298]

950L

Check Your Understanding

1. Describe two kinds of early shoes.

   _____

   _____

2. What happened when an American shoemaker sold his machine to a factory owner?

   _____

   _____

Reading Fluency Assessment Passage 3

As the sun sinks slowly behind the horizon each evening, darkness creeps across the land. For many animals, this hour is the time to wake up and become active. As you prepare for bed, these nighttime animals begin a busy day.

In a forest setting, as a person peers into[50] the growing gloom and hustles home before nightfall, small animals like the raccoon begin prowling around. These animals are on their nightly search for food. Red foxes, mule deer, and badgers join the raccoons on the hunt. All are as quiet as possible as they do not want to be[100] heard by those they hunt. Others are quiet to protect themselves from animals that hunt them.

The peacefulness of the night is rarely disturbed by loud animal sounds. If forest animals do make noise, they usually are raising an alarm. An enemy or a fire may have been sighted.

The[150] moon begins to gleam, revealing other creatures of the night. Bats whirr and swoop, feasting on mosquitoes. A barn owl glides gracefully through the night air, its white face shining. Its dive toward the ground will scatter all small animals aware of the owl's presence. They are afraid of becoming the[200] mighty bird's evening meal.

You might, one night, also spot a flying squirrel soaring through the trees until morning. It watches the action above and below its path. The flying squirrel's cousin, the tree squirrel, is active during the day and peacefully sleeps the night away in a snug nest.[250]

So, as you drift off into the land of dreams tonight, imagine creatures large and small roaming the night. If you listen very closely, you may hear the quiet whoosh of a squirrel or the soft patter of a fox.[299]

960L

Check Your Understanding

1. Why might animals make a loud noise at night.

_____

2. Name three animals that hunt for food at night in the forest.

_____

_____

_____

Reading Fluency Assessment Passage 4

In a wealthy British home during the 1800s, dozens of servants worked to make the household run smoothly. Male servants held the highest rank. The head female housekeeper was viewed as slightly inferior to the butler.

Truly, the head housekeeper ran the house. She handled everything from financial matters to[50] the supervision of cooking and cleaning. If any servants were viewed as lax in their duties, they would have to answer to the housekeeper. Yet, the butler was viewed as the "boss" of the servants. Why, then, was the housekeeper usually the one with the keys to every lock in[100] the house?

Discrepancies between male and female servants were also obvious in the kitchen. A male chef was considered much more desirable than a female cook. However, male chefs had to be paid higher wages. As a result, most cooks were female. Still, their employers liked to be able to[150] say that male chefs had trained the female cooks.

Sometimes, ladies of the house would insist on a French maid. However, an English maid who could speak a few French phrases was also acceptable. Young women training to be rich ladies' maids often heard potential employers say, "She curtsies nicely,[200] but does she speak French?" Learning how to say French words with a flawless accent greatly increased a young woman's chances of being hired.

Several funny movies have been made about the typical wealthy, hard-working Englishman who constantly had to deal with the problems of keeping his estate running. With[250] a look of confusion on his face, the man confronts his wife's complaints about nannies, maids, and footmen. In the England of the 1800s, wealthy men preferred to focus on business. They left all matters concerning the home to their wives. In this respect, then, the movies are true.[299]

970L

Check Your Understanding

1. In the 1800s, the head housekeeper held the highest rank among servants.

   True / False? Explain:

   _____

2. Why were most cooks female in the 1800s?

   _____

   _____

Reading Fluency Assessment Passage 5

Maya Ying Lin, the college student and architect who designed the Vietnam Veterans Memorial, had a strong idea about fitting the Wall into its surroundings. Her plans found an appropriate way to connect this new structure to the land and to the other memorials around it. Her ideas for the[50] site seemed as perfect as anyone could have hoped to see.

What Lin and others could not possibly have known was the deep level of emotion the memorial would stir in visitors. The coordinators of the effort hoped that the Wall would help to heal the political division caused by the Vietnam War. They have been thrilled with the results. Visitors[100] often let their feeling show, and many are stunned by the impact the memorial has on them.

Visitors bring things to leave behind at the Wall. Together, these objects are a huge tribute to the men and women who served our country. More than fifty thousand objects have been left[150] at the Wall. They are collected twice daily by the National Park Service. When the weather is bad, the objects are picked up more often, ensuring that the less durable items are not damaged. The items are carefully entered into the Vietnam Veterans Memorial Collection. Exceptions are flags and living[200] things, such as plants. The flags are given to hospitals for former soldiers and groups like the Boy Scouts or Girl Scouts. The flags are also given to people who are attending special events at the memorial.

The things often left are writings, such as poems or letters. Bracelets worn[250] to remember missing soldiers are numerous, too. Rubbings of the names carved into the wall are often left too. Things that soldiers owned and photographs are also among the most commonly deposited mementoes.[283]

970L

Check Your Understanding

1. How do visitors to the wall respond?

2. Which items are not entered into the Vietnam Veterans Memorial Collection?

   a. flags
   b. photographs
   c. poems

Reading Fluency Assessment Passage 6

When Fredrick Douglass was born, no one could have predicted that he would lead a life of greatness. Born in 1818 into slavery on a plantation in Maryland, he was sent by his owner to Baltimore at the age of eight.

Douglass might have grown into a sullen, illiterate young man, but[50] an unexpected gift filled him with hope. He learned to read, in defiance of the law. After years of being treated cruelly, Frederick, at eighteen, planned an escape. His plan was discovered, and he was imprisoned. Once out of jail, Frederick's dream of freedom became possible, and he fled north to[100] New Bedford, Massachusetts.

Douglass became active in anti-slavery organizations. At one abolitionists' meeting, he met the great speaker William Lloyd Garrison. Garrison's unconcealed hatred for slavery and his fiery speech greatly inspired Douglass.

A few days later, Douglass himself gave a speech at an anti-slavery convention. One observer wrote, "Flinty[150] [hard] hearts were pierced, and cold ones melted by his eloquence." Douglass's speech so stirred listeners that he was asked to become a lecturer. It was the start of a career that took him to many places in the North and to Europe.

Douglass also published an autobiography. Because it[200] gave details of his former life, he had to increase his vigilance for possible capture by his former owner. He soon left the country for a two-year speaking tour in the British Isles.

Douglass returned from Europe with enough money to buy his freedom and start his own anti-slavery paper,[250] the *North Star*. After the Civil War, he began fighting for civil rights for freed slaves and for women and later served in several government positions. Thus Douglass defied his those who believed he was not destined for greatness.[288]

980L

Check Your Understanding

1. Name two of young Douglass's acts that were against the law.

   _____

   _____

2. Why did Frederick Douglass leave the United States for two years?

   _____

Reading Fluency Assessment Passage 7

Over the centuries, wigs have been popular accessories. Since the earliest times wigs were used to enhance beauty. In ancient Egypt, both men and women of nobility wore wigs of human hair adorned with flowers and gold ornaments on special occasions. Paintings of the dead wearing wigs prove that wigs[50] were important to the Egyptians. They believed that everything needed in the afterlife must be buried with the dead.

The expression blonds have more fun may have originated in ancient Rome. Many Roman women believed that blond hair was more desirable than their own dark locks. The solution? Wigs were[100] fashioned from the hair of blond captives. Apparently, the Romans were slaves to fashion. A sculpture of one noblewoman was fitted with a sequence of different marble wigs, each succeeding the other as styles changed.

Throughout history, the wearing of wigs was a sign of prosperity. Only wealthy people and[150] members of the royalty could afford the elaborate headpieces that were fashionable. Unlike modern men's hairpieces, the wigs popular in 17th-century were not meant to disguise hair loss. It did not take much scrutiny to recognize that a king's long and curly locks were not his own.

In the 1700s, [200] wigs for women were designed with support wires that raised the hairdo three feet in the air. Some included cages with miniature ships or live birds. It would take an agile woman to move easily in such a headpiece without tipping over!

These days, wigs are mainly worn by entertainers[250] and those who have lost their hair due to illness. Some people donate their hair for wigs that are donated to cancer patients.[273]

990L

Check Your Understanding

1. In the 17th century, wigs were

   a. thought of as fashion accessories.

   b. primarily used to disguise hair loss.

   c. made out of marble and feathers.

2. Why might the expression *blondes have more fun* have originated in ancient Rome?

   _____

   _____

Reading Fluency Assessment Passage 8

Anyone who feels a moral duty to help those less fortunate will be drawn to the ideas of Make a Difference Day. This national day of helping others is run each October by USA WEEKEND Magazine. The magazine has an alliance with the Points of Light Foundation and the actor[50] Paul Newman, among others. They holds the event to encourage people to commit to a specific project that will help others.

Paul Newman and his nonprofit company pledge $100,000 to the program each year. The money that has been promised will be divided among ten participants whose good deeds are[100] chosen as the best of the year. More times than not, the winners pass on the cash they have received to the very people they helped on Make a Difference Day. The virtue of these acts is impressive. Such good deeds surely encourage others to join the program.

Over the[150] years, millions of people have taken part in Make a Difference Day. The effort might be one person spending a couple of hours reading to others. It might involve a whole town joining together to collect and deliver food to the needy. Truly, every deed is remarkable. Despite our busy[200] lives, surely we all can get behind the simple idea of the event. "Put your own cares on hold for one day to care for someone else." Before next October rolls around, get involved in your own pursuit of a solution to a problem in your neighborhood.

Make a Difference[250] Day is held on the last Saturday of the month. Make plans early to spend a few hours that day on the project of your choice. The sick, the poor, and other needy members of society will appreciate your help.[290]

1000L

Check Your Understanding

3. What do the sponsors of Make a Difference Day hope to achieve?

_____

_____

4. More times than not, what do winners of their part of the $10,000 prize do with the money?

_____

_____

Reading Fluency Assessment Passage 9

Billy was a daydreamer.

It started when he was in preschool. Billy would start doing a jigsaw puzzle, but his mind would begin to wander even before he inserted the first puzzle piece into the rectangular frame. At first, his thoughts would drift aimlessly, in no apparent direction. Then his[50] eyes would close, and a story would start to take shape in his mind. Soon Billy would be off on a great adventure in some distant land that was far more exciting than Miss Hannah's Preschool.

That's when Miss Hannah would tap him on the shoulder and ask why he[100] wasn't completing his puzzle like the other children.

When he got older, Billy learned to daydream with his eyes open. He would sit in class, carelessly doodling in his notebook, when suddenly his mind would drift. For a few fleeting moments, Billy would enjoy leading a squad of fearless soldiers[150] into battle or piloting a space shuttle through the treacherous rings of Saturn.

Then, like clockwork, the teacher would barge in, saying in a stern voice, "Time to rejoin the real world," and the whole class would laugh.

Billy didn't care, though. Sometimes, when his parents were bickering, Billy would[200] escape into a private world where people never argued or raised their voices. In Billy's daydreams, everyone got along.

When he reached high school, Billy began to write down some of his daydreams as stories. His teachers had to admit that the stories were good, even if Billy did have[250] trouble paying attention in class.

In his sophomore year, Billy suggested that he and other student authors begin a school literary magazine. In it, they would have the opportunity to share their daydreams with others. Before long, this particular daydream of Billy's became a reality![295]

1000L

Check Your Understanding

1. Students in Billy's classes often laughed at him because he

   a. wanted to start a literary magazine.
   b. got into trouble because he daydreamed.
   c. thought that everyone should get along.
   d. made funny doodles in his notebooks.

2. What traits and habits probably helped Billy to write great stories?

   _____

   _____

Reading Fluency Assessment Passage 10

People call swirling wind storms by many names, such as whirlwind, twister, tornado, and cyclone. This violent storm can occur at any time of the year, but they are most common during the spring and early summer. May and June are the most common months, but tornadoes occurring during April[50] are the deadliest. These storms have brought fatal consequences to an average of nearly thirty people a year.

Tornadoes occur mainly in the central and southern United States. This region is known as "tornado alley." It lies between the Rocky Mountains and the Appalachians, and runs from Iowa and Nebraska[100] down to the Gulf of Mexico. If you live in this region, you have probably experienced all kinds of extreme weather.

The level of destruction caused by a tornado depends on the speed of the winds. A level F0 tornado, with winds of 40–72 miles per hour, usually causes[150] light damage. Branches might be ripped from trees, and trees with shallow roots may topple over. Damage to signs, traffic signals, and chimneys might occur.

Almost half of all tornadoes fall into the F1 category. With winds of 73–112 miles per hour, this tornado usually causes moderate damage. Mobile[200] homes can be knocked off their foundations. Cars might be flipped over. Roofing materials might be damaged.

A level F2 tornado, with winds of 113–157 miles per hour, causes considerable damage. Solid, old trees are uprooted easily. Some homes are completely destroyed. Roofs are ripped off buildings. Train cars[250] can be knocked over.

Tornadoes labeled F3, F4, and F5 range from "severe" to "devastating" to "incredible damage." Only about one percent are classified as F5. The winds of one of these tornadoes can toss cars through the air and turn houses to piles of sticks and stones.[298]

1000L

Check Your Understanding

1. The worst tornadoes

   a. often occur in September.

   b. occur in the northeastern part of the United States.

   c. are classified as F5.

   d. are classified as F1.

2. What is the difference between a cyclone and a tornado?

   _____

   _____

337

Reading Fluency Assessment Passage 11

Long before the invention of airplanes and steam engines, people relied on wind power to travel great distances over the water. While sailboats are still used for fishing and for recreation today, sailing ships no longer play a prominent role in transportation and commerce.

Every sailing ship has a hull,[50] rigging, and at least one mast to support its sails. The hull is the framework upon which the ship is built. The rigging allows the crew to raise and lower the sails on the masts. Traditionally, a vessel with fewer than three masts was called a *boat* rather than a[100] *ship.*

Sailing across the ocean has always been a treacherous undertaking. A severe storm can blow a sailing ship off course. It can even lead to shipwreck. Seasickness can transform an otherwise pleasant ocean crossing into a nauseating experience. Although gazing at the beautiful, starry sky is a fine distraction[150] on a balmy evening, boredom can become another hazard. Passengers can grow restless on long and uneventful voyages.

Sailors on a traditional sailing ship had many projects at hand. All crew members would alternate hours, working four hours on and four hours off around the clock. They would take turns[200] steering the ship and navigating. Another daily responsibility was keeping the ship adequately maintained. Rigging and sails often needed repairs, and masts needed oiling. As guardians of the ship's safety, the sailors in charge of keeping lookout had one of the most important jobs of all.

Attacks by pirates were[250] not uncommon and, after many weeks at sea, sailors sometimes reported seeing such fantastic creatures as mermaids and sea serpents. Often, these sightings would turn out to be whale sharks or giant squid. Other times, they proved to be no more than figments of a bored sailor's imagination.[298]

1030L

Check Your Understanding

1. Sailing ships no longer play a prominent role in long-distance travel because

   a. airplanes and other modern vessels have replaced them.

   b. they required too much maintenance.

   c. people became bored during long voyages.

   d. people were scared of sharks and giant squids.

2. Describe the work of crew members on traditional sailing ships.

   _____

   _____

Reading Fluency Assessment Passage 12

In 1965, the first close-up picture of the planet Mars was revealed below its hazy pink sky. Since then, spacecraft traveling by and landing on the planet have shown us an amazing world. Exploration of Mars has brought us increasing knowledge of this cold, rocky wasteland.

Clues hint at past[50] conditions quite different from those today. For example, at one time, volcanoes erupted on Mars.

The big question today for most scientists is whether life ever existed on Mars. Operations managers at the United States space agency have developed a strategy called "follow the water" to answer such questions. Scientists[100] gather data from features such as the polar ice caps and dry riverbeds with the hope that their work will show that water once may have covered parts of the planet. Furthermore, they dream of discovering hot springs or pockets of water beneath the Martian surface.

Advancement in computer technology[150] enables Scientists to receive and study data from a Mars explorer that moves along the surface. If the explorer stops working properly, they can remotely correct its programs.

One problem that equipment on Mars has had is dust from the planet's surface. Dust forms a layer on the spacecraft's solar[200] panels. The panels sunlight and change it to the electricity the spacecraft needs. If the spaceship does not get enough power, the situation could turn critical resulting in an early-ending mission. Perhaps software engineers will develop a program to fix the problem. Imagine a robotic arm that can dust[250] off the panels.

Will people ever travel to Mars? Scientists need to know a lot more than they do now before sending humans there. If humans do walk on Mars, might they be able to discover more than any robot can? Maybe in your lifetime you'll find out![298]

1030L

Check Your Understanding

1. To determine if life existed on Mars, scientists are first looking for

   a. volcanic rock

   b. water

   c. dust particles

2. What feature of Mars causes problems for the equipment?

_____

339

Screening Test

Directions: *Read the following passages. Then answer the questions. Some items will have no passage. On the answer sheet, fill in the bubble for the answer that you think is correct.*

Metro's garbage haulers will pick up household garbage and yard refuse every other Friday beginning January 4th. On pick-up day, each household in the Metro area can set out one 32-gallon trash can, one paper yard bag, or one bundle of trimmings at no charge. Any additional cans, bags, or bundles will cost the household $1.50 each. Please note that each bag, can, and bundle cannot exceed 45 pounds.

---

1. Which statement is true about Metro's service?
   A. Each can, bag, and bundle cannot weigh more than 32 pounds.
   B. Household garbage is picked up at the same time yard refuse is.
   C. Every two weeks, one can, bag, or bundle is picked up for $1.50.
   D. The fee for a household's first 45 cans, bags, or bundles is $1.50.

2. What happens after a household puts out a second trash can, yard bag, or bundle?
   F. It will stay there because the trash haulers will not take it.
   G. The household will lose service for the year.
   H. It will be picked up the following Friday.
   J. The household will be charged $1.50.

All clothes are not created equal. That's why Windmark has made its latest washing machine, the T1100 Deluxe. With five speed settings, the T1100 can handle your heaviest denims and your most delicate hand-washable fabrics. The T1100 also offers a second rinse option for tough stains.

---

3. What is the main idea of this passage?
   A. Rinse muddy clothes twice.
   B. The T1100 Deluxe has five speeds.
   C. The T1100 Deluxe has many fine features.
   D. All clothes are not created equal.

4. This paragraph would *most* likely be found in —
   F. an advertisement
   G. an owner's manual
   H. a sales agreement
   J. a set of directions

Your Windmark T1100 Deluxe is covered under warranty for ten years after the purchase date of the machine. This warranty does not cover damages caused by natural disasters or damage to the washing machine due to the owner's mishandling. (See owner's manual for operating instructions.) The T1100 Deluxe will be serviced free of charge if any mechanical problems arise. The machine will be replaced if any problems continue after a service representative has attempted a repair.

---

5. This paragraph describes —
   A. where to find information about other Windmark washers
   B. how to fix a washing machine that someone has just bought
   C. why the washing machine might break down after a few years
   D. when the company will fix problems with the washing machine

6. When you connect the main idea of Passage 1 and Passage 2, you find that the T1100 —
   F. doesn't work well
   G. has many features and is covered by a warranty
   H. is very expensive
   J. is too complicated for most service representatives to fix

> Parents often tell stories about the past to their children. The stories may change over time and become more and more unbelievable. Ancient stories called myths are like family stories in many ways. Myths are stories about heroic warriors, magical worlds, and gods long ago. Like family stories, myths were passed down through history by storytellers. Though the stories may have happened, myths have many unbelievable characters and adventures.

7. According to the passage, as time passes —
   A. people forget the stories they tell
   B. stories may grow more unbelievable
   C. songs are written to tell the stories
   D. warriors become part of stories

8. What causes myths to be like family stories?
   F. They are passed down through history.
   G. They are meant for children.
   H. They are required to be very long.
   J. They have gods as characters.

> The snow had been falling for hours. Almost no cars were on the roads. Inside the house, the Lyons family was worried. The snow had knocked the telephone lines down, so they couldn't call anyone. They were supposed to go to the airport today and begin their vacation. "I think the roads are too dangerous," said Mrs. Lyons. "We should probably do the sensible thing."

9. What sensible thing will the Lyons family *probably* do?
   A. drive to the airport slowly because the roads are dangerous
   B. wait until the storm has ended to start their vacation
   C. call a taxi and have the driver take them to the airport
   D. walk to the airport and carry their suitcases

10. Based on the passage, which adjective *best* describes the Lyons?
    F. Lazy
    G. Cautious
    H. Wealthy
    J. Frazzled

> The hikers were getting close to the top of the mountain. They would set up camp there and spend the night. The next morning, they would hike back down to the parking area. The hikers carried supplies for themselves. They also carried things the group would share, such as tents, food, and cooking items. All of the members of the group had spent a great deal of time thinking about what they would need. They wanted this hike to be challenging but not dangerous.

11. Based on the passage, it seems reasonable to assume that the hikers —
   A. are college students
   B. are in Colorado
   C. work well together
   D. have a good leader

12. How do you know the hikers expect to have a safe trip?
   F. They are not far from the parking area.
   G. They are getting close to the top of the mountain.
   H. They spent a lot of time preparing for the trip.
   J. They knew the trip would be challenging.

13. If they did not spend a great deal of time thinking about what they would need, the hikers might —
   A. run out of supplies
   B. bring the wrong supplies
   C. bring duplicates of supplies the group could share
   D. all of the above

Mail in the American colonies was not what you might think. In 1753, Benjamin Franklin was put in charge of the postal service. He worked hard to improve everything. Even so, many people chose not to use the mail service. They believed it cost far too much. These people paid private carriers to bring their letters from place to place.

---

14. To show that the postal service wanted to do a better job, the author —
   F. says that it was expensive
   G. mentions 1753
   H. describes private carriers
   J. says that it put Benjamin Franklin in charge

15. Why did the colonists hire their own mail carriers?
   A. They were worried about people reading their mail.
   B. They knew the carriers would get there more quickly.
   C. They thought the postal service charged too much.
   D. They did not trust Benjamin Franklin to do a good job.

Discount Auto announces an unusual sale. All new cars on its lot will be sold at the amazing price of $1,000. These cars normally sell for $10,000 to $20,000, so this is a once-in-a-lifetime opportunity. This is a first-come, first-serve sale, so get there early. The price of the cars includes taxes and all other costs. Bring your checkbook and drive away in the car of your dreams.

---

16. Which of the following is an *opinion*?
   F. The cars normally sell for $10,000 to $20,000.
   G. This is a once-in-a-lifetime opportunity.
   H. This is a first-come, first-serve sale.
   J. The price of the cars includes taxes.

17. Which of the following is a *fact*?
    A. People should get to the sale early.
    B. You can drive away in the car of your dreams.
    C. $1,000 is an amazing price.
    D. Discount Auto announces an unusual sale.

> I believe that school uniforms are an all-around good idea. When students at our school started wearing uniforms, there was an immediate reaction. Student behavior began to change for the better. There were fewer classroom interruptions and hallway disturbances. Students seemed to care less about what they were wearing and more about what they were learning. Only one year after the school adopted uniforms, test scores had improved by 15 percent.

18. Which of the following is the *weakest* support for the belief that school uniforms are a good idea?
    F. Students test scores improved.
    G. There were fewer classroom interruptions.
    H. There were fewer disturbances in the halls.
    J. Students cared less about what they wore.

> **To Start Your Washer:**
>
> 1. Measure detergent and add to basin.
> 2. Add fabric softener to dispenser in the center of machine.
> 3. Close washer lid and set water level.
> 4. Set water temperature control and number of rinses.
> 5. Set speed control.
> 6. Close lid and pull wash cycle knob out to begin washing.

19. According to the instructions, what should you do after you add fabric softener?
    A. Set the water temperature control.
    B. Set the speed control.
    C. Close the washer lid.
    D. Measure the detergent and add it to the basin.

20. What information do you find in this passage?
    F. descriptions of temperature settings for a washer
    G. speeds and controls for a washer
    H. directions for starting a washer
    J. instructions for care and service of a washer

Favian Mercado thought it would be neat to run for student-body president, so he did. When the votes were counted, and Favian had won the election, he met with the vice principal to go over his new duties. Afterwards, Favian felt overwhelmed. He had no idea he would have to attend school-board meetings, write monthly reports, and organize the annual fundraiser. If he had known being president would be so much work, he might not have run.

21. The moral of this story is —
    A. nothing is worth more than freedom
    B. with greatness comes responsibility
    C. misfortune is the test of friendship
    D. common sense is a valuable treasure

When Wilma Rudolph was four, she got terribly sick and came down with polio. Wilma's doctors said she was crippled and would never walk again. But Wilma was determined to walk. With the support of her family and years of physical therapy, Wilma was not only able to walk but to play on the basketball team. A basketball championship eventually led Wilma to college and a successful career in track. Then, in 1960, the girl whom doctors said would never walk again earned three gold medals at the Olympic Games.

22. What *most* likely helped Wilma Rudolph stay determined to walk again?
    F. knowing that other people also struggled with polio
    G. not wanting to stay in the hospital
    H. her family's support
    J. not wanting to rely on other people to help her move from place to place

Directions: *Read the following questions. On the answer sheet, fill in the bubble for the answer that you think is correct.*

23. Which of these is an example of *simile*?
    A. The thunder boomed like a drum.
    B. Our crab apple trees were in full bloom.
    C. The dog heard the whistle and jumped.
    D. A blanket of dew lay over the fields.

24. Which of these is an example of *metaphor*?
    F. The poppies opened in the afternoon sun.
    G. The prairie was a sea of rolling green.
    H. The women chattered quickly and noisily.
    J. The small boat was tossed all night long.

Directions: *Read the following sentence. Choose the correct meaning of the underlined word. On the answer sheet, fill in the bubble for the answer that you think is correct.*

25. Many of us had learned to be cautious in dealing with representatives of the <u>press</u>.
    A. push against
    B. news media
    C. large machine
    D. move forward

Directions: *Read the following phrases. Then decide which of the four answers has most nearly the same meaning as the underlined word. On the answer sheet, fill in the bubble for the answer that you think is correct.*

26. To <u>utter</u> a word
  F. write
  G. speak
  H. teach
  J. spell

27. To hold a <u>grudge</u>
  A. package
  B. disappointment
  C. favor
  D. resentment

Directions: *Read the following words. Look for mistakes in spelling. For each item on the answer sheet, fill in the bubble for the answer that has the mistake. If there is no mistake, fill in the last answer choice.*

28. F. healthy
  G. lawndry
  H. quickly
  J. (*No mistakes*)

29. A. leest
  B. prowl
  C. quail
  D. (*No mistakes*)

Directions: *Read the following sentences. Look for mistakes in punctuation. For each item on the answer sheet, fill in the bubble for the answer that has the mistake. If there is no mistake, fill in the last answer choice.*

30. F. Our class is selling candy to
  G. raise money for our trip to
  H. Washington DC this spring.
  J. (*No mistakes*)

31. A. I remember it was November and
  B. the leaves had all fallen from the
  C. trees when we got a new dog?
  D. (*No mistakes*)

Name _____ Date _____

Practice Test 1:

Suppose that you and your classmates must write a persuasive speech about why you think the school should offer more after-school activities. You will begin by suggesting several activities and including reasons why they should be offered. You and your classmates will deliver the speech at the next school board meeting. Answer the questions that follow.

1. In addressing the school board, what should your vocabulary and style reflect?
   A. your disappointment with your school and your teachers
   B. your respect for community members
   C. your desire to leave the meeting after your speech is complete
   D. your lack of interest in more than one of the suggested activities

2. What is a good way to begin the speech?
   A. State the main idea.
   B. Give the names of students who will take part in a certain activity if it is offered.
   C. Provide details.
   D. Ask whether the audience has any questions.

3. What should you do if someone in your group forgets an important point?
   A. Interrupt and make the point yourself.
   B. Go whisper in his or her ear.
   C. Do nothing.
   D. Ask about that point during the question-and-answer session.

4. After dividing the speech so that several students may deliver different parts, what should you verify?
   A. that all parts support the main idea
   B. that everyone's opinion is expressed, even if several opinions do not support the main idea
   C. that no detail presented will be confusing to the audience
   D. both A and C

5. What is a good supporting reason to use in your speech?
   A. After-school activities make students stay up late to study.
   B. It will cost a lot of money to hire coaches and moderators for activities.
   C. Additional activities will be beneficial for students.
   D. The school is run by lazy people.

6. What tone is appropriate for addressing the school board?
   A. professional
   B. comical
   C. sarcastic
   D. informal

7. In addition to standing up straight, how can you communicate confidence during your speech?
   A. speaking the way you would with your close friends
   B. making eye contact with the audience
   C. making jokes throughout your speech
   D. quoting your favorite movies and songs

8. What might be the result if a speaker made very good points but had poor nonverbal skills?
   A. This would have no effect on how the audience evaluated the speech.
   B. The audience might pay more attention.
   C. The speech might be less persuasive.
   D. none of the above

Answer the questions that follow.

9. A television commercial shows a group of teenagers offering a certain brand of potato chips to members of a rock band, who then invite the teens to perform with them at a concert. What can you conclude is the message the advertisers want you to believe?
   A. The chips are delicious.
   B. The chips come in a variety of flavors.
   C. All good stores sell the chips.
   D. Extraordinary things will happen if you buy the chips.

10. What is correct about a radio advertisement that states, "We have just received a new shipment of sports cars, and they are by far the coolest cars you will ever see"?
    A. It has stated a fact.   C. both A and B
    B. It has expressed an opinion.   D. neither A nor B

11. In a television commercial, a girl wears a new brand of jeans. She is called onstage during a school assembly to accept a special award called "Everyone's Best Friend." Confetti falls from the ceiling and the girl smiles broadly. According to the commercial, which of these is the **best** reason to buy the jeans?
    A. Many students wear jeans to school.
    B. Jeans will be sold at school assemblies.
    C. Popular, well-liked young people wear the jeans.
    D. Jeans that are old are no fun to wear.

Read each of the sentences that follow. Then choose the word below that expresses the meaning of the underlined word.

12. The police officer said, "One of the best ways to protect your home against crime is to illuminate the area around it."
    A. patrol   C. light
    B. fence   D. wire

13. As soon as Nancy and Raymond met, there was <u>antipathy</u> between them.

    A. admiration   **C.** attraction

    B. competition   **D.** dislike

Answer the questions that follow.

14. Which sentence contains an analogy?

    A. A talented athlete is said to be poetry in motion.

    B. Sometimes colorful jellyfish make swimming in the ocean a stinging experience.

    C. Dancing couples swirled and twirled around the gym.

    D. Lie is to truth as knowledgeable is to ignorant.

15. Which sentence contains a simile?

    A. Words often come out of Tanya's mouth like water pouring from an open faucet.

    B. Ingrid and Tamara wonder if she ever thinks before she speaks.

    C. Public speaking ability should be required for a person who wants to be mayor.

    D. Try to be very quiet in the reference section of the media center.

16. What are the connotations of the underlined words in the sentence below?

David said that he'd love to take a trip to Paris, but spending <u>that kind of money</u> isn't possible right now.

    A. David doesn't want to use European currency.

    B. David thinks that the trip will cost too much.

    C. David doesn't like to carry hundred-dollar bills.

    D. David doesn't want to plan a trip to a foreign place.

Read the following passages. Then answer the questions that follow.

Kate and Buster

    All summer Kate and her dog Buster played in the backyard. One day, Kate sat on her back porch step with Buster. School was starting the next day. Kate thought about how unhappy Buster would be in the house all day long. Then she got an idea. Kate raced to the kitchen and got a length of rope and Buster's leash. She tied one end of the rope to the back porch railing. She put the rope through the loop at the end of Buster's leash. Then, she stretched the rope across the yard and tied it to a tree. When she put Buster on the leash, he could run up and down the yard. The leash, which was attached to the rope, kept him safe.

    "Now you can run and play until I come home from school!" Kate said.

17. What is the setting of this story?

    A. Kate's first day of school   **C.** the last day of school

    B. sometime in June   **D.** the day before school starts

18. What is the first thing that happens after Kate realizes that Buster will be lonely when she goes to school?
    A. She ties his leash to the railing.
    B. She gets ready for school.
    C. She gets an idea that will help Buster.
    D. She asks her mother whether Buster can go to school too.

19. What conflict does Kate face?
    A. She doesn't want to go to school.
    B. She thinks that she may have to give her dog to someone else.
    C. She fears that her dog will be sad when she leaves.
    D. She needs to find someone to walk Buster while the family is on vacation.

20. What inference can you make about Kate after reading this passage?
    A. She really cares about her dog.
    B. She doesn't like walking Buster.
    C. She is a good student.
    D. She has a very big yard.

> Break, break, break,
>   On thy cold gray stones, O Sea!
>
> — from "Break, Break, Break"
>   by Alfred, Lord Tennyson

21. Why does the poet repeat the word *break* so often in these lines of poetry?
    A. to show that waves are coming in again and again
    B. to show how much damage waves can do
    C. to show that the sea breaks the stones
    D. to show that the gray stones are cold and near the sea

22. What is the feeling created in the following line from a poem?
    As I stepped out into the warmth of the summer sun, my heart overflowed.
    A. excitement
    B. gloom
    C. misery
    D. joy

23. How is drama different from other kinds of literature?
    A. It is meant to be acted out as well as read.
    B. It has characters that seem like real people.
    C. It ends each line with a word that rhymes.
    D. It has a setting where the story takes place.

24. What is an advantage of writing nonfiction?
    A. You can create as many characters as you want.
    B. You can write using mostly your imagination.
    C. You can leave some of the punctuation out.
    D. You can focus on telling just facts.

25. What would be a *likely* subject for a fantasy story?

    A. why the dinosaurs disappeared

    B. the life of a real queen

    C. a famous musician

    D. an imaginary world

26. Which of the following words is spelled correctly?

    A. helthy

    B. healthey

    C. healthy

    D. heallthy

Practice Test 2:

Read the following passages. Then answer the questions that follow.

Montezuma, Emperor of Mexico

Montezuma looked out over the capital. The kingdom stretched as far as his eyes could see. As a boy, he had heard stories about his great grandfather's military strength extending these borders.

How he wished he had known his great grandfather! Montezuma's rule had been his great grandfather's legacy. He wondered often whether he could carry on his great grandfather's vision as he carried his name.

While Montezuma's thoughts wandered, his servant entered. "Strangers are reported near the city, my great emperor."

"Where are they?" Montezuma asked, still looking over the city.

"To the north, my lord. Two days at least."

"Do they carry weapons?" Montezuma's recent dreams about his great grandfather convinced him that the visions were warnings about men from foreign lands. The men carried weapons he had never seen and caused great destruction.

"Yes, my lord. They have powerful weapons. They also have with them some warriors from a neighboring people."

1. What is this story mostly about?
   A. an emperor who finds out about strangers coming to his kingdom
   B. a servant who meets strangers and brings them to his kingdom
   C. some visitors who come to a strange land to meet Montezuma
   D. an emperor's great grandfather and his military victories

2. If this story continued, what *probably* would be the main idea of the rest of the story?
   A. Montezuma welcomes the strangers and invites them to stay.
   B. The strangers come to make a peace treaty with Montezuma.
   C. Montezuma goes to war and loses his empire to the strangers.
   D. Montezuma and his great grandfather speak to the strangers.

3. What important idea in the story is shown by the sentence, "They also have with them some warriors from a neighboring people"?
   A. The strangers are coming for a peaceful visit.
   B. The neighboring tribes have joined the strangers to fight.
   C. The strangers have made friends among other people.
   D. The tribes want to talk to Montezuma.

Encyclopedia Article

The word *arena* comes from the Latin word *harena*, meaning "sand." The ancient Romans built many amphitheaters for combats and other athletic competitions. Roman sports tended to be violent, so the center of the amphitheaters where the action took place was often covered with sand. The sand helped soak up the blood so that the competitors wouldn't lose their footing. Eventually the word *harena* came to mean the area at the center of an amphitheater or stadium. In the seventeenth century, people speaking English began to use the word *arena* to describe the location of English sporting events.

Newspaper Editorial

Patrons attending sporting events at modern arenas probably do not realize just how appropriate the word *arena* is. The original arenas were home to the bloody competitions of Roman gladiators. Today's arenas host violent professional sports competitions. Football, wrestling, hockey, and boxing are among the most violent of modern sports. Even athletes in "non-contact" sports often abandon the game to fight with opponents. This use of violence for entertainment may have its roots in ancient history, but it is dangerous to modern society. Not only are athletes themselves violent, but also spectators may become dangerous mobs after witnessing the brutal competitions.

4. Which of the following is an opinion expressed in the newspaper editorial?
   - **A.** Some people who attend sports events do not know the origin of the word *arena*.
   - **B.** Violence in today's sports can be traced back to ancient times.
   - **C.** Violence in sports is dangerous to society.
   - **D.** The original arenas were home to bloody competitions.

5. Which of these statements **best** describes the newspaper editorial's discussion of arenas?
   - **A.** It is mostly fact.
   - **B.** It contains many opinions.
   - **C.** It shows that arenas are useful buildings.
   - **D.** It is easier to understand than the other source.

6. Which of the following phrases conveys the author's belief that sport spectators are sometimes irresponsible?
   - **A.** violent professional sports competitions
   - **B.** bloody competitions
   - **C.** violence for entertainment
   - **D.** dangerous mobs

7. Which of the following is the **best** summary of the encyclopedia article?
   - **A.** The word *arena* has origins in ancient Rome and refers to the sand used on the ground during competitions there.
   - **B.** People have enjoyed watching violent competition since ancient times.
   - **C.** English words often come from Roman and Greek words used long ago.
   - **D.** The ancient Romans built many amphitheaters for combats and other athletic competitions.

8. What is a good strategy for giving a speech in which you state your opinion of the newspaper editorial?
   - **A.** Totally disagree with the writer of the editorial.
   - **B.** Totally agree with the writer of the editorial.
   - **C.** Discuss the editorial's points and also add your own.
   - **D.** Compare and contrast today's arenas with those of ancient Rome.

9. How could you find more information to include in your speech?
   A. Look for information on the Internet.   C. Read articles in periodicals.
   B. Find books at the library.   D. all of the above

10. What is a good strategy to use in your speech after you have found three good sources of information?
    A. Use quotes only from the best one.
    B. Use information found only in all three of the sources.
    C. Explain to the audience that the authors do not present the same information.
    D. Take information from each source, being sure to cite it correctly.

11. Which of the following questions shows a good reader's response to the encyclopedia article?
    A. What kinds of weapons did ancient Romans use in combats?
    B. What sports did ancient Romans play?
    C. What are some different ways we use the word *arena* today?
    D. all of the above

Answer the questions that follow.

12. What kind of source is a diary entry written by a Civil War soldier?
    A. poetic   C. primary
    B. secondary   D. summary

13. What kind of source is a textbook about the Civil War?
    A. primary   C. advanced
    B. secondary   D. summary

Read the following passage. Then answer the questions that follow.

Who Invented Band-Aids®?

Although many people don't even know his name, Earle Dickson was responsible for creating one of today's most common household items. Dickson was the genius behind Band-Aids®.

In 1917, Dickson was a newly married man and a cotton buyer for a successful bandage company in New Jersey called Johnson & Johnson. As the story goes, Dickson's wife, Frances, was *accident-prone*. She often cut herself or nicked her fingers doing various household tasks. The regular bandages were too big and clumsy for Frances, so Dickson devised something better.

He folded pads of cotton gauze and placed them on long strips of surgical tape. He covered this with a material called crinoline. This prevented the tape from sticking to itself when it was rolled back together. Frances could unroll the bandage and cut off as much as she needed.

One day, Dickson mentioned his creation to a friend at work. Soon, Dickson was before the Johnsons, showing them what he had come up with. The Johnsons were especially impressed with the fact that you could put the new bandage on yourself. Up until that point, bandages had been difficult to apply without help.

Johnson & Johnson began producing Band-Aids®, but the bandages didn't take off until the mid-1920s when the company gave thousands of samples to the Boy Scouts. After that, Band-Aids® were a hit. Dickson was made vice president of Johnson & Johnson, and when he died in 1961, the company was selling $30,000,000 dollars' worth of Band-Aids® a year.

14. Here is a partial outline of the passage.

The Invention of Band-Aids®

    I.   Who Earle Dickson was
    II. _____
    III. How Dickson made his own bandage
    IV. What happened at Johnson & Johnson
    V. The success of Band-Aids®

Which information would fit **best** in the blank shown in the outline?

  A. Where Johnson & Johnson was
  B. What Dickson's wife's name was
  C. Why Dickson made his own bandage
  D. How Dickson met with Johnson & Johnson

15. Which of the following is the central idea of the passage?

  A. The Boy Scouts make Band-Aids® more popular.
  B. A housewife is finally able to bandage herself.
  C. A cotton inventor becomes head of a company.
  D. One man's homemade bandages become Band-Aids®.

16. In the passage, the author says that Frances Dickson was *accident-prone*. Why is this a **better** word choice than *clumsy* or *graceless*?

  A. It sets a more respectful tone.
  B. It describes how she acted.
  C. It helps the reader picture Frances.
  D. It shows that Frances needed bandages.

Answer the questions that follow.

17. Which is the **best** way to revise the three sentences that follow?

We go to the city. We meet our aunt and uncle. We have lunch with them.

  A. We have lunch with our aunt and uncle.
  B. Our aunt and uncle have lunch with us.
  C. In the city, we meet our aunt and uncle for lunch.
  D. We go to the city for lunch. Our aunt and uncle are there.

18. Which is the **best** way to rewrite the sentence that follows?

Shelley reads books with her family, which is important to her.

  A. Shelley reads books, and so does her family.
  B. Reading books with her family is important to Shelley.
  C. With her family, Shelley reads important books.
  D. Reading so many books, Shelley is an important part of her family.

19. Why is a word processor a good writing tool?
    A. You can type a rough draft on it.
    B. It is possible to make changes as you type.
    C. You can move whole passages around as you work on a final draft.
    D. all of the above

20. In what way can an idea web or other graphic organizer help you to arrange writing ideas?
    A. by identifying good sources
    B. by determining how long your essay will be
    C. by showing you grammar mistakes
    D. by focusing your main idea

Read the following sentences. Then answer the questions that follow.

The **long**, winding **road cuts across** the **brutally** cold land. **Ah**, how Shannon wishes **she** could be warm **and** cozy at home!

21. What part of speech is **long**?
    A. noun
    B. adverb
    C. conjunction
    D. adjective

22. What part of speech is **road**?
    A. adjective
    B. noun
    C. pronoun
    D. verb

23. What part of speech is **cuts**?
    A. adverb
    B. verb
    C. interjection
    D. conjunction

24. What part of speech is **across**?
    A. verb
    B. conjunction
    C. preposition
    D. interjection

25. What part of speech is **brutally**?
    A. adverb
    B. adjective
    C. verb
    D. interjection

26. What part of speech is **Ah**?
    A. verb
    B. pronoun
    C. preposition
    D. interjection

27. What part of speech is **she**?
    A. noun
    B. conjunction
    C. pronoun
    D. adverb

28. What part of speech is **and**?
    A. pronoun
    B. preposition
    C. interjection
    D. conjunction

My cousin didn't want their photograph to appear in the newspaper.

29. What is true about the pronoun *their* as it is used in the sentence above?
   A. It is correct because the cousin's gender is unknown.
   B. It is incorrect because *cousin* is singular.
   C. It is correct because *photograph* is singular.
   D. It is incorrect because *My* is singular.

   One of the jugglers _____ also a trapeze artist.

30. In the sentence above, which of these words belongs in the blank?
   A. are
   B. were
   C. is
   D. perform

   We were walking to the skate park when Lenny's father <u>drives</u> up and said, " I heard the park has closed for the season."

31. In the sentence above, which of the following verb forms should replace the underlined verb?
   A. was driving
   B. drived
   C. drove
   D. had driven

Writing Prompt 1

Imagine that the community park will soon be adding something new. What do you think should be added? Perhaps it should be a new piece of equipment, a court or field for playing a particular sport, or a spot where people can relax, talk, or read. The new feature may be meant for children, adults, or both. Write a letter to convince the director of the park that your plan is the one that should be adopted. Be sure to be specific and to give reasons why your plan is superior to other plans.

Writing Prompt 2

Think about your favorite place in the world. It might be a place you go every day or a place you have visited only once or twice. Consider reasons why this place is so special to you. Perhaps your fondness for it has to do with the beauty or excitement of the place. Or perhaps you faced challenges and learned something about yourself in this place. Write a journal entry in which you describe this favorite place, using specific examples, vivid sensory words, and figurative language to let readers share its specialness. Be sure to identify the place at the start of your journal entry, so readers can understand and appreciate your descriptive details.

Practice Test 3

Read the following short story and then answer the questions that follow.

from "*Reel* Time: How the Movies Portray History"

Some of the most successful Hollywood movies ever made have been historical films. There's something about being transported to another time and place that audiences find magical.

Making history come alive on screen requires a lot of preparation and dedication. Good historical films require a suspension of disbelief. Viewers watching a movie that takes place in ancient Greece know that it wasn't really filmed in ancient times. Yet, if the movie is made well, viewers allow the movie to **deceive** them. They believe they are seeing ancient Greece on screen.

How do moviemakers perform this amazing feat? It's a challenge that involves hard work—and often a cast and crew of thousands—to pull off. Attention must be paid to every detail: how characters looked, talked, and felt; how places looked; how events really happened; what the weather was like. That's as close to a time machine as any of us is likely to come.

A Moviemaking Primer

How **fluent** are you in the language of moviemaking? Take a look at some of the terms below.

The director: The person in artistic control of the movie. The director controls the actors, the set, and the filming.

The producer: The producer is the boss of the movie. A producer often does most of the hiring on a set. A producer also raises money.

extras: people who appear in movies but are not specific characters and speak no lines. Extras are usually parts of crowds or in the background of scenes. Most epic films use a lot of extras.

scene: a piece of a screenplay or story that is set in a particular location. Movie shoots are usually broken down into scenes.

The Set

In a historical film, all the scenes not shot on location are shot on a set. This means that the production designers (or set designers) play a key role in the movie. Their job is to establish the look and feel of a particular time.

Most set designers do a lot of research before coming up with sketches of what a set might look like. They work closely with the director to ensure that everyone's vision of how the film should look is the same.

One benefit of shooting on a set compared to shooting on location is that the moviemakers have more control. They can make things just as they want them and adjust them if they need to. Sets can also be more economical than locations. In the World War II movie *Saving Private Ryan,* an entire French village was recreated on a set in England. The same set was then used in a new context in the movie to represent a different French village.

The Costumes and Props

Costumes and props help reveal a movie's historical period. They can communicate a time period to audiences almost better than anything else. Are there hoop skirts on screen? Then the movie must be set in the mid-1800s. Are the men wearing togas? Think of ancient Rome.

Computer Generated Imagery (CGI)

CGI refers to special effects done on the computer. CGI can be used to eliminate unwanted modern details from a historical backdrop. It can be used to make seemingly impossible things happen. CGI can also be used to add extras to a scene. In the pictures from the battle scene that opens *Gladiator,* CGI was used to add soldiers to the scene.

1. Based on the context of the passage, what is the meaning of the word *deceive*?

   A. to explain

   B. to help

   C. to trick

   D. to please

2. Which of the following is *not* usually one of the jobs done by the set designers?

   A. determining the look of a particular time period

   B. making sketches of how the set will look

   C. giving actors recommendations about how to play particular roles

   D. working closely with the director

3. What is the *most important* reason for paying attention to every detail when making a historical film?

   A. to avoid being accused of deceiving the audience

   B. to transport the audience to a different time and place

   C. to provide challenges for the large cast and crew

   D. to win an Academy Award

4. What is one of the factors to consider when deciding whether to shoot a film on a set or on location?

   A. It is usually cheaper to film on location than on a set.

   B. The moviemakers have more control on the set.

   C. All scenes from a film must either be shot on location or on the set.

   D. The sets are expensive and never reused.

5. In a historical film, what are *usually* the most important elements needed to recreate the time period of the film?

   A. setting

   B. dialects and accents used by the actors

   C. costumes and props

   D. Computer Generated Imagery

6. In the "Moviemaking Primer" section, what is the meaning of the word *fluent*?

   A. to understand what is spoken or written

   B. to be able to write or speak smoothly

   C. to be unable to read or write

   D. to be tongue-tied

7. What is the main idea of the selection?

   A. Creating a great historical movie takes a lot of work.

   B. The set, costumes, and props are the main elements needed for a successful movie.

   C. Most historical films today use Computer Generated Imagery.

   D. Today historical films are not made very often.

8. What is *probably not* an advantage of using CGI (Computer Generated Imagery) in a movie?

   A. CGI could be used to create all props and costumes to be used in a film.

   B. Unwanted details can be eliminated.

   C. Fewer extras will be needed

   D. Impossible things can be made to happen.

9. Which of the following statements is *not* accurate?

   A. The director hires and controls the actors.

   B. Extras are often used in crowd scenes.

   C. The producer raises the money.

   D. The producer is the boss of the movie.

Name _____ Date _____

Read the following poem and then answer the questions that follow.

"Excelsior" *by* Henry Wadsworth Longfellow

(1) The shades of night were falling fast,
As through an Alpine village passed
A youth, who bore, 'mid snow and ice,
A banner with the strange device,
Excelsior!

(2) His brow was sad; his eye beneath
Flashed like a falchion from its sheath,
And like a silver clarion rung
The accents of that unknown tongue,
Excelsior!

(3) In happy homes he saw the light
Of household fires gleam warm and bright;
Above, the spectral glaciers shone,
And from his lips escaped a groan,
Excelsior!

(4) "Try not the Pass," the old man said;
"Dark lours the tempest overhead,
The roaring torrent is deep and wide!"
And loud that clarion voice replied,
Excelsior!

(5) "O stay," the maiden said, "and rest
Thy weary head upon this breast!"
A tear stood in his bright blue eye,
But still he answered, with a sigh,
Excelsior!

(6) "Beware the pine-tree's withered branch!
Beware the awful avalanche!"
This was the peasant's last Good-night.
A voice replied, far up the height,
Excelsior!

(7) At break of day, as heavenward
The pious monks of Saint Bernard
Uttered the oft-repeated prayer,
A voice cried through the startled air,
Excelsior!

(8) A traveler, by the faithful hound,
Half-buried in the snow was found,
Still grasping in his hands of ice

(9) That banner with the strange device,
Excelsior!

(10) There in the twilight cold and gray,
Lifeless, but beautiful, he lay,
And from the sky, serene and far,
A voice fell, like a falling star,
Excelsior!
Excelsior

10. Why is "Excelsior" a narrative poem?

   A. Because it rhymes.

   B. Because it tells a story.

   C. Because it is about a maiden

   D. Because it has several verses.

11. Based on stanza 2, what ***most likely*** is a falchion?

   A. a bird

   B. a stone

   C. a fire

   D. a sword

12. What is the young man warned about in stanza 4?

   A. a man

   B. a fire and a glacier

   C. a storm and the river

   D. a voice

13. What is the main idea of the selection?

   A. A young man saves his country from a terrible war.

   B. A young man is killed in war.

   C. A young man is sad and lonely.

   D. A young man dies as he tries to reach his goal.

Read the following selection and then answer the questions that follow.

Not All Lockers are Created Equal

Have you ever walked right past your locker in the hall without realizing it was your locker. At most schools all lockers look pretty much the same. Would you like for your locker to be special? You to can be the proud owner of a "one of a kind" individualized locker. A little bit of "home away from home." Read the following steps for creating a personalized locker that is a reflection of you.

Steps:

1) Find out what your school's policies are about decorated lockers. Some schools will allow decorations only on the inside of the locker.

2) After you have all the facts, begin to collect all the things that you think you might want to include. Pictures, a mirror, fabric trim, trinkets, or maybe even a bumper sticker. Remember that a variety of people (girls, boys, teachers, parents) will see inside your during the year, so keep it in good taste!

3) Before you actually begin to decorate, you need to draw out a design plan. You will need to keep books in your locker so be sure to leave plenty of room for them.

4) Attach your personal items to the locker with removable glue or with sticky putty. You will want to take your personal items with you when you move to a new hall next year.

5) Keeping your locker neat is an important part of your decorations. Your locker is a reflection of what you think is important. Show that organization and neatness matter to you. A note pad with a pencil attached to the locker door is a great way to keep track of important information or a way to remind yourself what you need to take home each day.

6) Decorating your locker isn't like a beauty contest. It is a place to show your character. Create a theme that will show old friends and new friend what you are really like.

14. What is the main idea of the selection?

   A. Decorating your locker can be fun and inexpensive.

   B. Decorating your locker can get you in trouble at school.

   C. A personalized locker will show friends and teacher who you are,

   D. Don't put anything in your locker that you don't want others to see.

15. Why should you check with your teacher *before* you begin?

   A. You will need his or her help.

   B. You don't want someone to copy your ideas.

   C. You will need to borrow things from your teacher.

   D. You do not want to violate school policies.

16. Why is it a good idea to develop a plan *before* you begin to decorate?

   A. You want to be sure you have enough room for your books.

   B. You need to get permission before you begin.

   C. You want everything to match.

   D. You want to win the contest.

Name _____ Date _____

Read the following play and then answer the questions that follow.

Scenes from The Adventures of Tom Sawyer *by* Mark Twain

Setting: Aunt Polly's house and yard
Characters: Tom Sawyer (*a boy about 12 years old, the son of Aunt Polly's dead sister*)
Aunt Polly (*An older lady who cares for Tom but is very strict.*)

Aunt Polly: (standing on the front porch yelling) **Tom!. Tomm!** (no answer) **Tom! . . . What's gone with that boy?** (Aunt Polly pushes up her glasses) **Well, I lay if I get hold of you I'll** . . . before she finishes she hears a noise and looks around)

Tom: (Sneaks on stage and stands behind Aunt Polly, then Meows like a cat) meow (Tom has a dirty face and hands)

Aunt Polly: **You-u Tom!** (she grabs Tom by the back of his shirt) **Look at your hands and your mouth! It's Jam. . . . that's what it is . . . Forty times I've said if you don't leave that jam alone...I'd skin you. . . . Hand me that switch.**

Tom: (urgently to Aunt Polly) **Look behind you!** (When Aunt Polly turns her back Tom runs away)

Aunt Polly: **Hang that boy, can't I never learn anything? Ain't he played me tricks enough? I guess there's no fool like an old fool . . . Can't learn an old dog new tricks** (she starts to sweep the porch) **but he never plays them alike two days. How is a 'body to know what's coming.** (she stops sweeping and looks at the audience) **he 'pears to know just how long he can torment me before I get my dander up, and he knows if he can put me off for a minute or two or make me laugh, it's all down again and I can't hit him a lick.** (She walks down stage) **Lord's truth, goodness knows. Spare the rod and spoil the child.**

Setting: Later that day at the dinner table in Aunt Polly's kitchen. Aunt Polly suspects that Tom played hookey from school. Tom is eating his supper and stealing sugar as the opportunity presents itself) Tom had played hookey from school and had torn the collar of his shirt.

Aunt Polly: (setting the table) **Tom, it was middling warm in school, warn't it?**

Tom: Yes'm

Aunt Polly: Powerful warm, warn't it?

Tom: Yes'm

Aunt Polly: Didn't you want to go in a swimming, Tom?

Tom: (squirming and looking uncomfortable) **No'm . . . well, not too much.**

Aunt Polly: (reaches over and touches Tom's shirt) **But you ain't too warm now.**

Tom: (not sure what to expect next) **Some of us pumped our heads....mine's damp yet, see?** (Tom leans over for Aunt Polly to touch his hair)

Aunt Polly: **Tom, you didn't have to undo your shirt collar where I sewed it, to pump your head, did you? Unbutton your jacket.**

Tom: (without worry because his collar was securely fastened takes off his jacket) **See, it is just like you sewed it.**

Aunt Polly: **Brother! Well go 'long with you. I'd made sure you'd played hookey and been a swimming. I reckon you're kind of a singed cat, as the saying goes** . . . (She pats Tom on the back) **I'm glad you stumbled into being obedient for once.**

Tom: (with a big smile looks up at Aunt Polly) **Yes'm**

Aunt Polly: (looking closely at Tom) **Well, now I don't think I sewed that collar with black thread...I'm sure it was white!**

Tom: (not waiting for Aunt Polly to finish, takes off for the door under his breath) **Confound it! sometimes she sews it with white thread and the other black. I wish to geeminy she'd stick to one or t'other.**

17. Why is the use of dialect appropriate for this selection?

   A. It makes it funnier.

   B. It makes it more realistic.

   C. The author talks this way.

   D. The author is making fun of the characters.

18. What *most likely* will happen next?

   A. Aunt Polly will send Tom to an orphanage.

   B. Tom will continue with his tricks.

   C. Aunt Polly will never believe Tom again.

   D. Tom will not get in trouble again.

19. Which of the following **best** supports the idea that Aunt Polly loves Tom inspite of his tricks?

   A. when she asked Tom about school.

   B. when she laughs to herself about falling for Tom's tricks.

   C. when she sews Tom's collar.

   D. when she asked Tom about swimming.

20. What is the effect of beginning the selection with Aunt Polly looking for Tom?

   A. It lets you know that Aunt Polly is mad at Tom.

   B. It lets you know that Tom is playing hookey.

   C. It lets you know that Tom is often in trouble.

   D. It lets you know that Aunt Polly fusses a lot.

21. How do the stage directions help the reader?

   A. They tell the reader where to stand

   B. They give expression to the lines.

   C. They provide directions for the actors.

   D. They help the reader visualize the play.

22. Which of the following *best* describes Aunt Polly?

   A. A caring person who is concerned for Tom's welfare.

   B. An old lady with loose glasses.

   C. Tom's strict Aunt.

   D. A hateful person who fusses all the time.

23. Which of the following **best** describes Tom?

A. A boy who likes to trick his Aunt.

B. A boy who plays hookey from school.

C. A boy who is full of fun and mischief.

D. A boy who likes to go swimming.

24. What **most likely** did Aunt Polly mean when she said, "Spare the rod and spile the child"?

A. A Tom needed a spankings

B. Adults have the right to punish children.

C. Tom was a spoiled brat.

D. Children need to be taught to behave.

Name _____ Date _____

Read the following poem and then answer the questions that follow.

The Little Ghost by Edna St. Vincent Millay

I knew her for a little ghost
  That in my garden walked;
The wall is high—higher than most—
  And the green gate was locked.

And yet I did not think of that
  Till after she was gone—
I knew her by the broad white hat,
  All ruffled, she had on.

By the dear ruffles round her feet,
  By her small hands that hung
In their lace mitts, austere and sweet,
  Her gown's white folds among.

I watched to see if she would stay,
  What she would do—and oh!
She looked as if she liked the way
  I let my garden grow!

She bent above my favourite mint
  With conscious garden grace,
She smiled and smiled—there was no hint
  Of sadness in her face.

She held her gown on either side
  To let her slippers show,
And up the walk she went with pride,
  The way great ladies go.

And where the wall is built in new
  And is of ivy bare
She paused—then opened and passed through
  A gate that once was there.

25. What is the rhyme scheme of this poem?
   A. ABCD
   B. ABBA
   C. ABAB
   D. AABB

26. Based on the context of the poem, how does the speaker feel about the Little Ghost?
   A. The speaker does not know the Little Ghost and is worried that she is there.
   B. The speaker does not recognize the Little Ghost, but finds her friendly.
   C. The speaker knows the Little Ghost and tries to stop her from leaving.
   D. The speaker recognizes the Little Ghost and seems happy she came.

27. Based on the context of the poem, what *most likely* is the Little Ghost feeling?
   A. The Little Ghost seems afraid.
   B. The Little Ghost seems worried.
   C. The Little Ghost seems happy.
   D. The Little Ghost seems sad.

28. Which of the following best describes the last stanza of the poem?
   A. The Little Ghost leaves the garden by the new gate.
   B. The Little Ghost tries to leave the garden but can not find the gate.
   C. The Little Ghost leaves the garden by opening a gate that is no longer there.
   D. The speaker leaves the garden by opening the gate with a key.

Name _____   Date _____

Read the following passage about dog intelligence and then answer the questions that follow.

How Emotionally Smart are Dogs?

Most dog owners and dog lovers would agree that dogs are good pets. One of the best reasons for this opinion is that dogs are smart. Almost anyone would like to have a great dog, like Lassie or Winn Dixie, but what about real dogs? If you have ever seen a seeing eye dog at work, or read about a family pet that saved someone's life, you realize that dogs can truly be man's best friend. According to Michael D. Lemonick, an ethologist, and writer for *Time Magazine*, animal behavior experts also think dogs are emotionally smart and have the research to back up their beliefs.

For many years scientists did not believe that animals had emotions. They believed that only humans could feel happiness, sadness, and frustration. Biologists now believe most social animals like dolphins, monkeys, dogs, and even some birds and rats have not only low level emotions, but also emotions such as envy, empathy, and a sense of "fair play."

In his article, Mr. Lemonick shares the research of scientist Mr. Marc Bekoff. Bekoff, who teaches at the University of Colorado, and has studied dogs, wolves, and coyotes for many years. He has documented numerous signals that these animals use to let other canines know that they want to play.

One of the signs of a playful mood is what Bekoff calls the "play bow." The canine puts his front feet forward and lowers his head while the hind-quarters stay in the air and the tail wags. In dog language, that means "let's have some fun." In another playful stance, the canines appear to be dancing. Both animals stand on their hind legs and hold on to each other with their forepaws. Bekoff even believes that dogs have a way of apologizing for any accidental pain they might inflict during their play fight. He goes on to say that dogs who cheat won't get invited to play again.

It just may be true that when you think your dog looks happy or embarrassed, he or she may truly be feeling these emotions. Bekoff worked for over ten years on his research and believes that canines have a very "complex social interaction." "I don't say dogs are fair the way you and I are fair, or have the same moral systems," said Bekoff. However, it does seem that many of the emotions that were once thought to be only human are, in fact, shared with other animals.

It makes this writer wonder what my old Dalmatian is thinking and feeling when he rides in the car. His head is out the window; his ears blowing in the breeze. Just maybe, part of the thrill for him is the attention he receives from passengers in other cars. Maybe it makes him happy to see the smiles on children's faces.

29. Based on the selection, what are social animals?

   A. animals that people keep as pets.

   B. animals that are called canines

   C. animals that live in groups

   D. animals that have feelings

30. Based on the selection, what is the meaning of "complex social interaction"?

   A. a certain kind of behavior

   B. many ways of dealing with each other

   C. different ways of fighting

   D. numerous ways of obtaining Food.

31. How did Mark Bekoff **most likely** make his discoveries?

   A. by observing and studying dogs

   B. by reading other research

   C. by watching wolves in the wild

   D. by owning dogs, monkeys and rats

32. What does Bekoff mean by the term **signals**?

   A. emotions

   B. actions

   C. canines

   D. thinking

33. Which of the following actions is not part of what Bekoff calls the "play bow?"

   A. The canine puts his or her front feet forward.

   B. The canine lowers his or her head.

   C. The canine barks loudly.

   D. The canine wags his or her tail.

34. Why is Bekoff's research important?

   A. It explains why people love dogs.

   B. It proves that dogs are man's best friend.

   C. Most people did not think dogs were smart.

   D. It helps prove that animals have emotions.

Read the following two excerpts and then answer the questions that follow.

Part 1

In the following excerpt from "Meet Ranger Nancy Muleady-Mecham," Nancy discusses some of the aspects of her job.

from Meet Nancy Muleady-Mecham

An Outdoor Classroom

Lacey: So what's a work day like for a naturalist ranger?

Ranger Nancy: Well, there is a lot of variety! Each day is different. In Sequoia and Kings Canyon National Parks, I led hikes high up in the mountains to lakes carved by glaciers. I even used real skins, skulls, and sometimes even live animals to illustrate diversity in animals. People got to see the difference between a bobcat and a mountain lion. They learned a bear is an omnivore—it eats both plants and meat—by looking at its skull and teeth.

In Death Valley and Grand Canyon National Parks, I led walks to identify birds. Fossils and geology were also subjects of my talks. More than 20 different kinds of amphibian and reptile fossil footprints have been found at the Grand Canyon. Also, it is a great place to talk about how rocks are formed. The walls of the Grand Canyon are over one-mile high. There are almost forty different kinds of rock layers. Many of them can be seen.

I took people canoeing in the Everglades. There people learned that alligators can live to be over 50 years old. People learned alligators can move fast, too. Did you know alligators can run up to 30 miles per hour?

Cultural history played a role in my talks too. In the Grand Canyon, I showed people gourd plants. Native Americans used the gourds to carry water and food. In Sequoia and Kings Canyon, people learned how Native Americans used reeds to weave baskets.

Lacey: What is one of the days you remember the most?

Ranger Nancy: That would be the day I had a "grand slam" at Death Valley. In baseball, that means a player is on every plate. When the batter hits a home run, each of those players scores a point. For a protection ranger, it's a 24-hour period of time when not only are you a policeman and fireman but you are a searcher and a medical responder too.

My grand slam happened while I was working in Death Valley. I had been searching for a man who disappeared in the middle of the desert. All we found was his car. When I left the search, I had to stop people from shooting guns where they weren't supposed to. Then I helped people whose car had caught on fire because it got too hot. After that, I had to go on a helicopter to help someone who had fallen and had a head injury. That was all in one hour! Luckily, everyone was alright though the man who left his car was never found.

Making a Difference

Lacey: What makes it all worth it?

Ranger Nancy: I feel like I am making a difference. People leave parks with a greater appreciation of our world. They are convinced of the need to take care of our community's natural, historical, and cultural areas.

Also, I am at home in these places. I get to watch animals go about their daily tasks in their communities. I don't hear traffic because I am listening to birds and rivers. The night sky and stars can be so bright that it feels like you can hit your head on them if you stand up too fast. And though the dollar pay is not much, I feel like I am paid in amazing sunrises and sunsets.

Part 2

In this excerpt from "A Winged Mystery," the narrator discusses bird watching.

from A Winged Mystery

Startling Sighting In February of 2004, a man named Gene Sparling was kayaking in the Cache River National Wilderness of Arkansas. The area he was in was a bayou. It was swampy, with many old trees. He saw a very large bird. It flew toward him and landed on a nearby tree. He watched it with the intent of identifying it. It was large and moved with a jerky motion. It looked to him like an ivory-billed woodpecker. This is a bird that has not been seen since 1944. Everyone thought it was extinct—that there were none left on Earth.

Shortly afterward, a birdwatcher captured the woodpecker on videotape. However, the quality of the tape was bad. Experts were not convinced. Ornithologists, scientists who study birds, looked at the tape. One said that the wings of the bird in the video had the wrong colors to be an ivory-billed woodpecker. He claimed it was a pileated woodpecker, a much more common bird. This bird is very similar in shape, size, and color to an ivory-billed woodpecker. Another ornithologist insisted that the bird in the video flew too quickly to be a pileated woodpecker.

Experts Join In Ornithologists came to the area to participate in a search. Several of them saw the bird, too. They described it. It had white wing edges. There was a narrow red crest on its head. A white line ran from its wings up its neck. One scientist heard the bird double-knocking on a tree trunk. He said this was a sound no other bird could imitate. It had to be an ivory-billed woodpecker.

Other ornithologists still did not think the bird was an ivory-billed woodpecker. They said it must be a pileated woodpecker. How could they determine which kind of bird it was?

There are six main ways that birdwatchers distinguish one bird from another. Their methods utilize the senses – sight and hearing – and they compare unknown birds to known birds. You can use these methods to identify birds, too. In fact, you can use them to decide for yourself if the mystery bird was a pileated woodpecker or an ivory-billed woodpecker!

... Be a Birdwatcher

With a pair of binoculars, a field guide to birds, and your own senses, you can probably identify almost any bird you see. The methods you've read about will help you. Notice a bird's habitat, size, shape, posture, color, and markings. Observe its behavior and flight. Listen to its voice. Each of these details will contribute to your identification. Even just a quick glimpse of a bird can give you enough information to hypothesize about its identity. If the bird will cooperate by staying in sight long enough, you can be even more certain of your identification. Watching and identifying birds can enrich your understanding of nature and the world around you.

35. In part 1, which of the following activities *best* describes the work done by a naturalist ranger?

   A. leading hikes in the mountains and around the lakes

   B. taking people canoeing

   C. giving history talks.

   D. all of the above

36. What *most likely* is *not* a reason that Ranger Nancy loves her job?

   A. She sees amazing sunrises and sunsets.

   B. She watches animals in their natural settings.

   C. She receives a large paycheck.

   D. She helps visitors appreciate our world.

37. What is Ranger Nancy's favorite part of her job?

   A. the nature walks

   B. helping the park visitors

   C. the variety of activities she does

   D. dressing up for the history talks

38. In part 2, Sparling sees a woodpecker. Why do the experts believe that it is most likely not the ivory-billed woodpecker?

   A. Sparling was no an expert on birds.

   B. The ivory-billed woodpecker was thought to be extinct.

   C. This woodpecker's colors were wrong, and it flew too slowly.

   D. The ivory-billed woodpecker was not native to Arkansas.

39. What is the meaning of the word *hypothesize* based on its context in the "Be a Bird-watcher" section of part 2?

   A. to propose a theory

   B. to prove a theory

   C. to gather evidence

   D. to observe with the five senses

40. What do both Ranger Nancy and Gene Sparling have in common?

   A. They can recognize different kinds of woodpeckers.

   B. They both work full-time caring for our natural resources.

   C. They are both very observant.

   D. They are both explorers.

41. Which of the following *most likely* describes how Sparling felt when he saw the ivory-billed woodpecker?

   A. worried that no one would believe him

   B. very surprised to see an ivory-billed woodpecker

   C. happy because he was looking for an ivory-billed woodpecker

   D. disappointed because he was looking for another type of bird

42. For what purpose is each passage written?

   A. to persuade the reader to work with natural resources

   B. to entertain the reader

   C. to inform the reader

   D. to interview a naturalist

43. In the "Be a Birdwatcher" section of part 2, what is the *most important* benefit of being a birdwatcher?

   A. the ability to quickly identify different types of birds

   B. the chance to travel to many places

   C. an increased understanding of nature and the world

   D. meeting new people during interviews

44. What is the meaning of the word *gourd* based on its context in the "Outdoor Classroom" section of part 1?

   A. green and ripened

   B. fruit with a hard shell

   C. vegetable which grows underground

   D. type of cactus

45. What is the meaning of the word *utilizes* based on its context in the "Experts Join In" section of part 2?

   A. to neglect

   B. to put to use

   C. to ignore

   D. to awaken

46. How many main ways are there for birdwatchers to distinguish one bird from another, according to the "Experts Join In" section of part 2?

   A. two

   B. three

   C. six

   D. nine

Read the following story and then answer the questions that follow.

from The Invisible Man, *by* H.G. Wells

H.G. Wells, (1866-1946), was a prolific writer, but he is best remembered for his science fiction. The Time Machine(1895), The Invisible Man (1897), and The War of the Worlds (1898), are his best known novels. Wells was a sociologist and historian. His satirical works reflected his views of society.

CHAPTER I

"The Strange Man's Arrival"

1)   The stranger came early in February, one wintry day, through a biting wind and a driving snow, the last snowfall of the year, over the down, walking from Bramblehurst railway station, and carrying a little black portmanteau in his thickly gloved hand. He was wrapped up from head to foot, and the brim of his soft felt hat hid every inch of his face but the shiny tip of his nose; the snow had piled itself against his shoulders and chest, and added a white crest to the burden he carried. He staggered into the "Coach and Horses" more dead than alive, and flung his portmanteau down. "A fire," he cried, "in the name of human charity! A room and a fire!" He stamped and shook the snow from off himself in the bar, and followed Mrs. Hall into her guest parlor to strike his bargain. And with that much introduction, that and a couple of sovereigns flung upon the table, he took up his quarters in the inn.

2)   Mrs. Hall lit the fire and left him there while she went to prepare him a meal with her own hands.

A guest to stop at Iping in the wintertime was an unheard-of piece of luck, let alone a guest who was no "haggler," and she was resolved to show herself worthy of her good fortune. As soon as the bacon was well under way, and Millie, her lymphatic aid, had been brisked up a bit by a few deftly chosen expressions of contempt, she carried the cloth, plates, and glasses into the parlor and began to lay them with the utmost éclat. Although the fire was burning up briskly, she was surprised to see that her visitor still wore his hat and coat, standing with his back to her and staring out of the window at the falling snow in the yard. His gloved hands were clasped behind him, and he seemed to be lost in thought. She noticed that the melting snow that still sprinkled his shoulders dripped upon her carpet. "Can I take your hat and coat, sir?" she said, "and give them a good dry in the kitchen?"

3)   "No," he said without turning.

4)   She was not sure she had heard him, and was about to repeat her question.

5)   He turned his head and looked at her over his shoulder. "I prefer to keep them on," he said with emphasis, and she noticed that he wore big blue spectacles with sidelights, and had a bush side-whisker over his coat-collar that completely hid his cheeks and face.

6)   "Very well, sir," she said. "As you like. In a bit the room will be warmer." He made no answer, and had turned his face away from her again, and Mrs. Hall, feeling that her conversational advances were ill timed, laid the rest of the table things in a quick staccato and whisked out of the room. When she returned he was still standing there, like a man of stone, his back hunched, his collar turned up, his dripping hat-brim turned down, hiding his face and ears completely. She put down the eggs and bacon with considerable emphasis, and called rather than said to him, "Your lunch is served, sir."?

7) She rapped and entered promptly. As she did so, her visitor moved quickly, so that she got but a glimpse of a white object disappearing behind the table. It would seem he was picking something from the floor. She rapped down the mustard pot on the table, and then she noticed the overcoat and hat had been taken off and put over a chair in front of the fire, and a pair of wet boots threatened rust to her steel fender. She went to these things resolutely. "I suppose I may have them to dry now," she said in a voice that brooked no denial.

8) "Leave the hat," said her visitor, in a muffled voice, and turning she saw he had raised his head and was sitting and looking at her. For a moment, she stood gaping at him, too surprised to speak.

9) He held a white cloth? it was a serviette he had brought with him? over the lower part of his face, so that his mouth and jaws were completely hidden, and that was the reason of his muffled voice. But it was not that which startled Mrs. Hall. It was the fact that all his forehead above his blue glasses was covered by a white bandage, and that another covered his ears, leaving not a scrap of his face exposed excepting only his pink, peaked nose. It was bright, pink, and shiny just as it had been at first. He wore a dark-brown velvet jacket with a high, black, linen-lined collar turned up about his neck. The thick black hair, escaping as it could below and between the cross bandages, projected in curious tails and horns, giving him the strangest appearance conceivable. This muffled and bandaged head was so unlike what she had anticipated that for a moment she was rigid.

10) He did not remove the serviette, but remained holding it, as she saw now, with a brown-gloved hand, and regarding her with his inscrutable blue glasses. "Leave the hat," he said, speaking very distinctly through the white cloth.

11) Her nerves began to recover from the shock they had received. She placed the hat on the chair again by the fire. "I didn't know, sir," she began, "that?" and she stopped embarrassed. "Thank

you," he said dryly, glancing from her to the door and then at her again?..

12) "The poor soul's had an accident or an op'ration or somethin'," said Mrs. Hall. "What a turn them bandages did give me, to be sure!"

13) She put on some more coal, unfolded the clothes-horse, and extended the traveler's coat upon this. "And they goggles! Why, he looked more like a divin' helmet than a human man!" She hung his muffler on a corner of the horse. "And holding that handkerchief over his mouth all the time. Talkin' through it! ... Perhaps his mouth was hurt too? maybe."

14) She turned round, as one who suddenly remembers. "Bless my soul alive!" she said, going off at a tangent; "ain't you done them taters yet, Millie?"

15) When Mrs. Hall went to clear away the stranger's lunch, her idea that his mouth must also have been cut or disfigured in the accident she supposed him to have suffered, was confirmed, for he was smoking a pipe, and all the time that she was in the room he never loosened the silk muffler he had wrapped round the lower part of his face to put the mouthpiece to his lips. Yet it was not forgetfulness, for she saw he glanced at it as it smoldered out. He sat in the corner with his back to the window-blind and spoke now, having eaten and drunk and being comfortably warmed through, with less aggressive brevity than before. The reflection of the fire lent a kind of red animation to his big spectacles they had lacked hitherto.

16) "I have some luggage," he said, "at Bramblehurst station," and he asked her how he could have it sent. He bowed his bandaged head quite politely in acknowledgment of her explanation. "To-morrow?" he said. "There is no speedier delivery?" and seemed quite disappointed when she answered, "No." Was she quite sure? No man with a trap who would go over?

17) Mrs. Hall, nothing loath, answered his questions and developed a conversation. "It's a steep road by the down, sir," she said in answer to the

question about a trap; and then, snatching at an opening, said, "It was there a carriage was up settled, a year ago and more. A gentleman killed, besides his coachman. Accidents, sir, happen in a moment, don't they?"

18) But the visitor was not to be drawn so easily. "They do," he said through his muffler, eyeing her quietly through his impenetrable glasses.

19) "But they take long enough to get well, don't they? ... There was my sister's son, Tom, jest cut his arm with a scythe, tumbled on it in the 'ayfield, and, bless me! he was three months tied up sir. You'd hardly believe it. It's regular given me a dread of a scythe, sir."

20) "I can quite understand that," said the visitor.

21) "He was afraid, one time, that he'd have to have an op'ration? he was that bad, sir."

22) The visitor laughed abruptly, a bark of a laugh that he seemed to bite and kill in his mouth. "Was he?" he said.

23) "He was, sir. And no laughing matter to them as had the doing for him, as I had? my sister being took up with her little ones so much. There was bandages to do, sir, and bandages to undo. So that if I may make so bold as to say it, sir?"

24) "Will you get me some matches?" said the visitor, quite abruptly. "My pipe is out." Mrs. Hall was pulled up suddenly. It was certainly rude of him, after telling him all she had done. She gasped at him for a moment, and remembered the two sovereigns. She went for the matches?

47. What is the meaning of the word *sovereigns* in paragraph 1?

   A. quarters

   B. money

   C. clothing

   D. bargain

48. What is the main purpose of paragraph one?

   A. to establish the time of year.

   B. to introduce the stranger and show how he looks.

   C. to explain that the stranger arrived on the train.

   D. to establish Mrs. Hall's Character.

49. What was unusual about the stranger's arrival?

   A. There were few travelers during winter.

   B. Mrs. Hall had closed for the evening.

   C. The stranger did not have a bag.

   D. The stranger was covered from head to foot.

50. Why *most likely* did the stranger wear his gloves when he ate?

   A. It was very cold in the room.

   B. He did not realize he was wearing them.

   C. his hands were covered in bandages.

   D. His hands were invisible.

51. Which of the following *best* explains the stranger reaction to Mrs. Hill's story of the carriage accident?

   A. He thought it was minor compared to his problem

   B. He had genuine concern for Tom.

   C. He thought it was a big joke.

   D. He didn't want to hear the story.

52. What *most likely* had happened to the stranger before he arrived at Mrs. Hill's inn?

   A. He had missed his train.

   B. He had met Tom on the train.

   C. He had been in a terrible accident.

   D. He had an operation.

53. Which of the following *best* describes the stranger's behavior at Mrs. Hill's inn?

   A. He was mysterious and reserved.

   B. He was rude and smoked too much.

   C. He ate a lot and wanted to talk.

   D. He laughed a lot and smoked.

54. Why *most likely* was the stranger wrapped in bandages?

   A. He had an operation.

   B. He did not want to be recognized.

   C. He was invisible.

   D. He was badly scared.

55. Which of the following techniques did the author use to make the story more realistic?

   A. dialect

   B. irony

   C. figurative language

   D. setting

Writing Assessment Sample Prompts

Use the following two prompts to practice for writing assessment.

Writing Prompt 1

You are walking down the street and you notice a wallet lying on the sidewalk. No one is around so you pick up the wallet and look inside. There is no identification, but there is a large sum of money inside. You look around to see if anyone appears to have lost a wallet. No one does. You don't know what to do.

Write an essay in which you think of a solution to your problem. In your essay, explain what you plan to do with the wallet and why.

As you write your essay to your principal, remember to:

- Focus on the problem that yozu face, and propose a solution for what to do with the wallet.
- Consider the purpose, audience, and context of your essay.
- Organize your ideas effectively.
- Include specific details that develop your essay.
- Edit your essay for standard grammar and language usage.

Use a blank sheet of paper to plan your essay. Anything you write on the blank sheet will not be scored. Write the final copy of your essay on the next page(s).

Writing Prompt 2

You are a teacher. For the past few months your students have not been completing their homework. You have established strict consequences in your classroom for those students who have not completed their homework. However, the consequences are not working. You are desperate to think of another plan to get your students to complete their assignments.

Write an essay explaining an alternate solution to the problem. Think of a creative way to encourage students to do their homework.

As you write your essay, remember to:

- Focus on the problem you face as a teacher, and propose an alternate solution.
- Consider the purpose, audience, and context of your essay.
- Organize your ideas effectively.Include specific details that develop your essay.
- Edit your essay for standard grammar and language usage.

Use a blank sheet of paper to plan your essay. Anything you write on the blank sheet will not be scored. Write the final copy of your essay on the next page(s).

ITBS PRACTICE TEST

Vocabulary

DIRECTIONS

This is a test about words and their meanings.

■ For each question, you are to decide which one of the four answers has most nearly the same meaning as the underlined word above it.

■ Then, on your answer folder, find the row of answer spaces numbered the same as the question. Fill in the answer space that has the same letter as the answer you picked.

The sample on this page shows you what the questions are like and how to mark your answers.

SAMPLE

S1 To <u>utter</u> a word
- **A** write
- **B** speak
- **C** teach
- **D** spell

ANSWER

S1 A B C D

Vocabulary

1 A <u>melancholy</u> guy

A friendly
B mean
C glum
D unhealthy

2 A dust <u>particle</u>

J desk
K piece
L highway
M walkway

3 To <u>emphasize</u> the point

A stress
B undermine
C approximate
D explain

4 A <u>baffled</u> detective

J grumpy
K confused
L lost
M brash

5 A severe <u>typhoon</u>

A snowstorm
B tidal wave
C hailstorm
D tropical storm

6 A <u>victorious</u> swimmer

J delighted
K triumphant
L ferocious
M fearless

7 An <u>approximate</u> number

A precise
B average
C inexact
D inferior

8 The rain <u>relented</u>.

J ceased
K renewed
L surged
M continued

9 A long <u>blockade</u>

A exile
B crusade
C barrier
D neighborhood

10 An <u>irregular</u> procedure

J normal
K awkward
L modern
M unusual

11 A <u>shrewd</u> businesswoman

A harsh
B clever
C annoying
D easy-going

12 <u>Utilize</u> a pencil

J use
K take
L bring
M provide

13 A dog <u>in pursuit</u>

A walking
B running
C chasing
D pointing

14 A <u>punctual</u> person

J stern
K sullen
L prompt
M resourceful

Reading Comprehension

DIRECTIONS

This is a test of how well you understand what you read.

- This test consists of reading passages followed by questions.

- Read each passage and then answer the questions.

- Four answers are given for each question. You are to choose the answer that you think is better than the others.

- Then, on your answer folder, find the row of answer spaces numbered the same as the question. Fill in the answer space for the best answer.

The sample on this page shows you what the questions are like and how to mark your answers.

SAMPLE

> I flew to Miami and had a wonderful time. The women only were able to compete on bars, beam and floor—and you didn't have to compete in every event if you didn't want to. We had four people on the team, and three had to compete in each event. I had planned on competing on the beam and floor.

S1 **What was the author doing?**

- **A** Dancing in a show
- **B** Competing in gymnastics
- **C** Playing a basketball game
- **D** Performing for her parents

ANSWER

S1 A B C D

"More Than Statistics" in *Discoveries: Path to the Present*

What Is Diversity?

Demographers are social scientists who study population. They look at numbers of people who fit into one or more of six categories. These include cultural and economic factors. They are race/ethnicity, foreign born, age, household composition, education, and income. There are studies of one geographic area over time and across different geographic areas. Depending on a community's similarities or differences, it may be called more or less diverse.

How Does Cultural Diversity Affect People?

You can look at cultural diversity in several ways. You can analyze it by region. You can consider it in a metropolitan area—a city and its suburbs. You can look within the city itself or in one of its ZIP Codes, even in one census tract. Does living in one of these diverse areas make a difference to some of its people? Does it make a difference to any of its people?

It really all depends. America was once thought of as a melting pot. People who came here from different countries were the ingredients. Throw them into the pot—and out came a soup or a stew. Individual ingredients were no longer important. Today, the variety of people from different backgrounds make up what we usually call a *cultural mosaic*. A mosaic is a pattern or picture made from different small pieces of tile. Although they form a whole, you can still see the separate pieces.

From Sea . . .

It is possible for people to live next door—even on the same floor of an apartment building—and have little or nothing to do with one another. In cases like that, diversity has little effect on people's daily lives. If they shop together, go to school together, and unite behind a common cause, then the value of learning to live with others unlike oneself serves a positive purpose.

---

1 With which one of the following statements would the author be most likely to agree?

   A Once someone arrives in the U.S. from another country, his or her individuality is no longer important.

   B Today America is considered a melting pot.

   C Today America is considered a cultural mosaic.

   D Today America is considered both a melting pot and a cultural mosaic.

2 According to the article, what activities do *not* help people learn to live with different people?

   J living next door to people unlike yourself

   K going to school with people unlike yourself

   L shopping with people unlike yourself

   M supporting a common cause with people unlike yourself

3 Based on the context of the passage, what is the meaning of the phrase *cultural mosaic*?

   A people of different backgrounds who come together while keeping their individuality

   B a new term meaning melting pot

   C a system of separate communities for within a large city

   D a collection of cultural and economic factors that make up a community

4 Based on the context of the "What is Diversity" section, what is the meaning of the word *metropolitan*?

   J in the city

   K economic

   L in the country

   M diverse

Morning by Emily Dickinson
1 Will there really be a morning?
2 Is there such a thing as day?
3 Could I see it from the mountains
4 If I were as tall as they?
5 Has it feet like water lilies?
6 Has it feathers like a bird?
7 Is it brought from famous countries
8 Of which I've never heard?
9 Oh some scholar, oh some sailor,
10 Oh some wise man from the skies,
11 Please to tell a little pilgrim
12 Where the place called morning lies.

---

5 **What is the rhyme scheme in this poem?**

A ABAB

B ABCB

C ABCD

D ABBC

6 **What best describes the speaker's tone in this poem?**

J childlike

K sad

L worried

M cheerful

7 **In lines 5 and 6, the speaker asks if "it" has feet or feathers. What does *it* refer to?**

A a bird

B water lilies

C the pilgrim

D morning

8 **In this poem, to whom is the speaker asking for help?**

J a scholar

K a sailor

L a wise man

M all of the above

9 **To whom is the author referring when she talks about "a little pilgrim" in line 11?**

A a traveler

B a scholar

C the speaker

D an unknown place

10 **Based on the context of the poem, what does the speaker desire?**

J to be as tall as mountains

K to sail to another country

L to fly freely like a bird

M to go to the place called morning

"The Iditarod: the Last Great Race on Earth" in *Discoveries: Trouble Ahead*

The Iditarod, a race that covers over one thousand miles, is grueling. But the distance is not the only thing that makes it so hard. The real challenge comes from the course itself, an unending stretch of cold, snowy, isolated, unpredictable Alaskan wilderness. Mushers are in a constant battle with the elements just to finish this incredible race.

Those who do survive and finish say there is nothing like it. The feeling of conquering both nature and human limits is glorious. That is why many mushers come back, year after year, to try their luck in crossing the unforgiving Alaskan terrain.

A Race to Save Lives

The origin of the Iditarod goes back over one hundred years, to the early 1900s. That is when gold was first discovered in the area around Nome, Alaska. The lure of gold brought thousands of people to Alaska. Towns like Nome and Iditarod grew rapidly.

The miners in these places needed a way to transport gold, mail, and supplies during the winter months when ships couldn't reach the harbor. So, they turned to dogsleds. Soon, dogsled trails traversed this remote area.

By 1920, the gold rush was over. People abandoned the town of Iditarod. Eventually, it was almost deserted. However, sled dogs still continued to use the trails that led to Nome, delivering mail and other important supplies during the cold winter months.

Then, in January of 1925, tragedy struck Nome. Two Native Alaskan children died of an infectious disease called diphtheria. Diphtheria is very contagious. The doctor in Nome was worried. His hospital didn't have the medicine he needed to fight the disease. Without it, hundreds of people would certainly die. The townspeople prayed that the doctor would locate some medicine and have it delivered quickly.

The problem was that nothing arrived quickly in Nome during January. Nome residents relied on a delivery system that used both a train and dogsleds. It took months for mail and supplies to arrive. Nome often received only two mail deliveries all winter.

Desperate to save lives, the doctor appealed to Alaskan officials. Together they hatched a plan. Teams of dogsled racers would relay the diphtheria serum to Nome. The relay could take up to two weeks, depending on the weather, but it was the best anyone could do. It would have to work.

The serum was first transported by train from Anchorage to Nenana. Then, on January 27, twenty mushers and their dogs got ready to rush the medicine the next 674 miles to Nome.

The mushers were stationed at intervals along the trail. One musher would complete his leg of the relay. Then he would hand off the serum to the next musher, who would set out into the cold, snowy wilderness.

The weather was worse than anyone had expected. The mushers endured numbing cold, strong winds, and storms. Through it all, they had to be careful that the medicine didn't freeze.

With their determination, the mushers accomplished the impossible. They got the serum to Nome in less than six days. The mushers became national heroes.

The Beginning of a Tradition

Though the mushers and their race to save lives became famous, the Iditarod trail eventually fell into disuse. Planes and snowmobiles made dogsleds unnecessary. By the mid 1900s, traveling by dogsled was considered old-fashioned.

Then, in 1967, a celebration was organized for Alaska's centennial year. It was the hundredth anniversary of Alaska's purchase from Russia. Looking for ways to celebrate, organizers decided on a dogsled race. They would recreate part of the historic relay that had saved so many lives in 1925.

It Must Be Love

Why do people race in the Iditarod? As the racers themselves point out, it's not for the money. It costs more to run the race than the winners get in prize money. There are dogs to train and there is equipment to buy and transportation to pay for. Every racer has to ship food for 16 or more dogs to each race checkpoint.

For most racers, competing in the Iditarod is a family affair. Family members help the racers pack and ship food before the race. They often meet racers at checkpoints along the way or wait for them at the finish line in Nome.

For many families, the Iditarod is an annual ritual. Racers compete in the Iditarod over and over again. Some have already won it and are looking for more victories. Others still seek that elusive first win.

11 In the early 1900's, what was the *most likely* reason a person went to Alaska?

A to participate in one of the first Iditarod races

B to look for gold

C to work in the Nome hospital

D to enjoy the unique living conditions

12 In the "A Race to Save Lives" section, what is the meaning of the word "traversed"?

J to slide

K to go across

L to drive

M to become lost

13 What could one expect during the Iditarod race?

A unending stretches of cold, snowy land

B a great feeling of conquering nature

C the possibility of winning prize money

D all of the above

14 In 1925, which of the following was *not* a reason that a doctor appealed to Alaskan officials?

J He needed help to get medical supplies to Nome.

K Hundreds would die without medicine to fight diphtheria.

L He did not have the money to pay for an airplane to transport the medicine.

M Two children had already died.

15 What was the main problem of transporting the medicine to Nome?

A The medicine had to be frozen during the trip.

B The Nome airport was closed during the winter.

C There were no quick methods of transportation during the winter.

D Most dog sleds were not available because they were in the Iditoral race.

16 What was the *biggest* reason that the medicine was transported to Nome in less than 6 days?

A The weather conditions were good.

B Every musher and every dog performed his best.

C The train from Anchorage to Nenana was on time.

D Nome residents joined in the relay.

17 Why *most likely* would someone participate in the Iditarod race?

J to win the trophy for the fastest dog sled in Alaska

K to enjoy the outdoors

L to win the cash prize

M to have the glorious feeling of conquering nature

18 Based on the context, what is the meaning of the word *endured*?

J enjoyed

K ran away from

L suffered through

M rejected

Spelling

DIRECTIONS

This test will show how well you can spell.

- Many of the questions in this test contain mistakes in spelling. Some do not have any mistakes at all.

- You should look for mistakes in spelling.

- When you find a mistake, fill in the answer space on your answer folder that has the same letter as the line containing the mistake.

- If there is no mistake, fill in the last answer space.

The samples on this page show you what the questions are like and how to mark your answers.

SAMPLES

S1
  A   bond
  B   churn
  C   feest
  D   notch
  E   *(No mistakes)*

S2
  J   healthy
  K   landry
  L   quickly
  M   stingy
  N   *(No mistakes)*

ANSWERS

S1 A B **C** D E

S2 J **K** L M N

Spelling

1
A accomplish
B anguish
C disagreable
D campaign
E *(No mistakes)*

2
J infinate
K elevation
L endurance
M stammer
N *(No mistakes)*

3
A handicap
B purchase
C sucessful
D guardian
E *(No mistakes)*

4
J venison
K torrent
L agreeable
M tangerine
N *(No mistakes)*

5
A valient
B cherish
C quench
D propel
E *(No mistakes)*

6
J production
K international
L parliament
M oblagation
N *(No mistakes)*

7
A parole
B mareshall
C latter
D veteran
E *(No mistakes)*

8
J sustain
K intensive
L ammendment
M qualification
N *(No mistakes)*

9
A ventillate
B survival
C tedious
D spectacular
E *(No mistakes)*

10
J reception
K repitition
L reaction
M pension
N *(No mistakes)*

11
A realm
B plight
C morale
D lapse
E *(No mistakes)*

12
J habitation
K evasive
L comedien
M deceit
N *(No mistakes)*

13
A curency
B defendant
C decipher
D encompass
E *(No mistakes)*

14
J fortell
K flexible
L fugitive
M discriminate
N *(No mistakes)*

Capitalization

DIRECTIONS

This is a test on capitalization. It will show how well you can use capital letters in sentences.

- You should look for mistakes in capitalization in the sentences on this test.

- When you find a mistake, fill in the answer space on your answer folder that has the same letter as the **line** containing the mistake.

- Some sentences do not have any mistakes at all. If there is no mistake, fill in the last answer space.

The samples on this page show you what the questions are like and how to mark your answers.

SAMPLES

S1
A When my family moves
B to Binghamton, New York, I will
C attend montgomery elementary school.
D *(No mistakes)*

S2
J Erma Bombeck, the author
K of *at wit's end,* was a beloved
L newspaper columnist for many years.
M *(No mistakes)*

S3
A Maria smiled and asked, "Do
B you think you can teach me to ice
C skate? I've always wanted to learn."
D *(No mistakes)*

ANSWERS

S1 A B **C** D
S2 J **K** L M
S3 A B C **D**

Capitalization

1 A Mark Twain wrote many stories
   B about adventures along the banks
   C of the mighty Mississippi river.
   D *(No mistakes)*

2 J I wish I had asked our elderly
     neighbor,
   K Mrs. Cruz, more about what our
   L Neighborhood was like when she
     was growing up.
   M *(No mistakes)*

3 A My Mother thinks that I
   B should play on a soccer team next
   C year, since I play soccer with my
     friends every day.
   D *(No mistakes)*

4 J Paulina had never vacationed in
     Seattle, Washington,
   K because she wasn't sure that the
     rainy weather there would
   L appeal to her as much as the
     sunny weather in southern
     Mexico.
   M *(No mistakes)*

5 A After Kyle had taken three years
   B of Spanish, he went on a class
     trip to
   C Puerto Rico and the Dominican
     republic.
   D *(No mistakes)*

6 J Santa Fe, New Mexico, is a city
     famous
   K for its Native american arts and
     crafts,
   L including jewelry, pottery, and
     textiles.
   M *(No mistakes)*

7 A The first thing Rodney wants to do
     when he travels to Washington,
     D.C.,
   B is visit the white house, and the
   C second is to visit Monticello.
   D *(No mistakes)*

8 J   5498 west 54th Street
   K   Minneapolis, MN 55419
   L   October 31, 2000
   M   *(No mistakes)*

9 A Ms. Jasmine Johnson
   B The Minnesota arboretum
   C Dear Ms. Johnson:
   D *(No mistakes)*

10 J   The seventh-grade class at
      Lincoln Junior High
   K would like to thank you for the
      great
   L tour you gave us of the arboretum
      on October 25.
   M *(No mistakes)*

11 A   You pointed out and
      explained which plants and
   B trees grow in Minnesota. We
      especially liked the
   C red and orange leaves on the
      Maple trees.
   D *(No mistakes)*

12 J Thank you again for the tour.
   K   sincerely,
   L   The Seventh Grade
   M *(No mistakes)*

Punctuation

DIRECTIONS

This is a test on punctuation. It will show how well you can use periods, question marks, commas, and other kinds of punctuation marks.

■ You should look for mistakes in punctuation in the sentences on this test.

■ When you find a mistake, fill in the answer space on your answer folder that has the same letter as the **line** containing the mistake.

■ Some sentences do not have any mistakes at all. If there is no mistake, fill in the last answer space.

The samples on this page show you what the questions are like and how to mark your answers.

SAMPLES

S1 **A** We told Jack that he
     B wouldnt like the movie, but he
     C insisted on coming along anyway.
     D *(No mistakes)*

S2 **J** I have three favorite
     K pastimes, running, skiing,
     L and reading historical novels.
     M *(No mistakes)*

S3 **A** The little boy stared at
     B the ground. "I don't know
     C where my kitten is," he said.
     D *(No mistakes)*

ANSWERS

S1 A **B** C D
S2 J **K** L M
S3 A B C **D**

Punctuation

1
A Have you heard that saying?
B It goes, "If at first you don't
C succeed try try again."
D *(No mistakes)*

2
J Mohammed Elshihabi,
K Environmental Protection Agency
L December 19, 2000
M *(No mistakes)*

3
A Dear Mr. Elshihabi,
B   Our science club at Live Oak
  Junior High School
C is interested in studying the
  endangered animals of Texas.
D *(No mistakes)*

4
J   Please send information
  about endangered species of
K Texas or the Southwest. We are
  especially interested
L in opossums and armadillos. Are
  they endangered.
M *(No mistakes)*

5
A Thank you for considering our
  request
B   Sincerely,
C   The Seventh Grade
D *(No mistakes)*

6
J Did you live in New Hampshire
  before?"
K Ewen asked Joshua as they rode
L the bus home on the first day of
  school.
M *(No mistakes)*

7
A Amy said to Kay in surprise
B "When did you call last night?
C My brother never gave me the
  message."
D *(No mistakes)*

8
J One of the most frequently sung
K songs is "Happy Birthday to You"
L written by Patty Smith Hill and
  her sister Mildred Hill in 1893.
M *(No mistakes)*

9
A The menu at Mama's Ristorante
  includes pizzas with
B your choice of toppings; cheese,
  artichokes, sausage, pepperoni,
C olives, anchovies, and
  mushrooms.
D *(No mistakes)*

10
J Although Simon Bolivar was born
  in Caracas Venezuela,
K he fought for the independence
L of much of South America from
  the Spanish.
M *(No mistakes)*

11
A Kim was walking toward her gym
  locker when she heard Mi Long's
B voice behind her saying, "Did you
C get my note? You didnt write me
  back!"
D *(No mistakes)*

12
J They sold Valentines Day candy
K at school this year, and Jamie
  received
L a box of it from a secret admirer.
M *(No mistakes)*

Usage and Expression

DIRECTIONS

This is a test on the use of words. It will show how well you can use words according to the standards of correctly written English.

■ You should look for mistakes in the sentences on this test.

■ When you find a mistake, fill in the answer space on your answer folder that has the same letter as the **line** containing the mistake.

■ Some sentences do not have any mistakes at all. If there is no mistake, fill in the last answer space.

The samples on this page show you what the questions are like and how to mark your answers.

SAMPLES

S1 A Neither the manager nor the
    B employees understands why the employee
    C summer picnic was canceled this year.
    D *(No mistakes)*

S2 J Although my friend Ryan
    K ran very quick, he finished
    L only third in the race.
    M *(No mistakes)*

ANSWERS
S1 A **B** C D
S2 J **K** L M

Usage

1
  A "Watch the road! If you was
  B paying attention, you wouldn't have
  C missed the exit," her cousin said.
  D *(No mistakes)*

2
  J I asked my parents if I could go, but they want
  K me to stay home and study because
  L their not happy about my grades this fall.
  M *(No mistakes)*

3
  A Leo asked Jessica, "How are you?"
  B Jessica gave him a bright smile and said,
  C "Just fine, and how are you?"
  D *(No mistakes)*

4
  J That baker is really creative. She makes cakes in all kinds
  K of shapes. She done kangaroos,
  L trucks, and deer with antlers.
  M *(No mistakes)*

5
  A It's not well known that,
  B in addition to making good grades,
  C Frampton painting quite well.
  D *(No mistakes)*

6
  J Every student knows the
  K location of their class in addition
  L to his or her responsibilities.
  M *(No mistakes)*

7
  A Their mother picked them up
  B from soccer practice as she
  C was on the way home from judo practice.
  D *(No mistakes)*

8
  J After they watched the movie,
  K they played soccer at the park
  L because they was in the mood for exercise.
  M *(No mistakes)*

9
  A The magazine article claimed that
  B the quality of the water in the
  C lake will only get worser.
  D *(No mistakes)*

10
  J The front of the yard doesn't get
  K no sunshine, but the back of the
  L yard gets far too much.
  M *(No mistakes)*

11
  A My baby sister like to watch
  B the neighborhood kids play
  C games together in the evening.
  D *(No mistakes)*

12
  J Although it does not get much
  K attention, the pancreas is a very
  L important part of the body.
  M *(No mistakes)*

Expression

DIRECTIONS

This is Part 2 of the test about the use of words. It will show how well you can express ideas correctly and effectively. There are several sections to this part of the test. Read the directions to each section carefully. Then mark your answers on your answer folder.

Directions: Use this paragraph to answer questions 13–15.

---

[1]Ogden M. Pleissner was born in Brooklyn, New York, in 1905 and began painting when he was eleven years old. [2]He studied at the Art Students League and sold his first painting to the Metropolitan Museum of Art when he was twenty-seven. [3]Pleissner's love for the outdoors led him to paint landscapes, many of which include fishing scenes. [4]He even has a painting of a rainy day and a man on a bicycle talking with a couple who have umbrellas. [5]He is noted for his ability to re-create the mood of <u>some</u> seasons or times of the day by varying the light in his paintings.

---

13 **Which sentence should be left out of this paragraph?**

- **A** Sentence 1
- **B** Sentence 2
- **C** Sentence 3
- **D** Sentence 4

14 **What is the best way to write the underlined part of sentence 5?**

- **J** certain
- **K** other
- **L** any
- **M** *(No change)*

15 **Which is the best concluding sentence for this paragraph?**

- **A** That is why you should go see a Pleissner painting at the New York Metropolitan Museum of Art.
- **B** If you do not share his enthusiasm for the outdoors, you will not find his work interesting.
- **C** Pleissner's works are featured in many museums and private collections.
- **D** His painting *Springtime Rain* is my favorite.

Name _____ Date _____

Expression

Directions: In questions 16–17, choose the best way to express the idea.

16
J   My mom, for my birthday, took me and my two closest friends to the movies.
K   My mom took my two closest friends and me for my birthday to the movies.
L   For my birthday, my mom took my two closest friends and I to the movies.
M   For my birthday, my mom took my two closest friends and me to the movies.

17
A   My little brother was born on November 10, right before Thanksgiving.
B   Right before Thanksgiving, my little brother was born on November 10.
C   Right before Thanksgiving, on November 10, my little brother was born.
D   On November 10, my little brother was born right before Thanksgiving.

Directions: In questions 18–19, choose the best way to write the underlined part of the sentence.

18   She **don't** listen when I ask her to help set the table.

J   do   K   doesn't   L   do not   M   *(No change)*

19   We **were** coming home from the hay ride when the bus got a flat tire.

A   was   B   are   C   is   D   *(No change)*

20   **Which of these would be most persuasive in a letter to the school board?**

J   Please change the rule and let us use the Internet. We are probably the only school in the city that doesn't have Internet access. We promise we'll be responsible.

K   We do not have any Internet access at our school. The Internet is an important source of information that we need to learn to use. We can only learn to use it responsibly if you will give us a chance to try.

L   Everyone I talk to at school does not agree with the Internet policy. We can't prove that we'll be responsible if you won't even give us a chance. Give us Internet privileges for a month, and we'll show you we can be good.

M   We, the students of Carver Junior High, are writing to say that it is so unfair that we don't have Internet access. There are lots of programs you could install to restrict the sites that we use. You could just try to use one and see if it works.

TERRANOVA PRACTICE TEST

Reading and Language Arts

Sample Passage

One-of-a-Kind Creations

Did you know that for every kind of tree and flower, there may be dozens—or even hundreds—of unique variations? Botanists are scientists who study and classify plants according to their characteristics. For most of us, a rose is a rose, but for botanists, there are actually hundreds of different types of roses—each one unlike every other one.

Sample A

This passage is mostly about

Ⓐ how botanists study different kinds of roses

Ⓑ how botanists study many different types of plants

Ⓒ how people know very little about trees and flowers

Ⓓ how some trees and flowers have many different variations

All-in-One Workbook: Standardized Test Practice
393

Name _____ Date _____

Directions

A student wrote a paragraph about his older brother. There are some mistakes that need correcting.

> [1]For as long as I can remember, my older brother Mark has been there. [2]Mark has always been there for me. [3]He taught me how to have faith in myself and to stand up for what I believe in. [4]I always knew that whenever I had a problem, Mark would be there for me, trying to make things better.

Sample B

Which of these best combines Sentences 1 and 2?

Ⓕ For as long as I can remember, my older brother Mark has been there for me.

Ⓖ My older brother Mark, for as long as I can remember, has been there for me.

Ⓗ Because my older brother Mark has been there, for as long as I can remember.

Ⓙ My older brother Mark has always been there for me, at least as long as I can remember.

Sample C

Where would this sentence best fit into the paragraph?

I know he'll also be there for me in the future.

Ⓐ after Sentence 1

Ⓑ after Sentence 2

Ⓒ after Sentence 3

Ⓓ after Sentence 4

Learning New Lessons

Everybody learns new things all the time. Whether you are discovering something about yourself, developing an artistic or athletic skill, studying a new language, or researching a topic that interests you—you are learning.

In this theme, you will find people to get to know, activities to investigate, and solutions to discover. Let's begin finding out about Learning New Lessons.

From *Barrio Boy* by Ernesto Galarza

Directions

Here is an excerpt from *Barrio Boy*, the autobiography of Ernesto Galarza, an acclaimed writer who emigrated at age eight from Mexico to Sacramento, California, along with his family. In this excerpt, Galarza remembers his first months in the Lincoln School in Sacramento when he began to learn English.

Like Ito and several other first graders who did not know English, I received private lessons from Miss Ryan in the closet, a narrow hall of the classroom with a door at each end. Next to one of these doors Miss Ryan placed a large chair for herself and a small one for me. Keeping an eye on the class through the open door she read with me about sheep in the meadow and a frightened chicken going to see the king, coaching me out of my phonetic ruts in words like *pasture, bow-wow-wow, hay,* and *pretty,* which to my Mexican ear and eye had so many unnecessary sounds and letters. She made me watch her lips and then close my eyes as she repeated words I found hard to read. When we came to know each other better, I tried interrupting to tell Miss Ryan how we said it in Spanish. It didn't work. She only said "oh" and went on with *pasture, bow-wow-wow, hay,* and *pretty.* It was as if in that closet we were both discovering together the secrets of the English language and grieving together over the tragedies of Bo-Peep. The main reason I was graduated with honors from the first grade was that I had fallen in love with Miss Ryan. Her radiant, no-nonsense character made us either afraid not to love her or love her so we would not be afraid. I am not sure which. It was not only

that we sensed she was with it, but also that she was with us. Like the first grade, the rest of the Lincoln School was a sampling of the lower part of town where many races made their home. My pals in the second grade were Kazushi, whose parents spoke only Japanese; Matti, a skinny Italian boy; and Manuel, a fat Portuguese who would never get into a fight but wrestled you to the ground and just sat on you. Our assortment of nationalities included Koreans, Yugoslavs, Poles, Irish, and home-grown Americans.

At Lincoln, making us into Americans did not mean scrubbing away what made us originally foreign. The teachers called us as our parents did, or as close as they could pronounce our names in Spanish or Japanese. No one was ever scolded or punished for speaking in his native tongue on the playground. Matti told the class about his mother's down quilt, which she had made in Italy with fine feathers of a thousand geese. Encarnación acted out how boys learned to fish in the Philippines. I astounded the third grade with the story of my travels on a stagecoach, which nobody else in the class had seen except in the museum at Sutter's Fort. After a visit to Crocker Art Gallery and its collection of heroic paintings of the golden age of California, someone showed a silk scroll with a Chinese painting. Miss Hopley [the principal] herself had a way of expressing wonder over these matters before a class, her eyes wide open until they popped slightly. It was easy for me to feel that becoming a proud American, as she said we should, did not mean feeling ashamed of being a Mexican.

1 **Choose the sentence that best describes the main idea of the passage.**

Ⓐ A boy finds many new friends from various backgrounds at his new school.

Ⓑ A boy has a difficult time with certain English words.

Ⓒ A boy is frightened of his new school.

Ⓓ A boy finds self-respect, with the help of a caring teacher.

2 **Near the end of the passage, Galarza writes, "I astounded the third grade with the story of my travels on a stagecoach. . . . " Based on the context of the paragraph, the word *astounded* probably means _____.**

Ⓕ frightened

Ⓖ amused

Ⓗ teased

Ⓙ amazed

3 **Why did Ernesto succeed in learning English?**

Ⓐ He was eager to please his teacher.

Ⓑ He found English very similar to Spanish.

Ⓒ He thought English sounded interesting.

Ⓓ He wanted to fit into his new surroundings and leave behind old ways.

4 **What is the major purpose of this passage?**

Ⓕ to reveal the many kinds of lessons the author learned at Lincoln School

Ⓖ to entertain readers with funny memories

Ⓗ to describe the different nationalities that live in Sacramento

Ⓙ to show the language problems that Galarza had in first grade

5 **According to the passage,**

    Ⓐ the teachers tried to pronounce the students' names correctly.

    Ⓑ the teachers did not worry about pronouncing the students' names correctly.

    Ⓒ the teachers had a difficult time pronouncing the students' names.

    Ⓓ the teachers tried to be available when parents called.

6 **Here are two sentences related to the passage:**

The students loved Miss Ryan.

They sensed that she was with them.

Which of these choices best combines the two sentences into one?

    Ⓕ The students loved Miss Ryan, and they sensed that she was with them.

    Ⓖ The students loved Miss Ryan because they sensed that she was with them.

    Ⓗ Miss Ryan was loved by the students although they sensed that she was with them.

    Ⓙ The students loved Miss Ryan sensing that she was with them.

All-in-One Workbook: Standardized Test Practice
397

Hang Gliding

Directions

Ms. Martino's class just finished reading a book about a young girl who traveled with her father in a hot-air balloon. Now the class is writing about other interesting ways to travel. Justin wrote about hang gliding, a sport in which a person sails through the air hanging from a glider. There are several mistakes that need correcting. Here is the first part of his report.

---

[1]Have you ever wondered what it would be like to fly like a bird? [2]If you have, you might want to try hang gliding. [3]When you hang glide, you hang from a strap connected to a glider, this is where the name hang gliding comes from. [4]People hanging from hang gliders take off from any slope that's not near anything they can get stuck on. [5]They run down the slope and take off when they feel a breeze of about 15 to 20 miles per hour.

---

7 The sentence that should be rewritten as two complete sentences is

- Ⓐ Sentence 1
- Ⓑ Sentence 2
- Ⓒ Sentence 3
- Ⓓ Sentence 5

8 Choose the best way to write Sentence 4.

- Ⓕ Hang gliders can take off from any slope that's clear of obstacles.
- Ⓖ So they don't get stuck on things, hang gliders take off from slopes.
- Ⓗ People going for a ride can take off from any slope that's not near nothing.
- Ⓙ Best as it is

Now read the second part of the report.

---

¹Once in the air, you can move the hang glider by moving forward, backward, or side to side. ²When you do this, you roll a little and turn the glider in the direction you are moving and the glider turns in that direction. ³It takes a while to be able to hang glide long distances. ⁴Holding the glider is like balancing a 40 to 60 pound weight on your shoulders. ⁵Experienced hang gliders can glide for a long time. ⁶People who have been hang gliding for a long time can glide for an entire day.

---

9 Select the best way to write Sentence 2.

ⓐ The glider turns in the direction you are moving when you roll a little and move that way.

ⓑ You roll a little and turn the glider in whatever direction you are moving when you do this.

ⓒ When you do this, you roll a little and turn the glider in whatever direction you're moving.

ⓓ Best as it is

10 Which of these best combines Sentences 5 and 6?

Ⓕ Experienced hang gliders can glide for an entire day.

Ⓖ Long-time hang gliders can glide for a long time or an entire day.

Ⓗ People who have been hang gliding for an entire day can glide for a long time.

Ⓙ Experience hang gliders can glide for a long time, and people who have been hang gliding for a long time can glide for an entire day.

Here is the last part of the report.

> [1]Although hang gliding can be a great deal of fun, it's dangerous if you don't know what you're doing. [2]At least 5 to 10 gliders are killed each year while riding hang gliders. [3]Hang gliders should be properly trained by an instructor who is certified by the United States Hang Gliding Association. [4]A good training program takes a really long time to complete.

11 **Where would this sentence best fit in the paragraph?**

However, most hang gliders fly all their lives without serious injury.

Ⓐ after Sentence 1

Ⓑ after Sentence 2

Ⓒ after Sentence 3

Ⓓ after Sentence 4

12 **Which is the best way to write Sentence 2?**

Ⓕ Hang gliders are killed each year, about 5 to 10.

Ⓖ At least 5 to 10 hang gliders are killed each year.

Ⓗ Nearly 5 to 10 hang gliders are killed each year, usually from hang gliding.

Ⓘ Best as it is

13 **Here is a paragraph about the planet Venus that Melanie wrote for science class. Choose the best topic sentence for her paragraph.**

> _____. Because Venus is very close to the sun, the temperature there is about 895 degrees. Pressure from the thick atmosphere that surrounds Venus is about 95 times greater than the pressure here on Earth. Most of Venus's surface is a rocky desert.

Ⓐ Venus is the brightest planet in the sky.

Ⓑ Human beings could not survive on Venus.

Ⓒ Venus is the Roman goddess of love and beauty.

Ⓓ Many astronauts hope to travel to Venus one day.

from Myths and Legends in American History

The Truth and Fiction of George Washington

Here are some things we know about George Washington: He led the Continental Army to victory during the American Revolution. He was elected the first President of the United States. Before he became president, he rejected the idea of becoming "king." He thought it was the antithesis–the complete opposite–of what the fight for independence was about. It was also Washington who decided that two terms as president was enough. He was aware that he was paving the way for what other presidents would do.

Those achievements say a great deal about George Washington. He was a strong leader. He was trusted and admired by others. He placed the good of his country above his own personal gain. They create a picture of a virtuous man with many qualities to respect.

Then there are those odd things we think we know about him. Did he really
o wear wooden teeth?
o throw a silver dollar across the Potomac River?
o chop down a cherry tree at age six—and admit it?
The answers is *no* on all accounts.

False Teeth, False Toss

Washington did wear false teeth. They were made of cow teeth, human teeth, ivory, and other materials. Scholars know this because a set of Washington's teeth have survived. The teeth fit him poorly and he was often in pain. It's not clear how the myth of the wooden teeth developed. Perhaps it was less of a challenge to imagine wooden teeth than the actual mishmash of stuff!

The silver dollar toss may also have a base in fact. Washington had no children—no direct descendants—but he had stepchildren.

A step-grandson reported that Washington once threw a piece of slate stone across the Rappahannock River in Virginia. The silver dollar story was meant to emphasize Washington's physical strength. So the stone may have become a dollar and the river the much wider Potomac. Historians know the coin is wrong. There were no silver dollars when Washington was a young man. The Potomac River is more than a mile across. Trace a mile where you live, then imagine if anyone could conceivably toss a coin that distance.

Parson Weems, Mythmaker

The most famous Washington myth is the cherry tree tale. It's all fiction. It was created by Mason Locke "Parson" Weems, a minister and traveling bookseller. He wrote a biography of Washington published in 1800, after his death. Weems's intention was to show Washington's honesty—strangely enough, by telling a lie. The book was wildly popular and widely read, which helps explain how the cherry tree legend became so well known. It appealed to qualities that people in the nineteenth century considered important. They valued honesty and humility—being humble. They wanted their leaders to be good and faithful people.

Many Americans were willing to believe this unlikely story about Washington precisely because he had behaved honestly as a leader. He didn't try to hold onto power. He resigned from the army after the revolution was won. He accepted the presidency because he believed in duty.

Weems wanted to enrich Washington's image by making him exceptional in boyhood, too. Yet, even Weems's myth got distorted with time. In his original tale, Washington only cut into the tree with his hatchet and damaged it by removing bark.

14 **Which of the following is *not* true about George Washington?**

F   He cut down the cherry tree.

G   He was trusted and admired by others.

H   He placed the good of his country above his own personal gain.

J   He wore false teeth.

15 **This passage is mainly about**

A   the history of the first president of the United States.

B   the truths and untruths concerning George Washington.

C   the cutting down of the cherry tree.

D   the importance of myths.

16 **Which of the following demonstrates George Washington's humbleness and honesty?**

F   He wanted to serve more than two terms as president.

G   He did not want to become "king" of the United States.

H   He resigned from the army after the revolution.

J   He accepted the presidency because he believed in duty.

17 **In the section "False Teeth, False Toss," what does the word *conceivably* mean?**

A   definitely

B   possibly

C   doubtfully

D   correctly

18 **Which of the following *best* describes Weem's reason for creating the cherry tree tale?**

F   He wanted to sell more copies of his book.

G   He wanted to show one of Washington's weaknesses.

H   He wanted to show Washington's honesty.

J   He wanted to show that as a boy Washington was not very exceptional.

19 **Which of the following are reasons that it is unlikely that Washington tossed a silver dollar over the Potomac River?**

A   It is very unlikely that anyone could throw a coin over a mile.

B   There were no silver dollars when Washington was a young man.

C   The river is more than a mile across.

D   all of the above

The Children's Hour by Henry Wadsworth Longfellow

"The Children's Hour" is a poem written by Henry Wadsworth Longfellow in which the speaker describes his children as they come into the room.

Between the dark and the daylight,
    When the night is beginning to lower,
Comes a pause in the day's occupations,
    That is known as the Children's Hour.

I hear in the chamber above me
    The patter of little feet,
The sound of a door that is opened,
    And voices soft and sweet.

From my study I see in the lamplight,
    Descending the broad hall stair,
Grave Alice, and laughing Allegra,
    And Edith with golden hair.

A whisper, and then a silence:
    Yet I know by their merry eyes
They are plotting and planning together
    To take me by surprise.

A sudden rush from the stairway,
    A sudden raid from the hall!
By three doors left unguarded
    They enter my castle wall!

They climb up into my turret
    O'er the arms and back of my chair;
If I try to escape, they surround me;
    They seem to be everywhere.

They almost devour me with kisses,
    Their arms about me entwine,
Till I think of the Bishop of Bingen
    In his Mouse-Tower on the Rhine!

Do you think, o blue-eyed banditti*,
    Because you have scaled the wall,
Such an old mustache as I am
    Is not a match for you all!

I have you fast in my fortress,
    And will not let you depart,
But put you down into the dungeon
    In the round-tower of my heart.

And there will I keep you forever,
    Yes, forever and a day,
Till the walls shall crumble to ruin,
    And moulder in dust away!

* bandits

All-in-One Workbook: Standardized Test Practice
403

20 **What happens during "The Children's Hour"?**

F   The children whisper and plan together.

G   The three children climb up the chair where the speaker is sitting.

H   The children hang on to the speaker and give him lots of kisses.

J   All of the above are true.

21 **Choose the sentence which best describes what the poem is about.**

A   The children are playing games by themselves.

B   Without the speaker noticing them, the children sneak into the study.

C   There is a great love between the speaker and his children.

D   The children enjoy playing in their castle.

22 **Which of these phrases belongs in Circle 1?**

F   implies a nearby castle

G   symbolizes that the children will always be in the speaker's heart

H   symbolizes an attack

J   indicates that the children entered the speaker's study

23 **This web was designed to describe the poem's**

A   meter.

B   rhyme.

C   symbolism.

D   setting.

Directions

Below is a web based on the poem. Use the web to complete items 22-23

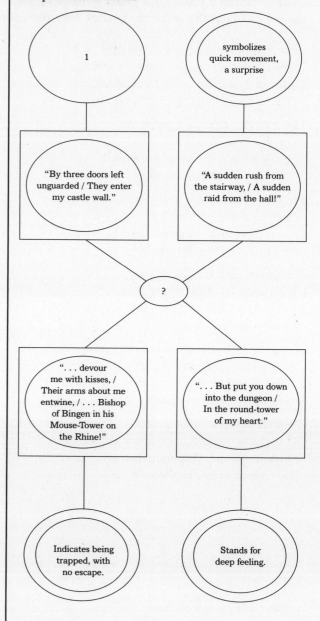

24 In the first half of the poem, the speaker is sitting in his study. In the second half of the poem, he discusses a castle which is being entered by "banditti," or bandits. Reread the poem and jot down details about the speaker, and details about the castle in the boxes below.

The Speaker

The castle

25 **Write a paragraph discussing how the speaker and the castle are alike. Use examples from the poem in your answer.**

For this answer, make sure you use complete sentences and check your work for correct spelling, capitalization, and punctuation.

_____

_____

_____

_____

_____

_____

_____

_____

_____

26 A student wrote a paragraph about in-line skating. He made <u>four</u> mistakes in grammar, capitalization, and punctuation. Draw a line through each part that has a mistake, and write the correction above it.

Last summer I learned how to in-line skate. This is much harder then it looks. At first, I fell and cut my leg, after that I scraped my arms. I thought learning to skate would have took me only a few days. Instead, it took me a whole month to get it right. Now, however, I can in-line skate real fast.

SAT 10 PRACTICE TEST

Vocabulary

Directions:

Look at each underlined word. Choose the word or group of words that means about the same thing.

1 <u>Gorgeous</u> means—

   A hungry

   B fat

   C beautiful

   D friendly

2 Someone who is <u>bashful</u> is—

   F lazy

   G excited

   H ugly

   J shy

3 To <u>create</u> something is to—

   A break it

   B make it

   C eat it

   D sell it

4 A <u>bouquet</u>—

   F feels good

   G smells good

   H tastes good

   J sounds good

Directions:

Read each boxed sentence. Then read the sentences that follow. Choose the sentence that uses the underlined word in the same way as in the box.

5

> Your spelling test is <u>perfect</u>.

In which sentence does the word <u>perfect</u> mean the same thing as in the sentence above?

   A I don't know him; he's a <u>perfect</u> stranger.

   B There are three <u>perfect</u> tenses in English.

   C Wally will <u>perfect</u> his invention for the science fair.

   D 100 percent is a <u>perfect</u> score.

6

> A triangle is a geometric <u>figure</u>.

In which sentence does the word <u>figure</u> mean the same thing as in the sentence above?

   F A simile is a <u>figure</u> of speech.

   G What <u>figure</u> has eight sides and eight angles?

   H The skater made a <u>figure</u> eight on the ice.

   J The <u>figure</u> of a snail is explained in the science textbook.

Name _____ Date _____

Directions:

This excerpt is from "Living History: Making History Come Alive." Read the excerpt. Then complete numbers 1 through 4 by choosing the best answer.

Living History As a Hobby

Some people want to fully immerse themselves in history. These people choose to become reenactors. They enjoy re-creating history by portraying a person from another time. First, they learn as much as they can about a certain period in history. Then they communicate what they learn as they act the part of this character. Reenactors dress in period clothes and use the speech of another era. They learn the appropriate behavior for that time, and obey the social rules. Some choose to transform themselves in order to portray actual historic figures, such as Abraham Lincoln. Others create their own fictional characters. These are often composites of real people from the era that they have researched.

Taking history in their own hands There are many different groups of reenactors. Some portray Pilgrims in Colonial America. Others portray soldiers in the French and Indian War. Still others might re-create parts of the journey of the explorers Lewis and Clark. By far the most popular subject for reenactments, though, is the Civil War. Tens of thousands of people take part in this hobby. Some join disorganized groups who meet once a year while others join highly focused groups who spend nearly all their free time on their hobby.

In fact, Civil War reenactors have names for each other that indicate their level of dedication. *Farbs* are reenactors who don't try very hard to be authentic. Farbs either don't know their history or don't take the hobby very seriously. *Stitch Counters* feel compelled to be authentic. They will sew or purchase handmade shirts, and count the number of stitches to make sure it's correct for the period. They sleep on the cold ground and eat food that most of us wouldn't touch. Between the Farbs and the Stitch Counters are the so-called *Mainstreamers*. The Mainstreamers like to look authentic but do not go to extremes. Often they like to talk to the people who come to see reenactments. That way they can spread what they know about history while they promote their hobby.

Some outside observers critique the reenactors, pointing out that many who portray Civil War soldiers are much heavier than the actual soldiers were. Other critics, especially veterans of actual wars, react negatively to reenactments because they worry that these events trivialize war. They maintain that no one will actually know what it feels like to be in the midst of a real battle while taking part in a scripted event. Reenactors might respond that they are not trying to join the army. They are role-playing—making creative decisions about who their characters are and how they behave.

1 In the passage, the reenactors "learn appropriate behavior for that time." The word *appropriate* means

A positive

B polite

C accurate

D historical

2 Which of the following statements does *not* accurately describe reenactors?

F They dress in period clothes.

G They portray only actual historical figures.

H They learn as much as they can about a certain time in history.

J The Mainstreamers look authentic, but do not go to extremes.

3 Some criticism of the reenactors includes the opinion that

A they trivialize the wars they are recreating.

B they are much heavier than the actual soldiers.

C they do not know what it feels like to be in a real battle.

D all of the above

4 Which of the following characters would not *most likely* be portrayed by a reenactor?

F a Confederate soldier

G General Lee

H George Bush

J Abraham Lincoln

Directions:

This excerpt is from "Early America: Through Europe's Eyes." Read the excerpt. Then complete numbers 5 through 8 by choosing the best answer.

America and France: Seeing Differences

1) On April 30, 1789, George Washington was sworn in as the first president of the United States. Two and a half months later, the French Revolution began. You might think that the earlier friendship between France and America, plus the common experience of overthrowing a monarchy, would promote a strong and trusting bond.

2) But just like relationships between people, the way that countries interact is seldom simple. For starters, France had helped the Americans fight for independence mainly as a way to make things difficult for its archrival, England. When the revolution threw out the French king and queen (and eventually beheaded them), it led to war with the British. The French were mainly concerned with who was on their side and who might be helping the English.

3) George Washington wanted to keep his new republic safe and decrease the danger of getting caught between these two old enemies. He tried to minimize the possibility of being sucked into war by declaring that America was neutral. It wasn't easy to stay on the sidelines because both sides tried to take advantage. The British created the bigger problem. They seized American merchant ships that they claimed were aiding the French and forced American sailors to fight for the British navy.

4) There were other issues that were still not settled from the time of independence, including the exact border between the U.S. and British Canada. So, in 1794, the Americans and the English negotiated a treaty. It's known as Jay's Treaty for John Jay, who represented America. President Washington thought the treaty was satisfactory. Some of the problems were solved and America stayed neutral. But many Americans didn't like the treaty because it gave England special rights to trade with the states.

5) For the U.S. and France, Jay's Treaty produced an impact that included a scandal and an undeclared war!

5 Choose the sentence that best describes what the passage is about?

   A George Washington's first term as President

   B a discussion of Jay's treaty

   C America's struggle to stay neutral

   D the issue of the border dispute between Canada and the United States

6 Based on this passage, which of these statements best describes France?

   F only interested in what was best for their country

   G eager to form a compromise with the United States

   H satisfied with Jay's Treaty.

   J concerned with freedom and independence for Americans

7 The answer you chose for number 6 is best because you learned from the text that

   A the United States and France were involved in negotiating Jay's Treaty.

   B after France's king and queen were killed, France formed a democracy like the U.S.

   C France helped the United States mainly to make it difficult for France's major rival, England.

   D France did not force American sailors to fight in their navy.

8 In paragraph 5, what does the word *impact* mean?

   F treaty

   G compromise

   H division

   J effect

Reading Comprehension

from *Stepping Out with My Baby* by Paul Reiser

Directions:

In this excerpt, Paul Reiser describes his first trip outside the house with his infant son. Read the excerpt. Then complete numbers 9 and 10 by choosing the best answer.

Finally we arrive at the mailbox—an exhausting block and a half from home. Dizzy with the victory of arriving at our destination in more or less one piece, I reach into my pocket, retrieve the now sweaty envelopes, and am about to toss them into the mailbox when I hear a voice. It's my wife's voice, echoing in my head.

"Talk to him."

"Hmm?" I say automatically, totally accepting that my wife might in fact be physically standing next to me, just for a follow-up evaluation on my performance.

"Talk to him. Explain to him what you're doing," the voice in my head suggests.

Sometimes I forget that part—talking to my child. Actually *being* with him. When I'm in charge of the kid, I tend to either stare at him like he's television or drift totally into a world of my own, running through my list of things-I-have-to-do-later-when-I'm-not-taking-care-of-the-kid. Or I take the job so seriously I become blinded by the severity of the responsibility, and panic. What I seem to miss is the middle ground—the part where you share, teach, learn, play—the part you can actually enjoy.

9 **What does the author mean when he says of his baby, "I tend to . . . stare at him like he's television"?**

  A The baby is interesting to watch.

  B The baby enjoys children's shows.

  C The baby has been in a commercial.

  D The baby is often very loud.

10 **From evidence in the passage, which of these descriptions best fits Paul Reiser?**

  F He tends to ignore the advice his wife gives him about their son.

  G He wishes his wife would spend more time with their son.

  H He has had a great deal of experience raising young children.

  J He worries about being a good father.

from Screaming in the Dark

Monsters have been in the movies almost as long as there have been movies.

Although many people view movies on television, monster movies are often more effective with a large, live audience in a movie theater. Part of the fun is being involved. When the monster suddenly appears, the audience's reaction is contagious. Screams ring in the dark as the audience confronts a pure burst of fear.

Alarming Changes

When everything stays the same, we feel comfortable. Surprises can be scary. Of course, surprises are also unavoidable. We can't control everything. Some movie monsters focus on our fear of sudden, dramatic changes. People who seem normal or average suddenly transform into ghastly creatures

Scare Tactics

No matter what the monster looks like, there are many ways a movie can be scary. Cinematography is the art of photographing and lighting a movie. With the right cinematography, a scary monster can become ever scarier.

One trick is to change the focus of the camera. At first, a shape in the background might be blurry because the camera is focused on a person. When the focus suddenly changes, we see that the blur is really a monster!

A jump cut is a sudden shift from one image to another. Jump cuts can increase the suspense. A chase scene might include dozens of jump cuts. These quick shifts make the scene feel more exciting.

The camera's point of view can also change. For example, a camera might change to show what the monster sees. This can be called "monster cam." *Predator* (1987) used a special kind of monster cam. The fierce alien did not see visible light. Instead, it sensed heat. Occasionally, the movie would show what the monster saw: an image of the human body's warmth.

The soundtrack can also exaggerate a fearful mood. Slightly audible groans or scraping sounds can put an audience on edge. A repetitive melody can also increase tension. The two-note theme from *Jaws* is just one example of a soundtrack that arouses shivers and shakes.

The Power of the Imagination

In some cases, film techniques alone can create true terror. *The Blair Witch Project* (1998) is a monster movie without a monster. The film seems like a documentary. The footage shows three young moviemakers lost in the woods. They record their own troubles as they encounter an unseen enemy. The hand-held camera makes the film seem unsteady and nervous. Soon, the audience is imagining a monster much worse that anything a special effects department could create. This film proves that the human imagination really does create the most terrifying monsters of all.

11 **What creates the most terrifying monsters?**

    A. the soundtrack
    B. the focus of the camera
    C. your own imagination
    D. the lighting

12 **Choose the phrase that best describes what the passage is mostly about.**

    F. the imagination as the most effective creator of scary monsters
    G. focusing the camera in a scary movie
    H. techniques used to make monsters scary
    J. the importance of the musical score

Reading Comprehension

Directions:

Read this excerpt from a textbook. Then, complete number 13 by choosing the best answer.

> Jacob Lawrence (1917–2000) is widely regarded as one of the most influential African American painters of the twentieth century. Most of his work focuses on the lives, history, and culture of African Americans. He has created many narrative series—collections of paintings or images that are often strung together with text from his own research.
>
> Lawrence was born in Atlantic City, New Jersey, but moved with his family to Harlem in New York City in 1926. His most famous work is *Migration of the Negro*, a collection of sixty paintings showing the flight of southern blacks to northern cities after World War II.

13 What is this passage mostly about?

   A the culture of African Americans

   B the life and work of Jacob Lawrence

   C the flight of southern blacks to the North

   D Harlem in 1926

Directions:

Read the following announcement. Then, complete number 14 by choosing the best answer.

> ### HELP WANTED: LIBRARY VOLUNTEERS
>
> How would you like a great job that helps you learn new skills while gaining valuable working experience? If you are interested, volunteer at the public library.
>
> Here is a list of volunteer jobs available.
>
> **General Library Assistant**
> Shelve books and help maintain the computer catalog. You will have the opportunity to learn the Dewey decimal system.
>
> **Story Time Supervisor**
> Read stories and poems to young children. You can practice your read-aloud and presentation skills.
>
> **Special Events Assistant**
> Help the coordinators of reading clubs, book drives, author visits, and other special events. You can improve your people skills.
>
> If you are interested in volunteering for any of these jobs, please fill out an application at the library circulation desk.

Reading Comprehension

14 If you would like to arrange books in order, which job would be interesting to you?

    F general library assistant

    G story time supervisor

    H special events assistant

    J none of the above

Directions:

Read the following passage. Then, complete number 15 by choosing the best answer.

> The most important reason playing video games is bad is that the players get little exercise. For example, instead of playing their favorite game, people could exercise for 30 minutes. If people spent less time playing video games and more time exercising, they could have healthier bodies. Obviously, playing video games can put a person's health in danger.

15 The main argument of this passage is that—

    A exercising is more fun than playing video games

    B playing video games puts one's health at risk

    C playing video games contributes to better health

    D exercising helps people play video games better

Spelling

Directions:

Read each group of sentences. For each item on the answer sheet, fill in the bubble for the answer that has a mistake in spelling. If there is no mistake, fill in the last answer choice.

1 **A** You can get a driver's <u>license</u> at age 18.

    B Jake spilled the juice <u>accidently</u>.

    C I hope it doesn't rain <u>tomorrow</u>.

    D No mistake

2 **F** Did you <u>recieve</u> a birthday card?

    G The <u>surprise</u> party embarrassed Mira.

    H The <u>capital</u> of Alabama is Montgomery.

    J No mistake

3 **A** The girls <u>cooperated</u> on the science project.

    B You can research Neptune at the <u>libary</u>.

    C Blue <u>whales</u> are huge.

    D No mistake

4 **F** Grace's new kitten is <u>mischievious</u>.

    G <u>Tomorrow</u> is Saturday.

    H Doctors have <u>knowledge</u> of medicine.

    J No mistake

5 **A** August is the <u>eighth</u> month.

    B The <u>colonel</u> was in charge of the troops.

    C Roses have a <u>pleasant</u> aroma.

    D No mistake

6 **F** Be careful when you use <u>scissors</u>.

    G Hank plays soccer on <u>Wenesdays</u>.

    H The movie <u>theater</u> is showing a double feature.

    J No mistake

7 **A** Von <u>bought</u> an apple and a banana.

    B <u>Aluminium</u> is a silver-colored metal.

    C Computer programming is a good <u>career</u>.

    D No mistake

8 **F** 100 percent is the <u>maximum</u> score.

    G Ellen's <u>niece</u> is six years old.

    H I ate a tuna <u>sandwitch</u> for lunch.

    J No mistake

9 **A** The bride wore a <u>viel</u>.

    B The scientists work in a <u>laboratory</u>.

    C Senator Watts was <u>reelected</u>.

    D No mistake

10 **F** Leonard had layer cake for <u>dessert</u>.

    G Grains of sand are <u>minuscule</u>.

    H Laura Ingalls Wilder wrote about life on the <u>prarie</u>.

    J No mistake

11 **A** The frisky dog was <u>unmanagable</u>.

    B How many cents are there in a <u>nickel</u>?

    C Tall tales always <u>exaggerate</u>.

    D No mistake

Spelling

12 F In my <u>opinion</u>, snakes are scary.

   G The Stone Age was a <u>primative</u> time in history.

   H To get good grades, it is <u>necessary</u> to study.

   J No mistake

13 A Cindy's arms <u>ached</u> after playing basketball.

   B It often snows in <u>Febuary</u>.

   C Bracelets and rings are <u>jewelry</u>.

   D No mistake

14 F The <u>ceiling</u> fell down during the hurricane.

   G Francisco <u>bandaged</u> the cut on his arm.

   H Put your clothes away in the <u>burau</u>.

   J No mistake

15 A <u>Answer</u> the question.

   B The Sahara <u>Desert</u> is in Africa.

   C Peas are my favorite <u>vegetable</u>.

   D No mistake

16 F A <u>skunk</u> has a bad smell.

   G The snowman <u>disapeared</u> in the sunshine.

   H It will <u>probably</u> snow this weekend.

   J No mistake

17 A Put the letter in an <u>envelope</u>.

   B End a business letter with "<u>Sincerely</u>."

   C Stay home if you have a bad <u>cough</u>.

   D No mistake

18 F The science fiction movie was <u>wierd</u>.

   G When you <u>criticize</u>, be polite.

   H Give the dog a <u>biscuit</u>.

   J No mistake

19 A <u>Ninety</u>-nine cents is almost a dollar.

   B <u>Apologize</u> if you bump into someone.

   C My brother is <u>ninteen</u> years old.

   D No mistake

20 F <u>Congratulate</u> the winner of the race.

   G Willie Mays was a great <u>athelete</u>.

   H My <u>bicycle</u> has a flat tire.

   J No mistake

21 A Do you like to study <u>grammer</u>?

   B The <u>dining</u> room was full by 7 o'clock.

   C It is wrong to <u>deceive</u> people.

   D No mistake

22 F My new <u>neighbor</u> has a pet rabbit.

   G Don't <u>misspell</u> "Alabama"!

   H The anniversary was a happy <u>occasion</u>.

   J No mistake

Language

Directions:

Read the passage. Then, choose the word or group of words that belongs in each space. For each item on the answer sheet, fill in the bubble for the answer that you think is correct.

In 1998, twenty-one-year-old Sarah Tueting ___(1)___ the dream of a lifetime—playing in the Olympic Games and winning a gold medal. Tueting was the goalie for the United States women's ice hockey team. Sarah almost ___(2)___ hockey two years earlier. Upset because she had never ___(3)___ to play on a United States national team, Sarah told everyone she was through with the game. Then she got a letter inviting her to try out for the women's Olympic team. Sarah ___(4)___ gave up all plans to stop playing hockey. Instead, she decided to chase her ___(5)___ dream—and it certainly paid off! After winning the gold medal, she knew she ___(6)___ the right decision.

---

1 **A** achieves

   B achieved

   C achieving

   D were achieving

2 **F** quit

   G quitting

   H quitted

   J is quitting

3 **A** was inviting

   B invited

   C was invited

   D been invited

4 **F** more immediate

   G immediate

   H immediately

   J most immediately

5 **A** special

   B specially

   C specialize

   D specialness

6 **F** makes

   G is making

   H will make

   J had made

Language

Directions:

Read each passage. Some sections are underlined. The underlined sections may be one of the following:
- **Incomplete sentences**
- **Run-on sentences**
- **Correctly written sentences that should be combined**
- **Correctly written sentences that do not need to be rewritten**

Choose the best way to write each underlined section and mark the letter for your answer. If the underlined section needs no change, mark the choice "Correct as is."

In the early 1800s, thousands of girls worked in the textile mills of Lowell,

Massachusetts. <u>At first, life at the Lowell mills was good.</u> <u>The girls worked hard for long</u>
               7   8

<u>hours. The girls also worked quickly for long hours.</u> However, they still found time to

learn. Some studied foreign languages or took piano lessons. Others attended lectures

and concerts. <u>Some of the girls decided to work together. In order to put out a magazine.</u>
                                9

<u>The magazine was called *Lowell Offering*, it included stories and sketches of mill life.</u>
10

---

7 A At first; life at the Lowell mills was good.

   B At first. Life at the Lowell mills was good.

   C Life at the lowell mills was good; at first.

   D Correct as is

8 F The girls worked hard and quickly in order to keep up their long hours.

   G The girls worked hard and quickly on their long hours.

   H The girls worked hard and quickly for long hours.

   J Correct as is

9 A Some of the girls decided to work together to put out a magazine.

   B Some of the girls worked on a magazine together, in order to do it.

   C To put out a magazine together, some of the girls decided to work together.

   D Correct as is

10 F The magazine was called *Lowell Offering*, which decided to include stories and sketches of mill life.

   G The magazine was called *Lowell Offering*, and the magazine included stories and sketches of mill life.

   H The magazine was called *Lowell Offering;* it included stories and sketches of mill life.

   J Correct as is

Language

Alex Haley, the author of Roots, spent several years tracing his family back to its first African ancestor who was brought to the United States as a slave. <u>Haley got the idea</u>
<u>of researching his ancestors from his grandmother.</u> When Haley was young, his
₁₁

grandmother would tell him about the "furthest-back person" in their family. This person was known simply as "The African." Years later, he decided to find out more about the history of his family. <u>His search for the "furthest-back person" began in the National</u>
₁₂

<u>Archives building in Washington. His search ended in a village on the Gambia River in</u>

<u>Africa.</u> Haley learned that this ancestor's name was Kunta Kinte. <u>Kunta Kinte left his</u>
₁₃

<u>village to chop wood to make a drum. When he was sixteen. His family never saw him</u>
₁₄

<u>again he was taken captive and then sent to America as a slave.</u>

11 A Haley got the idea. Of researching his ancestors from his grandmother.

B Since Haley got the idea of researching his grandmother's ancestors.

C Haley's grandmother, giving him the idea, had ancestors.

D Correct as is

12 F His search for the "furthest-back person" began in the National Archives building in Washington, and it was ending in a village on the Gambia River in Africa.

G His search for the "furthest-back person" began in the National Archives Building in Washington, and it ended in a village on the Gambia River in Africa.

H The beginning of his search for the "furthest-back person" was the National Archives building in Washington, but the ending of his search was in a village on the Gambia River in Africa.

J Correct as is

Language

13 A When he was sixteen, Kunta Kinte left his village to chop wood to make a drum.

   B Being sixteen, Kunta Kinte left the village to chop wood to make a drum.

   C Kunta Kinte left his village to chop wood to make a drum. When he left the village, he was sixteen.

   D Correct as is

14 F His family never saw him again and he was taken captive and then sent to America as a slave.

   G His family never saw him again, he was taken captive and then sent to America as a slave.

   H His family never saw him again. He was taken captive and then sent to America as a slave.

   J Correct as is

Directions:

Read the passage, and choose the word that belongs in each space. For each item on the answer sheet, fill in the bubble for the answer that you think is correct.

A recent survey showed that over half of all Americans who smoke do not

_____ 15 _____ that cigarettes are _____ 16 _____ for their

health. An additional statistic shows that on any given day, over 4,000 adolescents aged

from 11 to 17 will smoke their first cigarette. Approximately half of these youngsters will

become regular smokers.

15 A believe
   B believed
   C believes
   D believing

16 F worst
   G worse
   H bad
   J worser

Language

Directions:

Read the passage. Then, decide which type of error, if any, appears in each underlined section. For each item on the answer sheet, fill in the bubble for the answer that you think is correct. If there is no error, fill in the last answer choice.

January 15, 2000

Special Sneaker Company

<u>Dear Mr. Calvillo:</u>
17

   I am writing <u>to express my disatisfaction</u> with the sneakers that I recently purchased.
             18

<u>Because you are the President</u> of the Special Sneaker Company, I hope you can help me.
19

   The problem <u>I have is that the soul is coming off</u> the right shoe! I have owned the
             20

shoes for only three <u>weeks; this cannot be normal ware and tear.</u> <u>Living in boston, I do a</u>
         21   22

<u>lot of walking; however, this is ridiculous!</u> I didn't even notice the problem at first. <u>Then</u>
                                                      23

<u>my friend said Check out your shoes!</u> It was really embarrassing.

   <u>I would like your company to refund my money.</u> I will send you the sneakers in
   24

return. <u>I think thats a fair trade.</u> <u>Don't you agree.</u>
      25   26

Sincerely,

Craig Lancer

Language

17 A Spelling error

    B Capitalization error

    C Punctuation error

    D No error

18 F Spelling error

    G Capitalization error

    H Punctuation error

    J No error

19 A Spelling error

    B Capitalization error

    C Punctuation error

    D No error

20 F Spelling error

    G Capitalization error

    H Punctuation error

    J No error

21 A Spelling error

    B Capitalization error

    C Punctuation error

    D No error

22 F Spelling error

    G Capitalization error

    H Punctuation error

    J No error

23 A Spelling error

    B Capitalization error

    C Punctuation error

    D No error

24 F Spelling error

    G Capitalization error

    H Punctuation error

    J No error

25 A Spelling error

    B Capitalization error

    C Punctuation error

    D No error

26 F Spelling error

    G Capitalization error

    H Punctuation error

    J No error

Language

Directions:

Read the following question. Then, complete number 27 by choosing the best answer.

27 Suppose that you are writing an essay about the main ideas and supporting details in a selection. Which of the following organizers would be most useful?

    A character-change map

    B main-idea map

    C time line

    D character-trait web

Directions:

James is working on an essay about a Mexican legend. Several mistakes need to be corrected. Read the following paragraph. Then, complete numbers 28 through 30 by choosing the best answer.

---

[1]"Popocatepetl and Ixtlaccihuatl" is a legend that explains the origin of two volcanoes near present-day Mexico City. [2]A powerful emperor in the Aztec capital of Tenochtitlán has only one child, the beautiful princess Ixtla. [3]Ixtla loves a brave warrior named Popo. [4]The emperor has forbidden Ixtla and Popo to marry.

[5]Eventually, the aging emperor offers his daughter's hand in marriage. [6]The warrior who will defeat the Aztecs' enemies. [7]After a lengthy war, the emperor's men prevail. [8]Most soldiers agree that Popo has fought hard and is responsible for the victory. [9]Jealous soldiers hurry back to the city and report that Popo has been killed—news that causes Ixtla to fall ill and die. [10]Popo returns and responding by killing the guilty soldiers and refusing to become emperor. [11]He buries Ixtla near the peak of one and then takes his place atop the taller of the two, where he watches over Ixtla's body for the rest of his days. [12]The two volcanoes stand as reminders of the two lovers who dreamed of always being together.

Language

28 **Sentence 6 is not complete. Which of these best combines it with Sentence 5?**

F Eventually, the aging emperor offers his daughter's hand in marriage and the warrior who will defeat the Aztecs' enemies.

G Eventually, the aging emperor offers his daughter's hand in marriage to the warrior who will defeat the Aztecs' enemies.

H Eventually, the warrior who will defeat the Aztecs' enemies, the aging emperor offers his daughter's hand in marriage.

J Eventually, warrior who will defeat the Aztecs' enemies, and the aging emperor offers his daughter's hand in marriage.

29 **Choose the best transition to be inserted at the beginning of Sentence 9.**

A Therefore,

B For example,

C However,

D Finally,

30 **Where would this sentence best fit in the passage?**

He then builds two stone pyramids outside the city.

F before Sentence 9

G before Sentence 10

H before Sentence 11

J before Sentence 12

Listening

Directions:

Suppose that the following paragraph is being read aloud. Read the paragraph. Then, complete numbers 1 and 2 by choosing the best answer.

In the days before athletes had learned how to incorporate themselves, they were shining heroes to American kids. In fact, they were such heroes to me and my friends that we even imitated their walks. When Jackie Robinson, a pigeon-toed walker, became famous, we walked pigeon-toed, a painful form of <u>locomotion</u> unless you were Robinson or a pigeon.

—from "Was Tarzan a Three-Bandage Man?" by Bill Cosby

---

1 You can tell from the passage that the word <u>locomotion</u> means—

  A movement

  B imitation

  C inspiration

  D ridicule

2 Where did the speaker get the information for this passage?

  F from his own life

  G from a biography of Jackie Robinson

  H from his baseball coach

  J from one of his friends

Directions:

Read the following passage from an oral report. Then, complete number 3 by choosing the best answer.

Did you know that for every kind of tree and flower, there may be dozens—or even hundreds—of unique variations? Botanists are scientists who study and classify plants according to their characteristics. For most of us, a rose is a rose, but for botanists, there are actually hundreds of different types of roses—each one unlike every other one.

---

3 This passage is mostly about—

  A how botanists study different kinds of roses

  B how botanists study many different types of plants

  C how people know very little about trees and flowers

  D how some trees and flowers have many different variations

Listening

Directions:

Read the following message left on Mrs. Thorn's answering machine. Then, complete number 4 by choosing the best answer.

> Hello, Mrs. Thorn, this is Marc Green calling from Green Growers Nursery. I just wanted to let you know that we received the six-inch clay pots you ordered. When you come to pick them up, please ask for Janine, our warehouse manager. If you don't pick up the pots by next Wednesday, we will put them out on display for our other customers to purchase. You can give me a call me at 555-1098. Thank you.

4 In order to dictate this message for Mrs. Thorn, you would—

   F wait for Marc Green to call back

   G listen carefully to the entire message

   H ignore the information you think is unimportant

   J listen only for names you know

Name _____   Date _____

Answer sheet: Screening Test

1. (A) (B) (C) (D)	17. (A) (B) (C) (D)
2. (F) (G) (H) (J)	18. (F) (G) (H) (J)
3. (A) (B) (C) (D)	19. (A) (B) (C) (D)
4. (F) (G) (H) (J)	20. (F) (G) (H) (J)
5. (A) (B) (C) (D)	21. (A) (B) (C) (D)
6. (F) (G) (H) (J)	22. (F) (G) (H) (J)
7. (A) (B) (C) (D)	23. (A) (B) (C) (D)
8. (F) (G) (H) (J)	24. (F) (G) (H) (J)
9. (A) (B) (C) (D)	25. (A) (B) (C) (D)
10. (F) (G) (H) (J)	24. (F) (G) (H) (J)
11. (A) (B) (C) (D)	27. (A) (B) (C) (D)
12. (F) (G) (H) (J)	28. (F) (G) (H) (J)
13. (A) (B) (C) (D)	29. (A) (B) (C) (D)
14. (F) (G) (H) (J)	30. (F) (G) (H) (J)
15. (A) (B) (C) (D)	31. (A) (B) (C) (D)
16. (F) (G) (H) (J)	

Name _____ Date _____

Answer sheet: Practice Test 1

1. Ⓐ Ⓑ Ⓒ Ⓓ	14. Ⓐ Ⓑ Ⓒ Ⓓ
2. Ⓐ Ⓑ Ⓒ Ⓓ	15. Ⓐ Ⓑ Ⓒ Ⓓ
3. Ⓐ Ⓑ Ⓒ Ⓓ	16. Ⓐ Ⓑ Ⓒ Ⓓ
4. Ⓐ Ⓑ Ⓒ Ⓓ	17. Ⓐ Ⓑ Ⓒ Ⓓ
5. Ⓐ Ⓑ Ⓒ Ⓓ	18. Ⓐ Ⓑ Ⓒ Ⓓ
6. Ⓐ Ⓑ Ⓒ Ⓓ	19. Ⓐ Ⓑ Ⓒ Ⓓ
7. Ⓐ Ⓑ Ⓒ Ⓓ	20. Ⓐ Ⓑ Ⓒ Ⓓ
8. Ⓐ Ⓑ Ⓒ Ⓓ	21. Ⓐ Ⓑ Ⓒ Ⓓ
9. Ⓐ Ⓑ Ⓒ Ⓓ	22. Ⓐ Ⓑ Ⓒ Ⓓ
10. Ⓐ Ⓑ Ⓒ Ⓓ	23. Ⓐ Ⓑ Ⓒ Ⓓ
11. Ⓐ Ⓑ Ⓒ Ⓓ	24. Ⓐ Ⓑ Ⓒ Ⓓ
12. Ⓐ Ⓑ Ⓒ Ⓓ	25. Ⓐ Ⓑ Ⓒ Ⓓ
13. Ⓐ Ⓑ Ⓒ Ⓓ	26. Ⓐ Ⓑ Ⓒ Ⓓ

Answer sheet: Practice Test2

1. Ⓐ Ⓑ Ⓒ Ⓓ	17. Ⓐ Ⓑ Ⓒ Ⓓ
2. Ⓐ Ⓑ Ⓒ Ⓓ	18. Ⓐ Ⓑ Ⓒ Ⓓ
3. Ⓐ Ⓑ Ⓒ Ⓓ	19. Ⓐ Ⓑ Ⓒ Ⓓ
4. Ⓐ Ⓑ Ⓒ Ⓓ	20. Ⓐ Ⓑ Ⓒ Ⓓ
5. Ⓐ Ⓑ Ⓒ Ⓓ	21. Ⓐ Ⓑ Ⓒ Ⓓ
6. Ⓐ Ⓑ Ⓒ Ⓓ	22. Ⓐ Ⓑ Ⓒ Ⓓ
7. Ⓐ Ⓑ Ⓒ Ⓓ	23. Ⓐ Ⓑ Ⓒ Ⓓ
8. Ⓐ Ⓑ Ⓒ Ⓓ	24. Ⓐ Ⓑ Ⓒ Ⓓ
9. Ⓐ Ⓑ Ⓒ Ⓓ	25. Ⓐ Ⓑ Ⓒ Ⓓ
10. Ⓐ Ⓑ Ⓒ Ⓓ	26. Ⓐ Ⓑ Ⓒ Ⓓ
11. Ⓐ Ⓑ Ⓒ Ⓓ	27. Ⓐ Ⓑ Ⓒ Ⓓ
12. Ⓐ Ⓑ Ⓒ Ⓓ	28. Ⓐ Ⓑ Ⓒ Ⓓ
13. Ⓐ Ⓑ Ⓒ Ⓓ	29. Ⓐ Ⓑ Ⓒ Ⓓ
14. Ⓐ Ⓑ Ⓒ Ⓓ	30. Ⓐ Ⓑ Ⓒ Ⓓ
15. Ⓐ Ⓑ Ⓒ Ⓓ	31. Ⓐ Ⓑ Ⓒ Ⓓ
16. Ⓐ Ⓑ Ⓒ Ⓓ	

Name _____ Date _____

Writing Prompt 1:

_____
_____
_____
_____
_____
_____
_____
_____
_____
_____
_____
_____
_____
_____
_____
_____
_____
_____
_____
_____
_____
_____
_____
_____

All-in-One Workbook
432

Name _____ Date _____

Writing Prompt 2:

_____

_____

_____

_____

_____

_____

_____

_____

_____

_____

_____

_____

_____

_____

_____

_____

_____

_____

_____

_____

_____

_____

_____

_____

_____

Name _____   Date _____

Answer sheet: Practice Test3

1. Ⓐ Ⓑ Ⓒ Ⓓ	20. Ⓐ Ⓑ Ⓒ Ⓓ	39. Ⓐ Ⓑ Ⓒ Ⓓ
2. Ⓐ Ⓑ Ⓒ Ⓓ	21. Ⓐ Ⓑ Ⓒ Ⓓ	40. Ⓐ Ⓑ Ⓒ Ⓓ
3. Ⓐ Ⓑ Ⓒ Ⓓ	22. Ⓐ Ⓑ Ⓒ Ⓓ	41. Ⓐ Ⓑ Ⓒ Ⓓ
4. Ⓐ Ⓑ Ⓒ Ⓓ	23. Ⓐ Ⓑ Ⓒ Ⓓ	42. Ⓐ Ⓑ Ⓒ Ⓓ
5. Ⓐ Ⓑ Ⓒ Ⓓ	24. Ⓐ Ⓑ Ⓒ Ⓓ	43. Ⓐ Ⓑ Ⓒ Ⓓ
6. Ⓐ Ⓑ Ⓒ Ⓓ	25. Ⓐ Ⓑ Ⓒ Ⓓ	44. Ⓐ Ⓑ Ⓒ Ⓓ
7. Ⓐ Ⓑ Ⓒ Ⓓ	26. Ⓐ Ⓑ Ⓒ Ⓓ	45. Ⓐ Ⓑ Ⓒ Ⓓ
8. Ⓐ Ⓑ Ⓒ Ⓓ	27. Ⓐ Ⓑ Ⓒ Ⓓ	46. Ⓐ Ⓑ Ⓒ Ⓓ
9. Ⓐ Ⓑ Ⓒ Ⓓ	28. Ⓐ Ⓑ Ⓒ Ⓓ	47. Ⓐ Ⓑ Ⓒ Ⓓ
10. Ⓐ Ⓑ Ⓒ Ⓓ	29. Ⓐ Ⓑ Ⓒ Ⓓ	48. Ⓐ Ⓑ Ⓒ Ⓓ
11. Ⓐ Ⓑ Ⓒ Ⓓ	30. Ⓐ Ⓑ Ⓒ Ⓓ	49. Ⓐ Ⓑ Ⓒ Ⓓ
12. Ⓐ Ⓑ Ⓒ Ⓓ	31. Ⓐ Ⓑ Ⓒ Ⓓ	50. Ⓐ Ⓑ Ⓒ Ⓓ
13. Ⓐ Ⓑ Ⓒ Ⓓ	32. Ⓐ Ⓑ Ⓒ Ⓓ	51. Ⓐ Ⓑ Ⓒ Ⓓ
14. Ⓐ Ⓑ Ⓒ Ⓓ	33. Ⓐ Ⓑ Ⓒ Ⓓ	52. Ⓐ Ⓑ Ⓒ Ⓓ
15. Ⓐ Ⓑ Ⓒ Ⓓ	34. Ⓐ Ⓑ Ⓒ Ⓓ	53. Ⓐ Ⓑ Ⓒ Ⓓ
16. Ⓐ Ⓑ Ⓒ Ⓓ	35. Ⓐ Ⓑ Ⓒ Ⓓ	54. Ⓐ Ⓑ Ⓒ Ⓓ
17. Ⓐ Ⓑ Ⓒ Ⓓ	36. Ⓐ Ⓑ Ⓒ Ⓓ	55. Ⓐ Ⓑ Ⓒ Ⓓ
18. Ⓐ Ⓑ Ⓒ Ⓓ	37. Ⓐ Ⓑ Ⓒ Ⓓ	
19. Ⓐ Ⓑ Ⓒ Ⓓ	38. Ⓐ Ⓑ Ⓒ Ⓓ	

Name _____ Date _____

Writing Prompt 1:

_____

_____

_____

_____

_____

_____

_____

_____

_____

_____

_____

_____

_____

_____

_____

_____

_____

_____

_____

_____

_____

_____

_____

_____

_____

_____

_____

_____

Writing Prompt 2:

_____

_____

_____

_____

_____

_____

_____

_____

_____

_____

_____

_____

_____

_____

_____

_____

_____

_____

_____

_____

_____

_____

_____

_____

_____

_____

_____

_____

Name _____ Date _____

Answer Sheet for ITBS

Vocabulary

1. Ⓐ Ⓑ Ⓒ Ⓓ	4. Ⓙ Ⓚ Ⓛ Ⓜ	7. Ⓐ Ⓑ Ⓒ Ⓓ	10. Ⓙ Ⓚ Ⓛ Ⓜ	13. Ⓐ Ⓑ Ⓒ Ⓓ
2. Ⓙ Ⓚ Ⓛ Ⓜ	5. Ⓐ Ⓑ Ⓒ Ⓓ	8. Ⓙ Ⓚ Ⓛ Ⓜ	11. Ⓐ Ⓑ Ⓒ Ⓓ	14. Ⓙ Ⓚ Ⓛ Ⓜ
3. Ⓐ Ⓑ Ⓒ Ⓓ	6. Ⓙ Ⓚ Ⓛ Ⓜ	9. Ⓐ Ⓑ Ⓒ Ⓓ	12. Ⓙ Ⓚ Ⓛ Ⓜ	

Reading Comprehension

1. Ⓐ Ⓑ Ⓒ Ⓓ	5. Ⓐ Ⓑ Ⓒ Ⓓ	9. Ⓐ Ⓑ Ⓒ Ⓓ	13. Ⓐ Ⓑ Ⓒ Ⓓ	17. Ⓐ Ⓑ Ⓒ Ⓓ
2. Ⓙ Ⓚ Ⓛ Ⓜ	6. Ⓙ Ⓚ Ⓛ Ⓜ	10. Ⓙ Ⓚ Ⓛ Ⓜ	14. Ⓙ Ⓚ Ⓛ Ⓜ	18. Ⓙ Ⓚ Ⓛ Ⓜ
3. Ⓐ Ⓑ Ⓒ Ⓓ	7. Ⓐ Ⓑ Ⓒ Ⓓ	11. Ⓐ Ⓑ Ⓒ Ⓓ	15. Ⓐ Ⓑ Ⓒ Ⓓ	
4. Ⓙ Ⓚ Ⓛ Ⓜ	8. Ⓙ Ⓚ Ⓛ Ⓜ	12. Ⓙ Ⓚ Ⓛ Ⓜ	16. Ⓙ Ⓚ Ⓛ Ⓜ	

Spelling

1. Ⓐ Ⓑ Ⓒ Ⓓ Ⓔ	4. Ⓙ Ⓚ Ⓛ Ⓜ Ⓝ	7. Ⓐ Ⓑ Ⓒ Ⓓ Ⓔ	10. Ⓙ Ⓚ Ⓛ Ⓜ Ⓝ	13. Ⓐ Ⓑ Ⓒ Ⓓ Ⓔ
2. Ⓙ Ⓚ Ⓛ Ⓜ Ⓝ	5. Ⓐ Ⓑ Ⓒ Ⓓ Ⓔ	8. Ⓙ Ⓚ Ⓛ Ⓜ Ⓝ	11. Ⓐ Ⓑ Ⓒ Ⓓ Ⓔ	14. Ⓙ Ⓚ Ⓛ Ⓜ Ⓝ
3. Ⓐ Ⓑ Ⓒ Ⓓ Ⓔ	6. Ⓙ Ⓚ Ⓛ Ⓜ Ⓝ	9. Ⓐ Ⓑ Ⓒ Ⓓ Ⓔ	12. Ⓙ Ⓚ Ⓛ Ⓜ Ⓝ	

Capitalization

1. Ⓐ Ⓑ Ⓒ Ⓓ	4. Ⓙ Ⓚ Ⓛ Ⓜ	7. Ⓐ Ⓑ Ⓒ Ⓓ	10. Ⓙ Ⓚ Ⓛ Ⓜ
2. Ⓙ Ⓚ Ⓛ Ⓜ	5. Ⓐ Ⓑ Ⓒ Ⓓ	8. Ⓙ Ⓚ Ⓛ Ⓜ	11. Ⓐ Ⓑ Ⓒ Ⓓ
3. Ⓐ Ⓑ Ⓒ Ⓓ	6. Ⓙ Ⓚ Ⓛ Ⓜ	9. Ⓐ Ⓑ Ⓒ Ⓓ	12. Ⓙ Ⓚ Ⓛ Ⓜ

Punctuation

1. Ⓐ Ⓑ Ⓒ Ⓓ	4. Ⓙ Ⓚ Ⓛ Ⓜ	7. Ⓐ Ⓑ Ⓒ Ⓓ	10. Ⓙ Ⓚ Ⓛ Ⓜ
2. Ⓙ Ⓚ Ⓛ Ⓜ	5. Ⓐ Ⓑ Ⓒ Ⓓ	8. Ⓙ Ⓚ Ⓛ Ⓜ	11. Ⓐ Ⓑ Ⓒ Ⓓ
3. Ⓐ Ⓑ Ⓒ Ⓓ	6. Ⓙ Ⓚ Ⓛ Ⓜ	9. Ⓐ Ⓑ Ⓒ Ⓓ	12. Ⓙ Ⓚ Ⓛ Ⓜ

Usage and Expression

1. Ⓐ Ⓑ Ⓒ Ⓓ	5. Ⓐ Ⓑ Ⓒ Ⓓ	9. Ⓐ Ⓑ Ⓒ Ⓓ	13. Ⓐ Ⓑ Ⓒ Ⓓ	17. Ⓐ Ⓑ Ⓒ Ⓓ
2. Ⓙ Ⓚ Ⓛ Ⓜ	6. Ⓙ Ⓚ Ⓛ Ⓜ	10. Ⓙ Ⓚ Ⓛ Ⓜ	14. Ⓙ Ⓚ Ⓛ Ⓜ	18. Ⓙ Ⓚ Ⓛ Ⓜ
3. Ⓐ Ⓑ Ⓒ Ⓓ	7. Ⓐ Ⓑ Ⓒ Ⓓ	11. Ⓐ Ⓑ Ⓒ Ⓓ	15. Ⓐ Ⓑ Ⓒ Ⓓ	19. Ⓐ Ⓑ Ⓒ Ⓓ
4. Ⓙ Ⓚ Ⓛ Ⓜ	8. Ⓙ Ⓚ Ⓛ Ⓜ	12. Ⓙ Ⓚ Ⓛ Ⓜ	16. Ⓙ Ⓚ Ⓛ Ⓜ	20. Ⓙ Ⓚ Ⓛ Ⓜ

Name _____   Date _____

Answer Sheet for SAT 10

Vocabulary

1. Ⓐ Ⓑ Ⓒ Ⓓ	4. Ⓕ Ⓖ Ⓗ Ⓙ
2. Ⓕ Ⓖ Ⓗ Ⓙ	5. Ⓐ Ⓑ Ⓒ Ⓓ
3. Ⓐ Ⓑ Ⓒ Ⓓ	6. Ⓕ Ⓖ Ⓗ Ⓙ

Reading Comprehension

1. Ⓐ Ⓑ Ⓒ Ⓓ	6. Ⓕ Ⓖ Ⓗ Ⓙ	11. Ⓐ Ⓑ Ⓒ Ⓓ
2. Ⓕ Ⓖ Ⓗ Ⓙ	7. Ⓐ Ⓑ Ⓒ Ⓓ	12. Ⓕ Ⓖ Ⓗ Ⓙ
3. Ⓐ Ⓑ Ⓒ Ⓓ	8. Ⓕ Ⓖ Ⓗ Ⓙ	13. Ⓐ Ⓑ Ⓒ Ⓓ
4. Ⓕ Ⓖ Ⓗ Ⓙ	9. Ⓐ Ⓑ Ⓒ Ⓓ	14. Ⓕ Ⓖ Ⓗ Ⓙ
5. Ⓐ Ⓑ Ⓒ Ⓓ	10. Ⓕ Ⓖ Ⓗ Ⓙ	15. Ⓐ Ⓑ Ⓒ Ⓓ

Spelling

1. Ⓐ Ⓑ Ⓒ Ⓓ	6. Ⓕ Ⓖ Ⓗ Ⓙ	11. Ⓐ Ⓑ Ⓒ Ⓓ	16. Ⓕ Ⓖ Ⓗ Ⓙ	21. Ⓐ Ⓑ Ⓒ Ⓓ
2. Ⓕ Ⓖ Ⓗ Ⓙ	7. Ⓐ Ⓑ Ⓒ Ⓓ	12. Ⓕ Ⓖ Ⓗ Ⓙ	17. Ⓐ Ⓑ Ⓒ Ⓓ	22. Ⓕ Ⓖ Ⓗ Ⓙ
3. Ⓐ Ⓑ Ⓒ Ⓓ	8. Ⓕ Ⓖ Ⓗ Ⓙ	13. Ⓐ Ⓑ Ⓒ Ⓓ	18. Ⓕ Ⓖ Ⓗ Ⓙ	
4. Ⓕ Ⓖ Ⓗ Ⓙ	9. Ⓐ Ⓑ Ⓒ Ⓓ	14. Ⓕ Ⓖ Ⓗ Ⓙ	19. Ⓐ Ⓑ Ⓒ Ⓓ	
5. Ⓐ Ⓑ Ⓒ Ⓓ	10. Ⓕ Ⓖ Ⓗ Ⓙ	15. Ⓐ Ⓑ Ⓒ Ⓓ	20. Ⓕ Ⓖ Ⓗ Ⓙ	

Language

1. Ⓐ Ⓑ Ⓒ Ⓓ	7. Ⓐ Ⓑ Ⓒ Ⓓ	13. Ⓐ Ⓑ Ⓒ Ⓓ	19. Ⓐ Ⓑ Ⓒ Ⓓ	25. Ⓐ Ⓑ Ⓒ Ⓓ
2. Ⓕ Ⓖ Ⓗ Ⓙ	8. Ⓕ Ⓖ Ⓗ Ⓙ	14. Ⓕ Ⓖ Ⓗ Ⓙ	20. Ⓕ Ⓖ Ⓗ Ⓙ	26. Ⓕ Ⓖ Ⓗ Ⓙ
3. Ⓐ Ⓑ Ⓒ Ⓓ	9. Ⓐ Ⓑ Ⓒ Ⓓ	15. Ⓐ Ⓑ Ⓒ Ⓓ	21. Ⓐ Ⓑ Ⓒ Ⓓ	27. Ⓐ Ⓑ Ⓒ Ⓓ
4. Ⓕ Ⓖ Ⓗ Ⓙ	10. Ⓕ Ⓖ Ⓗ Ⓙ	16. Ⓕ Ⓖ Ⓗ Ⓙ	22. Ⓕ Ⓖ Ⓗ Ⓙ	28. Ⓕ Ⓖ Ⓗ Ⓙ
5. Ⓐ Ⓑ Ⓒ Ⓓ	11. Ⓐ Ⓑ Ⓒ Ⓓ	17. Ⓐ Ⓑ Ⓒ Ⓓ	23. Ⓐ Ⓑ Ⓒ Ⓓ	29. Ⓐ Ⓑ Ⓒ Ⓓ
6. Ⓕ Ⓖ Ⓗ Ⓙ	12. Ⓕ Ⓖ Ⓗ Ⓙ	18. Ⓕ Ⓖ Ⓗ Ⓙ	24. Ⓕ Ⓖ Ⓗ Ⓙ	30. Ⓕ Ⓖ Ⓗ Ⓙ

Listening

1. Ⓐ Ⓑ Ⓒ Ⓓ
2. Ⓕ Ⓖ Ⓗ Ⓙ
3. Ⓐ Ⓑ Ⓒ Ⓓ
4. Ⓕ Ⓖ Ⓗ Ⓙ

Answer Sheet

Short Answer/Essay

_____

_____

_____

_____

_____

_____

_____

_____

_____

_____

_____

_____

_____

_____

_____

_____

_____

_____

_____

_____

_____

_____

_____

_____

_____

_____

_____